ILLEGAL FORECLOSURE, TITLE THEFT, AND ITS CHAIN OF CORRUPTION

How America's Banks are Stealing Private Property and Feeding Homes to the Securities Market

ALEXANDRA CLAIR

I have quoted names and content from public documents. The crimes I report rely heavily on document fraud. Given the levels of corruption this book addresses, content read within some of these documents may be entirely made up or, in some part, false. Those responsible for production of these documents should be held accountable for any administrative mistake and, or, any untruths proposed within. All persons named in this book are innocent until proven guilty.

Number: 2178645
Create Space Independent Publishing Platform
ISBN Number: 978-0-9847059-4-8

Alexandra Clair, d.b.a., Diamond Hedge Productions, LLC
Website: www.alexandraclair.com

Other works by Alexandra Clair, d.b.a., Diamond Hedge Productions, LLC
Wood's End (fiction)
The Year Between the Wood (fiction)
Discerning Sprits: Visionary Gifts in Practice (nonfiction)
Clachan Maze (fiction)
Wood's End: Screen play
Patrick: Screen play (St. Patrick: Exorcist, Evangelist, Rebel Bishop)

Connect over Facebook.

This book is dedicated to the great grandchildren of
John Patrick Clair and Audrea Kearin Clair.
Two well-read students of history, independent thinkers, that warned against group-think while modeling a legacy that shunned the herd instinct to tumble off the edge of any cliff.

Victoria Faith Stafford, Angel Renea Bailey, Anna Marie Bailey, Zachary Rain Bailey. Colin Starbuck Moran, Regan Starbuck Moran, Macy Starbuck Moran. Katherine Mary Moran, Jack Robert Moran, Charlotte Cecile Moran. Katherine Clair Hanson, Caleb John Hanson, Andrew Patrick Hanson and Elizabeth Ann Hanson. Morgan La Von Clair, Alexander John Ubben, Eleanor Irene Ubben. Connor Michael Clair, Lillian Louise Clair.

A lot of people helped me. There are too many to name including some that would be at risk of retaliation if I did name them.
You were absolutely God-sent.
A forever thank you to Marj and Ray Pierce. I could not have done this without you. Thank you to: Ryan and Heather McCrillis, Joshua Morgan, Arnold and Nancy Roberts, Nina and Mark Haines, Slona Wallace Forbes.

Heartfelt gratitude to my brother, John Charles Clair.
Always ready with bits of wisdom, a shoulder to cry on,
and unshakable faith.

Table of Contents

Table of Contents

INTRODUCTION

"No State shall make or enforce any law which shall abridge the privileges or immunities of citizens of the United States, nor shall any State deprive any person of life, liberty, or property, without due process of law; nor deny any person within its jurisdiction the equal protection of the laws." United States Constitution: Fourteenth Amendment

As you read this book, you may ask, how could this senior citizen have been targeted for a level of corruption that started in the charming court square of Fayette County, Tennessee? So iconic of rural middle America that it could easily be chosen as a film location. Then spread its venom all the way up to the U.S. Court of Appeals for the Sixth Circuit? Is it possible that in writing about another scandal, Helen Davis Chaitman[1] who labeled our nation's largest banks the "new mafia" could be right? Do they have such power that they can subvert a Treasury investigation and interfere with the Constitutional Rights of ordinary Americans over a long span of time? Sadly, the answer is, yes.

For an illegal organization to thrive there must be contempt for ordinary people. There must be an indulgent rush of accomplishment when successfully plundering the assets and harming the welfare of others. For a RICO Criminal Enterprise to operate on a national scale many people must hold together and not crack. Crimes must be normalized as the cost of doing business. Such practices lead to widespread systemic corruption in institutions that no longer function for the public welfare. Two men, one of them a judge, did threaten the ongoing operations of the Criminal Enterprise described in this book. They were positioned as insiders with the power to bring down the entire house of cards. They are both dead.

My fight for recognition of these crimes ran counter to the rigid conception of how victims are scripted to fall into line. Potential victims are researched and profiled as unlikely to fight back. Skilled con-artists blame shift to victims causing them to feel extended trauma and harassment. The goal is to silence any person inclined to investigate theft of their home. I am alive today only because I have

---

[1] JPMadoff: The Unholy Alliance Between America's Biggest Bank and America's Biggest Crook. By, Helen Davis Chaitman and Lance Gotthoffer; copyright 2013.

been consistently underestimated. I did not accept at face value the mountain of document fraud that told a story at odds with reality. When I first sought to make sense of a tangled web of lies, I had a lot to learn.

Unequal application of justice that favors an elite class has become an epidemic in the United States. How does a mafia-like organization exercise such power? Within these pages we examine just how The Bank Theft Delivery System operates. The chain of theft is not difficult to spot when understood in the context of what federal investigators have dubbed a Property Flip – Equity Skimming – Title Theft Scheme(s).

Theft of private property under the umbrella of an illegal foreclosure is a billion-dollar industry. It is in recognizing where the bulk of these properties end up that we see the Racketeering Criminal Enterprise at work. I filed a Civil RICO Case pro se and under pauper status at the United States District Court in Memphis, TN. If you have a similar story to tell, I'll be describing how the Racketeer Influenced and Corrupt Organizations Act may work for you.

RICO: 18 U.S.C. § 1962I: It shall be unlawful for any person employed by or associated with any enterprise engaged in, or the activities of which affect, interstate or foreign commerce, to conduct or participate, directly or indirectly, in the conduct of such enterprise affairs through a pattern of racketeering activity or collection of unlawful debt.

The statute of limitations on Civil RICO start when victims recognize how they were harmed. Not when they were harmed. This is a distinction with a huge difference. This makes CIVIL RICO a viable alternative for those that have been told that it is too late to seek justice. That watershed moment of recognition may arrive as you delve into the pages of this book. With or without an attorney, the work you do to bring a Civil RICO case into a federal courtroom may lead to criminal charges.

I only recently discovered that I have an ancestor that fought as a colonel in the Revolutionary War of Independence. Hard won liberties were achieved at the cost of bloodshed; fighting another world-stage despot power. The dangers for us today come from within. Widespread corruption threatens our Constitutional Republic. This organized criminality has such a reach that it can obstruct what the United States Constitution and the Bill of Rights guarantee to every American. When we consider that this country just experienced a near successful coup d'**état** by federal employees who embarked on a treasonous endeavor to reverse a valid election it should be no stretch to consider that corrupt access to selectively block the due process rights of American citizens extends to our federal court system.

Mega corporations and the financial industry have no territorial boundaries. The world is their stage. A globalist worldview is not beholden to God given rights of individual thought, action, and liberty. The U.S. Constitution and in particular access of every American to due process represents a significant obstruction to greed fueled agendas. When Bank of America, JP Morgan Chase Bank, the Bank of New York Mellon and a corrupt judge conspired to obstruct my right to be heard in the open forum of a courtroom, the rights of every American were also endangered. The ease and expertise. The boldness by which obstruction of fundamental civil liberties slid forward to corrupt the appeals process per employees at the Sixth Circuit informs that I cannot be the only pro se victim denied basic and fundamental civil rights.

I did not follow the victim script that white-collar con-artists laid down for me. I wanted and needed to understand what turned out to be a chain of theft operating in every state. As I peeled back the layers, I saw a national scheme stealing homes on a massive scale. Doing so through a network of operatives; some local and some within the national footprint of the banking and securities industry. Many of these stolen properties end up pooled into securities. They are then bought and sold as a commodity on Wall Street or directly by banks to their investor-depositors. This cycle returns long term profit back to the criminal banks that put this pipeline in place.

Banks that have control over these homes pooled into securities have price-fixed the rental market leading to increased homelessness and the destabilization of families. Value is artificially inflated to back these securities keeping this a viable market. This may lead to the next financial meltdown. The entire operation is arrogantly fixated on the expectation of criminal banks that, once again American tax payers will bail them out. To thus, inform that we have a powerful mega globalist syndicate that considers itself above the law.

For these crimes against ordinary Americans to thrive the cooperation of certain federal agencies is needed. More locally appraisers, lawyers, loan officers, on board local bureaucrats, real estate agents and brokers and others. All ostensibly good people trying to make a living for their families. Or so some of them, told me when confronted. This system cannot exist except that everyone must agree. Corruption has a corroding impact on government. Crony corruptionism is all about the death of individuality. At some point it is safer to stay part of the raiding crew. To rationalize that a single perpetrator's contribution to the chain of theft is worth the fee, favor, and promise of future business, promotion, or patronage. Any that contemplate turning whistle-blower need only recall two deaths that I describe in this book. Message sent; breaking ranks may bring fatal consequences.

As I continued to speak out and seek exposure for these crimes I was marginalized, threatened, and slandered. I wrote and spoke to everyone from the United States Department of Housing and Urban Development (HUD). The Department of Justice. Departments within the State of Tennessee. The Internal Revenue Service (IRS). I did my best to make these crimes known to the white-collar crime unit at the FBI Memphis field office who in all effect slammed the door in my face. I concluded that, especially at HUD, unelected bureaucrats were fully invested in protecting the ongoing reach of the criminality, they had enabled by failing to do their jobs.

What other victims had suffered became evident in the wealth of document fraud dumped indiscriminately into the public land records. Poorly trained but duly elected Registrar(s) of Deeds and their staffs, even if they wanted to take steps to protect the public welfare, are hamstrung by antiquated laws that have not kept pace with the electronic age in which we live. After reading this book you will know exactly how to expose any chain of theft that resulted in the illegal seizure of your home in violation of the Fourth Amendment to the United States Constitution.

Other scandals have shown us that our government tolerates crime by a favored elite class of people. I have never given up the idea that others may be as invested as I am in exposing these same crimes, i.e., illegal seizure of private property on a, grand scale. Along the way I have met a few. Including a senior U.S. Treasury Agent whose investigation was shut down by the same powerful, Financial Industry Defendants named in my Civil RICO Law Suit.

This is not my story alone. The finely tuned, target-flexible, and methodically executed Bank Theft Delivery System that I describe in this book has impacted so many Americans that only after it is fully disclosed could a statistician come along to make an educated guess as to how many. These crimes cry out for recognition from law enforcement, legislators, and judges no longer bowing to a power hungry cadre of white-collar criminals. When corruption has overtaken authority, real change must come from the ground up. We need to make our voices heard. What is at stake is the preservation of property rights in the United States of America.

PART I

CHAPTER 1

"It is not our part to master all the tides of the world, but to do what is in us for the succor of those years wherein we are set, uprooting the evil in the fields that we know, so that those who live after may have clean earth to till. What weather they shall have is not ours to rule." J.R.R. Tolkien; Return of the King

The Back Story... It was night. Air kicked in through the vent and Brett turned over taking the cover with him. Cold air hit my legs as I snuggled against him. Declan, who had been sleeping on his dog bed near the door stirred. Me, awake changed the timbre of the room. By whatever watchful ability that we don't understand he knew that I was awake and considered it his job to mark such happenings in the minutiae of my life. No longer Brett's dog, by some process of osmosis like bonding, Declan has disengaged from Brett and attached to me. This dog I did not want became a loved and cherished friend.

Brett observed this change and remarked upon it only the week before. We were arguing about a bill that had not been paid, me in the wing chair and Brett on the leather sofa. Declan would normally be sitting at Brett's knee, looking back at me as if to say, "shut-up now, there you go, leave my man alone." Abandoning Brett, he had changed position to sit beside my chair.

Dog and owner shared a secret that Declan noted and did not like. It was the bodily internal change that had rendered Brett unreliable, even neglectful. That foreign chemical quotient escaping through pours in the skin. And by an avenue of partnership with sin, a spirit change, as well. Demons had caught the shirt tails of transference and followed my husband home hoping for greater gains of territory. For maximum impact, evil must rely on human conduits. Certain limitations were imposed on demons when they lost the war in heaven that is described in Revelation 12: 7-17. But that would be another book.

Brett was puzzled and a little hurt as he called Declan back to the other side of the room and dog refused to budge. In true enabling dysfunction I compensated, "He'll always be your dog first."

And with these words the argument that should have come to overdue resolution did not. Instead I recalled the day the breeder tied a red ribbon about the puppy's neck so that when next we returned, we would know which tiny bundle of inquisitive black fur was ours. We talked of this and how Brett had placed an unwashed sweatshirt in the puppy crate, bonding to the scent of a new owner. Brett named Declan after a character in an unfinished novel I'd written. Perhaps thinking the name would make me warm to the dog that initially I had not wanted. I finally conceded. "Okay, you take care of him." I did not imagine a Doberman.

Sensing these and other changes long before me, Declan had shifted parties and changed allegiance with no wooing on my part. I was amused that he seemed to consider me his new job as though I were crippled. As though I were wounded in a manner I did not recognize. Hours later he would be herding me down the steps, pushing me against the wall for ballast. But for now, on that fateful night, recognition was a few hours off. The secret was safe with the clock counting down the minutes. I turned on my side and closed my eyes. As I did so Declan rose from his bed. He turned in two or three quick circles and settled back sniffing in my direction, knowing I'd heard. Dog was on the watch. We exchanged this awareness as I slipped into sound and deep sleep.

When sound sleep falls on man, while they slumber in their beds, then He opens the ears of men and seals their instruction... (Job 33: 15a).

When I woke again a full moon had sent a bluish light into the room. I knew the approximate time by its position in the sky which made this possible. Simultaneously, I heard a voice and felt a presence standing by the bed. It was the solid place of space occupied, though my eyes saw nothing at all.

"Something is wrong."

I turned toward the voice, half rising on one elbow.

Because once was not enough and the tactical, world-centered part of my brain is wired to reject the supernatural, "Something is wrong."

I had just heard from an angel. He remained in that spot on my side of the bed, a, mid place between my head and my chest, communicating understated factual urgency. I didn't question this. Like many others I've experienced the unseen dynamics of Christian faith during certain junctures of life.

I've taught Bible for many years. Some have told me that my books would sell better if I did not insert my faith into the story. Others, with perhaps a denominational bias have not liked my take on the supernatural. In context to the back story I hope the reader will indulge me because the fact is, if we are people of faith, regardless of what form this takes, we are thought far more pliable to the whim and wiles of career criminals. My faith was used as an exploitive means to establish common ground upon which a pretense of friendship was established. Nothing about this friendship was genuine. It proved to have disastrous consequences still felt today.

Angels have three basic purposes in regard to humans. They are messengers like the angel Gabriel who announced to Mary that she would give birth to the Messiah. The angel Gabriel told both Mary and Joseph at different times exactly what they should name the unborn child. It is easy to imagine Mary and Joseph, their heads together talking about their mutual angel experiences, sharing the wonder of it all and coming together in agreement. The name was to be Jesus, and not as Hebrew tradition would have it, named after the supposed father, Joseph, the most famous step-father in the world.

It was also the angel Gabriel that calmed the fears of Joseph who, upon learning that Mary was with child thought to put her aside "quietly" so that Mary and her family would not be shamed.

Angels are organized in military like fashion with specific roles to fill. Some are warriors equipped for literal battle. One warrior angel identified himself as a, ***"captain of the host of the Lord."*** This warrior showed up on the eve of battle and let Joshua know that he was not alone in facing the enemy. The text itself informs our own battles; whatever they may be. ***Now it came about when Joshua was by Jericho, that he lifted up his eyes and looked, and behold, a man was standing opposite him with his sword drawn in his hand, and Joshua went to him and said to him, "Are you for us or for our adversaries?" And he said, "No, rather I indeed come now as captain of the host of the Lord." Joshua 5: 13-14b***

Another warrior angel account is described in 2nd Kings 6: 17. This account has always inspired my imagination. When I wrote the screen play to Wood's End, I wrote a similar scene into the last frame of the film I hope will someday be made.

This is what happened. Elisha's servant rose early and saw that in the night a great army had gathered and was about to come against them. The servant was struck with the paralyzing fear of doom. Greatly outnumbered he was certain that all would be lost and he would die.

Elisha comforted him with these words: ***"Do not fear, for those who are with us are more than those who are with them." Then Elisha prayed and said, "O Lord, I pray, open his eyes that he may see." And the Lord opened the servant's eyes, and he saw; and behold, the mountain was full of horses and chariots of fire all around Elisha (2nd Kings 6: 17).***

Those that wrote the New Testament read and repeated as unchanging bedrock wisdom and truth the Old Testament concepts using the same inspired imagery straight from the mind of God. In the following verse John's words are reminiscent of Elisha: ***You are from God, little children, and have overcome them, because greater is He who is in you than he who is in the world (1st John 4: 4).***

Angels are also guardians. Yes! We do have guardian angels that are specifically assigned to watch over the smallest detail of our physical welfare as we navigate a material world running parallel to what is not seen. ***For He will give His angels charge concerning you, to guard you in all your ways (Psalm 91: 11).***

Angels are not infallible. Though powerful beyond our imaginings they can be delayed or intercepted by evil spirit beings and fallen angels more generically called demons. It is good to pray for victory in the unseen realms. Special guardian angels assigned to your welfare, even when we are totally oblivious, are present in our lives. God assigns His angels specific duties. King David had a finely attuned sense of the supernatural dynamics of godly protection. David wrote: ***Let those be ashamed and dishonored who seek my life; let those be turned back and humiliated who devise evil against me. Let them be like chaff before the wind, with the angel of the Lord driving them on. Let their way be dark and slippery; with the angel of the Lord pursuing them (Psalm 35: 4-6).***

Obviously, the angel sent to me that night in 2010, to speak three simple words, "Something is wrong," was a messenger angel. God sent him because I had not been paying attention. You could say that my dog was better informed than I was. This is a failing of mine... to be so focused and intellectually engaged in what I'm doing that I do not always notice what I should.

"Something is wrong." I came fully awake. Brett was no longer beside me, though this was not a bit unusual. My husband of ten years suffered from chronic insomnia and as a routine slept no more than three or four hours at a time. I got out of bed. Some instinct told me not to turn on the lights. I walked through the living room into the kitchen area. Moved into the family room and checked the office. I walked to the back, door half expecting to see Brett standing on the patio, bathed in moonlight and smoking a cigarette, a habit he had taken back up.

I had lately become worried about Brett's health. I am going to be graphic in the hope it will help others recognize common signs I saw, but... call it denial, failed to see. His urine had a bad smell. I suggested he see his doctor. I did not know him as a full-blown Alcoholic, but this is how he described himself telling me in one of our first meetings that he had started drinking at age twelve and that alcohol was his drug of choice. At the time he was clean and sober and was over men's ministry at a ministry we worked at together. Ignorance caused me to take Brett's sobriety for granted.

I was oblivious of how fragile, how precious, was this "one day at a time," commitment to stay sober. Other changes were baffling but I was not connecting the dots. I was working long hours at this time in a new job. Conversations had become perfunctory and blandly superficial. Brett was always coming or going as was I. But while I was tired, ready to fall into bed at night, Brett was restless. Appointments he had took far longer than normal. There were prolonged unexplained absences. When making love, he could suddenly not come to climax; the emotional intimacy we shared was absent; the marriage bed no longer a shared experience. I had begun to feel lonely in my marriage.

It had been our habit to pray and read scripture together. Brett no longer initiated this as he had in the past. Church fell by the wayside. At this time, I worked as the operations manager at a Christian counseling ministry. This was a job change that Brett was against me making. There had been lots of turnover and though I was brought in to make changes, the director wanted no part of this. Brett resented that I had not taken his advice, leaving a secure position as Director of Development at a large Church. As it turned out he was right and I would soon lose this job, compounding the problems I would face ahead.

At different times in our marriage Brett or I paid the bills. Over the previous year he had taken on this responsibility. Only the week before

I had found a packet of mail ignored and unopened. Among the mail was a letter from a bank notifying Brett of an overdraft charge from an account I did not recognize. He was moving money and draining certain accounts for at least six months before I noticed.

"Something is wrong."

I turned my attention to the upstairs; three rooms. I reached for the light switch, but then just as quickly removed my hand. To my right was the closed bathroom door. Just as I knew not to turn on the lights, I knew not to knock or announce my presence. It was as if I were being guided and inaudibly instructed because, something was decidedly wrong and it was now well beyond the point that I should have noticed. In His very great kindness, God took the self-imposed, fear-based blindness off the table.

Brett jumped as I opened the door. Our eyes met in mutual shock. There was a plunge of my heart that I have never felt before and hope to never feel again. I can't say how my beloved husband would have described my expression. I only know that I was seeing Brett. How gaunt he had come to be and the thousand other shreds of broken glass that came together in a mosaic of recognition that was not exactly shock or surprise. I was seeing what I already knew to be true.

Brett sat on the edge of the tub, the needle still in the vein. Blood had spurted in an arch and landed a red stain on the white wall. Other spatters on that same wall.

I'm a fixer. I'm a list maker. When I'm writing I am disciplined enough to know that I can do some part of the writing process whether I feel the inspired creative juices or not. Being logical and proactive at times of crisis is my default speed. My mind raced ahead already planning how this man could be "fixed." I would turn back the clock and fix us. We both loved Jesus Christ. We loved each other. Even as my mind took me to this place my body betrayed the truth. I stumbled as I turned to walk down the stairs. But for Declan pushing his body against me toward the wall I would have fallen.

I wanted instant answers and diligently sought them. Trouble was Brett was not my fixing to do. No logical formulistic sequence of tasks would work beyond the superficial. God loved and was concerned about Brett, but He was just as much concerned about the log in my eye. ***So, then it does not depend on the man who wills or the man who runs, but on God who has mercy (Romans 9:16).***

This one event marked the beginning of a five-year spiral of multiple crisis and wrenching losses that would have been too much to bear if I'd been able to look into the future and see the path ahead. Not that I'm comparing... We don't know how many years Job's trials lasted. But we do know they did not begin and end overnight.

A year later Brett had been to, rehab and then entered an outpatient program that required my involvement. He was going sporadically to Alcoholics Anonymous more to manage my fears than for himself. Although I didn't know this, another woman had entered his life.

I then had another supernatural experience that rocketed me off dead center denial. I'd been invited to an evening church service at a church I was not familiar with to "share afterwards" with a few women that had read my book, Wood's End. These women had presold some of these books and I was to bring the signed copies with me. I imagined from the conversation and confirming email an informal non-event. Books were in the trunk of the car and I was so very happy to have Brett accompany me. I recall bending down to give him a quick kiss through the open window before he drove off to park the car.

When life with Brett was good it was very good colored by an unnatural intensity for that recognition that peace was unlikely to last. A pattern had emerged. When Brett relapsed, he could be gone with no word of his welfare for days on end. He held all power over my welfare... a power I had handed over and was struggling to take back. As he white-knuckled a fragile grip on sobriety, even at times of apparent calm I was taking nothing for granted, in a hyper-vigilant state of guarded optimism. We had moved into an unhealthy enmeshment. I desperately needed, but had not yet discovered Al-anon.

It seemed to be dawning on both of us that I was no longer what Brett wanted. I was no fun at all. I didn't drink and I was abhorrently against illegal drugs, had found some flushed them down the toilet and threatened to call the police if ever they showed up in our home again. Brett knew me well enough to believe that I would not hesitate to follow through. When he married me, he knew what he was getting and, in some way, he perhaps hoped I would be enough to keep him sober.

With addiction in the picture facets of our relationship disintegrated into one of parent and child; the untenable spot no wife wants to be. Operating as if my every happiness hinged on Brett's ability to stay sober was a formula for failure. I looked for reasons to trust when really and truly trust was impossible and the person I once loved had morphed into a stranger. But on this day the seeds of hope flowered anew. It was the cruel seduction of false hope, the Judas-kiss that flowed from periods of reprieve.

I didn't watch him drive off. Strange that I can regret that now, as if watching Brett, turn that car away from the church parking lot and into the road could make any kind of difference. Abandoning me at that church was not the most terrible thing Brett ever did to me. If his addiction were the topic of this book, I would describe this old story and completely unoriginal protracted litany of addiction and you would never select this one event as the number one most horrible. It finally just felt that way.

As the church filled up and the musicians tuned their instruments, I stood at the window watching the parking lot, knowing Brett was not coming back. Only people who have lived this understand it. I'd been abandoned miles from home with no transportation and none of the books that people had already purchased and he was not coming back. He might never come back. Then the ax fell.

"Alex, I've allowed you twenty minutes to speak. I'll introduce you and then you can share about deliverance."

Deliverance! I was to speak on deliverance! The irony did not escape as I'm sure it hasn't escaped the reader. It was the pastor of the church and I was stunned. Satan had lined up a few familiar triggers, abandonment being the sling and helplessness the arrow.

Sitting in the pew, waiting to be announced, my scattered brain could not focus. I felt like a hypocrite. I was about to fall apart. You know... that kind of melt down that builds like a wave taking on the force of an over powering surf. Huge breakers ready to shred the heart, drowning hopes and expectations that were never really prayers, but demands. A sob rose in my throat.

"Now if you will welcome, Alexandra Clair..."

I took a deep breath. I stood. I heard the voice of God. And He didn't tell me what I wanted to hear. You love Brett. He loves you. Don't worry, I'm giving you back your marriage and soon all will return to normal. No... that wasn't it. Not at all!

"I'm taking you somewhere Brett's not going."

And then a miracle took place. The earth didn't shake. Choirs didn't sing, but later I thought they should have and probably did at...

that place described by the prophet Jeremiah. ***A glorious throne on high from the beginning is the place of our sanctuary (Jeremiah 17: 12).***

A wonderful peace came over me. I can't say I pulled myself together because I had nothing to do with it. I rose from my chair and walked to the podium to share as authors do. When it was all over, I called my friend, Rosalyn, asking her to come pick me up. The woman who had invited me, along with her husband, were nice enough to stick around until my ride arrived. The summer sky grew dark as we sat on the steps and everything around us closed down. I don't know what we talked about. My mind was entirely elsewhere.

Though she is one of my best friends I did not tell Rosalyn that I had heard the audible voice of God. It was too precious to me. It was at least a year before I shared the experience with anyone. Not because I was afraid, I would be thought crazy, but because the indelible experience was supernaturally personal and intimate in a way that words fail. It was too wonderful.

After this I began to move toward acceptance. Did you get that? I can only say that I moved by incremental steps toward the understanding that my love for Brett was not going to be enough to save him. I could not control him. I could not cure him. And hardest of all. I did not cause his inherited allergy to alcohol and then his spiraling addiction to drugs.

After this my life with Brett quickly deteriorated. There was a violent incident in which he pushed me against a wall when I refused him money and threatened to call the police if he did not leave our home. Once he was so paranoid that he thought he was being watched from our neighbor's attic window. As we stood in the dining room and looked across the street and in all earnestness, he sought to convince me of what had no basis in reality, my heart broke for Brett. There were many, but in another incident, he was in the VA Emergency Room and I did my very best to have him admitted, desperate to get him help. I stood face to face with that ER Doctor arguing until finally someone from the Psych-Rehab area came to assess his condition. This man walked Brett around the ER and decided he was no danger to himself. With a near doctorate in psychology, just short of his dissertation, Brett knew just what he needed to say.

Friends were pushing me to divorce Brett. I was very ambivalent. At this point a mutual friend that Brett and I had both worked with,

Pastor Larry Brown, offered Brett another rehabilitation program. Three days later his drug addict girlfriend drove six hours to get him out. Larry did not want me to give up. He, and his wife Toni came for dinner and Larry said something that has stayed with me; even haunted me. He said, "Satan has your rib."

Six years later, I remember the man he was; the love of my life. Under the influence of drugs and alcohol, at the point that I stopped making his destructive slide possible, he found someone else who would. Eventually Brett was sentenced to eighteen months for a third DUI. His booking photograph broke my heart. He was unrecognizable as the handsome man with a lock of shiny black hair falling over his forehead, his green eyes and striving intelligence all absent from the face that looked back from that photograph.

Eventually circumstances separated us to the extent that I held no influence. He no, longer called me in the dead of night to cry on my shoulder promising to get help. In love, mercy, and foresight God took out of my hands what I lacked the human strength to let go of. And letting go, really that's a metaphor. Life takes us to another place. Pain dims and becomes something else. We can never completely let go of those we have loved and lost.

"I'm taking you somewhere Brett's not going." There are very good reasons why we cannot know the future. One of the most valuable lessons I learned during this time came from Al-Anon. Although it wasn't labeled as such, they taught me the biblical principal of how to disengage from Brett with love. I had to change myself. I had to let go so that God could work. This was a process by which my emotions and unrealistic expectations were untangled and viewed with realism.

On March 3, 2011 our divorce was final. Brett signed a quit-claim deed, deeding our home to me on December 21, 2010. He elected not to be present for the divorce proceedings. Like most addict endings I was left to face financial consequences.

Even before our divorce was final, talk in my neighborhood had drawn the attention of a dangerous group of white-collar criminals. This group weighed the equity skimming potential of my home. They learned that I was not upside down on my loan but had placed a significant cash deposit at time of purchase in April 2005. As a result of the turmoil surrounding Brett's destructive slide into addiction,

I was profiled as the perfect victim. So beleaguered that I was unlikely to fight back.

What this evil group failed to consider is that loss was not preparing me to fold my tent, curl into a fetal position and give up on life. Though many times I wanted to do just that, God had another plan.

The Rock! His work is perfect, for all his ways are just; a God of faithfulness and without injustice. Righteous and upright is He (Deuteronomy 32: 4).

CHAPTER TWO

"This country's major financial institutions are sick to the point of being toxic. JPMC (JP Morgan Chase Bank) is the biggest bank in the United States and the best example of the problem. But it is not alone. As the news media confirm virtually every week, the major financial institutions are routinely pleading guilty to violations of criminal laws- with absolute impunity. And the recidivism rate of banks at major financial institutions is truly shocking."[2]
Helen Davis Chaitman

The Racketeer Influenced Corrupt Organization Act (RICO), 18 U.S.C. §§ 1961-1968 was enacted on October 15, 1970, as Title IX of the Organized Crime Control Act of 1970. When Congress enacted RICO, they included a civil remedy provision for ordinary American citizens like you and I. It reads that we are empowered to act as citizen prosecutors. This challenges the elitist bias that equates pro se to mean no lawyer equals no case.

Its purpose was initially to deal with the mafia, but later served a far broader application to address mafia-like criminal activity as exercised by an "association-in-fact" criminal group or enterprise. RICO allows prosecution and civil penalties for racketeering activity performed by and as part of an ongoing, organized, criminal enterprise. If law enforcement is ignoring those crimes committed against us, we are empowered under the RICO Statutes to file a civil case in federal courts.

Organized crime, including those crimes committed by the banking industry are obviously not fans of Civil RICO. They would like nothing better than to place restrictions which legislators at the time left deliberately broad. In the corrupt culture of today some have learned to do an end run around legislators, law enforcement, and courts. I ran into many of these obstacles.

Under Civil RICO a private plaintiff is allowed to sue for injuries to their business and, or, property caused "by reason of" a defendant's

---

[2] JP Madoff: The Unholy Alliance Between America's Biggest Bank and America's Biggest Crook. By, Helen Davis Chaitman and Lance Gotthoffer. Opening words from Chapter Nine.

violation of RICO; (18 U.S.C. § 1963). The set of laws, when broken carry both criminal and civil penalties. Further along I've listed some. Only the feds or states attorney generals can bring a criminal case. These laws are very clear. When two or more of these laws are violated, they are part of the criteria that establishes a valid case filed under the RICO statutes. These violations are called, RICO Predicate Acts. Predicate means foundation. They are the foundation upon which a Civil RICO Case can survive a challenge by the opposition. Though I reference some of these laws you can go on line and download the list.

Many judges have a bias against lawyer-less Americans filing Civil RICO cases. They take up a lot of time, cost a lot of money, and challenge the prejudicial attitude that only if federal prosecutors consider a case worth investigating should it be brought into a federal courtroom. This rationale is Orwellian double-speak to say that ordinary Americans do not have the right to stand in the open forum of a courtroom and decry those crimes perpetrated upon the public by a mafia-like Criminal Enterprise. The truth is there are not enough regulators, investigators, and federal prosecutors with the will and freedom to put any more than a dent in these crimes.

All of us that paid attention in civics class know that the United States Constitution was not written for a select few. It is upon the fundamental right of access to due process that a healthy democracy survives. When government is overwhelmed by corruption or societal out of control levels of white collar crime individual Americans, under Civil RICO, are empowered to act. If we cannot afford the costs associated with such a case, we can file for pauper status. The American government will incur the cost and upon request, may even appoint the plaintiff an attorney.

Criminals hate that RICO is open to ordinary American citizens. In direct proportion to unchecked corruption more and more people like you and I will bring these cases to the federal system. The statute of limitations is liberal. Those that crafted the RICO statutes recognized that it takes time, sometimes years, before these crimes surface and can be recognized.

Thus, the Civil RICO clock starts ticking not when the crimes occur or end, but when victims of these crimes recognize how they were defrauded.

You may suspect you were defrauded. Every instinct tells you that your home was stolen. The foreclosure was a complete travesty.

This is not the same as knowing what happened. Having the language that ferrets out the criminal actions, knowing what laws were broken, laying out the very specific chain of theft, and naming the multiple bad actors.

After I appealed my Civil RICO case to the Sixth Circuit, Magistrate Judge Vescovo, with no explanation, arbitrarily changed the date that she declared my RICO case to be time barred. She recognized that I knew the foreclosure was a complete sham and that she could not hang her dismissal on this date. I had too much evidence and had dug too deeply into how these crimes operated. Covering for herself she failed to admit errors though she repeatedly and persistently slandered my claims. If corruption would win, she needed to block my case from achieving due process. She therefore forwarded that date so as to mislead the sixth circuit judges. She need not have bothered. Judges never read a word of my appeal. Trailing forward, denial of my right to be heard at the second highest court in the land was already in the bag.

All this to say expect a challenge premised on the RICO statute of limitations. Be prepared to meet that challenge head on. Courts are biased to think any foreclosure is the fault of the home owner. You will need to educate on how these crimes operate behind the scenes with no disclosure to homeowners.

Create a timeline. Fix the dates informed by facts. I did not begin my investigation until August 2012, four months after the brutal and illegal seizure of my home. Only then did the process begin by which I could begin to flesh out and recognize the chain of theft described in this book.

March and April of 2012 I had no clue that REO Investors had owned my home for the previous three years. I also did not realize that every dollar I sent, beginning in 2009 did not go to pay down a mortgage. Mortgage payments were being skimmed and labeled assignment of rents. This money went directly into the pockets of the private investor group; local white-collar criminals having targeted my home for theft in 2009. The local Jones, Kelley, Boyd Perpetrator Nexus – REO Private Investor Group had secretly acquired my mortgage from Bank of America premised on a forged Certificate of Abandonment and very low first appraisal. They had control of my Property Title. Over a three-year period, Bank of America made no disclosure to me holding up their end of the deal by pretending that nothing had changed. Thus, the REO secret Note-Holders were able to masquerade as Bank of America in all communication with me. They became the secret Note-Owners/Note Holders. This is Title Theft. The digital title to real property must then be laundered in much the same way that drug assets are laundered. This is not done overnight. It takes time. The big picture, seen in where many of these homes end up, is what I've come to label and describe as The Bank Theft Delivery System.

Whatever stage of the assault you are experiencing. Whether you are still in your home or not this book will tell you how to defend your property title and physical premises from outright illegal seizure. Despite what you may be told it is not too late. You are not helpless. Nothing you did or did not do was deserving of criminal acts that targeted your home, moving that theft-asset into the coffers of a RICO Criminal Enterprise. Federal investigations have dubbed the needed chain of theft a Property Flip – Equity Skimming Scheme.

PROPERTY FLIP SCHEME: "A fraudulent property flip is a scheme in which individuals, businesses, and/or straw borrowers buy and sell properties amongst themselves, normally within a short time frame, to artificially inflate the value of the properties."[3]

Many of the property theft examples I describe were initially undervalued before the flipping sequence began. This allows the secret Note-Holders to take out home improvement loans with the funds not used for the stated purpose. It is in the interest of these white-collar criminals that the property flip scheme not take place, *"within a short time frame"* as described above. The theft step process is the same, but in the twist, I describe takes place while homeowners are still living in their homes having no idea of what is going on behind the scenes.

Property title says who is the lawful owner of the home. This record has to be corrupted before your home can be stolen. A flip of a property title includes a transfer of authority, a sale, or transfers of the digital property title amongst the same members of the REO Investment Group. They do not yet have physical possession of the

---

[3] The Detection and Deterrence of Mortgage Fraud against Financial Institutions: A White Paper; FFIEC Fraud Investigations Symposium, page 36. Download and read this document. Found at: www.ffiec.gov/exam/Mtg_Fraud_wp_Feb2010.pdf

home because the eviction and illegal seizure has not yet taken place. It is the electronic title over which fraudsters have complete control. It is hard to believe but these transfers and transactions take place every day with no disclosure whatsoever made to home owners. Your lender has a fiduciary duty to hold up their end of the contract that is your Deed of Trust. They knowingly off load selected mortgages to these Private Investor Groups whose sole intent is theft.

The theft schemes I describe cannot take place without the knowing cooperation of our nation's largest banks. To distance themselves from complicity the Banks allow the private investor groups to assume the mortgage, no disclosure to homeowners. The new and secret Note-Holder now has the power to drive the mortgage into default. But first, as payoff for services rendered, they will skim real and fictitious equity. Their job is to guide the mortgage toward default per use of The Bank Theft Delivery System.

Much of this signed and notarized paper cannot surface in the public land records. If it did you would recognize that your, mortgage no longer existed. For all intents and purposes, you become a renter long before the charade of foreclosure takes place. This Property Flip interim period between secret assumption of the mortgage and the phony foreclosure is highly lucrative for the Private Investor Groups.

We get into the details further along in this book, but a lot of people help out. It takes a fully functioning predatory Criminal Enterprise working in tandem to streamline and perfect these thefts. Any that enable these crimes, regardless of what level of intent or participation are considered part of the RICO Criminal Enterprise. The RICO Statutes seek to root out corruption at its source by bringing consequences to those that make the criminal operations successful.

In regard to another case where some defendants tried to say they were innocent, and yet had helped perfect these crimes, in regard to the RICO statutes a federal judge in Maine ruled: **Participation in a conspiracy is presumed to continue until all activity related to the conspiracy is ceased. Accordingly, each defendant is presumed to be a participant for the duration of the conspiracy unless he can overcome the presumption by providing withdrawal. A conspiracy may be deemed to continue as long as its purposes neither have been abandoned nor accomplished. United States v. Battle, 473 F. Supp. 2d at 1205.**

You may feel overwhelmed. Here is a suggestion. Form a group of two or more families targeted by the same group of locally situated Private Investors. Pool your skills and gather the proof needed to undergird a set of RICO claims. The chain of theft is listed below.

1. Premised on a fraud narrative banks allow private investor groups to assume mortgages for the sole purpose of driving those mortgages into default. No disclosure to homeowners that a change has taken place.
2. Victims are carefully profiled and selected as unlikely to fight back.
3. The private investor identity replaces the homeowner identity.
4. Homeowners are defenseless since they never know what entity controls any outcome related to the mortgage.
5. The private investors launder the chain of property title, skimming equity, establishing a secret dual claim of ownership to thus, bury the original homeowner Deed of Trust under a mountain of document fraud.
6. Finally, the theft commitment requires that a very specific series of documents are filed in the public land records leading to the charade of an illegal foreclosure. These filings are described in Part 111.
7. The majority of these homes then end up as rentals, pooled into securities, bought and sold on Wall Street, returning long term profit back to the criminal banks that put this theft structure in place via bank approved vendor-partners.
8. The chain of theft begins and ends with the banking industry.
9. There are six key players to identify. They conspire and network to flush the stolen property title through the pipeline of The Bank Theft Delivery System. You need to understand the roles that each played in the theft of your home. Expanded more upon later they are:
   (a) Your Original Lender who under the contract of your Deed of Trust loaned you money to buy your home; that money secured by the physical premises of your home. Who then offloaded your mortgage to criminals – no disclosure to you, premised on a fraud narrative that slanders you and the title to your property.

(b) Mortgage Electronic Registration System, MERSCorp Holdings, Inc., the MERS E-Registration System.
(c) The third-party mortgage servicer companies.
(d) The boots on the ground, secret, REO Private Investor Groups to whom the bank secretly off-loaded your mortgage long before you knew there was a problem.
(e) The Title Insurance Companies hired by the REO Fraudsters to lie to each bank or lender that plays a role in laundering the chain of title; much the same way that drug money is laundered. Though it is not true, and they know it is not true, they assert that the secret Note-Holders claim to your property title is free and clear of doubt and fraud.
(f) Lastly the foreclosure mill attorneys. They knowingly file forged, reformed, theft concealing endorsements (signed and notarized instruments) into the public record. They are hired by the REO secret Note-Holders.

Much more about each of these mafia-like players further along. Together they form a RICO Criminal Enterprise. This book will show you where to find the needed proof and what to look for in the mountain of document fraud; much of it withheld from the public record.

CHAPTER THREE

"How about, instead of trying to design new and better regulation, we go with the regulation we've got and enforce it to the hilt? Ferguson (Charles Ferguson, Predator Nation**) says that if we did that, we would get the culprits one way or another. Except, of course, that they've got the whole regulatory system in their pockets." America's Criminal Crony Capitalism by, Michael Edesess**

From May thru August 2012 a pervasive inertia had trapped me in a cloud of depression. I was pretty sure that this level of self-pity must be a sin. There had been too many loses and with them came the invitation to believe the lie that nothing would or could change. I had lost job, home, and marriage. Then a different kind of grief stole sleep and appetite as I watched a good friend and creative partner fight the return of a fatal cancer.

Ambushed by a brutal eviction I was facing homelessness. Nina and Mark Haines offered me a place to live in a small apartment above their garage where I stayed for almost a year. It, was here that I grounded myself and made some monumental decisions. Would I move near my family and away from the scene of the crime? Or would I stay in West Tennessee, investigate and expose these crimes? This was not the kind of work I imagined for myself; no pay and no benefits. But the decision was pretty much taken out of my hands. God opened doors a crack and shut others with a resounding crash. Sometimes destiny is all about going in the last direction we would willingly choose.

For the first months it was a massive struggle to force myself each day to go through the motions required of daily life. On this particular morning I dragged myself to the computer. I typed in the address of the home I had been evicted from on April 25, 2012. I had no idea that I had been targeted over the prior three years by white collar scam artists. My very limited understanding told me that Bank of America had lied. Mistakes were made. I needed an attorney who would fix these mistakes. Yes, I was naïve. But what bled through to my computer screen on that fateful day in August acted like a catalyst. It shocked me out of a life-stealing, paralyzing stupor.

This was an industry only website that I needed a password to access. The information appeared just long enough for me to read it.

I was never able to print the page. The screen suddenly went blank. I had to restart my computer, but the words provided the first reasonable context to the confusion and harassment I had experienced. This first glimpse of truth would send me down a long road of investigation blocked at every turn by those that were committed to keep secret what I came to call, The Bank Theft Delivery System. Though others told me I was wrong, I clung to what I read that day. 65 Pinehurst Drive was purported to be valued at $100,000. A ridiculous sum, far less than fair market value. My home was claimed to be an REO Owned property beginning in 2009. Here was a history that was imbedded into a record that was absolutely untrue.

I asked the next logical question. To whom had I been communicating with over the prior three years if not Bank of America? To what entity had I sent money? To whom had I mailed HAMP Applications? Despite everything I believed to be true that entity was not Bank of America. Bank of America entered into a conspiracy to hide the fact that they had illegally off-loaded my mortgage to criminals. Mail continued to come on Bank of America letterhead though they were no longer the owner or the servicer of my loan.

By design of how this theft-step-process works there was almost no paper trail to be found in the public land records. Enter the bank created MERS E-Registry System, MERSCorp Holdings, Inc., a.k.a., the Mortgage Electronic Systems, Inc., collectively known as MERS. How this shell company functions to disenfranchise victims from the ability to protect their property title is explored in Chapter Nineteen.

I also asked myself. What did REO stand for?

(REO) Real Estate Owned Property. REO private investors are people who buy and invest in at risk real estate directly from the bank. Combined with the Keller Williams eEdge paperless system and the MERS E-Registry there is by design of the Bank Theft Delivery System described in this book a very reduced paper trail. A little further along we look at Core Logic and their Equator platform which serves to keep all the REO secret Note-Holders on the same page in the buildup to illegal seizure of countless homes across America.

Victims are profiled as unlikely to fight back. Death of a spouse, divorce, or any absence from the home due to illness were common themes. REO Investors take over, these mortgages considered easy targets directly from banks. Selling what may or may not be at risk mortgages, at least not until the REO Fraudsters get involved, there is a sales pitch. Local boots on the ground REO Investor Groups are needed. At minimum they include lawyers, real estate agents, and appraisers. The sales pitch to getting these criminal groups up and running, inviting REO fraudsters into the mix goes like this. *"The REO purchasing process can be quicker and simpler than a regular foreclosure."*

In other words, there is no foreclosure. The mortgages are assumed prior to the foreclosure charade. The cost is borne by the REO Private Investors creating a layer of distance from the criminal banks. The REO Fraudster groups hire the foreclosure mill attorneys to walk the pretense of a foreclosure into the public record. Homeowners never learn that banks have off-loaded their home to criminals who will then drive the mortgage into default, having every incentive to do so.

Going on to write: *"When buying an REO property there is no lengthy waiting period. REO's are as easy to find as other properties, but finding foreclosures can often be a comparatively daunting challenge."* Banks provide the information to those they let into the theft system. This is Keller Williams inviting their realtors to buy into and assist in growing this fraud scheme... more properties fed to the Wall Street Securities Market, returning long term profit back to the Financial Services Industry. These REO Fraudsters make money also. Not only are they able to skim equity, but some will eventually manage groups of rentals pooled into securities propped up by a theft structure. More about this further along.

Linking to REO fraudster partners: *Banks are willing to sell hastily in order to expedite the process of getting the property off their books. Available for far less than their market value."* ***Far less than their market value*** is code for fraudulent appraisals accepted by banks because there is an end game. This phrase is an invitation. It invites the Property Flip – Equity Skimming Scheme. Title Theft is the precursor. Title offloaded to criminals, no disclosure to home owners, still living in their home and just beginning to experience the scripted harassment in whatever form is fitted to the personal circumstance of victims. The theft field is open because banks are willing. Working through partners they sell this scam; *"REO's offer a myriad investment prospects."*

When an unregulated financial services industry was given cart blanc to commoditize American mortgages what did we think was going to happen? The mortgage, which may or may not be in trouble, is then driven into default.

Because homeowners do not know what is going on behind the scenes, they cannot defend their property title in real time as a foundation of document fraud is layered into official records. Document fraud going unchallenged paves the way for illegal seizure of private property.

Once targeted communication is strictly controlled. The banks are fully complicit. They put this operative highway in place. At some point house payments become assignment of rents. Though victims of these schemes don't know it, they are no longer a homeowner and the money sent to a third-party mortgage servicer company does not go to pay down the principal on the loan under the original Deed of Trust.

Only today, in hindsight do I know why Bank of America aggressively told me I could not apply for HAMP. They had already sold my mortgage at an unnecessary loss to REO fraud partners. A not quite with the program of deception, Bank of America employee, told me I could not apply for HAMP because I was already in the "turn down department." When I asked her supervisor what this meant I was told that there was no such department. There is. Whistle blower bank employees later acknowledged the truth though no Bank board chair or executive ever went to jail. More about this later.

Many others turned down for HAMP after being preapproved to apply already had their mortgages off-loaded to REO Investors long before the charade of foreclosure took place. HAMP is no longer with us, but the bones of this scam are operating today. The delay between the secret assumption of the mortgage by white collar criminals and the illegal seizure gives time for the REO criminals to skim real or fictitious equity; payment for services rendered.

REO Groups may be institutional investors. They may be smaller groups imbedded into local communities as was the case with the Jones, Kelley, Boyd and Keller Williams Realty group of bad actors that targeted me.

REO Groups are assigned a number identifier by HUD. The number identifier confers a façade of legitimacy, kind of like the Good Housekeeping Seal of Approval. In a theft context this becomes the cover under which some of these criminal groups operate. If the federal government says you are legitimate you must be. Right?

The Jones, Kelley, Boyd Perpetrator Nexus – REO Investment Group included a HUD licensed appraiser, lawyers, two real estate firms, two local title companies and a certified public accountant. These were the boots on the ground local bad actors that directly impacted my life. They were morphing mortgages into pools of rental properties, even before the foreclosure charade played out. This represents millions of dollars in assets. Seen in context to the national scope of these crimes this is a billion-dollar theft industry and set up for the next financial crisis. It is the REO Private Investor job to supply residential property to the Wall Street Market by any means possible including outright theft. More about securities fraud later on.

Upon reading that as early as 2009, three years before the illegal seizure, my home was "REO owned," the screen went blank. I had to close and restart my computer. Doing so I started over moving onto the next search choice. Now my home's value had increased. It was now undervalued by, $80,000. Better than the previous devaluation by $134,000. Both appraisals were prominent red flags denoting fraud. An appraiser working as part of the theft-crew had come up with this figure.

I set to work on that afternoon and all of the next day trying to track down the appraiser. Which led me to Keller Williams Realty. Which led me to the Dallas Corporate Office. Which led to me being aggressively threatened by the Keller Williams Realtor and straw buyer, Sherry Boyd. And by extension, her husband, Vernon "Wayne" Boyd.

Let's be clear. I still own 65 Pinehurst Drive. There is no clean chain of title to this property. Criminals had conspired to corrupt the property title. They took possession of what can only be called the, "theft asset," via an illegal seizure. Not only did I lose the equity, but I lost future value as the housing market stabilized. And I wasn't alone. The ongoing investigation into Fayette County land records revealed that what had happened to me was just the tip of the iceberg. In its totality a billion-dollar theft industry operating within a national footprint. In all effect a RICO Criminal Enterprise networked to local white-collar criminals and launched by our nation's largest banks.

I clicked on the next search choice. Now my home was claimed to have sold thirteen months later for $171,000. Now called an "REO repossession." Reading a little differently from the prior statement, "REO Owned." I was now seeing for the first time the bones of what federal investigators have labeled a Property Flip – Equity Skimming Scheme. The same REO Investor group were now claiming to repossess a home that per document fraud they already owned. This was my money. I was never upside down on my loan. But here was an explanation for why my home had never sold during the six months that I had it on the market. There was a secret history out there in the ether world. There was a dual claim of ownership. I did print this document. It became Exhibit Number twenty-eight in the Civil RICO Case I would file pro se under pauper status four years later.

Before any record can go public. Before any claimed valuation or sale price to straw buyers can emerge out of the Registry of Deeds Office where victims of this theft-scheme can find, copy, and read them the REO scam-artists have to incrementally increase the price. This to appear more in keeping with comparative housing values in your area.

If a victim, post foreclosure charade, went to a lawyer with proof that the property was undervalued by 30k this would not seem like such a big deal. There could be any number of reasons to explain a not quite right appraisal. However, if the same homeowner shows that same attorney proof that their home was devalued by say, seventy percent below fair market value. With any lender accepting and affirming what is a day-glow, neon-flashing fraudulent appraisal premised on a specific set of lies. That is a different story. That lawyer might decide you have a case he/she might be willing to take on. This is the last thing the fraudsters want.

The first set of transactions take place in secret. You are still in your home. Fraud perfecting signed and notarized endorsement grease the chain of theft. They are nowhere where you can find them even though you are a legal party, under the contract that is your Deed of Trust to what is taking place. A wall of secrecy and strict code of silence surrounds these fraud schemes. The goal is to slander and bury the homeowners Deed of Trust under a mountain of document fraud. This is a form of identity theft.

There is a beginning, a middle, and an end to this fraud scheme. It is planned and methodically executed. Victims are profiled. In my case the local group entered my life to monitor what I did and did not know. What actions I might take so that they could formulate a plan to obstruct those efforts. How these secret flips of the property title are accomplished and where to look for proof of them is described throughout this book. Examples other than my own are described in Part 111 of this book. Start a task list.

For me it was a long road to recognition. Upon reading this book it will be a far shorter journey for you. As you investigate the history of your property title you will want to identify the Appraiser(s) working with the

REO boots on the ground investment group of bad actors. The Criminal Enterprise appraiser involved in theft of my home was licensed by both the State of Tennessee and the United States Department of Housing and Urban Development (HUD). The role of the Appraiser in perfecting these schemes is crucial to their success. Every bank transaction that succeeds in smothering the property rights of the actual owners requires a series of fraud perfecting appraisals.

Submitting a fraudulent appraisal to any lender is bank fraud. It is a federal crime. It is also a RICO Predicate Act. Document the appraisal history of your home as tied to any loan taken out by the REO Private Investor Group of criminals. Very little (if anything at all) in the public domain will actually name them. Homeowner consumers are entirely disenfranchised from any ability to fight back by the stranglehold over information that would not be allowed by any other debt holder. As you shall see this is very much an extortionist debt scam.

Every loan using your home as collateral. Every secret assignment of authority over disposition of your mortgage represents another flip of the property title taking place amongst the REO Fraudster Group of bad actors.

"Detection and Deterrence of Mortgage Fraud" – Illegal Appraisal – Fraud type: For profit/for housing reads: ***Appraisal fraud involves an appraiser (often in league with other parties involved in the transaction) deliberately providing an inaccurate report on a property, <u>either inflating or deflating</u> the value or otherwise listing misleading information. Fraud may also occur in the form of a person inaccurately representing themselves as a state-licensed appraiser. An artificially <u>overvalued property</u> may be used to increase an agent/loan officer's commission or to create "phantom equity" for the borrower; it may also indicate a builder buyout (see below) or a potential Ponzi scheme in the works. An <u>undervalued property</u> could be a sign that the appraiser is assisting with <u>a short sale or loan modification fraud scheme</u> (again, see below). Review appraisal reports and make sure employees know what to watch out for. Red flags include incomplete/ vague reporting, photos not matching the property details, or a lack of accurate or recent comparables. From Federal Financial Institutions Examination Council (FFIEC).***

Many Property Flip Schemes include a short sale fraud as described above. There were five known flips of my property title amongst the same REO, boots on the ground, local bad actors. Due to the stranglehold over disclosure it took me awhile to discover them. Reading this book, you will have far less trouble.

Each flip helps to push forward the identity theft REO Note-Holder claims. Magistrate Judge Vescovo was persistent in stating that there had been a short sale. Explaining it out of context to facts I could not defend since I did not yet know them. If allowed discovery I would have found there was a short sale, just one never applied for by me. When I contradicted her statement, asserting that there was no short sale she wrote that assertion back into her conclusions. She was undermining my integrity to say she had privileged information I did not yet have; painting me as an unreliable witness to what I could and did prove. The fix was in. More about this later.

Every FHA loan requires HUD-1 closing documents. This is a kind of real estate closing disclosure form. Those who assisted in theft of your home are at least in part illegally paid at closing, from these closing funds. The HUD-1 will itemize these financial payouts. Every company and individual name are significant. Where fraud is involved the HUD-1 provides a wealth of information to any citizen-investigator. The information allows you to flesh out a picture of those that came together, lending their professional credentials and names to, for a fee, accomplish any one flip of your Property Title; skimming equity as title to stolen property is laundered through various transactions.

Neither HUD nor the lender will just hand these forms over to you. I expected a battle from those lenders assisting to launder the chain of property title, but given my claims of fraud and theft, certainly not from my own government. The Freedom of Information Act (FOIA) exists to provide transparency to American citizens for the very reason that corruption and illegal coverups by government must not be allowed to thrive in a culture that encourages law breaking by federal employees. When leadership does not want to know what is going on that culture gets communicated downline; a fundamental abdication of responsibility.

Over and over again the privacy of white-collar criminals enabled by HUD was the excuse offered for why I could not have what I was entitled to under the rule of law. HUD's Distressed Asset Stabilization

Program allowed Bank of America and the REO Investors to pool my home into one of these programs and then repurchase it out of that program making no disclosure to me – the resident homeowner at the time. My home was just one within a "batch" of other Fayette County Homes fitting within the same chain of theft. Investigating fraud and theft I wanted those records. You will find flips of your property title going on long before you recognized there was a problem. What HUD provided to every lender and criminal flipping the property title was the HUD Seal of Approval. Far better than the Good House Keeping Seal of Approval. HUD has made no effort to hold employees, banks, and REO investors accountable. Those I sought help from were resistant to any notion of justice.

The fact is that no bank or closing attorney would supply the HUD-1 closing documents. Especially not to an off the street citizen with a story that if proven true would expose bank fraud. Implicating the bank, loan officer, underwriter, closing attorneys whomever performed the title search for the part they played in perfecting theft of private property by failing to perform even a modicum of due diligence.

I did manage to acquire the Evolve Bank & Trust HUD-1 under a FOIA request. That was in the beginning, before I was labeled a pest and threat to ongoing institutionalized corruption. After that I could get no other. I kept asking HUD for the same information over and over again continuing up to today.

Among my requests, I wanted the identity of REO Identity Number: 00906148. HUD assigns these numbers to REO Private Investors. Look for these REO numbers in documents you uncover. Hiding behind a number identifier in commission of a financial crime is a RICO Predicate Act. These numbers offer an excuse to the banks who allow stolen property title to be laundered so as to avoid the required fraud detection protocols and practices they are mandated to follow. They do an, end run around federal regulations which they regard as an irritating mosquito bite.

To say that HUD, as a federal program has already done the work when nothing could be further from the truth. This is criminal collusion between our federal government and the financial industry operating a fraud and deceit upon the American public. In a 2014 email HUD employee Gregory Newberry replied: *A copy of the HUD-1 would have to come from the bank's loan file or the closing attorney's file associated with the property. Are you talking about the HUD-1's for Mr. Boyd's closings?"*[4]

This response is HUD lying as they routinely did; having a lot to hide. You can request these HUD-1's under a FOIA Request. Please note the plural use of "HUD-1's" and "Mr. Boyd's closings." They have repeatedly protected Vernon "Wayne" Boyd though he is a key player in the local REO Investment Group that targeted me and many others. Upon belief REO ID Number 00906148 conceal the Boyd's identity and by extension the RICO Criminal Enterprise.

What about HUD telling the simple truth should be hard. Why not, during that six-year period that I filed multiple FOIA Requests just answer the questions? Why aren't these REO ID numbers a matter of public record? The answer is that HUD federal employees have used tax payer money to make the rich richer. Homes that should have gone to homeless families, homeless vets, and low income struggling families whose pride of ownership would contribute to stabilizing neighborhoods, have missed out. To unprecedented levels, corruption has infiltrated federal programs. Though I cannot prove it, it is my belief that the HUD Memphis field office have taken bribes or otherwise been compensated for their role in failing to report property theft. Civil servants have been infected with the notion that the American Public does not matter. Sadly, for me obstruction of justice under the HUD umbrella extended to other field locations, including Atlanta.

You need the HUD-1 tied to any loan as a "flip" of your property title. HUD should send you copies of every HUD-1 tied to your property address. Same seller, same buyer, same broker, a decoy real estate company is information they already recognize as a red flag and yet fail to report as bank fraud. Every loan or transfer is a flip of the property title amongst the same bad actors buying and selling your home amongst themselves. The HUD-1 itemize the fees that are charged to the borrower by the lender when applying for a loan. The HUD-1 must feign an "arms-length-transaction;" no conflicts of interest. It is not that there are minor conflicts of interest tied to these flipping transactions. As you investigate the relationships you will find that

[4] Email from HUD employee, Memphis Field Office, Gregory Newberry, Wednesday, June 4, 2014; 2:28PM to Alex Clair. Subject: Time Line / Call Log. Many of these multiple properties alluded to ended up parked within one of the Kelley Family Trusts. Lennie Faye Kelley is sister to Vernon "Wayne" Boyd.

there are screaming out, dayglow, flashing conflicts that, if internal protocols and laws were followed these loans would be denied. Meaning that out of town, corporate ownership of residential property would not be harming families looking for a safe and affordable place to raise their families while price fixing the rental market.

Every loan and secret assign of authority amongst conspirators adds a layer of distance from the source document that is your original Deed of Trust. Each layer is meant to supplant your rights and identity with that of the REO Fraudsters. Sometimes corruption is so great and so imbedded in a system, having hijacked the original intent of a federal program, that people need to be fired and whole departments need to be done away with.

The HUD-1 closing documents will name many of the key players that helped perfect the theft of your home. Having these names will allow you to flesh out the local crew tied to the broader enterprise. Where fraud is involved, everyone on the same page, the, HUD-1 assigns to co-conspirators a role they did not perform. Or a title they have no real claim to so as to robotically comply with the requirements dictated by the forms they are filling out for the sole purpose of deception. The HUD-1 closing documents will reveal payments for services rendered in the commission of the theft of your home. Use the FOIA laws to go after every secret HUD-1 of record during the period you lived in your home and at least for the following year after, since there will be at least one other flip of the property title to straw buyers. Do not give up asking.

Start a letter file. Keep copies and document every request for information. Being organized saves time. You will need to refer to past requests for information documenting your outrage that you, as an American tax payer, are being ignored.

The fraudsters often propose a different set of facts in a decoy second HUD-1 related to the same transaction. Larry Lane Billings, submitted a second HUD-1, in defense of one of several fraud perfecting appraisals to the State of Tennessee.[5] A decoy and altered version of the original support fraudulent write offs at year end. These are cash heavy theft schemes. Every possible write off needs to be claimed. The IRS is routinely defrauded. They are also the one agency that no REO Investment Group wants looking over their

[5] State of Tennessee Department of Commerce and Insurance. Tennessee Real Estate Appraiser Commission; Complaint No.: 2015011901. My Civil RICO Exhibit No.: 19.

shoulder; delving into the theft of private property involving bank fraud, identity theft, securities fraud sharing information with other federal agencies also defrauded.

The HUD-1 must list other property sales of similar condition and value. The comparable examples are carefully selected for the sole purpose of validating the theft agenda. I found that some were homes subjected to the same chain of theft and also owned by the same REO Private Investor Groups. Create a file for each. Obtain copies of what is filed at the Registry of Deeds Office. Look up the sale history. Knock on the door, and strike up a conversation with the occupants. Are they renters or homeowners? Are they straw buyers? To mean a future flip and illegal bank loan is in the works.

Upon determining what was obviously not an arms-length-transaction Evolve Bank & Trust should have declined to approve what the title history informed was an attempt to re-vest the physical premises of 65 Pinehurst Drive with the same REO Investor-criminals. They knew that the buyers were REO previous owners and stated so, but chose to ignore what they'd been trained to recognize about a conventional Property Flip Scheme showing reckless disregard for their depositors. I later linked the loan officer with the fraudsters. Become expert at doing back ground checks.

Only after the physical seizure of the theft-asset has taken place is it considered safe for the secret REO Note-Owners to step out of the shadows At this point overwhelmed and harassed victims have already been forced from their homes.

The physical seizure of what has long been a digital theft asset cannot take place until certain documents are selectively forged, signed, notarized, and filed into the local Registry of Deeds Office. The foreclosing party must file the Assignment of the Deed of Trust. They must remove the original trustee and appoint a new, cooperating Trustee. There are state laws that force this exposure; otherwise the theft crew would not bother. The REO Note-Holders are never named in any document where defrauded homeowners can learn their identity. We look at these documents, how to read them and what they tell us about the chain of theft in Part 111 of this book. There is no originality in these property thefts. Get copies of all the signed and notarized paper dumped into the land fill of your county Registry of Deeds Office. Everything else is hidden away to mean that right from the start you are looking at Broken Chain of Title assisted by the county in which you live. Secret sales, assigns of authority to bank vendors, and transfers of the digital property title amongst members of the REO fraud-crew (skimming equity) are concealed in the bank created MERS E-Registry System. I devote an entire chapter to MERS (MERSCorp Holdings, Inc.) later on.

The last Evolve Bank & Trust transaction vested my home with Keller Williams straw buyers, Vernon "Wayne" Boyd, aka, REO ID No.: 00906148 and his wife, Sherry Boyd. This was a conflict of interest, arm in arm transaction, illegal on several fronts.

When you find proof that banks have failed in basic due diligence and perfected flips of your property title write a letter to those banks. Insist that they file a Suspicious Activity Report (SAR) with federal regulators. These reports are compulsory. The Office of the Comptroller of the Currency (OCC) regulates banks. Upon getting your report the bank is required to make that report known. Small and large banks have helped flip many other homes at the whim of criminals. Everyone is fairly convinced that the lack of legally required information flowing to consumers of mortgage loans has hamstrung their ability to recognize and push back against these crimes. Copy any letter of complaint to the OCC fraud division. Add to your letter file. Calendar when you think you should expect a response and follow-up. I found that no one expected me to follow-up and when I did, they were ill equipped to explain why nothing was being done about the crimes I reported. Cover-up was the scripted response.

Your home may or may not have been illegally pooled into a HUD program as mine was. This was the modus operandi of the Jones, Kelley, Boyd Perpetrator Nexus in regard to some of their thefts. HUD absorbs massive amounts of tax dollars. HUD employees facilitate the REO theft of private property.

In a wholly incomplete FOIA request of mine, in 2018, the Memphis Field Office sent their response to 65 Pinehurst Drive. The physical premises were illegally seized in April 2012. I had not lived there since. The address did not appear as my return address in any HUD communication. My home is still occupied by Keller Williams straw buyers, Vernon "Wayne" Boyd and Sherry Boyd. The FOIA response mailed directly to them needed to be signed for. It was accepted and not returned to HUD though the envelope would have been addressed to me. I know this because I stood in the tiny reception area of the

Memphis HUD Field Office, treated as if I were the criminal, as I asked for an explanation as to why I had not received a response.

Sending the extremely limited FOIA outcome to 65 Pinehurst Drive was a back door warning to conspirators. In effect the Memphis Field Office found a way to alert dangerous white-collar criminals that I was persisting in my investigation. With two people dead. Having been threatened myself. I did not take this lightly. The actions of the Memphis Field Office put my physical welfare at risk.

Use of Federal Housing Administration Transactions to commit fraud is a fraud upon the federal government, the American tax payers, and a RICO Predicate Act(s). A forged Certificate of Abandonment was presented to Bank of America. As a fraud device it was blindly accepted. It then trailed forward slandering other records. This same fraud device was used by the same criminal network to steal property title to other West Tennessee homes. You will want to verify if a forged Certificate of Abandonment has surfaced as a fraud device in the chain of theft that impacted you.

CERTIFICATE OF ABANDONMENT: This is a notarized statement that along with the phony appraisal allows the bank to retitle the property in the name of the REO Private Investor Group whose sole intent is theft.[6]

Almost simultaneously my home was then pooled into the HUD program. HUD took possession of my property, along with all those appearing in the same Fayette County "batch" rubber stamping the claim that these homes were abandoned and derelict.

Claim of abandoned property is a possible red flag that requires vetting for the truth. Evolve Bank & Trust in perfecting the post foreclosure flip of 65 Pinehurst Drive failed to follow any fraud detection practices. Which includes: **Obtain a title search and review for: the types of property titles shown (such as, abandoned title), type of deed transferred (quit claim or warranty deed), the owner of record, the dates of deed transfers, and amount and dates of any prior mortgages.** Cooperative lenders greasing the chain of theft did not: **Require a signed perjury statement that the documents**

---

[6] The Detection and Deterrence of Mortgage Fraud Against Financial Institutions: A White Paper. FFIEC Fraud Investigations Symposium; page 36. http://www.ffiec.gov

submitted (including the HUD-1's) are true and accurate. If they did, when I reported these frauds, no one bothered to act in any manner that curtailed widespread theft of West Tennessee homes.

HUD helps out. They did not file the transfer of 65 Pinehurst Drive (nor others) into this HUD program anywhere, where I, or any other victim could find them. This transfer of my Property Title did not appear as part of the title history at the Registry of Deeds Office. This failure resulted in, Broken Chain of Title. This transaction did not appear linked to my address, as it should have, in the public records three years before the illegal seizure took place.

REO Investors are required to hold onto these homes before they can sell them. Giving time to skim equity. And of course, these homes are never actually offered to the buying public on a level playing field. That would defeat the end game of feeding property to the financial industry. From Atlanta, to Oklahoma, to Memphis HUD employees were aggressive at denying every FOIA request. They were obstructing recognition that what happened to me was no isolated instance of theft.

What happened next? HUD allowed the Criminal Enterprise to almost immediately repurchase my home and the others in that same "Batch" out of that same HUD program. HUD allowed the Jones, Kelley, Boyd Perpetrator Nexus, now formally designated the secret Note-Holder three years before the illegal seizures took place to perfect title theft. It is no random accident that homeowners are rendered unable to defend against what the system fails to disclose.

Under, 18 U.S.C. 1010 a HUD statute reads in part: ***Prohibits the making, or publishing any statement, knowing the same to be false, or altering, forging, or counterfeiting any instrument, paper, or document, or willfully overvaluing*** (or undervaluing) ***any security, asset, or income, for the purposes of obtaining any loan, with the intent that such loan will be offered to the Department of Housing and Urban Development (HUD) for insurance, or otherwise attempting to influence in any way, the action of the Department.***

Link any claim of REO ownership to whether HUD ever held your property title making no disclosure to you, performing no due diligence, no follow-up, and failing to file notice where you could find it with the County Register of Deeds Office.

It seems only just and logical that HUD should immediately charge REO Fraudsters with defrauding a federal program. In doing so they would have to admit and deal with the fact that their employees helped to streamline these thefts via the national scope of operations. They should return all properties in that Fayette County "batch," including 65 Pinehurst Drive to rightful owners. Even if it means backing my home and the many other theft-asset homes out of the securities they were illegally pooled into. Restoring integrity must start somewhere.

The State of Tennessee Cover Up. I filed a complaint with the Tennessee Real Estate Appraisers Committee. The outcome was critical of the Appraiser, Larry Lane Billings. It is filed as Exhibit No.: 19 with my Civil RICO Complaint. This was independent proof of fraud. As a pattern of practice, it undergirded my RICO Claims. It was thus, ignored by a corrupt Magistrate Judge at the *screening for merit* blockade discussed further along in this book. No measurable reform came from the crimes I reported or helped other Tennessee victims. In hindsight it seems clear that the appointment of an independent reviewer I had no access to, was not allowed to inform with other evidence, could not even have his/her name was merely an empty exercise designed to appease and get rid of me.

In a conference call with the Tennessee Office of Legal Counsel I accused these state officials of sitting on proof of bank fraud and doing nothing about it. They too were obligated to report what they knew. Protecting the income streams of persons far better connected than I, took a back-seat to the welfare of hardworking Tennesseans' similarly defrauded.

Powerful companies and people are behind The Bank Theft Delivery System. I am not the only victim whose cries for justice have fallen on deaf ears. The cadre of criminals that targeted my home as one example of many conspired with Tennessee state employees to keep me from attending a scheduled meeting with the Appraiser Committee. I wanted to go and made plans to be there. Once again, I was denied the right to speak and be heard in any forum that would produce a record that could arm other victims to fight back. And, or, lead to prosecutions.

I was abruptly told that the December committee hearing would be a closed-door session. I could suddenly not attend. There would be an anonymous outcome. I would have no access to any determinations coming out of that meeting. I would not know what evidence was or was not presented. By this time, I was very familiar with damage control, cover-up, and violations of my civil rights. Growing frustrated with the bureaucratic insider catch and kill mentality of protecting criminals I sent the following reply.

From: Keeling R. Baird [mailto:Keeling.R.Baird@tn.gov]
Sent: Friday, December 04, 2015 9:14 AM
To: alex_clair@... No longer my email address.
Subject: FW: Complaint #201501190-Billings, Larry Lane

RE: Complaint #201501190-Just to be sure I understand what you are saying. 'Keeling R. Baird'
Fri 12/4/2015 2:43 PM

Are you saying that I will not have a copy of this anonymous report? And... I will not have a copy of your legal summary extrapolated from my file and from any defense made by others from which conclusions are drawn in creation of this anonymous legal report? And this file. Is that too anonymous? I will not have any copy of any written or verbal defense made by any party connected whom you might decide to interview based on information I supplied and which inform decision regarding next steps. That too is anonymous? Lastly, I will share in no resolution of the complaint and since this report is secret, I can't dispute... cannot dispute any wrong or erroneous statements made by the perpetrators who stole my property with additional proof. Why? Am I right? Because... its anonymous and I won't have a copy? And you are not interested in other proof I've accumulated upon which fraudulent appraisals are needed in order to achieve a Property Flip/ Cash out Equity Skimming Scheme which is a crime. Is this the United States of America? Is your department accountable to taxpayers? However... this is something. I can sit passively by and listen to what? Identity of what's on your agenda of 12/14/2015. But I'm not allowed to speak. And outcome is determined by your committee behind closed doors. Please correct me where I am wrong. It is important that I <u>not</u> fail to interpret conclusions I've drawn by what you have described. I stand ready to be corrected where I am wrong.

Which leads me to ask. Have you interviewed any persons I named in my answers to your questions? Is that too anonymous? And in sharing my information with these persons and my charges I am prevented from knowing any defense that was offered to your department and I'm not afforded the same privilege on a level field. So here we have a huge imbalance of power that disenfranchises consumers. Thank you in advance for your reply. I look forward to clarity. Alex Clair

From: Keeling R. Baird [mailto:Keeling.R.Baird@tn.gov]
Sent: Friday, December 11, 2015 10:20 AM
To: alex_clair@comcast.net
Subject: Regarding the Tennessee Real Estate Appraiser Commission meeting

Hi Ms. Clair,

I wanted to let you know that legal counsel has decided to look further into your case and have the appraisal report sent to an expert reviewer for possible compliance issues. Because this will take a little extra time, I have decided to remove your case from the December 14 Commission meeting agenda. Therefore, your case will not be presented on that day. It is my hope that we will have this issue resolved in time for the January Commission meeting, and it will hopefully be ready for presentation at that time. I wanted to let you know so that you don't make a trip down to Nashville on Monday for nothing. Please let me know if you have further questions.

Keeling R. Baird | Assistant General Counsel, Regulatory Boards
Legal Division
Davy Crockett Tower, 5th Floor
500 James Robertson Parkway
p. 615-741-3072

I was then prevented from attending the next scheduled meeting. A summary by the expert reviewer whose name they refused to disclose was a significant obstacle. Though the report is critical of Larry Lane Billings one cannot say it was a legitimate independent process since Tennessee officials placed a choke hold over the very limited evidence provided to him/her. Among the "mistakes" Larry Lane Billings was censored for: *The property was previously listed between the dates of 5/5/2011 and 11/5/2011 for $234,000, which falls within the twelve months of the effective date of 7/29/2012. No analysis of this listing was presented.*

As absolute proof of theft this MLS listing falling within that date range could not appear in any HUD-1. This is because on May 16, 2011 JP Morgan Chase Bank handed over $100,000 of my equity to the Jones, Kelley, Boyd Perpetrator Nexus. This loan established the dual claims of ownership complained of by other victims. This loan obstructed me from selling my own home. The mystery "independent reviewer" was selectively fed information with the goal of protecting white collar criminals and the ongoing theft of Tennessee homes. They asked, did I want this report? Heck, yes!

The appraiser is an important actor, within the Criminal Enterprise. Larry Lane Billings presented photographs taken by my real estate agent in May 2011; passing them off as his. This to falsely assert that the 100k of stolen equity per the JP Morgan Chase Bank Loan had made improvements to 65 Pinehurst Drive. I somehow think I would have noticed if in May 2011 contractors suddenly showed up to make unneeded repairs on a home, I was living in and had just listed for sale.

In a letter Larry Lane Billings complained that I had too much information and that this represented a violation of his privacy. In Orwellian double speak he was the victim and I was the perpetrator. I continued to ask for a real and comprehensive investigation. Doing so in desperate hope that the State of Tennessee would protect their citizens over the interests of powerful REO white collar-criminals, working under the auspices of powerful corporations and the Financial Services Industry bad actors. I sent the following with attachments; some of which had already been sent but consistently ignored.

TN Department of Commerce and Insurance
Ms. Keeling Baird
Davy Crockett Tower, 5th Floor
500 James Robertson Parkway
Nashville, TN 37243

TN Complaint # 201501190
Subject Property: 65 Pinehurst Drive; Oakland, TN 38060

January 30, 2016

Dear Ms. Keeling:

This is a formal letter meant to convey my expectation that I will be fully included, appraised, and copied per any investigation conducted as a result of my complaint. Please affirm that no information will be withheld which disenfranchises me from ability to defend myself in an upcoming Civil RICO Case. And where a crime has been committed you, your department, and generally the State of TN whom you serve are as interested in justice as I am.

Not just for myself but for the many others harmed by the same Criminal Enterprise. If transparency and disclosure is not a reasonable expectation when crimes have been committed, I would like that clarified along with copies of whatever laws or policies in which that practice is rooted.

I am requesting a full copy of my complaint file. I am requesting copy of a former complaint made in 2013 and any resolution of that complaint which I never received. Also, a copy of any defense made and identity of whom the TN Real Estate Appraiser Commission interviewed and from whom information was requested as your department moves toward resolution; not possible without transparency per your department and accountability directed toward those that break the law. Copies and Information gleaned from any attempt to resolve my complaint and my claim of Theft by Deception, with timely updates of progress. I expect unedited copies of any reports generated, copy of any photographs presented as evidence to substantiate false appraisals and slanderous claims of an abandoned and derelict Subject Property. Copies of Appraisals upon which the Real Estate Fraud Scheme(s) depended.

Please send me a copy of the Appraisal Report you referenced in a prior email.

I am also requesting the last two Audit Reports for Kelley Mortgage Company, LLC #172569. I am requesting the last two Audit Reports for AMS Servicing, LLC #41578 / License active in 2012, but perhaps no longer active and now operating as Seneca Mortgage Servicing, LLC.[7]

I would like a meeting with the TN Attorney General's office, property fraud investigative unit if there is one. If there isn't one then the appropriate investigative unit attached to the TN Attorney General's Office. Reason: The 32 other properties that have experienced the same assault / modus operandi per criminal pattern and practice.

Seven (7) Enclosures:

- The liquidation record / Countrywide Home Loans for CWALT / Bank of New York Mellon. Clearly shows false claims based on fraudulent

[7] Now Nationstar Mortgage. When the heat threatens exposure of criminal patterns of practice spanning many decades these third-party mortgage servicer companies and others are allowed to pay a fine while accepting no blame; receiving no jail time. How does this serve the public welfare? There is no real or fair compensatory restitution to victims.

appraisals per Criminal REO Investors that ruthlessly targeted my home for Theft by Deception. Note the realized loss column where no loss should be evidenced given the true value of the property. Highlighted Line.

- HUD-1 Uniform Residential Appraisal Report / FHA Fraud Scheme. Highlighted area. Raises lots of questions.
- Price History for 65 Pinehurst Drive / Zillow
- Email / Carole Ann Burns. Only legitimate listing 3/25/2012 – 11/07/2011 / Reference for 1/12/2012 piggybacks fraudulently on this listing. I'm still in the home 1/12/2012 and have not yet been informed by the Criminal Enterprise that I've been turned down for HAMP. This attempt of Keller Williams MEM 2, LLC to hide their role and identity behind Crye Leike Realty.
- 1099A / Please note the discrepancy between what was claimed by BANA[8] / REO Criminals and what Bank of New York Mellon received. Discloses a deliberately undervalued property and bank fraud.
- Bank of America. Exhibit 7
- As a reminder my startled response to your claim that I can expect no disclosure regarding my compliant; its disposition, and resolution. I repeat. I look forward to clarity.

In looking at the list of members of Tennessee Real Estate Appraisers Commission it does not appear that there is a "real" "Public Member." My understanding is that this person would be an unbiased member; lending a voice that is not connected to the industry per Real Estate or Mortgage Banking and therefore with no agenda to protect. Please clarify the commissions understanding and the state's definition of "public member."

Thank you in advance for your response.

Larry Lane Billing kept his license. If I'd met him, I may have been able to put to rest questions about his identity. Is the name Larry Lane Billings an alias for Jeffrey L. Kelley? Just, as he and REO ID No.: 00906148 (Keller Williams and Vernon "Wayne" Boyd) have been protected by HUD the larger scope of these crimes, have gone unrecognized by their victims and thus, by design, are not prosecuted.

[8] BANA, aka, Bank of America.

Too many people are just making too much money. Crony corrupt accommodation operating in state government has worked over time to conceal these crimes.

I am still praying that someday I can stand in a courtroom, before an unbiased judge. I imagine a jury of my peers. Having an attorney passionate about the Bill of Rights and finally presenting my evidence. I recently woke from a dream with tears in my eyes and this image in my mind.

CHAPTER FOUR

"The United States is increasingly controlled by an amoral oligarchy that has progressively corrupted the federal government and the political system." Charles Ferguson from his book, Predator Nation.

How it works... As already stated, the chain of theft can be seen in the bones of a Property Flip Scheme. In these schemes the Property title has to be corrupted before the physical premises of a home can be illegally seized by white collar criminals.

The actual homeowner identity cannot just go away. This is because there is a Deed of Trust which is a legal contract between you and your original lender. It is filed at the Registry of Deeds Office within the county that you live. Unless it has been illegally removed or buried, it should come up in a transparent computer search by both name and address. It is a crime to tamper with or alter official records.

My limited income was most certainly an impediment to my investigation. I printed hundreds of documents from the Somerville Registry of Deeds Office and some from neighboring counties. I used these instruments to build pattern-example-groupings of other Fayette County homes that fit any one of the three categories I began to see. I documented these commonalities on spread-sheets. It is a gratifying experience to do this work and then have an ah-ha moment in which something unknown before, but very important to any investigation, jumps from the page into sharp relief. Each theft example revealed adaptations of the same chain of theft fitted to each victim profile.

I filed a Scrivener's Error Affidavit,[9] with the Fayette County Registry of Deeds Office on November 6, 2017. This is a notice of a mistake in another filing. You should file notice of any proven forgery or fraud. When I presented this notarized Affidavit there was a certain

[9] Affidavit of Scrivener's Error; Pursuant to: T.C.A. § 55-3-138. Notice of: Broken Chain of Title. Fayette County Instrument No.: 17006968. If in fact, it can still be found under address: 65 Pinehurst Drive, Oakland, Tennessee or under my name. Any victim of the schemes that I describe where secret sales, assigns, and transfers of authority are concealed in the MERS E-Registry System or otherwise withheld from the public land records can and should file a similar affidavit asserting broken chain of title. The fraud requires multiple deeds and other instruments be filed to perfect the theft. More than would otherwise be necessary. File this affidavit identifying any forgery or creative alterations upon examination of what is filed in the public land records. Examples are discussed in Part 111 of this book.

amount of whispering which I imagine centered on whether this affidavit could be rejected. As it turned out the solution was to file this instrument under last name Alexandra and first name Clair. Thus, to ensure that under any title search this filing instrument, claiming theft, broken chain of title, and lies from other filings would not show up. When I later decided to verify its filing, I found that it also did not appear under the property address: 65 Pinehurst Drive, Oakland, TN.

This was obstruction. I was filing notice that there was not a clean chain of title. Of mistakes within previous filings. That the foreclosure was a non-event used to conceal the illegal sale to REO Investors three-years before. That my home had been illegally seized in violation of the Fourth Amendment to the United States Constitution. This was something important for any future buyer and lender to know. Presumably the Registrar could forward my claims to the Tennessee States Attorney's Office for investigation. But this wasn't happening. Certain Fayette County employees had been covering for these crimes for a long time. In the end they accepted the Affidavit, but passive-aggressively took steps to be sure it could have no useful purpose. It could not expose the broader theft goals nor reflect on Keller Williams Realty straw buyers, Vernon "Wayne" Boyd and Sherry Boyd nor on the Criminal Enterprise "muscle" carrying out an illegal eviction; ERA Chamberwood Realty Group.

I wrote a letter to the Fayette County Mayor and afterwards met with him; evidence in hand that the Affidavit of Scrivener's Error, Instrument No.: 17006968 had been buried. You may know that there will be no just outcome or appropriate steps taken by those agencies and people you report these crimes to. This was the case here. I knew that this mayor would do nothing. The point is that just as they had buried my rightful ownership claims under the mountain of document fraud, I was building a record of my own efforts to expose these crimes. Whether that Affidavit is today properly accessible by both the property address and my name I cannot say. Best guess? It won't be found.

Letters are the official means of communication. This was among the best advice I received. Therefore, I have written lots of letters followed up by phone calls.

"Did you get my letter of April 5, 2019?"

"Yes, we did?"

"And do you have any plans to investigate what I have charged in this letter?"

"We have forwarded your letter onto the appropriate..."

"And who was that?"

Repeated intentional deflection... Followed by your next questions. Among them: "Was an official reporting form filled out and may I have a copy of that form and the name of whomever it was you forwarded my complaint onto?"

Ineffective bureaucrats invested in protecting a dysfunctional status quo do not expect you to follow-up with anything. It is simply your job to trust that they are doing their jobs. Some that I talked with had an inflated sense of importance, clearly offended if I pushed for action. Most were limited by constraints built into their job descriptions. A few, not immune or blind to the levels of corruption weighing heavily on their hearts did more for me than was asked.

One of the first letters I sent was to Tennessee Senator Lamar Alexander who in true passive-facilitator style failed to act. Why would he? He helped craft the 2011/2012 settlement between the banks and the State of Tennessee that in no way went far enough to protect mortgage consumers against future theft.

Start a letter file. Letters document who and what entities you have asked help of. Those with authority electing to give a, pass to criminals. Looking back, you will see the numbers of people who decided that protecting well-connected white-collar criminals was preferable to risking the solution. Don't worry about being a great letter-writer. Don't preach. Premise all claims on hard cold facts.

Criminals are skilled at projection. They will accuse you of what they themselves are guilty of. Deflecting out of context blame to the victim (you) comes directly from the con artist play book. Successful methods may be tweaked, but do not change. You cannot control every effort to characterize you as an out of control zealot who may be dangerous. You are not the danger. They are. State the facts, stay calm, and ask for help. That said, I did not always follow my own best advice. Hopefully, someday you or your lawyer may have one of these passive-facilitator bureaucrats to whom you have addressed repeated well-founded pleas for help on the stand.

While the more recently elected Registrar of Deeds, Sissy Dowdle, was an improvement over the last, she had no training in how to recognize sophisticated white-collar theft schemes. As I write this, she was recently re-elected for a second term. But is no longer in that position. What excuse was used to move her out of a duly elected position? Putting in her stead that person that lost the election and under whose watch years of corruption thrived? There is lots here that I do not know. I must wonder if this maneuver was even legal.

Because the original Deed of Trust cannot be removed (which may not mean that it has not been removed) it must be buried under the weight of forged documentation to thus supplant the homeowner identity with that of the secret Note-Owner/Note-Holder. Although they were the Note-Holder of record stemming from the Bank of America-HUD fraud, the Jones, Kelley, Boyd REO fraudster identity was concealed behind a proxy identity like Bank of New York Mellon or MERS.

In these theft examples there is a fraud narrative that provided the excuse for the original lender to knowingly off-load your mortgage to criminals with no disclosure to you. This event took place before you knew there was a problem because obviously, if you knew, you would recognize Title Theft and fight back.

That initial fraud narrative will trail into and slander other records. Going unchallenged due to the choke-hold over disclosure the many lies appear as fact. The date that criminals became the secret Note-Holder, controlling any outcome related to your mortgage is forward-dated within those endorsements that are later dumped into the Registry of Deeds Office. The initial title theft seen in when the mortgage was assumed is vigilantly guarded. That date is forward-dated to fit the later pretense of a foreclosure when in fact the theft itself pre-dates the foreclosure charade. If you knew what date criminal banks allowed their REO fraud partners to assume your mortgage you would recognize the crime of "Title Theft" and fight back.

Lots of boots on the ground local fraud partners are needed. Real Estate firms can select whom within their company are amenable to breaking the law. The local players profile likely victims. They know best which mortgages can be safely fed to the yawning jaws of the securities industry.

Thus, the sales pitch, drawing other REO Investors into this theft structure, is described as: *The REO purchasing process can be quicker, far simpler than a regular foreclosure purchase... no lengthy waiting period...* because acquisition of the mortgage as set up for the Property Flip – Equity Skimming scheme (laundering the chain of title) takes place in secret, no disclosure to homeowners, while bypassing the rule of law.

Once the REO Private Investors become the secret Note-Holders they have the power to drive the mortgage into default. Their authority is the homeowners original Deed of Trust that was acquired by fraud; no disclosure to you. Default will surface in the form of harassment and unfixable problems. It is never disclosed to you who it is you are actually communicating with. It may be the third-party mortgage servicer company, but it is never disclosed who hired them or what exactly they have been hired to do. The criminal enterprise – REO secret Note-Holders/Note-Owners are debt collectors, breaking numerous state and federal laws.

The initial fraud narrative that greased theft of 65 Pinehurst Drive long before the charade of foreclosure took place was that my home was abandoned and in derelict condition. Pertaining to theft of 35 Lewis Fairway Circle a forged Power of Attorney was used as authority to fabricate a Warranty Deed and phony Deed of Trust. Over 40 Valley Oaks Cove it was a fictitious loan and a fictious lien. Whichever set of lies led to assumption of your mortgage this is different from the lies that begin to pepper the record so as to justify the upcoming engineered default.

The end game is securities fraud seen in where most of these homes end up, pooled into groups of rentals, managed by out of state corporations whose primary focus is protecting the value of the securities, not the actual homes. Thus, we have a growing problem of substandard housing impacting socio-economic and health outcomes for many Americans. Absentee landlordism has never worked out for any community, nor for any country. Ireland is a prime example leading to mass evictions, famine, and forced immigration.

During that interim period between secret assumption of your mortgage by criminals and the foreclosure charade the electronic property title was laundered via secret assigns of authority, transfers amongst the same group of white-collar criminals, sales and home improvement loans that have skimmed equity. The original fraud narrative linked to that prior and secret date that your lender first allowed criminals to assume your mortgage making no disclosure to you, this is the date that you and your lawyer are on the hunt for. The financial services industry that put this pipe line in place, need the fight to be about something, almost anything else. In the contentious back and forth defense becomes a shell game hiding the big picture seen in what I describe as The Bank Theft Delivery System. Plaintiff attorneys must be sent in useless pursuit of questions and answers that deflect from what really took place under the umbrella of a Property Flip – Equity Skimming – Title Theft step process; laundering the chain of title. And of course, there are judges to deceive.

Trust your instincts. You knew at the time that something was very wrong. This centered on your frustration that you could never fix any of the disputes you were having with the so-called lender or that third-party mortgage servicer company. Promises are made. Two months later the same issues surface. The fraud narrative you don't recognize will never be expunged from bank and financial servicer records. You cannot dispute what by design and intent you do not know exists. In all effect you are speaking to a brick wall, swatting flies as side issues they easily defend.

If you are currently in the throes of this planned and very strategic harassment start a call log. Ask for the employee number of each person you speak with. Keep every letter. I later found that one AMS, third party mortgage servicer employee played three roles going by three different names. Start today. Obtain every document filed in the public land records. Make a list of every trustee, every bank, every company. Have they been sued in the past? Are they even who they claim to be?

Note the proxy identity use of any version of the MERS identity. They function as a shell company concealing from you the secret Note-Holder identity. Look into the back grounds of every lawyer, every title company that may have had a hand in creating and filing signed and notarized paper that in all effect function to perfect title theft; laundering the chain of title through various transactions.

It is not on the mind of most homeowners that they should periodically perform a title search of their property. Doing so in today's electronic age is vital. The Bank Theft Delivery System is designed, to ensure that homeowners never have enough information that they can defend their property title during that period between illegal assumption of the Mortgage by the REO Investors up to the physical seizure of the highly prized theft-asset; your home.

During this interim period specific theft goals are accomplished. These are:

1. First that your Deed of Trust is buried under a mountain of conflicting claims by the criminal REO Investors.
2. Second that your identity is supplanted by the white-collar criminal, REO Secret Note-Holder/Note-Owners, claims of

ownership. A property flip scheme is a form of identity theft; a RICO Predicate Act.

3. Third that the mountain of document fraud is indiscriminately accepted into both the MERS E-Registry System and the Registry of Deeds Office no questions asked. A lot of people have to be coerced or positioned not to do their jobs.
4. That the property title is so corrupted under layers of document fraud that overt lies and complete lack of transparently in the sequence of official looking documents obstruct homeowners from fighting back.

Theft of American homes has to start with title theft. Before physical acquisition of the home takes place the REO Fraudsters must first supplant the name of the real homeowner as it appears in the original Deed of Trust. Sometimes this step would appear as a temporary "Assignment of Authority" over the mortgage in the form of a signed and notarized endorsement concealed in the MERS E-Registry System. It cannot be made public. Title theft is the first crucial step needing to be accomplished. The Note-Holder, then holds all the marbles. They can launder the chain of title by flushing it through the Bank Theft Delivery System described in this book.

PROPERTY TITLE

Property title refers to who has legal ownership and the right to use a piece of land. "Chain of Title" refers to the ownership history of real estate, i.e., string of title or line of title. The ownership rights must be proven via an unbroken document trail of notarized paper that is traceable through the endorsement of those that sign these documents either as the Trustee, the Note-Holder, or the Note-Owner or some other proxy-beneficiary granted temporary authority to act in an assigned capacity. Courts have ruled that these signed and notarized documents have the weight of a contract. When any part is not true all assignments, transfers, sales subsequent to and pertinent to, falsifications within, render tailing documentation unenforceable; null and void.

Failing to protect land rights has historically led to the destabilization of cultures and civilizations not to mention wars being waged somewhere on the globe, uninterrupted throughout human history. Moses outlined land use and boundaries. God established specific regions by tribe comprising the land that was Israel. The preservation of land records goes back thirty-three thousand years before Christ. The Sumer civilization meticulously marked property lines even maintaining a bureau of records. These records were recognized as invaluable to keeping the peace. Details of purchase and transfers within the Sumer civilization were written on clay tablets and fired to the hardness of stone. Today we have computers and an easily compromised data system.

These schemes are so lucrative that residential homes are targeted by foreign investment interests. I found evidence that a Chinese national tied to Siemens Bank set up a shell company through which to funnel stolen properties. Siemens Bank does not offer financial services to retail-banking customers. They are an international financial services conduit for foreign corporate interests. In another instance the management company address, Turnkey Real Estate, Inc. was tied to a securities broker connected to Pretium Partners, LLC. The registered agents address turned out to be an empty lot in Lenoir, TN. Other local Memphis firms managed these rentals for large corporations heavily invested in this market. These connections require price fixing rentals in order to back a securities market fueled by fraud and theft. Globalist free for all land grabs should alarm every citizen of this country. Common sense leads us to consider that China and even sophisticated cartel gangs may, benefit from a few safe-houses in America. There are situations when, in the absence of morality, greed can and should be interpreted and prosecuted as treason.

Any change in the Mortgage Servicer Company or any abrupt change in how you are treated, may be the first red flag that something is wrong. Even if you think you know, confirm the identity of the Mortgage Servicer and who hired them. I experienced an abrupt rise in my house payment by $300 followed by forced placed insurance. Bank of America repeatedly promised to fix these issues. They had no authority to fix anything. Having let the REO Fraudsters assume my mortgage in 2009 their only interest in the outcome was to feed another home as a rental to the Wall Street securities market. Their job was to string me along, keeping me in the dark, appeasing my fears as lead up to illegal seizure of my home premised on a forged, Fayette County Judges Order of Eviction.

Harassment in the form of unfixable issues, and bullying tactics are part of the plan. This harassment is specifically tailored to the circumstances of each victim. If the target is in a nursing home and the adult children live in a different state much less care is needed. If a contentious divorce is brewing. If cash is being spent on getting a family member into a substance abuse program. If a spouse has just died everyone will be distressed and grieving. The boots on the ground locally situated REO Investment Groups heartlessly trade on tragedy knowing that victims will be less likely to, notice that a new third-party Mortgage Servicing Company, secretly hired by the REO Note-Holders for the sole purpose of driving the mortgage into default, is now claiming to be processing house payments.

In the world of title theft nothing claimed to be true, actually is true. This is 1984, the book,[10] not the year. The language spoken is Doublespeak. *"It was a bright cold day in April, and the clocks were striking thirteen."* Corruption relies on confusion and the tendency of most people to dismiss out of hand what they do not understand. When we are scared and threatened, we tend to believe what we want to believe. If you find that you are told problems are fixed only to find that they are not. If everything you are told breeds confusion it is time to go on the offensive; "man the barricades." Your home, your property title, your future peace is all under attack.

Your next logical question may be: "Is it too late for justice? No, it is not! The statute of limitations for a Civil RICO Case begins, not on the date of the illegal seizure of private property in violation of the Fourth Amendment to the U.S. Constitution. The clock starts ticking on that date that you recognize you were in fact defrauded by an organized chain of theft per the actions of a mafia-like criminal group of operatives.

Crotella v. Wood. In 2000 the Supreme Court found that the statute of limitations in civil RICO actions begins as soon as a plaintiff discovers his injury, regardless of when the fraud causing the injury took place.

Vague suspicion is not the same as knowing. Even before the foreclosure charade I knew that something was very wrong. I was exhaustively

[10] 1984, by, George Orwell written in 1949. A dystopian plot describes a future society in which the population is brain washed and controlled by its government.

shadow boxing, deprived of all legally required information, routinely lied to. As you read this book, if you have an awakening of recognition, journal the date. The record you keep in real time carries a lot of weight. Get yourself a highlighter. Mark up these pages. There is healing in knowing and pursuing the truth. There are others who cannot speak for themselves. They need your efforts to expose these schemes including the lapse of law enforcement in protecting private property rights in America. Some of these people have died and their heirs were defrauded. They too are covered under the Crotella v. Wood ruling.

Among the conspirator banks tied to theft of my home were: Bank of America, JP Morgan Chase Bank, Evolve Bank & Trust, and Bank of New York Mellon. A bridge loan was provided by a Core Logic subsidiary; a licensed Tennessee Mortgage Company. Because the Core Logic name appears in so many of the Pattern Example Files they should be barred from ever doing business in the State of Tennessee. The third-party mortgage servicer company was AMS Servicing, LLC. Each time federal investigators threatened operations these third-party servicer companies have closed shop, reformed, and changed their name. Today AMS Servicing, LLC is Nationstar Mortgage Company. Board chairs, CEO's, and CFO's need jail time.

This massive white-collar fraud scheme is lead driven. A continual stream of possible victims deemed unlikely to fight back must be fed into the pipeline. Those at the bottom of the rung are promised residuals or finders-fee for successfully identifying potential victims to the boots on the ground REO Investor Groups.

Pyramid Schemes, like the Ponzi Scheme are unsustainable. Group participants are unduly pressured and manipulated with grandiose promises as incentive to produce. Some of the local group that targeted me belonged to a church that some have called a cult. As I dug deeper into the broader network cult like practices of control and intimidation, having nothing to do with religion, had filtered into the operative structure.

From: Rick Alan Ross; *CULTS INSIDE OUT: How People Get in and Can Get Out*. From Chapter 4: Defining A Destructive Cult, page: 120. *"To define a destructive cult, distinctions are made based on behavior rather than on beliefs."*

To keep the chain of theft functioning there has to be a steady erosion of morals and critical thinking skills. Loyalty to the group dynamics must take precedence over any other, better or healthier commitment.

From False Profits: Seeking Financial and Spiritual Deliverance in Multi-Level Marketing and Pyramid Schemes by, Robert L. Fitzpatrick and Joyce Reynolds we read: *"Pyramid Schemes are structured to inevitably fail. They take money from those at the bottom and feed it to those at the top. I pointed out that the initial success of such a business is an illusion. That eventually the base grows too large and is not sustainable. And that's why they are illegal. That's what the fraud is all about."*

Rick Alan Ross makes the point that cults can include business schemes. He writes: "*But the truth about destructive cults is that if you remove their outer veneer, they are in fact quite similar. That is, they most often have the same basic structure of authority and rely on virtually an identical process of persuasion and corresponding group dynamics to gain undue influence."*

There were people around me that knew our Fair Oaks neighborhood had been targeted. Some were drawn into the toxic group dynamics. Most were educated. They were not persons one would think easily swayed or drawn into criminality. Some invested in Deeds of Trust before these same theft assets were fed by Warranty Deed to companies like Pretium Partners, LLC. They were sold on the notion that they had invested in pools of rental property. Bait and switch tactics are common. Some were destined to lose their investment in one or more of the engineered defaults. It was never disclosed that eventually these pools would be controlled by out of town mega corporations. This scheme operating in West Tennessee was the gift that kept on giving to groups like the Jones, Kelley, Boyd Perpetrator Nexus. Some properties appearing in multiple (different) pools of rental property made up these marketable securities.

Anyone of these people, some coming in regular contact with me, could have said, "Hey, Alex. I happen to know that Max Jones and others that work with him already own your home. You are not dealing with Bank of America. There is no HAMP Application. You cannot sell a home that on paper you don't own. Nothing you believe to be true is true." Why didn't they? Such betrayal has continued to bother me.

Foot soldiers are needed feeding leads to the theft structure. A community appearance of legitimacy is carefully cultivated. Professional expertise and personal relationships that the, fraudsters themselves lack are set in place. This is the stuff of crony corruptionism. Some take part thinking one thing, but end up practicing behaviors different from what was initially sold. Tools of manipulation and coercion induce people to cut corners so as to meet the performance scripts until many feel they are in too deep, there is no turning back. But what I usually found was a level of self-deception that struck me as astonishing.

The REO groups functioning in Western, Tennessee, selling investment in Deeds of Trust not actually owned by the REO Investment Group operated creative adaptations of a Ponzi Scheme.

We might ask, what drives the selection process deciding what families and what homes get targeted? The answer should scare every American.

1.) Homes with equity. Real equity the brass ring and therefore many senior citizens, like me, more likely to be targeted. Homes with equity are undervalued per the first appraisal at the start of the Property Flip sequence. This secures the inflated home improvement loan since any brain-dead loan officer can see the loan is fully collateralized by the theft-asset, aka, your home.
2.) Homes with no equity; mortgages perceived as already in trouble. Every option normally open to those in trouble with their mortgage is blocked. The Property title acquired by fraud, is already secretly vested with the REO Private Investors before the redundant foreclosure charade plays out. Acting as aggressive debt collectors (another RICO Predicate Act) they will threaten and coerce house payments with tacked on servicing fees for as long as homeowners can be manipulated to feed the coffers of criminals.
3.) With or without equity any victim profiled as unlikely to fight back. This vulnerability is leveraged. Acquisition of the mortgage needs to take place when targeted victims are vulnerable and situationally distracted.

There comes a point when theft perfecting endorsements have to emerge into the public record at the local Registry of Deeds Office. All the prior secret sales, assigns of authority, and transfers are missing and remain concealed, usually in the bank created MERS E-Registry System. Broken chain of title is no accident. The foreclosure charade conceals the theft that has already taken place. This is what makes the foreclosure an, empty exercise used only to deceive courts, judges, bank regulators and beleaguered victims of these fraud schemes.

Are some foreclosures legal? Yes, but in the absence of prosecutions many are not legal. This is a breach flooded by white-collar crime enabled by our nation's largest banks. Exacerbated by crony corruption seen in how the feds and states fail in their duty to enforce laws already on the books. Understanding why and how an increasing number of homes are fed to the rental market, undermining private property rights in America, needs to be recognized, dealt with and stopped.

When the REO Fraudsters interfere with your original Deed of Trust, supplanting your identity with that of the secret Note-Holder this is called: **TORTUIOUS INTERFERENCE.** This should be among the charges you name in any case you file. ***Tortuious interference, also known as intentional interference with contractual relation occurs when one person intentionally damages someone else's contractual or business relationships with a third party causing economic harm."*** Wikipedia.

Your Deed of Trust is a contract between you and your original lender. It was not only interfered with and slandered, its existence was obliterated from recognition. No disclosure to you.

CHAPTER FIVE

"Judges are the weakest link in our system of justice and they are also the most protected." Alan Dershowitz

I filed the Civil RICO Case pro se under pauper status at the Federal District Court in Memphis, TN on April 20, 2016. As much as possible I am sticking with and quoting from the first Civil RICO filing, filed with the District Court for the Western District of Tennessee. Exceeding the *screening for merit* guidelines Judge Vescovo in all effect ruled that I could not add defrauded federal agencies, enjoining them as co-plaintiffs. I believed her and submitted a condensed version of the first which, as she intended, weakened my case and deflected attention away from any possibility of a federal investigation.

In describing what happened I was guided by the very specific RICO criteria. This dictated the structure of what was written. Would a lawyer have done better? Of course. But courts do not operate for any certain class. They exist for, "We The People." Having no lawyer was never intended to be leveraged as a weakness traded upon by powerful judges with budgets, ideologic personal bias, and crony relationships to protect.

Driving away from the federal court house I felt an enormous sense of relief. I trusted that the system would work for me. I had requested a jury trial, not a bench trial. I wanted to address a jury of my peers not relying on a single judge to make the ultimate decision. I had no idea that before having access to due process my case would be pre-screened by a corrupt magistrate judge. She alone would write the dismissal. That dismissal would be rubber stamped by her superior. Both decided that the crimes I described did not rise to the level that due process should be granted.

If something about this sounds inherently unconstitutional it is. At the *screening for merit juncture* a pro se litigant does not appear before a judge. In this huge imbalance of power there is enormous opportunity for any judge to dig their heels in and refuse to address any objection. Which is exactly what happened to me. No opportunity to stand before the bench and be heard in one's own words, to look a judge in the eye creates an echo chamber. Before a biased judge, decisions are, an external manifestation of tyranny. Additionally, no physical appearance blocks an entire repertoire of how we as human beings communicate. For these reasons, due process, the right to appear and be heard, is fundamental to our justice system. It is meant to stand as a deterrent to tyranny.

Screening as a barrier to the free and equal access of my right to be heard by a jury of my peers was not explained to me by the filing clerk. There was no handy little three-fold pamphlet offered. If I had understood the screening exercise I don't know if I would have sold the little, I had left and somehow managed to come up with the filing fees. Because screening was not explained I did not recognize the risk in that my voice could be quashed before my case ever made its way into a court room. All District Courts are not alike. Some are run and managed better than others. Key information could have so easily been shared with me, but wasn't.

The District Courts are the first tier in our federal court system. The next are the Circuit Courts of Appeal. Finally, there is the United States Supreme Court. As you probably know very few cases are ever heard at the Supreme Court; the highest court in our land. These three courts dovetail while also having quite different functions. What they have in common is that The United States Constitution provides the guiding principles. Due Process is guaranteed by the Fifth and Fourteenth Amendments to the United States Constitution. Due process is a safeguard against vague or poorly applied secondary laws that may be used as a tool to subvert Constitutional Rights.

It is my firm belief that once Magistrate Judge Diane Vescovo looked at the defendant list there was no intention of ever screening my case as the law requires. I was shocked when I read her dismissal. She had not only overtly slandered my claims, but she omitted key information that in the absence of that information overwhelmingly favored the financial industry defendants while cutting the legs out from under the RICO Claims. I filed an objection with the District Court. I cited fourteen errors filing: *Objection to the Report and Recommendations 8/02/2016 District Court Case Number: 16-02263; Docket No. [14].*

Judge Vescovo arbitrarily decided not to address my objections. In doing so she smothered free speech. District Court Judge Sheryl Lipman, as her superior, was required to review and sign off on the dismissal making it official. Both judges treated the fourteen errors I cited as if they did not exist in the realm of fact. This tactic provided free license for Magistrate Judge Vescovo to keep writing the same errors into each of her subsequent conclusions. Judge Vescovo had concocted an alternate timeline and rendition of events that contradicted my statements. My Civil RICO case was witness to a very specific chain of theft impacting many other homeowners across this country. In all effect she smothered the voice of me, the witness to those crimes. No one else could speak for me, but in rewriting content and slandering my claims she sought to do just that.

It was then my job to follow the pro se script and forego defending my constitutional right to be heard. The fourteen errors and omissions I citied elicited a hyper-sensitive response. When self-will, "I shalt not be declared wrong," reigns supreme over the ethical requirements of a powerful and privileged position we no longer have a process capable of delivering any fair standard of justice. What we have is an agent(s) of government leveraging cruel and unreasonable use of power for reasons that have nothing to do with the law.

Screening for Merit. To read the statute: **SCREENING / 28 U.S. Code § 1915 – Proceedings in Forma Pauperis**

At the screening juncture all claims are to be accepted as true. This is because the *Screening for Merit* barrier is not due process. It is never intended to be an arbitrary exercise that functions outside the law, at the whim of a single judge. In the broader context screening is applied only to those who are so poor that they cannot afford to pay the filing fees. At the time I was living on approximately $900 per month.

How could a straightforward, simplistic process, go so wrong? Why was it so easy for a corrupt judge to slander with apparent impunity my claims so that she could deliver the outcome that my case would never make it beyond the screening blockade?

Let's be clear. This was not about me. This was about the criminal nature of the case that I filed. It was about the West Tennessee system of theft and pipeline of profit it could dismantle. This was about the public record that any court action produces. And the agreement among power brokers that there cannot be exposure of the national stage of operations. This was about protecting an income stream going to Vescovo-McLaren family members and the corrupt Memphis cabal of attorneys.

Corruption eventually reaches a saturation level. Repeated coverups lead practitioners and enablers self-destructively toward rapidly trending consequences that can no longer be delayed. Authoritarian systems as sub-groups hiding within bureaucratic agencies come with a smile before they come with a club. We are at the place where many are unashamedly wielding the club. Wherever we stand politically, more and more of us have noticed.

There is a line from the film the Devil's Own. In the context of a similar distortion of what is profoundly detrimental to the general welfare. What we as human beings let flourish, at least up to that point in time that manifested evil stares back to shock our sensibilities leading to fundamental, core upheavals of change. In this film the Brad Pitt character who is an IRA operative on the run, now on assignment in New York describes how his father was assassinated sitting with his family at the dinner table. The plot is set within the sectarian violence of Northern Ireland. Harrison Ford plays the New York police detective in this film. His character naturally wants to know, "Did they get the fuckers?" The fictional Frankie, played by Pitt replies, "They are the fuckers."

You'll excuse my quoting the profanity. Here is the core issue. Judges Vescovo and Lipman, by their actions, evidence disdain for the United States Constitution. The rights afforded to ordinary Americans are an impediment to personally held ideologic principals at odds with what they are sworn to uphold. Their actions were not nebulously rationalized. The growing reach of the Criminal Enterprise and those income streams would be protected. Lots of retirement money is invested in the mortgages of ordinary Americans sold and resold over the securities market. Even more money in those securities backed by rental income. There is massive incentive to keep these investments profitable.

To quote American poet and song writer, Bob Dillon, *"Well it may be the devil or it may be the Lord. But you're going to have to serve somebody."*[11] It is important to understand what Screening for Merit is. First off, it is not considered all that important a judicial exercise regardless of the fact that for me and many others the life and death fate of our Constitutional Rights, hang in the balance.

Obviously, I like film because here I go quoting another script, this one from a television series. In the Good Wife there is a telling statement made by a fictional character. Temporarily off the bench;

[11] Bob Dillon, Slow Train Coming; 1979.

"in the penalty box." The fictional Judge Cuesta is in danger of having one of his decisions reversed. He is offended that his superior intellect will be relegated to reviewing (screening) pauper petitions.[12] This most often means cases and, or, appeals filed by prisoners, but also by average Americans that cannot afford to pay the filing fees or maintain the costs of an ongoing trial. I fit this later, category.

Money provides immediate access to due process. Lack of it sustains the uneven playing field that reinforces a bigoted stereotype. Our founding fathers did not write the screening option into the Bill of Rights. If they had imagined the *Screening for Merit* provisions to mean no Due Process, they would have said NO! Screening equates being poor to mean a case that does not justify the courts time. This is the work that the fictional Judge Cuesta felt he was being punished with. With that attitude one would certainly tend toward blaming those that bring such cases. Judges inclined to abuse power can all too easily trade on this bias to deliver for themselves or others predetermined, personally motivated outcomes.

Screening a case before it is allowed to move forward is fairly new. Not allowing a good deal of these cases access to due process is intended to free up judges for more important work. To mean those cases that enhance reputations leading to status. Perhaps even a seat on the highest court in the land. What has incubated is a system that rejects self-assessment and any criticism as a weakening of the Judiciary itself. History has shown us that any dual system of delivery results in the subjugation of fundamental rights while predisposing cultures of those institutions to cross the line from expediency to unfair, from unfair to misuse of power, misuse of power leading to tyranny. Exactly what our founding fathers had escaped and did not want replicated in the newly formed United States of America. Addressing criticism is justice and an essential ingredient of any privileged position.

I did not recognize that there were no conditions by which Magistrate Judge Vescovo would allow my case to pass through the screening filter to be heard by a jury. It was assumed that I would follow the pro se script, accept my fate, sufficiently intimidated by the huge imbalance of power, fail to challenge slander of my claims. And certainly, never file an appeal with the Sixth Circuit Court of Appeals.

---

[12] The Good Wife season three, episode 23; created by Michele King and Robert King.

On appeal at the Sixth Circuit. The Appellants Brief is the main document that the appeals process must address. Within this five-page document, in your own words, you make clear what questions are before the panel of three judges appointed to hear your appeal. In part, among the appeal questions I raised was abuse of the screening procedures. The failure of the district court to address my objections. Slander of my claims. Denial of my right to Due Process. Judge Vescovo's conflicts of interest with the defendants and Judge Lipman's failure of oversight over her junior.

The circuit courts have an error correction duty. Errors that abridge your Constitutional Rights or were mistakes in the application of the law and, or, administrative procedure are some of the appeal questions that might be addressed. The circuit courts are not ruling on your case. They are addressing the specific errors that you cite. If they find that mistakes were made, they will reverse the dismissal of the lower court and send your case back to be revisited at the district court level.

When you bring any appeal to the circuit courts you will state why the lower court's decision was wrong. Not that it was unfair, but why under the rule of law it was wrong. Many things in life are unfair, but they are not lawfully wrong.

Judges are not pleased when their decisions are reversed. Everyone makes mistakes, right? Though they should not take a reversal personally, shielded by the intoxicating accoutrements of power, steeped in a profound lack of structural accountability some judges are prone to see any reversal as a personal attack on the godhead. That said, judges have immunity from law suits for good reason. We would have chaos without judicial immunity. And yet, when any one judge believes they are above criticism, unable to self-reflect they are a danger to the positions they hold. The near total lack of transparency regarding complaints invites corruption. Failure to address my complaints later filed with the circuit executive is just more abuse stemming from a culture that considers any criticism an indictment of the judiciary. A very dangerous and inherently anti-American bias to hold.

Due to the sabotaging efforts of the sixth circuit clerk's office my Appellant's Brief was never read. Therefore, the questions I raised were not ruled on. I could not file it until I was granted permission to do so. Upon receiving notice that I planned to appeal I was assigned a sixth circuit case number (first Case Number: 16-6672) and a first case manager (Karen Fultz). I waited rather impatiently to hear when I could file the quintessential Pro Se Appellants Brief. I filed it under the single case number I was aware of. When a new case number and new case manager were appointed, I did not recognize this as a violation of Procedural Due Process. I did not know that this meant a separation of filings. I therefore did not know enough to object. I trusted that the trail of corruption had not followed me to, of all places, the second highest court in the land.

Those in support positions in any federal agency have a lot of power. Corruption in how the policies of government are unequally applied by bureaucrats have abridged the rights of ordinary Americans throughout our history. Corrupt administrators at the sixth circuit had custody and control over my filings. In the separation of filings, they could control what judges saw, and did not see.

According to trusty Wikipedia: **Procedural Due Process is the legal doctrine in the United States that requires government officials to follow fair procedures before depriving a person of life, liberty, or property.**

Transparency International is a global anticorruption watch dog group. They have defined corruption as, *"the abuse of entrusted power for private gain."* *www.transparency.org*

How involved the first or second panel of judges at the sixth circuit, innocent or just so lazy that they failed to verify the information they were fed, I just cannot say. What I do know is that following earlier strategy, as a pattern of practice, I was not heard. At the screening precursor to due process, my objections were not addressed. On appeal my appeal questions were not addressed. Procedural Due Process run amok in the hands of corrupt sixth circuit employees subverted my right to be heard and delivered the scripted outcome that once again there would be no public record of these crimes running unchecked in Tennessee.

Screening as a precursor to due process is a kind of sacred cow. Most do not want to see it weakened by challenges. Others have written, taught, and believe that a Supreme Court decision that would clarify the ambiguities, close loopholes, adding to the weight of case law is long overdue. With or without an attorney one must ask, how often has the United States District Court for the Western District of Tennessee mitigated or foreclosed outcomes that touch on theft of private property.

How often have they used screening as a tool to improve their budget, improve their statistics by selectively winnowing cases considered problematic to the financial services industry.

Every case is lawfully entitled to the protection of Procedural Due Process seated in fair and uniform delivery of administrative practices. Employees of the federal court system are government employees. Their salaries are paid by American tax payers. Corruption goes well beyond these practices being a human resources matter. Sixth circuit case managers Karen Fultz and then decoy second case manager Jeanine Hance and others failed to follow the rules. In doing so they made lots of mistakes. So many in fact that the totality of these mistakes, obstructing my right to be heard, cannot be construed as innocent nor random.

These mistakes ran the gamut from outright forgery to "editing" relabeling a particular heading as a request for rehearing when in fact, there was nothing yet to rehear since I had not yet been granted permission to file the quintessential Pro Se Appellant's Brief. The "edited" rehearing blunder by the first case manager was used as a ploy to remove my case from the first panel of judges so as to declare that case closed. The first panel of judges had custody of the Assignment of Errors. The intrusion of a proxy appeal question that I never raised could not survive if a list of Judge Vescovo's many errors was read.

I've wondered what it was about the makeup of the first panel of judges[13] that could not be counted on to deliver and abridge my right to have my appeal questions addressed? Why a second case number that

---

[13] First Panel of sixth circuit Judges: Senior Judge Alan E. Norris. Judge Alice M. Batchelder and Judge Julia Smith Gibbons. First Case Number: 16-6672; appeal filed 2/24/2017. Sent back to the district court for ruling on an outstanding issue; 2/24/2017. *"This court lacks jurisdiction over this appeal. No final or appealable order terminating all of the issues presented in the litigation has been entered by the district court."* Note issues; plural. It was not clear what "issues" remained outstanding. As far as I was concerned, every objection, not a one of which was addressed, remained outstanding at the district court. At this point I had not yet been granted permission to file the Pro Se Appellants Brief with the sixth circuit. The appeal questions were not before the first panel of judges. Adding to confusion, right or wrong, I believed this first panel recognized the district court failure to address: *Objection to the Report and Recommendations [14] filed by me on 8/2/2016, District Court Case No.: 16-2263.* Judges Vescovo and Lipman ignored any directive to address what was outstanding. They hoped, and I believe contrived that this appeal would die on the vine of inaction and confusion. Flagrant rule breaking with no fear of correction provides the culture in which intimidation and coercion thrive. "I have the power, you don't, shut up, go away."

reassigned my appeal to a second case manager and a second panel of judges before the Pro Se Appellants Brief could even be filed?

Sound conclusions reside in facts. They flow from recognized patterns of practice. They emerge in the same outcomes and goals successfully abridging the rule of law. This second panel of judges were fed a forged appeal having nothing to do with what I listed in the summary Appeal from list and nothing to do with what was fleshed out in context in the Pro Se Appellant's Brief. Perhaps most significant, if the primary agenda was to shield the district court judges Lipman and Vescovo, and thus the Bank Theft Delivery System's ongoing operations from the attention of federal prosecutors the real appeal questions must not be before the decoy panel of judges. The Assignment of Errors was thus, effectively buried under the first case number. Never to be seen and where referenced by me, not found so as to communicate just another troublesome and unreliable pro se applicant singing to the already established prejudices.

Separation of filings is a flagrant breach of Procedural Due Process. And yet no person at the sixth circuit would entertain the notion that they had failed in a fundamental care of duty where important Constitutional questions centered on illegal seizure of private property and *screening for merit* abuses hung in the balance.

Just as Judge Vescovo treated my objections as if they did not exist in the realm of fact sixth circuit employees contrived a separation of filings and supplanted my appeal questions with a forgery. In doing so they sabotaged free speech. They chose to shield two district court judges from criticism and by extension a RICO Criminal Enterprise. Tanking my appeal lastly concealed flagrant abuse of the screening provisions under the auspices of a district court that had a committed and publicly stated agenda to limit and dispense quickly with pro se cases.

Protecting the district court judges required that the sixth circuit judges not address my clearly stated appeal questions. The risks taken to deliver this outcome tell us that abuse of administrative power and being comfortable in exercising those levels of corruption were in place long before my Appeal showed up in the sixth circuit mail room. It takes a lot of people deciding that they will not do their jobs for deep state corruption to flourish.

The dysfunctional system of judges robotically deferring to those who are not judges is little understood by most Americans. After granted permission to file the Pro Se Appellants Brief I did so on

07/24/2017. The second sixth circuit Case Manager, Jeanine Hance, claimed that no judge ever read the Pro Se Appellant's Brief upon which any appeal depends. Judges must not learn that the cabal of corruption were feeding them a fictitious case that had nothing at all to do with the appeal questions I submitted.

An essential appeal question centered on abuse of the Screening Guidelines. I quote below from the Pro Se Appellant's Brief. Doing so because this may be helpful to any that come after me and find themselves assaulted by a similar experience. *Second Case No.: 17-5618, Docket No.: [5]; 7/24/2017.* As is customary you will notice that I refer to myself in the third person; last name Clair.

G.) The law that governs "screening for merit." There is a duty to read the complaint(s) to the extent that content is quoted correctly. Not doing so, inserting statements contrary to the Factual Allegations is to exceed the screening requirement. Screening is not a fair procedure if used as an arbitrary tool to deny due process. 28 U.S.C. § 1915(e)(2) rule applies only to "In Forma Pauperis" suits. The exercise of this rule over already disadvantaged and beleaguered persons must guard against bias, filter personal inclinations that infringe upon the right of persons to file Civil Cases while guarding the Constitutional, protected interest of Cases to be heard. In the exercise of screening Clair was not accorded a liberal construction of her case. This standard was impossible to exercise given the pattern of omitting and altering fraud informing facts and circumstances. No Court can countenance a lack of good faith in any case, even a pro se, in forma pauperis suit, brought before it, where there is already a huge imbalance of power and in the exercise of that power, biased intent to dismiss.

H.) Due Process... applies to all judicial proceedings whether criminal or civil, that might deprive someone of "life, liberty, or property." In part, Clair is addressing illegal seizure of her home accomplished per absence of Due Process as a step-theft requirement as perpetrated by a RICO Criminal Enterprise. She is also addressing denial of Due Process and right of defense at the screening juncture. Due Process is denied if a litigant is denied a meaningful opportunity to be heard in a court of law;[14] "granted at a meaningful time and in

---

[14] Logan v. Zimmerman Brush Co., 455 U.S. 422, 437 (1982). Little v. Streater, 452 U.S. 1, 5-6 1981. See section III.B.I.

a meaningful manner."[15] Due Process rights denied Clair include: the right to a neutral decision maker. Right to have the factual allegations believed. Screening cannot be construed as due process. Screening is not to exceed the screening requirements so as to rule on the case itself. Clair was denied the rights to present evidence, to confront and cross examine witnesses per a slanderous reframing of the Civil RICO Complaint(s). This denial of due process served the conflict of interest Defendants and, in part, to improve the District Court statistics.[16] As a fundamental tenant of the fairness standard, upon screening, belief equates to an honest and factual rendering of the Compliant until such time that facts are confirmed or proved otherwise per due process. Not by a judge acting for the Defense.

You probably caught that I reversed letters. "Compliant" when I meant Complaint. Spell check catches many of my mistakes, but if the word is spelled correctly it doesn't. I did this in other examples. As in "trail" for trial. When I re-read documents, especially if under pressure, I don't catch these mistakes. Because I have a minor learning disability, I requested that an attorney be assigned; an option that may or may not be agreed to in pro se cases like mine. The last thing Judge Vescovo and Judge Lipman wanted was a legal mind looking at and preparing to present the massive amounts of evidence in my possession. Continuing to quote from the Pro Se Appellants Brief never read by any panel of sixth circuit judges.

E.) The Seventh Amendment has been interpreted to mean that Plaintiffs in a federal civil trial have the right to have their case decided by jury. The same premise that places limits on a Judge overriding a jury, applies to Judges obstructing the facts so as to override the right of due process abridged at the Screening juncture.

In the corrupt culture of our times we really do have a two-tiered system of justice in America? One for those with resources. Another for those that are well connected. One for those that can afford to hire an

[15] Logan v. Zimmerman Brush Co., 455 U.S. 422, 437 (1982), quoting Armstrong v. Manzo, 380 U.S. 545, 552 (1965). See also Little V. Streater, 452 U.S. 1, 5-6 (1981).
[16] Commercial Appeal: "Federal Court in Memphis takes steps to speed up pro se cases," by, Daniel Connolly, 4/4/2015.

attorney skilled at defending even the indefensible. Another for those that have access to none of the resources that money can buy.

So as to tank my case at the screening juncture Magistrate Judge Vescovo rewrote my content. Claims were overtly slandered. Independent proof of fraud stemming from three government sources were omitted. All this to justify denial of the right to be heard in a court of law, before a jury of my peers to thus shield a RICO Criminal Enterprise that also happened to be feeding an income stream to her family members; lawyers at four prestigious law firms.

West Tennessee can be thought of as the prototype of what is happening elsewhere. If you were a disease control scientist working to track the source of a dangerous virus Fayette County and Shelby County, Tennessee would be identified as ground zero for at least one major outbreak of the disease.

Complaints of Judicial Misconduct that follow were filed with the Circuit Executive at the Sixth Circuit Court of Appeals on November 1, 2018. They appear in the following four chapters. I've made a conscious decision to make them public. Feel free to consider this an act of civil disobedience. My right to freedom of speech has been continually, even aggressively obstructed. Some may elect to skip these chapters altogether. But I hope you don't.

In Part 11, we look more at what I experienced as the Criminal Enterprise and corrupt local players fought back. Much of this will resonate with other victims. I want readers of this book to know how they can be equipped to defend against The Bank Theft Delivery System and its stranglehold of crony corruptionism that makes the national scope of these property thefts possible.

So far nothing has come from these formal complaints. An unbiased judicial counsel with no conflicts of interest are to be appointed to review them. As of this writing I've not heard that any process has gotten underway. For all I know my complaints will suffer the same fate as everything else I filed at the Sixth Circuit Court of Appeals. Any risk I assume in making these complaints available to any who will read them, far outweighs the greater risk that these abuses will continue in any form, impacting any other pro se litigant.

As you read these complaints please consider the lengths gone to and the risks taken by federal employees willing to rig the system. It can only be that prior history told these people that no internal oversight would catch them out and hold them accountable. What happened to me was a broadside assault on every Constitutional Protection that promises to deliver a level playing field, the right to be heard, to weak and powerful alike.

Sadly, for Judges Lipman and Vescovo I had actually listened in civics class during a time when the United States Constitution and the Bill of Rights were taught. During a time that the Gettysburg Address had to be memorized and every morning we stood to recite the Pledge of Allegiance, hand over heart, and facing the flag that hung in every school room. At a time when my fourth-grade teacher read us the twenty-third psalm from the Old Testament every morning. Because of her I memorized my first passages of scripture which, as I grew older led me to faith. I wish I could remember her name.

The dawning realization that the same criminal network that had threatened me and sought to block my investigation at every turn now had access to subvert my right to be heard in a federal district court was unacceptable. To date, unless the Sixth Circuit hears my last motion for a void judgment, decides to address the appeal questions they've ignored, none of the evidence described in this book or in any filing, not any page of the 162 exhibits will be seen by a jury of my peers. This outcome is directly linked to, and the work of the Criminal Enterprise trading upon a dangerously prevailing culture of corruption.

Think! Think what this means for every other pro se litigant. An out of control Clerks Office at the Sixth Circuit conspired with the lower, District Court, to deliver the outcome that my actual appeal questions would never be addressed. I would say, "wake up America," but I'm fairly convinced that in growing numbers we are.

CHAPTER SIX

Judge Sheryl Lipman is a United States District Court Judge at the United States District Court for the Western District of Tennessee. She was nominated by President Barak Obama on August 1, 2013. Senator Harry Reid brought her nomination to the floor of the senate for a vote. Her nomination was confirmed by a senate vote of 58-39. She assumed office on May 1, 2014. Her prior work as an attorney centered on white-collar defense work. She additionally represented the University of Memphis.

For ease of reading I have increased the font of these complaints from eleven to twelve. There could be no more than five pages. Every word mattered and eleven seemed to be the standard front size.

Brief Statement of Facts: Judge Sheryl H. Lipman

In filing this Complaint, I intend to invoke procedures under 28 U.S.C. § 351 (a).

Information to Help Investigator Check Facts. For ease of back and forth between complaints attachments referenced in each complaint share the same numbers. Example: The Amended Assignment of Errors 5/02/2017, District Court Case No. 16-2263 [37] first appears as Attach. No. 3 in the complaint filed against Magistrate Judge Vescovo. There after it appears as Attach. No. 3 in every other complaint where referenced. Attach. No. 15 provides a complete list of attachments.

"When" and "Where it Happened." On 04/20/2016 Clair filed a Civil RICO Case, pro se, at the District Court for the Western District of TN. The case was assigned to Magistrate Judge Vescovo for screening on 4/20/2016 [4]. Leave to proceed in forma pauperis was granted on 4/25/2016 [5]. Judge Lipman signed Order Adopting 7, 8 Report and Recommendations, docket No.'s [9] and [10], affirming the dismissal on 7/14/2016. Every dismissal written by Judge Vescovo and adopted by Judge Lipman is premised upon changed dates, misstatements of fact, overt contradiction of claims, and fatal omissions. Among the omissions is independent proof of fraud from three government sources; addressed in the complaint filed against Judge Vescovo. Supporting the RICO Claims, also omitted is evidence of past criminal behavior by the REO Perpetrator Nexus Defendants. Judges are duty bound by law and ethics to be truthful. There was no honest rendering of the claims. Result: Deprivation of Rights Under Color of Law,18 U.S.C. 242.

A corrupt sequence of obstructions to this case achieving due process began with: Clair signed NOTICE to receive Electronic Filings 4/20/2016 [4], first to her comcast account which Clair believes may have been hacked and then to Outlook which was hacked. Four electronic communications from the district court were not received. One notice later arrived to Clair's phone (also hacked); unable to print or open so as to read, page-two of Attach. No. 17. Thus, by design Clair did not receive notice that her case had been dismissed. Clair was told that these notices had been electronically sent to her to state that she had somehow overlooked them. Clair knew that she would not have "overlooked" them.

Clair wrote a letter to the district court; 7/18/2016 [11]; Attach No.: 16. She wrote: *It is my belief that the criminal elements named in my Civil RICO Private Right of Action, have co-opted my email account. This fits the past pattern of behavior in another case in which the same defendants hacked into the computer system of a rival company for an extended period of time with the IP Address traced back to Keller Williams – MEM 2, LLC. Prudential Collins-Maury, Inc., Realtors v. MEM 2, d.b.a., Keller Williams Realty, aka, Keller Williams Realty East. Docket # CH 11 – 1860 Part 3 / Chancery Court in Shelby County, TN.*

TechAnywhere confirmed that the electronic emails had not been received; Attach No.: 17. Four electronic notifications were not seen at the precise-exact juncture that Clair could recognize and object to the many overt errors written into: Amended Report and Recommendations for Sua Sponte Dismissal [8] 6/27/2016; Attach. No. 1. It seems that the district court did not require a read receipt failing to apply whatever process was in place to communicate failed electronic communication to the Pro Se Plaintiff. They also did not report a potential federal crime, reasonably supportable in the past hacking conduct of the Association-in-Fact-Criminal Enterprise, to the appropriate federal agency for investigation?

Clair was then able to file: Objection to the Report and Recommendations 8/02/2016 [14]; in which she first raised the issue of recusal; page-11, page-12; Line No. 235 thru 239; Attach No.: 2. Clair listed fourteen selected errors upon which Judge Vescovo premised her dismissal. These errors are each singularly addressed in the complaint filed against Judge Vescovo; Attach No. 21. Judge Lipman failed to exercise oversight of her junior. Judge Lipman did not insist that the objections be addressed. She allowed lies and out of context manipulation of content to masquerade as fact under cover of judicial authority. Doing so, she empowered, and for all intents and purposes gave permission for the Magistrate Judge to write the same errors into future conclusions/ dismissals. She allowed Judge Vescovo to operate with impunity in over-riding and fatally quashing Clair's First and Fourteenth Amendment Rights for reasons that can have nothing to do with the law.

Contrary to Case Management Procedures the sixth circuit Clerk's Office severed a first set of filings from a second. Between 2/24/2017 and 6/01/2017 Clair's Appeal was back at the district court for ruling on: *This court lacks jurisdiction over this appeal. No final or appealable order terminating all of the issues presented in the litigation has been entered by the district court;* **First** Sixth Circuit Case No. 16-6672, 2/24/2017 {8}. Clair lacked an attorney to explain which appealable order the first panel of judges referred to. As far as she was concerned, for failure to address the objections, every dismissal that denied the objections a voice was outstanding. After sending a first letter, request for clarity, and not receiving an answer Clair filed: Pro Se Motion/ Request for Clarity 4/13/2017 [33]; Attach No.: 23. Clair believes that, but for this Motion her case would have died at this juncture hinged on the "edited" and slandered label of the previous letter regurgitated as a request for rehearing.

Clair had not yet been granted permission to file the Pro Se Appellants Brief. Thus, there was no sixth circuit order to re-hear. A ridiculous request used to discredit Clair. The relabeled sixth circuit request for rehearing qualifies as document fraud. It was dropped into the district court docket, 4/07/2017 [32]; *The Petition for Rehearing is Denied.* Originating from: *The Petition for Rehearing is Denied"* 4/07/2017, {12} **first** sixth circuit case number 16-6672. How this contrived denial was later utilized by the sixth circuit Clerks Office to justify a new docket concealing and replacing the Appeal from filing, please read the complaint filed against Chief Judge Cole and the Second Panel of Judges. This re-titled and "edited" Petition for Rehearing was utilized by the district court as a fraud device to cut the legs out from under any obligation to address Motion for Recusal 5/02/2017 [36] and

Amended Assignment of Errors [37]; Attach. No. 3. This demonstrates early corrupt collusion between the district court and the sixth circuit clerk's office to obstruct access to due process. This is a serious charge that requires investigation.

Judge Lipman failed in her duty of oversight of the magistrate judge. *...where it has been shown that the magistrate judge's order is clearly erroneous or contrary to law; 28 U.S. Code § 636 (b)(1)(A).* During the interim period that this Civil RICO Case had been sent back at the district court Clair filed: Motion for Recusal 05/02/2017 [36]. Motion to Reverse Judgment 05/02/2017 [38]. Amended Assignment of Errors [37], 5/02/2017, Attach No. 3, written and filed in response to Judge Vescovo's claim that Clair had not filed an Assignment of Errors. To wrongfully communicate that those fourteen errors first cited in the Objection to the Report and Recommendations [14], having gone unanswered since 8/02/2016, do not exist so as to muzzle and quash free speech. Addressing errors in August 2016 would have required voluntary recusal. Recusal was counter-productive to the predetermined intent and ongoing collusion between Judge Lipman and Judge Vescovo and then with clerk-staff at the sixth circuit, that this Civil RICO Case never move beyond what functioned as a screening blockade.

Judge Lipman chose <u>not</u> to protect the free speech right of the objections to be addressed. *...objections to such proposed findings and recommendations as provided by rules of the court. A judge of the court shall make a de novo determination of those portions of the report or specified proposed findings or recommendations as provided by rules of the court.* <u>And... *to which objection is made;*</u> *28 U.S. Code 636 § (b)(1)(C).*

And that... *however, the statutory obligation of the district court to arrive at its own, independent conclusion about those portions of the magistrate's report* <u>*to which objection is made is not satisfied by a mere review of the magistrates report itself.*</u> *Hernandez v. Estelle.*

Conflicts of Interest: Judges are required to disclose conflicts of interest to the court. Clair did not initially think to investigate what would later be recognized as overwhelming bias to dismiss rooted in Judge Vescovo's conflict of interest ties to the Financial Industry Defendants. "*The neutrality requirement helps to guarantee that life, liberty, or property will not be taken on the basis of an erroneous* *or distorted conception of the facts or the law ... At the same time, it preserves both the appearance and reality of fairness ... by ensuring that no person will be deprived of his interests in the absence of a proceeding in which he may present his case with assurance that the arbiter is not predisposed to find against him." 286. Fourteenth Amendment – The Requirements of Due Process.*

The responsibility to assign Clair a fair judge rested with the district court. Right to, and access to, an unbiased judge did not rest with the Pro Se Litigant at last thinking to research until finally recognizing the toxic extent of the conflicts of interest and bringing them to Judge Lipman's attention. Rather the neutrality requirement resides: *"in a Constitutional order grounded in the rule of law..."* Clair's right to a fair arbiter who is: *"unclouded by personal bias or conflicts of interest." Judicial Disqualification: An Analysis of Federal Law; 2010.*

Vescovo-McLaren attorney-family-members, Attach No. 18, share clients, returning profit and favor to those respective law firms where they are employed. To not one, but with every named Financial Industry Defendant. Bias to protect family income streams exists on behalf of Judge Vescovo's husband and therefore her immediate household. Also, her son, nephew, and step-son. Judge Vescovo was well equipped to recognize a Property Flip Scheme where the property title is illegally flipped amongst same fraudsters, laundering the chain of title. Well known to federal investigators and courts the term, "Property Flip – Equity Skimming Scheme" evokes a word picture that conveys a particular chain of theft. Omitted from the conclusions to dismiss, rubber stamped by Judge Lipman, its significant omission served to put forth out of context conclusions that favored the Financial Industry Defendants.

Judge Vescovo's attorney-husband admits: *"We talk about the law a lot. She tells me some of her cases and I tell her about some of mine;"* Attach No. 19. This is an admission of corresponding propensity for bias. The fraudsters required an insurer/grantor so as to communicate to cooperating lenders a property title free of fraud. First American Title Insurance Company, a client of Michael McLaren's firm filled that role. Conflicts extend to two subsidiaries of First American Corporation that played crucial roles in perfecting the ongoing chain of theft. These are Core Logic Services and their communications platform, Equator. The Equator work order, submitted as an exhibit, is important bridge-evidence. Its description was suppressed and ignored by Judge Vescovo.

This served the agenda to undermine the RICO Claims; shielding defendants. The Equator Work Order functioned to preserve the fraud narrative that Clair had abandoned her home in 2009 and thus, purports to evict a renter from an REO owned property and not Clair the resident home-owner.

Judge Vescovo was also biased to dismiss this case per her assignment to improve the district court statistics, low compared to other federal district courts. A Commercial Appeal article blame-shifts to the high proportion of poor and disadvantaged citizens residing in western TN; Attach No.: 5. Solution is not to adapt the performance of the court, offering help to pro se litigants as other federal courts have done (Federal District Court in Brooklyn, NY) but to dispense quickly with pro se cases considered a drain on the resources of the court. The appearance exists that this particular Magistrate Judge was appointed by Judge Lipman knowing that she would be predisposed to a quick turn over of this case? Have there been other similar complaints filed against Judge Vescovo involving obstruction of the right to be heard, failure to address objections, and abuse of screening procedures as a pattern, enabled by the district court? Was Judge Vescovo appointed by Judge Lipman?

Allowing due process for this costly and time-consuming Civil RICO case would have proved a setback to the statistical gains already made. Solicited by the district court content of this article is slanted to deter pro se litigants from pursuing due process when what pro se litigants already experience is a mine-field of legal and procedural obstacles. The communications opportunity communicates shame by association to the case-examples noted. It denigrates the one win as insignificant when to that prisoner shaving time off his sentence would have seemed almost a miracle. The elitist attitude communicates that no legal representation equates to a case not worthy of due process. Readers are invited to commiserate with Judge Vescovo's work-load. Message sent: Any pro se case will be a burden to this district court and *especially if you also happen to be poor.*

Functioning as a passive-facilitator Judge Lipman remained ostensibly blind to multiple violations of Clair's constitutional rights. She failed to enforce procedural protections at the screening juncture. *"...it is the duty of the courts to be watchful for the constitutional rights of the Citizen and against any stealth encroachment therein"* (Bryers v. United States 273 US R 28 (1927).

Judge Lipman failed in a care of duty when she signed and adopted every dismissal, ignoring: *The Supreme Court held that because there was an objective appearance of bias, due process required recusal (Caperton) and that the guarantee of fair procedures is a right (Matthews 424 U.S. at 332; (explaining that due process prevents government from freely depriving individuals of liberty or property).*

As a limitation upon abuse and over-reach of government, under both the Fifth and Fourteenth Amendments the district court was required to preserve procedural due process *"which requires the government to follow certain procedures before it deprives a person of life, liberty, or property."* Judge Lipman did not enforce screening procedures. She did not require the Magistrate Judge to address and correct Slander of the Claims. Her passivity played a crucial role in perfecting the goals of the RICO Criminal Enterprise; illegal seizure of private property absent due process. Ensuring that this Civil RICO Case never inform those federal agencies also defrauded. Never to inform bank fraud or any federal investigator screening Civil RICO Cases. Nor multiple targeted victims defrauded per the same chain of theft.

Upon failure to screen for merit, Constitutional Rights and procedural protections denied Clair were: **1.)** Right to have the factual allegations believed. **2.)** Right, to a liberal construction of the case. **3.)** Right, to a factual rendering of the claims. **4.)** Right, to a fair arbiter. **5.)** Right of the opportunity to be heard. Failure to protect constitutional rights within the framework of fair screening procedures made a mockery of: *All factual allegations of the plaintiff are to be believed and the claims must not be dismissed unless it appears that the plaintive can prove no set of facts pursuant to his or her allegations which would entitle the plaintiff to relief.* Windsor v. The Tennessean, 719 F.2d 155, 158 (6th Cir. 1983), cert. denied, 469 U.S. 826, 105 S.CT. 105, 83 L.ED.2d 50 (1984); Chartrand v. Chrysler Corp., 785 F. Supp. 666, 669 (E.D. Mich. 1992).

Judge Lipman allowed the Magistrate Judge to repeatedly write the fraud narrative into the record; both judges apparently ascribing to: *"If you repeat a lie often enough, people will believe it."* This strategy is born out per many examples including: In Amended Recommendations for Sua Sponte Dismissal [8] 6/27/2016 Judge Vescovo wrote: *On March 19, 2012, Recon Trust Company, BANA's Foreclosure Trustee, conducted a foreclosure of the Property.* This lie was repeatedly objected to by Clair though her words, the only voice one has at the screening juncture, was utterly and completely ignored. Please read: Amended Assignment of Errors [37] page-7; page-10; page-14; Attach. No. 3. Clair resorted to writing in capital letters: "There was **NO FORECLOSURE.**"

The district court contradicting the phony foreclosure, began on the day this case was filed. Ignoring the Civil RICO heading this case was labeled: **Nature of Suit: 220 Real Property: Foreclosure**; Attach No.: 20. This false label trailed forward to taint the perceptions of every person and entity having reason to look at this case. To communicate a mere foreclosure dispute, i.e., that judges of the district court do not believe the RICO Claims.

Like the foreclosure-lie Clair wrote in capital letters: There was "N**o SHORT SALE,"** ever applied for by Clair; Amended Assignment of Errors, page-17, Attach No. 3. Judge Vescovo conceals the Cooperative Short Sale Confidence Scheme sold to Clair as a Bank of America program for seniors with equity in their homes that did not exist. This is an essential RICO claim; Attach No.: 7. Quashing Clair's voice she inserts the needed defense to the benefit of the Financial Industry Defendants with whom she has conflicts of interest. A short sale did occur as one of five flips of the Property title, but never applied for by Clair. She inserts information that the Pro Se Litigant would not have until discovery and at the screening juncture cannot dispute with evidence. No due process equates to no discovery.

Failure to follow screening procedures is a form of corruption. Judge Lipman failed to protect Constitutional rights and screening procedures. The Due Process Clause essentially regulates procedure; even screening procedure. *Thompson v. Louisville, 362 U.S. 199; "it essentially regulates procedure."* Also: *Sniahdach v. Family Finance Corp., 395 U.S. 337; Wisconsin v. Constantineau 400 U.S. 433. A judgment or decree is invalid where it has no foundation of procedural due process. As where there is an absence of notice <u>or opportunity to be heard.</u> 16A C.J.S. Constitutional Law, § 625; Yellowstone Pipe Line company v. Drummon, 77 Idaho 36, 287 P.2d 288.* By no application of any measure was I heard.

No officer of any court should be estranged from those lines of defense guaranteed to every American. "*No provision of the Constitution is designed to be without effect;" "Anything that is in conflict is null and void of law;" "Cleary, for a secondary law to come in conflict with the supreme Law was illogical, for certainly the supreme Law would prevail over all other laws and certainly our forefathers had intended that the supreme Law would be the basis of all law and for any law to come in conflict would be null and void of law, it would bare no power to enforce... for unconstitutionality... It operates a near nullity or a fiction of law. Marbury v. Madison: 5 US 137 (1803).*

Fraud invalidates every decision. Every order that adopted the distorted claims as fact. That denied every opportunity to be heard. That served to contrive a slanderous and dishonest dismissal is a void judgement. *A void judgment is a nullity, and no rights can be based thereon; it can be set aside on motion or can be collaterally attacked at any time. Garren v. Rollis* 375 P.2d 994 (Idaho 1962). *Courts lose jurisdiction if they do not follow Due Process Law. Title 5, US Cod Sec. 556(d), Sec. 557, Sec. 706.*

I DECLARE UNDER PANALTY OF PERJURY THAT ALL STATEMENTS ARE TRUE.

I then signed and dated this complaint.

CHAPTER SEVEN

In the United States federal court system, magistrate judges are appointed to assist district court judges in the performance of their duties. Magistrate Judge Diane Vescovo operated under the authority of District Court Judge Sheryl Lipman. Diane Vescovo has deep roots into the Memphis legal and business community.

Brief Statement of Facts: Magistrate Judge: Diane K. Vescovo

In filing this complaint, I intend to invoke procedures under 28 U.S.C. § 351(a).

"When" and "Where it Happened." Alexandra Clair filed a Civil RICO Case, pro se, under pauper status at the District Court for the Western District of Tennessee on 4/20/2016. This case was assigned to Magistrate Judge Vescovo for screening.

Judge Vescovo slandered the claims. She rewrote content to favor powerful financial industry defendants that feed an income stream to Vescovo-McLaren family members. Persistent efforts to achieve recognition of the slandered claims, right to a fair-arbiter, to have her objections addressed Clair filed: Objection to the Report and Recommendations [14], Motion for Disqualification [21]; Motion for Recusal [36], Amended Assignment of Errors [37]. At no time were the actual stated objections addressed, acknowledged, or corrected.

Judge Vescovo operated under the assumption that it is not in the repertoire of perception that anyone will believe a powerless, discredited pro se litigant over a federal judge. That no party will bother to read what Clair actually stated as the Civil RICO Claims.

Background and Context. Judge Vescovo omitted the term: Property Flip – Equity Skimming Scheme. Absent all legally required disclosures, based on a forged certificate of abandonment, Bank of America secretly off-loaded Clair's mortgage to an REO Investment Group in 2009. Unknown to Clair her home was then pooled into a HUD program. Skimming equity, the REO Group took out a loan against Clair's home May 2011 for 100K. This secret JP Morgan Chase Bank loan and the secret dual claims of ownership were concealed in the MERS E-Registry System. This resulted in tortious interference with Clair's Crye Leike Realty sale contract of 5/5/2011. In August 2011 Clair contacted Bank of America with the intent to apply for HAMP. Rather than reveal the truth Bank of America entered into a conspiracy with the secret REO Note Owners and the third-party servicer to posture a phony HAMP Application; The HAMP Fraud Scheme. The chain of theft included a phony foreclosure with forged documents dropped into the public land records. Secret loans and assigns of authority were concealed in the MERS E-Registry system. HUD, Treasury, and the IRS were also defrauded. Because Clair had enough equity that she could have sold her home and paid all debt the fraud scheme contrived a loss to the investors in the CWALT securitized trust additionally equating to Securities Fraud.

Abuses of Judicial Power.

1.) Judge Vescovo did not screen the case upon its merits, an impossible bar to achieve given selected omissions and material alterations of content.

2.) As a practice she elevated out of context details favorable to the Financial Industry Defendants.

3.) When Clair objected to slander of her complaint(s) Judge Vescovo, rubber stamped by Judge Lipman, failed to acknowledge the existence of blatant errors which stand today to corrupt the federal record under cover of judicial authority.

4.) She violated procedural due process each time she failed to address the objections; quashing Clair's First Amendment Right to be heard.

5.) Judge Vescovo was assigned the task to improve the district court statistics dispensing quickly with pro se cases; Attach. 5. Clair's Civil RICO Case, if allowed to move forward, would have proved a set back to the statistical gains already made.

6.) Whether, Clair's right to act under RICO as a citizen-prosecutor would have survived a challenge at time of trial was the domain of that trial judge to rule on. Judge Vescovo acknowledges this right. Amended Report and Recommendations for Sua Sponte Dismissal [8] 6/27/2016; Line 321 thru 327, Page-14; Attach. No. 1. On the other hand, ruling rather than screening, she denies Clair this right despite: *The Object of Civil RICO is thus not merely to compensate victims but to turn them into prosecutors, 'private attorneys general,'*

> *dedicated to eliminating racketeering activity."* Judge Vescovo articulates this denial, Line 207 thru 248 Page-10, Page-11; Attach. No. 1. Manipulating Clair to remove federal agencies from the plaintiff list served to shield the Financial Industry Defendants with whom Judge Vescovo has conflicts of interest (addressed in the complaint filed against Judge Lipman). To impede federal law enforcement, scanning Civil RICO Cases, the district court labeled this case: "Nature of Suit: Foreclosure"; Attach. No. 20. THERE WAS NO FORECLSOURE.

Clair dropped the co-plaintiffs after Judge Vescovo claimed she had no right to include them. Not having an attorney Clair felt she had done something wrong. Additionally, having been previously denied the right to add to her exhibits by a clerk at the District Court, Clair wrongly believed that somehow this was not her right at the screening juncture to inform the judge with additional exhibits. Obstructing proof from informing any judicial opinion is a violation of Clair's Civil Rights and demonstrates the predetermined intent to dismiss.

The six abuses of power stated above produced: <u>Amended Report and Recommendations for Sua Sponte Dismissal [8] 6/27/2016; Attach. No. 1.</u> Judge Vescovo's decision not to screen Clair's case, but in all effect to rule on this case, more in the role of an aggressive defense attorney, foreclosed the risk of trial to the benefit of the conflict of interest Financial Industry Defendants. At the screening juncture where the imbalance of power is perhaps greatest the outcome seated in failure to accept the claims as true served to perfect the goals of the Association-in-Fact Criminal Enterprise, i.e., illegal seizure of private property absent due process. The *...state shall* (not) *make or enforce any law which shall abridge the privileges or immunities of citizens of the United States; nor shall any State deprive any person of life, liberty, or property, without due process of law nor deny to any person within its jurisdiction the equal protection of the law.* 14th Amendment to the U.S Constitution.

When Judge Vescovo charges that Clair failed to file an Assignment of Errors with the Motion for Disqualification [21] 10/25/2016. A term unfamiliar to Clair upon first reading this term. In clever Orwellian double-speak she communicates that the fourteen-errors that are cited in Objection to the Report and Recommendations [14] Attach. No. 2, do not exist. Failing to accept the claims as true, failing to address and, or, correct the original Fourteen Errors overcame Clair's voice. For failure to address objections. Continuing to write the same errors into future dismissals informs that this is an open case as of [14] 08/02/2016. Every dismissal premised on slander is a void judgement.

Information to Help Investigator Check Facts: Clair quotes below from: Amended Report and Recommendations for Sua Sponte Dismissal [8] 6/27/2016; Attach. No. 1. And from: Objection to the Report and Recommendations [14] 8/02/2016; Attach. No. 2. For ease of coordination between these two filings Clair has numbered each line. Of the fourteen-errors listed below none where ever addressed, acknowledged, or corrected. Those errors that by omission propose a rendition of events that deliberately mislead so as to materially alter the claims are numbered **(7, 8, 10, 11).** Others are blatant contradictions of content. These errors mirror the white-collar criminal fraud narrative. They serve to foreclose due process. They serve to drown-out the First and Fourteenth Amendment Rights of the pro se litigant to state the facts of her case as she understands them; informed by evidence that a jury has not yet seen. And if Judge Vescovo can help it they never will. These errors are numbered below as: **(1, 2, 3, 4, 5, 6, 9, 12, 13, 14).**

1.) Stated by Judge Vescovo Line 90, 91, Page-5; Attach. No. 1. *Clair contacted BANA in an attempt to short sell the property.* Objected to by Clair beginning at Line 37, Page-2 Attach. No. 2. Excerpt from Civil RICO [1] Complaint of 4/20/2012; Attach. No. 7: Cooperative Short Sale Confidence Scheme omitted; never accurately described.

2.) Stated by Judge Vescovo, Line 20, 21, Page--2, Attach. No. 1: *"frequently digresses into sweeping allegations about the "Wall Street Market."* Objected to by Clair beginning at Line 72, Page-4; Attach. No 2.

3.) Stated by Judge Vescovo, Line 21, 22, Page--2; Attach. No. 1. Frequently digresses (about) *...the validity of MERS.* Objected to by Clair beginning at Line 90, 91, Page-5; Attach. No. 2. Excerpt from Civil RICO Complaint [1] MERS; Attach. No. 8.

4.) Stated by Judge Vescovo, Line 22, 23, Page-2; Attach. No. 1. ... *and various fraud schemes perpetrated by the Fayette County*

Register of Deeds Office. Objected to by Clair beginning at Line 116, 117, Page-6; Attach. No. 2. Excerpt from Civil RICO Compliant [1]; Fayette County Land Records. Not leaving this to a jury Judge Vescovo concealed and suppressed claims/ proof of document fraud while attempting to discredit Clair as a credible witness to the crimes committed against her. Blaming the victim is a defense strategy and not that of a fair arbiter screening for merit.

5.) Stated by Judge Vescovo, Line 50, 51, Page-3; Attach. No. 1. *On March 23, 2012 Clair received notice that an eviction had been ordered.* Objected to by Clair beginning at Line 129, Page-7; Attach. No. 2.

6.) Stated by Judge Vescovo at Line 40, thru Line 42; Page-3; Attach. No. 1. *On December 21, 2011, Stancil transferred his interest in the Property to Clair via a quitclaim deed in compliance with their divorce agreement.* The fraud scheme required forward dating events. Judge Vescovo helps out forward dating this event by one year. She conflates the timing with the fraudsters manipulation of Clair to send, whom she thought was Bank of America, validation a year later upon claims that they had lost the original and needed it before approving HAMP. Objected to by Clair beginning at Line 140, 141, Page-7; Attach. No. 2. Excerpts from Civil RICO Compliant [1] Attach. No. 9

7.) Stated by Judge Vescovo at Line 48 thru 50, Page-3, Attach. No. 1. *On March 19, 2012, ReconTrust Company, BANA's foreclosure Trustee, conducted a foreclosure sale of the property.* And: *Public records also indicate that the property was sold on March 19, 2012.* Objected to by Clair beginning at: Line 159, Page-8, Attach. No. 2. THERE WAS NO FORECLOSURE; Amended Assignment of Errors [37] Page-7; Page-10; Page-14; Attach. No. 3. The phony foreclosure is lynchpin document fraud.

8.) Stated by Judge Vescovo at Line 52, 53; Attach. No. 1. ... *public records also show that the property was sold again via Warranty Deed on June 29, 2012 to Vernon and Sherry Boyd.* Judge Vescovo conceals that these are flips of the property title amongst same secret REO Note-Owners. Doing so, she suppresses recognition of a Property Flip – Equity

Skimming Scheme; covertly undermining an essential claim. Objected to by Clair beginning at Line 160, 161; Page-8 Attach. No. 2.

9.) Stated by Judge Vescovo, Line 71 thru 74, Page-4; Attach. No. 1. *It appears that the fraud alleged by Clair relates to BANA's refusal to approve Clair for HAMP..."* Objected to by Clair beginning at Line 182, 183; Page-9; Attach. No. 2.

10.) Stated by Judge Vescovo at Line 75 thru 78; Page-4, Page-5; Attach. No. 1. *Clair alleges that at some point during the time that she applied for HAMP, BANA told Clair that she no longer owned the property, that the property has already been sold, and that she could not stop the foreclosure.* Objected to by Clair beginning at Line 192 thru 194; Page-10; Attach. No. 2.

11.) Stated by Judge Vescovo, Line 83 thru 85, Page-5; Attach. No. 1. *Clair states that she believed BANA ultimately rejected her application for HAMP on February 10, 2012.* Objected to by Clair beginning at Line 199, 200, Page-10; Attach. No. 2. Excerpt from Civil RICO Case [1] Attach. No.10. Judge Vescovo offers a slanderous interpretation while omitting claims regarding the delay of notification of when Clair was turned down for HAMP. There never was a valid HAMP application process, just as there never was a foreclosure or a traditional short sale. Omitting context Judge Vescovo codifies lies that mirror the fraud narrative into the record.

a. To mislead regarding the HAMP Fraud Scheme Line 64, 65, Page-4, Attach. 1; Judge Vescovo writes: *According to Clair, she applied for a loan modification under HAMP from March 2, 2011 to August 15, 2011.* Pertaining to the HAMP Fraud Scheme, Clair applied for HAMP starting, not ending on August 15, 2011. Excerpt from the Civil RICO Case [1] Attach. No. 10 and Attach. No. 14.

12.) Stated by Judge Vescovo, Line 112, 113, Page-6, Attach. No. 1. *It appears that Clair's lawsuit in the state court was also a Civil RICO lawsuit.* This blatant contradiction is objected to by Clair beginning at Line 207, 208, Page-10; Attach. No. 2.

13.) Stated by Judge Vescovo, Lines 116 thru 120, Page-6; Attach. No 1. *It appears from the minimal allegations in her complaint that three law firms represented Clair at various* *points in her state court proceeding...* Objected to by Clair beginning at Line 219, 220, Page-11; Attach. No. 2.

a. *Minimal Allegations:* On June 3, 2014 Crislip, Philips & Associates filed a "Motion for Sanctions" against Webb Brewer; Attach. No. 4. This is evidence that validates Clair's claim that Brewer was moving her case toward dismissal in service to the REO and Banking Defendants; lying to her about what had and had not been accomplished.

14.) Stated by Judge Vescovo Line 330 thru 332, Page-14; Attach. No 1. *All the fraudulent Schemes alleged by Clair occurred prior to April 20, 2012, and therefore, Clair cannot recover for injuries based on acts outside the limitations period.* Objected to by Clair beginning at Line 232 thru 234; Page-11: Attach. No. 2. Later Judge Vescovo changed the date that the case was time barred; addressed in the Pro Se Appellant's Brief.

a. A primary goal of the Criminal Enterprise was not met until physical acquisition of the theft-asset was accomplished. This could not take place until the three-year HUD retention period had ended in 2012. Illegal seizure of Clair's home took place on 04/25/2012 via threats and misrepresentations of authority including forged documentation that claimed a Fayette County Judge had ordered Clair's eviction. No such order existed a fact entirely omitted. Clair filed her case on 4/20/2016; within the four-year statute of limitations for Civil RICO Cases.

b. Judge Vescovo does not repeat the term: Property Flip Scheme. She fails to describe the flipping sequence; fraudsters laundering the chain of title. Flip No. four, excerpt from the 06/22/2012 TN Residential Property Exception Notification, Attach. No. 6, claims Clair has not lived at the Property Address any time in the prior three years. This lie maintains the fraud narrative of an abandoned property conveyed under the HUD Contract to the REO Perpetrator Nexus in 2009.

Independent proof of fraud from three government sources scrubbed from recognition. Judge Vescovo acknowledges a standard that in practice she fails to follow. *The court construes the complaint in a light most favorable to (the) plaintiff" and "accepts all factual allegations as true" to determine whether they plausibly suggest an entitlement to relief;"* Page-8, line 168 thru 171; Attach. 1. When Judge Vescovo wrote: *However, "pleadings that ... are no more than conclusions are not entitled to the assumption of truth; Line* 172 thru 174, Page-8; Attach. No. 1, she, by omission, conceals and suppresses independent proof of fraud from three government sources. Quashing Clair's right to present this and other evidence to a jury equates to Fraud Upon the Court and Deprivation of Rights.

1.) **State of Tennessee Department of Commerce and Insurance.** TN Real Estate Appraisers Commission. Complaint No.: 2015011901; Attach. No. 12. Excerpt from Civil RICO Complaint [1] Attach. No. 13.

2.) **United States Department of Housing and Urban Development (HUD).** There are two HUD-1's tied to the same 8/15/2012 Evolve Bank and Trust final flip to REO straw buyers. The one contradicting the other. Proxy signers masquerade as what they are not; all tied to the REO Perpetrator Nexus. Both HUD-1's attempt to conceal same buyer, same seller, same note-owner, same realtor; the REO Perpetrator Nexus flipping – claiming to buy a property that on paper, per document fraud, they have owned since 2009. The first HUD-1 was acquired under a FOIA Request directly from HUD. The altered-decoy HUD-1 came from the State of TN. Two HUD-1, same transaction, is independent proof of fraud.

3.) **United States Department of the Treasury.** Money Management International (MMI) is a nonprofit, in part funded by banks, but answerable to Treasury as a government contractor. Between August and December 2011 Clair describes conference calls taking place between MMI, the MHA dept. within Bank of America, and Clair. At no time during these calls did Bank of America disclose that Clair's home had been off-loaded to REO Investors in 2009 premised on a forged Certificate of Abandonment. That there was no viable HAMP Application ever in process because they no longer legally authorized to execute one on Clair's behalf. Per the MMI Call notes acquired from MMI Attorney,

> Zynda Sellers. After the illegal seizure of 4/25/2016. These call notes revealed that MMI employees had escalated Clair's case for fraud on three occasions to Treasury. Hard evidence ignored, concealed, and suppressed at the screening juncture by Judge Vescovo.

Prejudicial statement: Judge Vescovo wrote: *Clair alleges that all thirty-four defendants formed a criminal enterprise and used various schemes with <u>the sole purpose to deprive Clair of her home</u>;* Lines 54 thru 56; Attach. No. 1. This statement suppresses the RICO Pattern Examples. Thirty-two homes transferred by Warranty Deed to Pretium Partners, LLC; Case-Exhibit #: 84. All acquired per same chain of theft by the same network. Clair is <u>NOT</u> a single victim defrauded by a RICO Criminal Enterprise for a "sole purpose." She is one of many victims selectively targeted as unlikely to fight back. Senior citizens, death of a spouse are commonalities among the three pattern example groupings developed via painstaking research that justice and the public welfare requires be heard by a jury.

Judge Vescovo failed to address Slander of the Claims raised in Motion for Disqualification 10/25/2016 [21]. She failed to address Amended Assignment of Errors [37]; Attach. No. 3. This same agenda to treat Slander of the Claims as if overt errors did not exist in the realm of fact began with the 8/02/2016 Objection to the Report and Recommendations [14]; Attach. No. 2. This conduct allowed her to continue writing the same errors over and over again into each subsequent order. To thus, drown out any and every opportunity of the pro se litigant right to be heard. Judicial conduct not consistent with Constitutional Protections.

I DECLARE UNDER PENALTY OF PURJURY THAT ALL STATEMENTS ARE TRUE.

I then signed and dated this complaint.

CHAPTER EIGHT

The same thread of corruption followed me to the United States Court of Appeals for the Sixth Circuit. Think about this. It is scary, stunning, abhorrent, and overwhelmingly unacceptable all at the same time. A mafia-like Criminal Enterprise had access to deliver an outcome at the second highest court in our land.

In this complaint I misspelled the first name of the second case manager. Her name is Jeanine Hance. I also use the term, *objection*, when more accurately I should be writing, *appeal questions*. Not a single one of the appeal questions I raised were ever addressed. Addressing actual appeal questions is the primary duty of the appeals process. Abuse of procedural due process and corruption within the clerk's office contrived that freedom of speech was quashed and my appeal questions were never addressed.

BRIEF STATEMENT OF FACTS – CHIEF JUDGE COLE

In filing this complaint, I intend to invoke procedures under 28 U.S.C. § 351(a).

Information to Help Investigator Check Facts: Attachments in common to each complaint share the same numbers. A complete list of all Attachments; Attach. No. 15.

If any party connected to the Clerk's Office at the sixth circuit is in a position to exercise influence and, or, control over disposition and, or, outcome of those complaints lodged against Magistrate Judge Vescovo, Attach. No. 21. Judge Lipman, Attach No. 27. The Second Panel of Judges and Chief Judge Cole they must be replaced by an unbiased party not connected to the sixth circuit. The shear-numbers of "mistakes," in service to common motive and goals to protect the Magistrate Judge from Slander of the Claims, and therefore, by extension the RICO Criminal Enterprise cannot be construed as simple error, but as fraud.

Separation of filings occurred under the management of the Chief Clerk. Chief Judge Cole is ultimately responsible to ensure that there is an unbiased application of controls rooted in rules and regulations of the court which govern procedure. What transpired per a series of obstructions that orchestrated concealment of the questions and objections to be addressed on appeal was an unequal, second class standard of care. The "less than" standards absent all oversight and accountability was utilized as a tool to perfect denial of the right to be heard. Such conduct endangers every pro se litigant. Administrative safeguards meant to guarantee procedural due process utterly failed under the watch of the Chief Judge.

Opening a new docket midstream was a deliberate decision rooted in a specific act contrary to normal Case Management Procedure. First Case No.: 16-6672. Letter Assigning the First Case No., Attach. No. 24; Case Manager Ms. Karen Fultz. Second Case No.: 17-5618. Letter Assigning a Second Case No., Attach. No. 25; Case Manager Ms. Jeanne Hance.

The second panel of judges did not have a full record before them. Proven in that Judges Keith, Cook, and Thapar at no time addressed the questions/objections presented on appeal. For failure to execute the error correction duty of the appeals process: **We AFFIRM {7}, 11/14/2017; under Case No.: 17-5618** is a void judgment inconsistent with the U.S. Constitution. As is: **Order {9} denying the En Banc Petition; 1/18/2018;** Attach. No. 30.

The re-titled and therefore forged Rehearing Order {12}, 4/07/2017 **under Case No.: 16-6672;** served three purposes:

1. **First:** That Judge Vescovo is under no obligation to address the objections filed between 2/24/2017 and 6/01/2017; the interim period that the case was back at the district court for ruling on the outstanding appealable order never actually named.
2. **To falsely posture** that the appeal has been reheard and dismissed thou the first panel of judges had not yet ruled on the quintessential Pro Se Appellant's Brief; not yet filed. Thus, logic would reveal nothing to rehear.
3. **Later** to withhold the Assignment of Errors and the Appeal from list from the second panel of judges. Who not only do not address the objections they don't recognize them. Like a horse to water they are led to rule on a proxy issue postured as the single only questions/objection before them.

After the interim period ended that Clair's case was sent back to the district court by the first panel of judges Clair gave notice to the sixth circuit that her appeal should resume; Attach. No. 26. The Facing Page reads: **6th Circuit Case No. 16-6672.** Ignoring Case Number: **16-6672** this notice was filed by the Clerk's Office as: *{1} Civil Case*

Docketed. Notice filed by Appellant Ms. Alexandra Clair... **Case No.: 17-5618.** The second case number served as a decoy to supplant and suppress the actual objections from recognition.

Clair had become wary of failure to address the objections utilized as a tool to obstruct due process at the screening juncture. She therefore stated the questions to be addressed on appeal. What publicly and officially substituted, and therefore concealed those clearly stated questions/ objections qualifies as document fraud; Attach. No. 38. The actual page-1 is replaced by the letter assigning the second Case Number. What replaces page-2 is the list of defendants. Persons at the sixth circuit decided that protecting the Magistrate Judge took precedence over Clair's right to be heard seated in the error correction duty of the appeals process to address clearly stated questions/objections; quoted below.

Notice is hereby given that Alexandra Clair, hereby appeal to the United States Court of Appeals for the Sixth Circuit from: Final judgment of the District Court of May 22, 2017. Appeal from: Judge Vescovo personal bias and conflict of interest in favor and protection of banking-defendants. Appeal from: denial of due process. Appeal from: culture of prejudice against pro se litigants. Appeal from: failure to accord a liberal construction of Clair's case. Appeal from: failure to quote accurately the factual allegations. Appeal from: failure to screen the case, in all effect, ruling on the case itself in the manner of a defendant-attorney, resulting in obstruction of a meaningful opportunity of the case to be heard before a jury. Appeal from: Obstruction of, and, refusal to add, JP Morgan Chase Bank as a defendant based on new evidence. And refusal to add REO ID#: 00906148; a number identifier used to conceal theft a RICO Violation. Appeal from: Stripping of independent collaboration of fraud documented per the U.S. Dept. of the Treasury and the State of TN Dept. of Commerce and Insurance. Appeal from: Abuse of judicial power in the failure to correct and acknowledge significant and overt misquotes of content codified into the record in support of the biased intent to dismiss. Appeal from: failure to grant Clair a fair judge-decision-maker. Appeal from: Omission of content that support the RICO claims and which in the totality of those selected omissions did materially alter and slander Clair's complaint(s). Appeal from: failure to voluntarily recuse for conduct noted within the: Objection to the Report and Recommendations [14], Motion for Disqualification

[21]. The Assignment of Errors, dated November 5, 2016... Also, the Amended Assignment of Errors [37], which addresses additional errors. Appeal from: *Denial of the Motion to Reverse Judgment of December 28, 2016 [38] for in part, the judicial abuses raised herein.* Appeal from: *District Court slanderous label of case (in part) as a "foreclosure" when, in point of fact, there was no foreclosure; an error repeatedly codified into the court records. ...Entered this action on the 1st day of June, 2017.* Attach. No. 26.

Why did this case not go back to the first panel of judges? That they expected this to happen is informed by: *This matter is before the court upon initial consideration to determine whether this appeal is properly before the court;* Order Filed Feb. 24, 2017; Attach. No. 22. The answer resides in that the successful derailment of this appeal by the Clerk's Office required concealment of the: **Assignment of Errors {6} 12/08/2016;** filed under: **First Case No.: 16-6672.** It required that the Appeal from list was never seen. Clerks deciding what judges will and will not see was perfected in the detour of a second docket. This paved the way for intrusion of a side-issue elevated to supplant the true objections from recognition. Absent all due diligence the second panel of judges were then led to those limited filings singularly visible under Second Case No.: 17-5618.

How the separation of filings functioned as a fraud tool to sabotage the appeal process is seen, in part, that filing No. {5} under the second Case No. (17-5618), docketed as the Pro Se Appellants Brief, appears under the first Case No. (16-6672) as {5} Correspondence. Thus, it would appear to the first panel of Judges Norris, Batchelder, and Gibbons that Clair never filed the Pro Se Appellants Brief. To wrongfully convey an end to their assigned duties.

The Assignment of Errors is another appeal-essential-filing. It serves to substantiate Slander of the Claims, by the Magistrate Judge. If looked for by the second panel of judges it would not be found and, or, could be reported as not found. Filing No. {6} appears under the second Case No. 17-5618 not as the Assignment of Errors, but as "Correspondence."

The Assignment of Errors is referenced on page-one of the Pro Se Appellants Brief; Attach. No. 28. This informs that at this juncture Clair is totally unaware that a second case number equates to no single continuous record of filings before the judge decision-makers.

Consistent with this plan the mailing label attached to the Pro Se Appellants Brief is numbered as page-31; Attach. No. 43. This to mimic that Clair had exceeded the designated page count and therefore no obligation of any judge to actually read it. No other filing includes the mailing label as a sequentially numbered page. The bold nature of employee staff engineering the outcome that the error correction duty of the appeals court is sabotaged informs a culture entirely at odds with Constitutional Protections.

Failure to follow rules and regulations of the court is a form of corruption. No wonder what functions as the gag-order of 11/14/2017, {7}; Case No.: 17-5618, states: *"unanimously agree that oral arguments are not needed."* That nothing from the "Appeal from" list. Nothing from the Assignment of Errors. Nothing from the Pro Se Appellant's Brief is ever alluded to, articulated, quoted, or in any way addressed by the second panel of judges. Denial of oral arguments fits the pattern that Clair must be denied her First Amendment Right to be heard both written and oral. Perfection of this fraud upon the court centers on actions of the Clerk's Office. It required that judges are fed conclusions premised on an incomplete record of filings.

Desperate for restoration of her First Amendment Right to be heard Clair then filed: **Petition for Rehearing – En Banc Filing; filed on 11/28/2017 {8}; Second Case No.: 17-5618;** Attach. No. 29. This filing must not be confused with the phony rehearing order retitled and "edited" by the first Case Manager Ms. Fultz; docketed under first case number: 16-6672, 3/08/2017 {9}. The plan to protect Judge Vescovo anticipated that Clair might complain that her objections were never addressed. But also anticipated that any investigator would be predisposed to believe that the docket would not be manipulated to contrive a nefarious outcome that the error correction duty of the Appeals Process is sabotaged; the objections never addressed. A superficial view of the docket without reading repeated pleas to have her objections addressed, serves to discredit any complaint Clair might lodge.

Clair was predisposed to trust the appeals process. Lacking an attorney, she was disenfranchised from recognizing how her appeal was sabotaged in real time as sophisticated machinations to corrupt and obstruct procedural due process were taking place. She did not realize that mid-stream the appointment of a second panel was unusual. She was never told that pacer would supply her free copies of what was filed. Not until February 2018, upon reading what was purported to be a complete docket, did Clair recognize the separation of filings as being fatal to her appeal and the reason why, trailing forward from the district court as the same chain of conduct, her objections were never addressed.

What followed: **Order issued 1/18/2018 {9}; Second Case No. 17-5618**; Attach. No. 30. To claim: "*The Original panel has reviewed the petition for rehearing and concludes that the issues raised in the petition were fully considered upon the original submission and decision of the case.*" The first original panel who had access to the Assignment of Errors never ruled on the Pro Se Appellant's Brief. By document fraud the second panel were offered an excuse not to rule on the Pro Se Appellant's Brief and never read/saw the Appeal from list.

Clair does not believe that actual judges at the sixth circuit colluded with the Clerk's Office, with RICO Defendants, and Judge Vescovo to orchestrate a confluence of toxic mistakes so as to deny Clair's First Amendment Right to be heard. Clair does believe that the second panel of judges rubber-stamped what they were dishonestly fed. That when Clair recognized the separation of filings as being fatal to her appeal Ms. Hunt followed the script and gagged Clair perfecting the goal to silence everything she wrote and said. Doing so she engaged in cover-up rather than file whatever functioned as an error report.

After viewing what was purported to be a full docket and noting that the Assignment of Errors was not present Clair phoned Ms. Hance who claimed there were not two dockets. Ms. Hance then instructed Clair to write a letter, 2/09/2018; Attach. No. 33. This is the date that Clair recognized the separation of filings as being fatal to her appeal. Did Ms. Hance report the separation of filings to her direct supervisor? Did there follow an internal inquiry to ensure that such a breakdown of Case Management Procedures would not impact any other pro se litigant? After 2/09/2018 Clair spoke to: Jeanne Hance, Susan Rogers, Yvonne Henderson, and En Banc Coordinator, Beverly Harris. Employing Orwellian-logic, seated in disdain for the rights of pro se litigants, statements were made to convince Clair that failure to address the objections did not impact outcome of her appeal. Though no order actually addressed the questions/objections presented on appeal Clair should accept the lie that never-the-less, somehow, they had been addressed. No lawyer would have been so treated.

Judge Cole cannot claim ignorance of what transpired resulting in: Deprivation of Rights Under Color of Law,18 U.S.C. 242. Clair wrote two letters to Chief Judge Cole. The first letter is dated 2/22/2018; Attach. No. 31. Timing the letter to Judge Cole to arrive in conjunction with: MOTION FOR RELIEF FROM A JUDGMENT of November 14, 2018 for Violations of FEDERAL RULES OF CIVIL PROCEDURE; RULE 60 (b)(1)(3)(6); Rule 60 (d)(3) and Rule 79 (a)(1). A motion that the Clerk's Office initially claimed they did not receive.

In this letter Clair wrote: *"Having questions, I spoke to, Ms. Yvonne Henderson yesterday. She related that the assignment of two Numbers and two case managers, and violations of Federal Rules of Civil Procedure Rule 79(a)(1) did not impact outcome of my case; to infer normal administrative procedure, i.e., no obligation to supply one continuous record to sixth circuit judge decision makers. Rule 79, which she stated did not apply is referenced under FRAP 4, Appeal as Right (7), "Entry Defined" (i) makes reference to Rule 79. In contradiction of what she told me, the exception that may result in separation of filings is not a case, like mine, but a second jury trial. As a direct causal outcome, separation of filings, no continuous record, my procedural due process rights were violated. This stems forward from 08/02/2016 [14] at the district court, my objections, including slander of my claims, abuse of screening procedures has never been addressed by either the district court or the sixth circuit. I have read that you can suspend the rules in exceptional circumstances. <u>I'm asking that you read what the sixth circuit should have in their possession today."</u>* Attach. No. 31.

Clair was told by Ms. Hance that the Motion referenced in the letter to Judge Cole was not received to the mail room. If looked for it would not be found by Judge Cole. The "not found tactic" was utilized to dissuade any investigation into the actual facts charged in the letter to Chief Judge Cole. To contrive that Clerk's, not duly appointed judges decide whether a motion will be heard or not heard. Clair mailed a replacement Motion on 3/13/2018. She included a new introduction and proof that the original Motion was received to the sixth circuit on 2/22/2018. Upon receiving the replacement copy, the original Feb.22nd – Rule 60b Motion was then miraculously found by Jeanne Hance. In the interest of truth and fairness was the original motion reported as found to Judge Cole? Since the aborted error correction duty of the appeals process never got off the ground, one must conclude that ongoing corruption, conspiracy, and cover-up by the Clerk's Office was allowed to operate unchecked.

Placing another barrier to justice, Clair was told by Jeanne Hance that her only option to having her appeal actually heard and ruled on at the sixth circuit was to appeal to the Supreme Court. This to convey that the sixth circuit would never hear Motion for a Void Judgement. Clair filed Motions for a Void Judgement, facing pages stamped received, Attach. No. 35. All but the last were sent back to Clair. This last Motion likely fed to a paper shredder and so attached here as Attach. No. 34. Consistent with other withheld filings perfecting the commitment to deny Clair the opportunity to be heard none were ruled on.

I do not read anywhere that the appeals courts are exempt from entertaining a Motion to Overturn and, or, a Motion for a Void Judgement. No restoration of procedural due process informs that Judge Cole either remained blissfully uninformed and, or, accepted superficial explanations. Failing to investigate corruption and deprivation of rights taking place under his management? As an avenue to inaction it appears that he elevated secondary laws or arbitrary rationalizations with intent, or in effect, to protect his court from criticism.

In spite of: *"No provision of the Constitution is designed to be without effect;" "Anything that is in conflict is null and void of law;" "Cleary, for a secondary law to come in conflict with the supreme Law was illogical, for certainly the supreme Law would prevail over all other laws and certainly our forefathers had intended that the supreme Law would be the basis of all law and for any law to come in conflict would be null and void of law, it would bare no power to enforce... for unconstitutionality... It operates a near nullity or a fiction of law. Marbury v. Madison: 5 US 137 (1803).*

Clair wrote to Ms. Hunt 4/25/2018; Attach. No. 36. Mrs. Hunt responded 5/02/2018; Attach. No. 37. Trading on the presumed ignorance through which pro se litigants can be manipulated to abandon defense of their Constitutional Rights Ms. Hunt used language that established an alternate history by which failure to address the objections could be concealed from any who later examined the record. She wrote: *As was explained to you in prior correspondence from this office, the mandates have issued in both your appeals. Upon the issuance of the mandate, this court's action is terminated. Thus, your subsequent motions were not received for filing because these appeals are closed. Your submissions are noted on the docket, but there will be no further action.*

1.) "prior correspondence" What correspondence? **2.)** "both your appeals..." there are not two appeals though document fraud states otherwise. **3.)** "this court's mandate is terminated." There was a complete failure to execute the error correction duty of the appeals process. Thus, there has been no valid mandate with the authority to terminate the appeal. **4.)** "your subsequent filings were not received for filing." If they had been filed transparency would have exposed sabotage of the appeal. **5.)** "Because the appeals are closed." Failure to address the objections is rooted in the failure of the Clerk's office to ensure a complete record of filings to either panel of judges. Every order tainted by obstruction of the right to be heard is a void judgement. Objections never addressed prove that the appeal (singular) is not closed.

A coordinated strategy to obstruct the right to be heard appears grounded in the expectation that the Chief Judge could be counted upon to superficially over-trust persons not deserving of such trust. And, or, conviction of perpetrator-staff that he would place concealment of a fraud upon the court above the Constitutional Rights of the pro se litigant. In either event corruption within his court transpired. Corruption requires a full investigation. It requires that the right of appeal, its full record be heard for the first time. That the Motion for a Void Judgement; Attach No. 34 come before actual judges of the court.

I DECLARE UNDER PANALTY OF PERJURY THAT ALL STATEMENTS ARE TRUE.

I then signed and dated this complaint.

CHAPTER NINE

What, follows is the last complaint.

BRIEF STATEMENT OF FACTS
Senior Judge Damon J. Keith, Judge Deborah L. Cook, Judge Amul R. Thapar

In filing this complaint, I intend to invoke procedures under 28 U.S.C. § 351(a).

Information to Help Investigator Check Facts: For a complete list of attachments see Attach. No. 15. Attachments referenced in any complaint share the same numbers. For this reason, they do not appear sequential within this document.

What Happened: Judges Keith, Cook and Thapar failed to verify and ensure equal delivery of administrative controls rooted in clearly stated rules and regulations of the court. There was a careless absence of oversight and due diligence afforded this pro se appeal. Clair's First Amendment Right to be heard was effectively denied. Judges were led to rule on a side issue never raised by Clair. The right to state what questions were to be addressed on appeal and have those questions adjudicated as the fundamental error correction duty of the appeals process was sabotaged by the separation of filings and other manipulations which buried, edited, and withheld selected filings from the second panel of judges.

Clair does not believe that the second panel of judges conspired to achieve denial of the right to be heard. Clair does believe that there was an utter failure to implement controls that if applied would have rooted out corruption. Trust but verify would have uncovered the altered page count of the Pro Se Appellants Brief; Attach. No. 28; Attach. No.43. Where a quintessential filing could be thrown out on a technicality there must have been a measure in place to verify the veracity of that reasoning. An internet search by name would have uncovered the Assignment of Errors referenced in the Pro Se Appellant's Brief. It would have revealed continuity of objections repeatedly articulated and just as consistently concealed and withheld. Conspiracy to withhold records to contrive an outcome, so as to suppress the Appellants First Amendment Right to be heard is a form of document fraud.

The separation of filings severed a first set of filings from a second set; Attach No. 24, Attach No. 25. This served the agenda that the second panel of judges Keith, Cook, and Thapar were deprived of the appeal-essential Assignment of Errors {6} 12/08/2016; First Case No. 16-6672. When looked for, the Assignment of Errors, referenced in the Pro Se Appellant's Brief would wrongly appear to the second panel, under Case No: 17-5618, as {6} Correspondence. For a complete picture of what Clair believes was a coordinated plan to conceal what questions were to be addressed on appeal. To feed Judges an incomplete record of filings please read Complaints filed against Judge Vescovo; Attach. No. 21. Judge Lipman; Attach. No. 27. Judge Cole; Attach. No. 39.

When questioned Jeanne Hance told Clair that the Pro Se Appellants Brief was not read; Attach. No. 28. What she did not tell Clair is that the mailing label was attached as page 31. This to posture the fiction that Clair had exceeded the designated page count; failed to follow instructions. Thus, no obligation to read and rule on the Pro Se Appellant's Brief.

Clair trusted that structural safeguards would ensure equal and fair procedural due process; right to be heard. One cannot timely object to what one does not recognize. On 2/09/2018, upon viewing what the Clerk's Office purported to be the single docket under Case Number: 17-5618 Clair recognized for the first time the absence of the appeal-essential Assignment of Errors. When questioned Ms. Hance at first denied the existence of an earlier docket. She then instructed Clair to write a letter; Attach. No. 33.

Clair later filed an Amended Assignment of Errors, Attach. No. 3, with the district court during the interim period that her case had been sent back for ruling on an outstanding "*appealable order*" by, the First Panel of Judges Norris, Batchelder, and Gibbons; 2/24/2017 {8} first case No.: 16-6672.

Clair remained confused about which appealable order had not been ruled-on at the district court. In Clair's mind every district court order was void for failure to address and correct the many errors, omissions, and slanderous statements codified as fact into the federal record by Magistrate Judge Vescovo. Disadvantaged in not having an attorney, Clair sent a letter to the district court. She copied this letter to the sixth circuit as: 3/08/3017 {9}. Then Amended {11} 3/09/2017. First Case Manager Fultz, having custody of the first set of filings, **entered this inquiry as what it was NOT. This act furthered**

the operational plan to derail this appeal. How, does a clerk have power to smother Clair's voice? If there was a question why not just pick up the phone and call Clair. The answer resides in that this opportunity was provided by a culture anesthetized against any idea that the administrative arm of the sixth circuit could engage in any form of corruption. Judges were therefore not guarding against it. They were failing to, "trust but verify." *Appellant Motion... to clarify order dated 02/24/2017...* was "**edited"** by Ms. Fultz and entered as 3/09/2017 {10} **Motion for Rehearing**. Having not yet been granted permission to file the Pro Se Appellant's Brief; Attach No. 28, Clair knew better than to petition the first panel of judges for a "rehearing" on what had not yet been delivered. The retitled phony "rehearing" order, "edited" by Ms. Fultz and which Clair did not have a copy of, since if she were sent a copy, she would object, qualifies as another example of document fraud and administrative corruption.

The fabricated outcome followed. The phony 4/07/4017 {12}; *The Petition for rehearing is DENIED.* Was there any requirement for the first panel of judges to actually read what was filed to then realize that Clair is not, nor was she ever, asking for a rehearing, but for clarity of what appealable order remained outstanding at the district court? *The Petition for Rehearing is Denied* was entered as [32] into the district court docket 4/07/2017. During the interim period that this case was back at the district court this ploy served the fraud-contrived agenda that granted illegal authority for Magistrate Judge Vescovo to forego addressing: Motion for Recusal [36]; Amended Assignment of Errors [37]; Motion to Reverse [38]; District Court Case No. 16-2263.

Having not received an answer to: *Appellant Motion... to clarify order dated 02/24/2017.* Still confused about which appealable order remained outstanding at the district court Clair then filed Motion/ Request for Clarity 4/13/2017 [33]; Attach. No. 23. That she needed to do this informs that Clair had been successfully denied real time knowledge and disclosure of the "edited," effectively retitled and therefore forged, Motion for Rehearing.

This example of document fraud served to deceive the first panel of judges. Served to ostensibly justify a second docket. Prematurely closing the appeal with no notice to Clair served to sever the Assignment of Errors referenced in the later filed Pro Se Appellants Brief; never read by the second panel of judges. Served to withhold case essential filings from the second panel of judges. All to achieve the predetermined agenda that this Civil RICO Case never see the light of a courtroom. That Judge Vescovo skate on, Slander of the Claims.

On 6/01/2017 Clair filed notice to the sixth circuit that her appeal should resume. The first Case Number 16-6672, as the only Case Number Clair was aware of at the time, is clearly noted on the facing page; Attach. No. 26. Premised on the forged rehearing order the Clerk's Office opened a second docket assigning what functioned as the decoy Case Number: 17-5618. This paved the way for the Clerk's Office to remove the case from the first panel of judges whom, having access to the Assignment of Errors... that bell could not be un-rung. So as to assign the appeal to a second panel who presumably would never see the Appeal-essential Assignment of Errors. So as to focus them on the single proxy side-issue never raised by Clair as an objection but weaponized as the single only objection.

On 6/01/2017 Clair filed notice to the sixth circuit that her appeal should resume. Clair included an Appeal from list. Since Judges Keith, Cook, and Thapar must never recognize the true and actual questions before them. Must not recognize the glaring absence of the Second Amended Complaint from this list; like the Assignment of Errors, the Appeal from list needed to be withheld.

This notice was docketed as: 6/01/2017 *Civil Case Docketed {1}* new Case No. 17-5618. What was filed to replace the actual 6/01/2017 notice is a forgery quashing the right to be heard. Attach. No. 38. What substitutes for page-1 is the letter assigning the second case number. What substitutes for page-2 is the Defendant List. The actual copy does not appear over: www.pacer.gov. It was never seen by the second panel of judges proven in that not a one of the Appeal from questions/ objections were addressed. Because rogue employees of the sixth circuit went to great lengths and considerable risk to substitute and conceal these questions for reasons that can have nothing to do with the law, they are quoted below.

Notice is hereby given that Alexandra Clair, hereby appeal to the United States Court of Appeals for the Sixth Circuit from: Final judgment of the District Court of May 22, 2017. Appeal from: Judge Vescovo personal bias and conflict of interest in favor and protection of banking-defendants. Appeal from: denial of due process. Appeal from: *culture of prejudice against pro se litigants.* Appeal from: *failure to accord a liberal construction of Clair's case.* Appeal from: *failure to quote accurately the factual allegations.* Appeal from: *failure to screen the case, in all effect, ruling on the case itself in the manner of a defendant-attorney, resulting in obstruction of a meaningful opportunity of the case to be heard before a jury.* Appeal from: *Obstruction of, and, refusal to add, JP Morgan Chase Bank as a defendant based on new evidence. And refusal to add REO ID#: 00906148; a number identifier used to conceal theft a RICO Violation.* Appeal from: *Stripping of independent collaboration of fraud documented per the U.S. Dept. of the Treasury and the State of TN Dept. of Commerce and Insurance.* Appeal from: *Abuse of judicial power in the failure to correct and acknowledge significant and overt misquotes of content codified into the record in support of the biased intent to dismiss.* Appeal from: *failure to grant Clair a fair judge-decision-maker.* Appeal from: *Omission of content that support the RICO claims and which in the totality of those selected omissions did materially alter and slander Clair's complaint(s).* Appeal from: *failure to voluntarily recuse for conduct noted within the: Objection to the Report and Recommendations [14], Motion for Disqualification [21]. The Assignment of Errors, dated November 5, 2016... Also, the Amended Assignment of Errors [37], which addresses additional errors.* Appeal from: *Denial of the Motion to Reverse Judgment of December 28, 2016 [38] for in part, the judicial abuses raised herein.* Appeal from: *District Court slanderous label of case (in part) as a "foreclosure" when, in point of fact, there was no foreclosure; an error repeatedly codified into the court records. ...Entered this action on the 1st day of June, 2017.* Attach. No. 26. Stamped received by the district court 06/01/2017.

The issue of the Second Amended Complaint was raised by Clair in the letter to first Case Manager, Karen Fultz: 11/28/2016; Attach. No. 40. Her reply to Clair 12/02/2016; Attach. No. 41. Proof that Clair respectfully accepted this is seen in that the Second Amended Compliant does not feature in the Appeal from list. Clair believed that once due process was achieved, she could ask that presiding future judge for permission to inform her case with additional proof; some of which the district court would not allow her to file. Logic suggests that at this early juncture a plan was conceived to weaponize the Second

Amended Complaint as a fraud device to falsely posture the fiction that every objection was addressed in this single proxy-decoy-issue elevated to suppress and conceal the actual questions before the appeals court.

How often has this same unchecked highway of corruption been facilitated by lack of oversight? Misplaced trust in clerks not deserving of that trust? Failure of quality controls utilized to deceive other judges while derailing other Pro Se appeals?

Protection of the fraudsters began when the district court labeled this Civil RICO Case: **Nature of Suit: 220 Real Property: Foreclosure;** Attach. No. 20. There was NO FORECLOSURE. The Foreclosure lie trailed forward to style this appeal as NOT intellectually challenging or precedent setting to actual judges. On one occasion Second Case Manager Hance used the first person singular leading Clair to question if Ms. Hance had authored the dismissal. This led Clair to research this shocking possibility. Clair learned that a high proportion of pro se cases are delegated to clerks and staff attorney's to be rubber stamped by appellant-judges. The wrong label provided the excuse to facilitate an unequal standard of care and custody of filings of a "less than" worthy appeal. So unimportant that it could be fed to a recent institutional structure at odds with Constitutional Protections. A structure within which, lacking judicial oversight, not applying administrative controls, what transpired is a fraud upon the court. By design to deprive Clair of her Right of Appeal seated in the Constitutional Right to be heard.

From the late law professor, Penelope Pether, "Sorcerers, Not Apprentices: How Judicial Clerks and Staff Attorney's Impoverish U.S. Law;" 39 Ariz. St. L.J. 1 (2007) *...that the corpus of clerk and staff attorney-authorized opinions is not merely likely to be sloppy or wrong, but that it has structurally subordinating effects. On the rare occasion that they register the kind of second-class treatment that is likely to produce injustice, they* (federal courts) *do not make the connection between <u>flawed procedure and its result: systemic injustice somehow becomes invisible.</u> FJC Report; supra note 82.*

For failure to address the objections. For, failure to execute the error correction duty of the appeals process: **We AFFIRM {7}, 11/14/2017;** under **Case No.: 17-5618** is a void judgment inconsistent with the U.S. Constitution. As is: **Order {9} denying the En Banc Petition; 1/18/2018.** How the sixth circuit second panel of judges were duped to affix their names to what they thought had addressed the actual objections (appeal questions) is informed by what is quoted from paragraph twenty-two from, Motion for a Void Judgment. Likely fed to a paper shredder; never coming before any judge of the court. Submitted herein as Attach. No. 34.

22.) *It took planning, coordination to replace the actual objections* (appeal questions) *with a facsimile.*

- *To begin with the case needed to be removed from Case Manager, Ms. Fultz leaving her in custody of the filings and motions that, by design, no party will see and, so informed, rule on.*
- *There needed to be a second case number so as to establish the pretense of one docket sheet. To posture transparent containment of all case essential motions and filings accessed from one electronic file.*
- *Under Ms. Hance's watch, Clair's objections were at no time present to inform the author of the November 14, 2017 Order [7] Case No.: 17-5618. Not to be confused with {7} under the first Case No.: 16-6672. Thus, Clair's objections could not inform Senior Judge Keith or Judges Cook and Thapar. Proven in the outcome that none* (of the appeal questions) *were at any time addressed.*
- *A proxy objection* (appeal question) *was needed to hang the dismissal on. This proxy objection, having nothing to do with the actual objections, provided the means of walking this case toward the inevitable dismissal that would protect Judge Vescovo. The charade of what on the surface appeared a lawful process was crafted to deceitfully slide under the bar of sixth circuit judicial oversight.*
- *The un-ruled upon complaint addressed in the Order of February 24, 2017 {8} Case No.: 16-6672, provided the convenient scapegoat issue dusted off and weaponized to quash the actual objections* (appeal questions) *from recognition. As needed, this back and forth between the case numbers shows knowledge and intent to derail this case.*
- *Thus, at the case summarization juncture, Senior Judge Keith, and Judges Cook and Thapar were spoon fed an incomplete record; manipulated to affix their names to what, by design, was in every sense a void judgment.*

- *The segregation of filings and motions guaranteed no judicial oversight and therefore, no threat of ensuring accountability. Court disparagement of pro se litigants, called in one publication, "Relief for Pro Se Headaches," establishing bias that litigants cannot overcome. To cloak this case as not worthy of judicial involvement and Clair as a persistent crackpot disrespectful of judicial authority.*
- *Lastly Clair must not recognize until it was deemed too late, if ever the fatal danger of two case numbers, two case managers, no complete record at any time before any sixth circuit decision-maker. Clair is not the only party assaulted by clerks usurping judicial power; described herein. Every future pro se litigant and every judge is compromised by such bureaucratic over-reach evidenced in disdain for constitutionally, conferred rights.*
- *Goal Accomplished. A corrupt magistrate judge with an almost overwhelming conflict of interest to protect the financial industry defendants that are, and have been feeding a significant income stream to Vescovo-McLaren family members, will survive to quash the due process rights of the next case that challenges the criminality of banks.*

A consistent pattern of conduct in pursuit of the same goal at both the higher and lower courts inform that outside influence was exerted to place protection of the Magistrate Judge, and by extension, the RICO-Defendants, over the First, Fourth, and Fourteenth Amendment Rights of the Pro Se Appellant. It is not outside the pale to consider this. The U.S. Circuit Court for the Tenth Circuit held that Clair's Defendant, Bank of America, could be labeled an unlawful racketeering enterprise. Criminal attempts at infiltration of federal institutions is well documented. Most recently by partisan FBI leadership and DOJ lying to a FISA Court.

The Clerk's Office has a protected interest in derailing these four complaints. Chief Judge Cole has demonstrated inept application and oversight of quality controls. As a culture of bias this lower standard of care, filtered down to the second panel of judges. The four complaints must be fully investigated as a fraud upon the court. No conflict of interest party can be allowed access to influence any outcome. Although the docket itself, by document fraud misleads and therefore dissuades any attorney from helping Clair, she knows that her Constitutional Right to be heard is worth fighting for. Motion for a Void Judgement must be heard. The following does not state "except for an appeals court." *A void judgment is a nullity, and no rights can be based thereon; it can be set aside on motion or can be collaterally attacked at any time. Garren v. Rollis* 375 P.2d 994 (Idaho 1962). *Courts lose jurisdiction if they do not follow Due Process Law. Title 5, US Cod Sec. 556(d), Sec. 557, Sec. 706.*

I DECLARE THAT UNDER PENALTY OF PERJURY ALL STATEMENTS ARE TRUE.

I then signed and dated this complaint.

I am not an attorney. I have never tried to be one. I've always known and felt keenly that I was disadvantaged in not having ethical legal representation. At the very least I trusted that those rights conferred on every person, rich and poor alike, would frame a just outcome under the rule of law. It might not be exactly the outcome I wanted. But the process itself would give me a voice. I am smart enough to recognize that the same pattern of practice to deny me a voice in any forum that could produce a record was modus operandi that followed me to Sixth Circuit Court of Appeals.

I was still living with my friends Marj and Ray Pierce at Deerwood. We had become a family, but it was time for me to leave. We said an emotional goodbye in August of 2018. I had lived with them for over four years. Marj and I had often sat on the screened in porch looking over her English cottage garden talked and prayed about next steps. When the February 24, 2017 decision from the first panel of judges came in the mail I skipped to the last page and thought my fight was ended with no outcome that in any way resembled justice. Tears filled my eyes.

Marj took the pages and read the salient passage out loud, letting me know that the first panel had sent the appeal back to the district court for a ruling on what remained outstanding. Meaning that it was not over. When the November 14, 2017 decision came in the mail, addressing the second amended complaint as the primary appeal question. Writing of recusal out of context to Judge Vescovo's conflicts of interest. Not addressing slander of my claims, abuse of the screening procedure, and failure to address the fourteen errors cited in: Objection to the Report and Recommendations 8/2/2016 district court docket No.: 14. I hit another brick wall.

Once again I asked, did God want me to continue this fight? My thoughts always took me back to the conviction that it did matter. It mattered for other pro se litigants. It mattered to the many other victims of this same Bank Theft Delivery System. It struck me that those filing under pauper status, whether they were in prison or on the street, must be able to trust that there is not a, dual system of justice operating in America. The bias that I experienced had reached toxic levels. If I did not fight for the fundamental right to be heard at the district court and then at the second highest court in the land others would be harmed by the same levels of corruption.

I halfheartedly called the second case manager, Jeanine Hance. I asked her for a complete list of filings needed as I organized my files and began writing the appeal to the United States Supreme Court. I had the docket list from the district court, which they always readily supplied, but not from the sixth circuit. I believe today that in providing this they were keeping me away from use of the Pacer System. Not understanding the Pacer System, I did not realize that there was a way that I could download this information without having to pay for it.

The first significant red flag at this juncture is that there was subtle and then increasing resistance to sending what I asked for. Why was that? After going over the head of Case Manager Hance and appealing to two other persons, with very clear reluctance it was sent. The interesting point here is that no person said, “hey it’s a matter of public record. Learn to use the pacer system, dummy.” When it comes to pro se litigants far too much is assumed.

When I was finally able to see what was claimed to be the complete docket of filings, I was shocked. On that fateful day of, February 9, 2018 I realized for the first time that the second panel of judges did not have a full company of filings before them. Most notably they did not have the Assignment of Errors buried under the first case number. For the first time I realized that two case numbers and two case managers equated to no one continuous electronic record of filings before the second panel of judges. It was only later when I learned to download the actual filings that I realized how the docket itself had been used to contrive a story that was not true.

I asked myself the question that next cried out for an answer. What else had been withheld from those judges? For the first time I had an explanation that made sense, but now I needed the first docket list of filings.

A series of sophisticated and well-planned maneuvers had sealed the fate that I would never be heard. I began to see the sneaky, underhanded way that my appeal was blatantly sabotaged by the Clerk's Office at the Sixth Circuit Court of Appeals. Motive emerged out of the pattern exposed in separation of filings; two dockets. The goal was to protect a corrupt judge and by extension The Bank Theft Delivery System. What happened to me could not shed light on how other victims coming up against a mafia like criminal enterprise had been treated. It could only be that the same crony corruption brand of criminality had been pulling strings.

"Administrative Corruption refers to a set of behaviors by a group of public servants who ignore the rules and regulations to achieve non-organizational goals. In other words, administrative corruption is an illegitimate tool to satisfy illegal needs." Samuel P. Huntington, Political Scientist.

Was it now too late? As it turned out, God led me to a solution. I could file a Motion for a Void Judgement. Having read the complaints filed against Chief Judge Cole and the decoy, second panel of judges you know how this turned out. Two of the filings were returned to me. The third was buried. I doubt the third could even be found; likely fed to a paper shredder. Failure to address actual appeal questions, my right to be heard, and restoration of my civil and Constitutional Rights would not be addressed. In publishing these complaints, I exercise my right of free speech.

CHAPTER TEN

"But this is what you must do. Tell the truth to one another. Render verdicts in your courts that are just and that lead to peace. Do not make evil plots to harm each other. And stop this habit of swearing to things that are false. I hate all these things says the Lord" (Zechariah 8: 16, 17.)

The changes in how federal appeals are superficially evaluated and then assigned to second-class standards of care made what happened to me possible. My appeal to the sixth circuit was delegated to federal employees that are not judges. The practices that have allowed appellate judges to selectively delegate their authority to those that are not judges has ushered in an institutional structure that is a threat to the delivery of equal justice under the rule of law.

I had filed a complaint against Chief Judge Cole for failing to guard against administrative corruption. For this reason, an acting Chief Judge needed to be appointed to oversee the complaints. What follows is my letter to the Circuit Executive addressing the conflict of interest appointment of Judge Alice M. Batchelder. At the very least her appointment informs the blind spot at the sixth circuit. At most it informs cover up and containment.

Alexandra Clair
PO Box 334
Spring Hill, KS 66083

Office of the Circuit Executive
100 East Fifth Street; Cincinnati, Ohio 45202-3988

RE: Complaint of Judicial Misconduct No: 18-90103/104/105/106/107/108

December 14, 2018

To Whom It May Concern:

I did not file a complaint against the first panel of judges; Case No. 16-6672; Judges Norris, Batchelder, and Gibbons. I determined and was hopeful that the culture that precipitated denial of my right to be heard on appeal was aptly described in the complaint(s) filed against the second panel of judges.

First Case Manager Karen Fultz forged, "edited" and retitled my letter/ motion; request for clarity of what "appealable order" remained outstanding at the district court. The alteration of the title misrepresented the intent of what was filed by me, morphing that request for clarity into the edited Rehearing Order {12}. This change of title occurred under, in part, the oversight of Judge Bratchelder. She and her fellow judges failed to read the docket (Clerk's) admission that this request for clarity was edited as a potential red flag. The retitled Motion for Rehearing served as the premise to accomplish the premature close of my case absent all disclosure to me, before I had even been granted permission to file the Pro Se Appellants Brief. Therefore, there was nothing to rehear. The outcome was entered into the district court docket under the forged title. This served to grant a rationale by which Magistrate Judge Vescovo might never address my objections. The retitled Rehearing Order opened the door for assigning my appeal to a second panel of judges who would then be operationally deprived of the appeal essential Assignment of Errors buried under the first case number.

Judge Batchelder was among the first panel of judges that failed to exercise oversight of my appeal. The first panel accepted what was falsely proposed, altered, and edited within the first docket; abdicating authority and responsibility to those who are not judges. There never was a request for rehearing at this juncture. To falsely posture such a request informs bias used as a tool to manipulate an outcome upon belief that there would be no safeguarding of Constitutional protections. If indeed confused, Karen Fultz could have, but never did pick up the phone to ask the intent of my first Letter/Motion request for clarity. Not having an answer, the first request for clarity was repeated. Neither request was ever answered; likely never read by any actual judge which allowed the fabricated rehearing request to stand; corrupting the docket. It escaped attention of the first panel that there was a dishonest agenda served by assigning a different title born out in the operational events that followed.

I must register that the Circuit Executive has not assigned whatever outcome will be determined to an entirely unconnected Acting Chief Judge. Unconnected to the events that led to the very serious abuses described in my complaint(s). Though I am sure Judge Batchelder would make every effort to be impartial I am also concerned by what appears a fundamentally unwise choice of a judge with a decided appearance of bias; predisposed to limit any investigation. Given your choice it seems prudent to appoint an acting Chief Judge not residing at the sixth circuit. I am now residing in Kansas. Perhaps even at the tenth circuit. Please let me know of whatever action will be taken and, or, not taken as a result of this request that you appoint an Acting Chief Judge with no appearance of bias. Thank you for your attention to this request.

I believe today that this "edited" rehearing title was a kind of test. Could employees of the court get away with using the docket to sabotage the appeal of a pro se litigant? What was my level of ignorance? Could, they get away with replacing my questions with a, decoy question I never raised? As of the writing of this chapter I've still not had any response to this letter. It is over a year that I filed these complaints. I am not considered important to the process. If concealment and damage control win out, I am already positioned as ancillary, unessential to any outcome, effectively silenced.

Logic told me that due to the separation of filings and failure to read and rule on the Pro Se Appellant's Brief, I still had an outstanding appeal at the Sixth Circuit Court of Appeals. The bold nature of what occurred were not simple administrative mistakes. Fear that any checking mechanism might curtail the behavior of the administrative staff, and particularly Case Manager Hance, seems to have been nonexistent. This suggests a past history of getting away with similar acts.

What did I do that was so offensive that my appeal needed to be buried?

- I was not sufficiently intimidated by the entitled imbalance of power.
- I persisted in asserting my right to have my actual appeal questions addressed within the framework of the error correction, fundamental responsibility of the sixth circuit.
- I dared to charge that Magistrate Judge Vescovo had slandered my claims so as to block my Civil RICO Case from achieving due process.
- I had charged that in doing so she had also protected a RICO Criminal Enterprise, i.e., powerful financial industry players with whom she and her family members have conflicts of interest.
- I had named Memphis attorneys (law firms) that perfected title theft, skimming equity, followed by a, brutal illegal eviction and seizure of my home absent due process.
- I had included in the defendant list three attorneys whose job it was to catch and kill my case; I was never their actual client.
- In doing so I had inadvertently shed light on the stranglehold of crony corruptionism operating in Western Tennessee; shutting out honest lawyers while rewarding those that conspire to limit and, or, derail a defense.
- Not getting the message that I should forgo defending my Constitutional Right to be heard, I persisted by filing the last three motions. Not only were the appeal questions not addressed,

but the En Banc Petition[17] was never presented to other judges at the sixth circuit. If it had been some other smart sixth circuit judge might have actually noticed the separation of filings.

- I had rejected the sixth circuit clerk staff Orwellian rationale that though my appeal questions had never been addressed and there was no record of them ever being addressed I should somehow accept that actual judges had mysteriously addressed them.
- I should accept no complete electronic record before the second panel of judges. I should accept manipulation of the docket so as to communicate a story inconsistent with the truth. Which biased future access to legal representation.

After February 2018 I realized how the docket was used to prematurely close my appeal before it could be heard. This was a shock of realization. It isn't that I should appeal to the Supreme Court it is that the, sixth circuit has a duty to rule on the void judgement. Just as they had a duty to rule on the Pro Se Appellants Brief, delivering to me an equal standard of care. A common sense word picture is helpful. You take your car in for an oil change. The receipt says that the oil was changed. It wasn't. Were the essential elements of the contract between you and the mechanic met? The Bill of Rights is a contract between American citizens and government operating on our behest. Not a one of the elements owed my appeal were met. What may

[17] Petition for Rehearing – En Banc Filing; Case No.: 17-5618; Docket No.: 8. Hand delivered to the attention of Case Manager Hance. Filed: 11/28/2017. Stamped filed by: Clerk, Deborah S. Hunt who failed to forward this petition to judges of the sixth circuit. Reading in part: *The questions presented in Clair's appeal to the sixth Circuit addresses violations of the Due Process Clause of the Fourteenth Amendment was violated. That Judge Vescovo did exceed screening requirements, ruling on the case rather than screening the case. That Judge Vescovo prejudiced the claims through multiple examples in which she misquoted the content of Clair's complaints. And that this practice extended to actual alteration of the...* Once again, my voice was smothered and powerful financial industry defendants were off the hook. As was David Osborn and the Jones, Kelley, Boyd Perpetrator Nexus group of operative – white collar criminals. This En Banc Petition is not the Karen Fultz forged and "edited" non-existent rehearing motion addressed earlier. The Karen Fultz alteration of a filing was the retitled order used to contrive removal of my case from the first panel of judges; calling that case closed before granted permission to file the Pro Se Appellants' Brief. At that time, I had not yet filed the En Banc Petition which was sent to the attention of second Case Manager Hance under the second case number. The En Banc petition was also buried never addressed by sixth circuit judges as was required. Appeal questions never addressed, administrative corruption, violations of procedural due process, abdication of judicial oversight and responsibility delivered the outcome that I was never heard. Subversion of due process rights is a significant civil rights violation(s).

appear as an arbitrary series of mistakes does not negate the responsibility to fulfill a contract. The answer on both counts is, NO! You are owed an oil change. I am owed a decision. Authoritarian misuse of power asserting that my appeal questions were addressed when there is no evidence that the appeal questions were ever addressed does not make it so.

My last, though not final attempts to have my appeal questions addressed centered on the last three filings. First for reversal and then after reading more on what constitutes *a void judgment*, two submissions for a void judgment. Why three? The first two were mailed back to me unfiled.

There was now a different tone. I was uncooperative in pushing for my right to be heard, and the clerks were the victims. Painting pro se litigants as too zealous, even a bit crazy is a tool of reprisal that is all too easily excused by underlying and existing bias. Irritation with me bled through. I was not respectful of authority. I hadn't fallen into line as was expected by elitist, arrogant bureaucrats that had callously fielded the huge imbalance of power and informational gaps as a weapon. In my last conversation with Jeanine Hance I was fairly certain that I was being recorded. It was then that I moved on to filing the complaints with the Circuit Executive.

If this kept up, I planned to take the pages out of the returned envelope, make the required date adjustment, pour it into another envelope and mail it back as Motion for a Void Judgement numbers 4, 5, 6... If anyone cared I had the United States Constitution on my side. Told that the first filing for reversal was lost, never received to the mail room... Here was another invitation in a long line of such bureaucratic machinations to subvert any chance I could be heard. I wrote the following.

What follows is a copy of what was mailed to the sixth Circuit Court of appeals on 2/20/2018. I spoke to Case Manager Ms. Hance today; 03/13/2018. She informed me there is no record of this filing being received to the Sixth Circuit Court of Appeals. It has therefore not been docketed. Please note, added to the attachments-list, is the receipt of overnight delivery; U.S. Postal Service (Attached as Exhibit No. 7) and confirmation that the original 2/20/2018 filing/Motion for Relief of Judgment as captioned above was received/delivered to the sixth circuit on 02/22/2018 (Attached as Exhibit No. 8.) Please also note Letter to Chief Justice Cole noting the arrival of this Motion: Relief from a Judgment... Re: separation of the filings into two case numbers. Strategic outcome of which

was denial of due process, right to be heard, and recognition of what objections were to be addressed on appeal; (Attached as Exhibit No. 9). The FIRST of those last three filings looked like this.

THE UNITED STATES COURT OF APPEALS
FOR THE SIXTH CIRCUIT

Two Case Numbers One Case. Please file as one complete record linking both Case Numbers to this Filing.

Alexandra Clair, et al.,	)	
Plaintiff	)	District Court
	)	CASE NO. 16-02263-SHL-dvk
v.	)	
	)	U.S. 6th Circuit CASE NO. 16-6672
Bank of America, N.A., et al,	)	U.S. 6th Circuit CASE NO. 17-5618
Defendants	)	

MOTION FOR RELIFE FROM A JUDGEMENT of November 14, 2018 for Violations of FEDERAL RULES OF CIVIL PROCEDURE; RULE 60 (b)(1)(3)(6); Rule 60 (d)(3) and Rule 79 (a)(1).

Why would judges not have wanted to clean up systemic corruption that if ignored in the face of knowledge would make them complicit? After doing some research, finding that there is no statute of limitations on a void judgement. What would be more "void" than failing to address the elements of any appeal? I then filed two motions for a void judgment. The heading of the Third filing, the only one retained looked like this. I doubt it is anywhere where it can be read.

THE UNITED STATES COURT OF APPEALS
FOR THE SIXTH CIRCUIT

Two Case Numbers One Case. Please file as one complete record linking both Case Numbers to this Filing.

Alexandra Clair, et al.,	)	
Plaintiff	)	District Court
	)	CASE NO. 16-02263-SHL-dvk
v.	)	
	)	U.S. 6th Circuit CASE NO. 16-6672
Bank of America, N.A., et al,	)	U.S. 6th Circuit CASE NO. 17-5618
Defendants	)	

MOTION FOR VOID JUDGMENTS OF NOVEMBER 14, 2017 and JANUARY 18, 2018; VIOLATIONS UNDER THE U.S. CONSTITUTION OF PLAINTIFF'S FIRST AND FOURTEENTH AMENDMENT RIGHTS; FOR FAILURE TO RULE ON THE OBJECTIONS; USUPTION OF JUDICIAL AUTHORITY; BIAS AGAINST PRO SE LITIGANTS; VIOLATIONS OF PROCEDURAL DUE PROCESS VIA CLERK-STAFF WITHHOLDING CASE ESSENTIAL DOCUMENTS FROM JUDGE DECISION-MAKERS.

Exhibits – An additional twenty-one pages. (48 Pages with Exhibits 1 thru 15)

Just imagine what a nightmare it would be to write the performance measures that allow Clerks and Staff Attorneys to function in place of judges. Have they been written? If so, they have not been challenged except by various law professors writing and speaking to the insider echo chamber. Human resource departments within government can do a lot to impede administrative corruption. They appear outgunned by behind the scenes agendas to undermine the Constitution and Bill of Rights. These tendencies have congealed in the growing acceptance of employees of the court acting in place of judges.

In attempting to formalize such practices into policy it would be clear that they are inconsistent with Constitutional Protections. The general public of voters must never fully realize how this institutionally imbedded dual system of care can be adapted to shred the civil liberties of themselves and their children. This country is faced with a constitutional crisis. Not the kind raised as an alarmist sound bite that desensitizes from a fundamental threat to civil liberties, but in fact, a real crisis.

Lawyers that have had their cases detrimentally impacted by these practices are afraid to speak out for fear of offending the system. Pro se appellants like me are never told that... *"Hey, judges are too busy for you. Your appeal is not intellectually challenging, career building, or precedent setting. Therefore, the system will assign your appeal to employees of the court who have never been to law school. And, or, to staff attorneys who hold no federal appointment to act as they do. In the assignment of your appeal to lower standards of care scripted outcomes are communicated. But don't worry. There will be a kind of cursory review meeting to document this outrage. Judges that have never actually read the filings will then rubber-stamp, sign off on these second-class, second-party decisions."*

We have consumer laws in this country that require disclosure. The fact is that given a choice, even minimally aware, any plaintive-appellant that has poured their heart and soul into the herculean effort to seek justice.

Doing so, not by choice, but many times out of deeply held convictions would shout back some version of: *"NO! You're the judge. Get your act together. Perform the sacred duty you are privileged to exercise and give my case the same care and attention you would any other. If for some reason you are not willing to meet performance standards please retire on the life-time salary with full benefits that tax payers subsidize."*

President Trump has appointed more federal judges to the bench, filling vacancies than any other President in our history. I cannot speak for him, but I do believe that he has recognized the swamp motives to undermine what the United States Constitution guarantees by holding up judicial appointments. Over worked federal judges lead to lower standards of care. This has opened the door for what I believe is corrupt and intruding outside influence. If all the vacancies were filled there would be less opportunity to sideline selected cases and appeals to a, second class standard of care. Just as a plaintiff will write, *jury trial requested.* When submitting an appeal to any circuit court they should declare, *this appeal to be addressed by judges, not employees of the court.*

Among those that have criticized this lesser standard of care, as already quoted, is the late Dr. Penelope Prether; Villanova University School of Law. Her powerful series of three articles challenged and exposed the unconstitutionality of this system.[18] I quoted one of her articles in the Complaint of Judicial Misconduct directed to the second panel of Judges at the sixth circuit: Senior Judge Keith, Judge Cook and Judge Thapar. The title itself is a clarion call for needed reform. I must wonder if these judges, having read the complaints I filed, looked back at how procedural due process was shredded under their watch? I cannot answer that. No outcome, no answer, is the answer of incubating tyranny under cover of law.

From the late law professor, Penelope Pether, "Sorcerers, Not Apprentices: How Judicial Clerks and Staff Attorney's Impoverish U.S. Law;" 39 Ariz. 9h. St. L.J. 1 (2007) ***...that the corpus of clerk and staff attorney-authorized opinions is not merely likely to be sloppy or wrong, but that it has structurally subordinating***

---

[18] About Penelope Pether at: https://digitalcommons.law.villanova.edu. When I read a reference to this article in another filing, I then had difficulty tracking it down. The Villanova law library claimed not to have a copy. For the benefit of the public welfare Villanova may decide to compile selective writings and make them available in a single publication. Here is where I did finally obtain what every pro se litigant should read before filing their case in federal court. Or in theory in any court. Arizona Law Journal; University of Arizona.

***effects. On the rare occasion that they register the kind of second-class treatment that is likely to produce injustice, they* (federal courts) *do not make the connection between flawed procedure and its result: systemic injustice somehow becomes invisible*.** *FJC Report; supra note 82.*

Please note that Professor Pether, writes: "on the rare occasion." The sixth circuit did an end-run around Constitutional Protections and was then offended when I objected. Our founding documents stand as an affront and very real obstacle to those globalist agendas that would like to tear down barriers of personhood and nationhood. The Financial Industry has a global reach. They are in essence a country without borders. I cannot speak to the leanings of those judges that abdicated their responsibility, failing in their duty to actually read and rule on my Pro Se Appellants Brief. If they had exercised even a minimal degree of oversight, they would have recognized that they were being fed a forged record that by design induced them to rule on a fictitious appeal to thus, shield powerful financial industry criminals from risk. This level of corruption does not just show up smartly dressed, ready and able to thwart justice. It arrives preceded by a thousand unremarked failures incubated in the culture that allows it.

In the next paragraph I wrote: For failure to address the objections. For, failure to execute the error correction duty of the appeals process: **We AFFIRM {7}, 11/14/2017;** under **Case No.: 17-5618** is a void judgment inconsistent with the U.S. Constitution. As is: **Order {9} denying the En Banc Petition; 1/18/2018.** How the sixth circuit second panel of judges were duped to affix their names to what they thought had addressed the actual objections is informed by what is quoted from paragraph twenty-two from, Motion for a Void Judgment. Likely fed to a paper shredder; never coming before any judge of the court. Submitted herein as Attach. No. 34.

On September 27, 2019, in a Fox News interview with Sean Hannity, Jay Sekulow speaking about something else, but applicable to what I experienced. What I believe other pro se litigants and some attorneys have experienced at the United States District Court for the Western District of Tennessee. Trailing forward, out, and under as unchecked corruption always does. **"It is a dereliction of Constitutional duties if you ignore the Constitution."**

PART II

CHAPTER ELEVEN

"There are two modes of invading private property, the first, by which the poor plunder the rich...sudden and violent; the second, by which the rich plunder the poor, slow and legal." John Taylor, *An inquiry into Principals and Policy of the Government of the United States (1814).*

Up to the time that I filed the Civil RICO Case, pro se and under pauper status, I had separately been represented by three attorneys. The first for a matter of days. The second, Webb Brewer, up to the day that I fired him shortly after a deposition when I realized he had lied to me about what he had and had not accomplished. The last attorney was Kathryn Maceri. Informing how deeply a culture of crony accommodation and corruptionism has seeped into the Memphis legal community, each had played a role in containing and misdirecting my defense.

My last hope was the Civil RICO Case I filed at the federal district court in Memphis, Tennessee. Given the cesspool of corruption that I had already experienced I was not going to turn any outcome over to a single Memphis judge. I therefore requested a jury trial. I knew of course that not everyone connected to the West Tennessee legal community was corrupt, but experience counts. I had been too willing to give people that said they would help me the benefit of the doubt. In the end I had to alter my default thinking, learned trust, moving a few degrees toward functioning paranoia to believe almost nothing that I read or was told until tested for myself.

The decision to request a jury trial was informed by another case that named the same white-collar criminal defendants that had targeted me. Keller Williams Realty – MEM 2, LLC functioned as an arm of the Jones, Kelley, Boyd Perpetrator Nexus – REO Investment Group. What RICO calls, "Enterprise plus Relationship."

I connected what happened to me to the local and then the national theft structure. Very soon one group became three and though they overlapped in the services they used I had to back off. I had to narrow my investigation to the core group that targeted me. Out of your own personal investigation you will single out those individuals and entities that made the theft of your home possible. **One important ruling clarifies that each person and entity, no matter how small the role, is**

culpable. The appraiser, the foreclosure mill attorney, the title company, the various lenders, the title insurance company, the straw buyers or any others that lent their professional credentials to making theft of private property possible could not say they were innocent if by their actions they had helped accomplish the goals of the Criminal Enterprise. Predicate act refers to the laws that were violated in commission of the crime(s). To say that: ***"A sufficient nexus or relationship exists between the racketeering acts and the enterprise if the defendant was able to commit the predicate acts by means of, by consequences of, by reason of, by agency of, or by instrumentality of his association with the enterprise." Marino vs. ME Department of Corrections; First Circuit Court of Appeals.***

Vernon "Wayne" Boyd and Sherry Boyd are Keller Williams realtors. Under HUD Vernon "Wayne" Boyd was an approved investor buying and selling at risk real estate through HUD programs. He had acquired my mortgage in 2009, buying, selling, and flipping the property title (secretly laundering the chain of title) that on paper, per document fraud, he and his REO criminal cohort claimed to own. Today they are still squatting at 65 Pinehurst Drive.

Certain other individuals associated with Keller Williams and David Osborn played very specific roles in furthering the theft goals of the Criminal Enterprise. I am not saying that every Keller Williams agent was part of this group. Nor that by blanket statement they are all engaged in illegal theft of private property. What I was able to prove is that some Keller Williams agents from other states that included Texas, Florida and Colorado acted as signing agents, claiming authority they did not have, signing fraud perfecting paperwork. The unifying link was that all, including Vernon "Wayne" Boyd and Sherry Boyd, worked for or with David Osborn. David Osborn is a multiple Keller Williams franchise owner.[19]

---

[19] David Osborn is the Keller Williams regional operating principal of four market centers including (Memphis) North Texas and New Mexico. He is involved in real estate activities from Los Angeles California to Tampa Bay, Florida; "fifteen states in the United States and Canada." He helped launch the Keller Williams Franchise Systems Orientation programs. The Jones, Kelley, Boyd Perpetrator Nexus operated under his direction. David Osborn was raised in Europe and educated in Great Britain. His wife is an attorney. He is linked by association to Michael Harlow and Judge Oscar Carr; both dead by gunshot wound.

The theft schemes were the brain child of banks and financial industry players. But as it most directly targets and assaults victims like myself, the chain of theft could be tracked back through the illegal seizure of targeted properties by the boots on the ground, locally situated REO Investment Group(s). What I came to call the Jones, Kelley, Boyd Perpetrator Nexus operated as just one of these groups.

The Collins-Maury Case was filed against this Memphis based Keller Williams franchise, by, Farris, Bobango, PLC; hereafter referred to as Farris-Bobango. This case alleged that Keller Williams – MEM 2, LLC engaged in corporate espionage.[20] The plaintiff attorneys, Farris-Bobango, wrote that Keller Williams hacked into a rival company computer system, ostensibly in search of leads. Doing so undetected over an extended period of time. There are two case numbers. The salient description of these crimes, written before the case was dumbed-down, is filed under Case Number: CH-11-1860 / Part 3; Chancery Court of Shelby County, TN; filed November 10, 2011. This filing was written after discovery had produced proof of internet hacking activity engaged in by rival realty company Keller Williams Memphis East. Also known as MEM 2, LLC. The other Case Number is: CH-09-2341.

This is a case that went on for nine years, I believe, giving time for the kill agenda to play out over my Civil RICO Case. Clever attorneys managed to waste the time and resources of the court delivering the outcome that there was no real resolution making its way into the public record. The case ended with a dismissal on November 8, 2018. Reading between the lines there was a back-door settlement taking place before the published dismissal. Crony corruptionism; Chancery Court judges allowed manipulation of the justice system by a RICO Criminal Enterprise averting public attention away from a pattern of illegal activity. Incessant delay, waiting for ancillary cases to be resolved or tanked, as a strategy to derail federal attention is the theme. Which might have led to consideration of motive. Why these computers, this

[20] Collins-Maury, Inc., d/b/a Prudential Collins-Maury, Inc., Realtors Plaintiff vs MEM 2, LLC d/b/a Keller Williams Realty a/k/a Keller Williams Realty Memphis East, first filed November 24, 2009; CH-11-1860. This is a case that went on for nine years, by intent and strategy, wasting the courts time and ending, November 8, 2018 in what appears to be a backdoor settlement and dismissal. One intended outcome of contrived delay is to prevent other victims from recognizing any possible pattern of assault having also impacted how they were harmed. At every opportunity where information could arm other victims to fight back choke-holds over disclosure is leveraged as a bargaining chip.

company, this rival? No deep dive into title theft; wholesale theft and illegal seizure of private property.

My investigation informs that the corporate espionage engaged in by Keller Williams – MEM 2, LLC (the defendant) their hacking of the rival, Collins-Maury Prudential Realty computers (the plaintiff), went far deeper than what was described in the filing of November 10, 2011; *Chancery Court Docket Number: CH-11-1860; Part 3.* When the number of legitimate foreclosures could not keep pace with demand for product the need was to increase the victim pool by any means possible. Including the hacking of rival realty company computers for leads. In showing an ongoing pattern of prior bad acts by the same RICO Criminal Enterprise I went in search of other cases. Some of them are referred to in this book.

Judge Oscar "Bo" Carr, III was assigned to take over this corporate espionage case. Unlike Magistrate Judge Vescovo, it would appear that he took one look at the defendant list and recused himself. Attorneys who are elected or appointed to the bench have 180 days from taking the bench under state law to wrap up any active cases in their law practice. Judge Carr's decision to recuse himself was followed by his untimely death three months later.

Six Degrees of Separation is the theory that a maximum of six steps connect any two people. I have marveled at all the pieces that came together in the course of my investigation. This is not entirely down to the crony corrupt partnerships embedded into a toxic West Tennessee legal community. Both Farris-Bobango and Oscar Carr, had each separately represented me. This was one degree of separation and I believe divine synchronicity.

When I looked at each party that had lent their professional credentials to perfecting these property thefts they all overlapped; some more tightly entwined than others. If one is breaking the law the circle of risk needs to be limited to select insiders. Some were directly tied to the Jones, Kelley Boyd Perpetrator Nexus – REO Investment Group that had targeted my home. Others were peripherally connected. Judge Carr's law firm had been pooling some of these properties into securities through brokers at Sun Trust Bank, Inc. The shared Keller Williams defendant(s) connected the Collins-Maury Case to my Civil RICO Case on a number of fronts.

I filed the Civil RICO Case seven years after the Collins-Maury Case, filed November 24, 2009, *"Complaint for Injunctive Relief and*

Monetary Damages." No mention then or ever in any docket heading of the chief offense, Corporate Espionage and internet hacking; both a federal crime. Mislabeling a case is common practice which impedes any data search. My RICO Case was labeled as a foreclosure dispute. There was no foreclosure. Title theft pre-dated the foreclosure charade.

What I wrote in my Civil RICO Complaint exposed a dangerous confluence of shared illegal acts. It heightened the risk of "Enterprise" exposure. It had potential to inform, under the umbrella of RICO, the thousands or so other victims in West Tennessee that also had their homes fed as fodder to The Bank Theft Delivery System. My case, if allowed to move forward might catch the attention (finally) of federal prosecutors and the broad scope of practice operating within a national footprint. Taking our victim count from thousands in Tennessee to millions nationwide.

Before Judge Carr was appointed to the bench he had represented me when my car was rear-ended at a traffic light. Doing so while I was still in my home. When I discovered that an unknown entity had paid my property taxes, I copied my then attorney, Oscar Carr, on correspondence seeking answers for how this could have happened. He had a vested interest in misleading me. He let me think this was simple oversight on the part of Bank of America. I promptly reimbursed Bank of America for the taxes I was led to assume they had paid in error.

I was thus, maneuvered to miss a valuable opportunity by which, if I'd pressed on with the thread of that inquiry, I would have discovered that white collar criminals had assumed control of my mortgage in 2009 from Bank of America and with no disclosure to me. I would have recognized, been able to expose and dispute the fraud narrative that my home was abandoned and in derelict condition premised on the 2009 forged Certificate of Abandonment. The crime of Title Theft would have entered my vocabulary. As it was, I would not learn how The Bank Theft Delivery System, enriching so many Memphis attorneys, worked until after I fired my second attorney, Webb Brewer in June of 2014.

As you will read in more detail further along in this book, stepping in to pay property taxes is a common first step. The property title cannot be stolen until the identity theft piece is established. This is because the homeowner identity under the original Deed of Trust has to be supplanted and replaced in prominence with the REO Fraudster identity. Oscar Carr knew this.

When the REO Investors step in to pay property taxes on a mortgage they have just acquired by fraud this lays down a layer that establishes authority over the mortgage as the new, but fictitious Note Holder. Trouble is that homeowners have no idea a change has taken place. If they did have any of the information, they were legally entitled to they would not allow criminals any access to corrupt the property title to their homes. Homeowners are consumers. The mortgage debt is collateralized by title to real property. Consumer protection laws are ignored in the arena of title theft by previously trusted professionals empowered by the financial industry and aided by select federal agencies.

The tax money is not credited as coming from the homeowner escrow funds. It cannot be because at this point the former bank mortgage-holder is no longer authorized to make an assignment of funds over a mortgage, they have just allowed the so-called Private Investor Groups, sometimes called Institutional Investors, to assume.

The source of funds from which the property taxes are paid is not credited as coming from the homeowner escrow funds. The secret REO Note-Holder goal is to position the homeowners as being delinquent on their property taxes. Bank of America could not return the money I reimbursed them, money they had no legal right to accept. This is because they are entirely invested in protecting the chain of theft from recognition. Judge Carr was making money from these same thefts. As a partner in his law firm, even after he was appointed chancellor, able to hear cases, he shared in the profits of his law firm. A low-level client, like myself, lacking prestige and connections could not compete with the income producing services and legal needs of the RICO Enterprise bad actors.

My letter, copied to Oscar Carr, became an exhibit in my Civil RICO Case. Judge Vescovo would have recognized that at a time when he was obligated to me as his client, seeking his advice, Oscar Carr had covered-up what I believe would have led me to an early understanding of what was taking place. That explanation would have saved me a river of grief. Judge Carr's documented and provable connection to me and to the RICO Criminal Enterprise moved the *Enterprise Plus Relationship* confluence of bad actors into a precarious position. Any federal investigator will acknowledge that smaller cases, those like the Collins-Maury, vs. Keller Williams corporate espionage case, opens the door to expose broader criminal activity; even larger cases. Where corruption flourishes everyone agrees to limit such exposure.

Judge Vescovo was biased to protect the RICO Criminal Enterprise feeding an income stream to law firms at which her family members were employed. She was a poor choice for the role of magistrate judge when as set up for indulging bias she was given the job of dispensing quickly with pro se cases so as to improve the District Court statistics. Shielding Judge Oscar Carr at the *screening for merit* blockade also impeded recognition of his law firm having perfected the final steps in the chain of theft for some of these properties. If allowed due process certain connections would have surfaced. These kinds of conflicts leave a judge vulnerable to blackmail or extortionist strong arm tactics.

A history of prior bad acts and more about the Collins-Maury Case.

U.S. Code, Title 18; Chapter 96 Racketeer Influenced and Corrupt Organizations; Section 1961, Definitions. **Simply put a racket is an organized criminal act. Pattern of racketeering "requires at least two acts of racketeering activity, one of which occurred after the effective date of this chapter (1970) and the last of which occurred within ten years (excluding any period of imprisonment) after the commission of a prior act of racketeering activity."**

You will be endeavoring to show an ongoing pattern of bad acts by the same criminal enterprise. In the operation of the crimes that I describe there are multiple RICO predicate acts as laws that are routinely broken. Read and download the list at: **https://www.law.cornell.edu/uscode/text/18/1961**.

I chose to focus on the Collins-Maury Case because it was substantially tied to my own case. I had named the Collins-Maury case as evidence of prior bad acts by the same RICO Criminal Enterprise. It doesn't matter that this case was not yet adjudicated. You can still name cases like this and will need to because often the settlements allow criminals to avoid any acceptance of blame. At every possible juncture where exposure could inform and arm others to fight back, the goal of white-collar criminal defense attorneys is to achieve a minimal public records footprint for their clients. These prior bad acts were relevant to my case. They informed an ongoing reckless disregard for the rule of law as an embedded and accepted pattern of practice.

My second attorney, Webb Brewer was aware of the Collins-Maury Case filed against Keller Williams Memphis East. It was a matter of public record when filed on November 24, 2009. He had been playing a weekly basketball game with the Boyd's attorney, John "Bucky" Phillip. Valuable content documented within the Collins-Maury filing of November 10, 2011 under the "original" complaint number of CH-11-1860 predated the state case filed on my behalf by Webb. It was his duty to keep up with other cases filed against any same defendants. Keeping its existence from me served the aim that I never recognize Keller Williams – MEM-2 and the straw buyers, Keller Williams agents Vernon "Wayne" Boyd and Sherry Boyd as the secret REO Note-Holders pre-dating the foreclosure charade.

Perfection of these theft schemes are lawyer-heavy. When a lawyer performs a service for a client and in so doing commits fraud the attorney client privilege is no longer in place. Attorneys that facilitate fraud for these REO Investment Groups step over the line to become the criminals. On the defense side, disguising the actual chain of theft is set-up for playing both ends against the middle. Seated in the crony corrupt culture of the Memphis legal community the limited defense is not about what actually took place. This is an immoral but highly lucrative game if lawyers can get away with it. And it seems in Memphis, TN too many routinely do.

Webb Brewer had been moving my state case toward dismissal up to the day I fired him. In doing so he extorted quid pro quo leverage and whatever else he could from the other side. The second attorney, Kathryn Maceri, conned me into removing the state case that Webb had filed and destined for dismissal, selling me on Civil RICO as a better alternate. Claiming to have cancer she then promptly disappeared. She knew that I had bought her lie that the statute of limitations on Civil RICO was three years, not four years. That as a lawyer-less, pro se plaintiff it was impossible that I could learn enough about RICO and file a case on my own in a matter of months.

Judge Carr was well familiar with the enterprise operations taking place in his back yard. He understood the chain of theft that laundered property title to countless homes. He knew where the bulk of these homes ended up. Each time the digital property title was flipped (laundered) amongst the same REO Investment Group of bad actors needed distance was established that nudged forward the secret REO Note-Holder, identity theft, claims of ownership.

Success requires that homeowners remain entirely ignorant of what has taken place behind the scenes. Up to that strategic moment that the charade of foreclosure takes place followed by illegal seizure. Each step is carefully choreographed.

1. There is a start – Title Theft predating the foreclosure charade.
2. There is a middle – Skimming Equity.
3. There is an end – Illegal Seizure of the theft asset.
4. There is the ultimate goal. Another home fed to the Wall Street securities market via the Bank Theft Delivery System having made the Title Theft "start" possible.

In Part 111 of this book we look at the filings dumped by foreclosure mill attorneys into the public records. We look at how targets of these theft schemes can recognize fraud within these signed and notarized endorsements and where to find what is buried. Upon reading this book you will know exactly where to start your investigation. After doing this work for yourself, a service to your community would be in helping others to sift through documentation to the extent that the chain of theft can be recognized. It is certainly the case that some lawyers could focus a practice on the victim side.

Judge Carr's firm perfected the last steps. After all possible equity could be skimmed by their clients, via illegal flips of the property title, they bundled selected homes, some acquired by robbery, into pools. Brokers then transformed these pools made up of rental properties into marketable securities. Just as the SEC were asleep on the Bernie Madoff Ponzi scheme, they are asleep on this one. Laundering of monetary instruments and fraud in the sale of securities are RICO Predicate Acts. The physical premises of the home and its digital property title is a monetary instrument bought and sold many times over as a commodity.

Judge Carr was assigned the Collins-Maury case and then almost immediately recused himself. The original judge appears to have been Kenny Armstrong. It is not clear why the case was shifted from Chancellor Armstrong to Chancellor Oscar Carr, 111 on January 15, 2015. One would have to be brain dead not to entertain the notion that the criminal cohort of bad actors hoped he would orchestrate a favorable outcome to the Keller Williams defense. Judge Carr chose the moral and right course of action. Was this seen as a slap in the face to the cabal of corruption benefiting from, representing, protecting, and streamlining the Bank Theft Delivery System described in this book?

If he was fed up, what other damage could he do? Did he have some federal investigator on speed dial? These white-collar criminals with a lot to hide, living under the cloud of possible prosecution, continuing to skim the surface of recognition had not escaped consequences by adopting a wait and see attitude.

The Collins-Maury Case was subjected to interminable delay. It did not serve the ongoing viability of these theft schemes enriching so many Memphis attorneys that any final outcome or any documented settlement become a matter of public record. I had linked my Civil RICO case to this case as proof of ongoing and prior bad acts engaged in by the same defendants. When I moved from Memphis in August 2018 the Prudential Realty Collins-Maury Corporate spying case, though it was conveniently never called that, was still outstanding.

Denise Martin worked for Collins-Maury before purchasing her position as a Real Estate Broker within what many believe is a Keller Williams pyramid scheme. Farris-Bobango separated the defendants into two cases. They then consolidated the cases toward the very end in preparation for the dismissal. This limited the public record exposure via any superficial review of docket(s). Sound familiar? The docket final order reads: *Final Disposition Per Consent Order of Dismissal with Prejudice Entered on 10/26/2018...* Dumbed down are the Keller Williams Corporate pressure-practices that invited and fueled the Denise Martin behavior; appearing in other cases as a documented pattern of practice. David Osborn does not appear among the list of defendants though he is the Keller Williams franchise owner. Limiting exposure of internet hacking and other federal crimes... *With Costs Equally Assessed Against the Defendant MEM2, LLC and Defendant Denise Martin See Docket # CH-11-1860-1.* Deflecting from CH-11-1860-3 (part: 3).

Lawyers that are more concerned about how a vigorous defense of their clients might impact peer group approval corrupt our entire justice system. Our founding fathers did not envision due process as an instrument to separate, minimize, or discourage a plaintiff from achieving reparations obviously due them. Or to drive a victim of white-collar crime into decisions, not in their best interests, but more amenable to settlements that limit the public records exposure and can later be spun into a disjointed story that in no way resembles the truth.

When threatened with exposure the RICO Criminal Enterprise I describe in this book will invite that threat into the quid pro quo web of operation. I believe that when my first forty-eight-hour attorney, Farris-Bobango (also representing Doug Collins) agreed to represent me that boat had already sailed. The Collins-Maury corporate spying case predates the illegal seizure of my home. Upon belief that Farris-Bobango had already decided to limit the Collins-Maury defense in favor of the deep pocket David Osborn, Keller Williams Defendants. Playing both sides of the street they acted in very much the same way that my second attorney, Webb Brewer, would with me. Corruption depends on people being demoralized, giving up only to be absorbed to varying degrees of complicity into the very criminality they at first decried. Such is the stuff of crony corruptionism operating like a disease in West Tennessee.

The role played by Farris-Bobango must have seemed easy. After evaluating my level of knowledge, drop me as a client making no referral to any other attorney. I was left to believe there really was a Fayette County Judges Order of Eviction since neither Farris-Bobango nor Webb Brewer ever challenged it.

As the illegal seizure of my home went off without a hitch it was believed that with the Farris-Bobango departure I would follow the well-worn path trod by other homeowner-victims. I would move away. This was the question repeatedly put to me. Why hadn't I moved? Didn't my children want me to move closer to them? When was I moving? The real threat from me was that once I was free of my last corrupt attorney I very quickly focused on other victims, compiling proof that what happened to me was just the tip of the ice berg.

A lot of shame comes with the loss of one's home. Shame is part of the script that predatory arrogance expected me to follow. It was not in the repertoire of experience that I would unearth the trail of document fraud. But even if I did, no problem. Systemic corruption functioned to limit any defense delivering the outcome that victims are never heard in any venue that leaves a public records footprint.

Doug Collins of Collins-Maury Realty was an industry professional. He was in a completely different category from me. As a well-respected business owner with deep roots in the Memphis community he had resources, connections and prestige. He could not be conned and maligned without push back leaving some kind of an informative record for other victims. Thus, the very careful labeling of his case as it appeared in the docket. This not only impeded any internet search it sent a message.

I do not think Keller Williams wanted another public relations debacle like that that backfired with their assault upon Iowa Realty. Keller Williams had underestimated the Iowa Realty pushback against the Keller Williams over the top bullying tactics, designed to sucker punch and eviscerate any opponent. This strategy did not quite work out as planned in the Des Moines Iowa market region.[21] Iowa Realty left a record that exposed commonalties between these two cases.

Once filed the Collins-Maury legal defense had to appear to be legitimate. Attorneys had to play-act working within the parameters of the law upholding the ethics of their profession. Time was needed for Doug Collins' initial outrage to abate in an atmosphere of incessant strategic delay wearing down the client. Bringing them in line with lower expectations.

Everyone waltzes. But this is no ordinary masked ball. All the players are drunk on the special allure of group collusion, power and greed. Nothing is what it seems. The Collins-Maury Case was filed and Judge Oscar Carr was assigned to "catch" this case. He immediately dropped that hot potato sending a message to a mafia like criminal enterprise that does not take kindly to rebellion within the ranks. Especially by those they already consider to be bought and paid for. In his new position Oscar Carr sent the message that though his prior law firm was for sale, helping to perfect some of these thefts, he no longer was.

---

[21] The Iowa Realty filings and local reporting are worth reading. They inform a bullying pattern of behavior indicative of those with a lot to hide.

CHAPTER TWELVE

"...victims of federal crimes have rights, including the right to be heard in a court, and most particularly, not to be precluded from court proceedings, and the right to be treated fairly." Crime Victims' Rights Act, (CVRA) [title 18, section 3771, of the US Code].

Other cases filed against Keller Williams Corporate have claimed that they use a, pyramid-like business model. Farris-Bobango, at least at the start were willing to state their agreement. Quoted in bold text from: Collins-Maury, Inc., d.b.a. Prudential Collins-Maury, Inc., Realtors vs. MEM 2, LLC d.b.a. Keller Williams Realty, a.k.a, Keller Williams Realty Memphis East; filed Chancery Court of Shelby County, Tennessee; November 10, 2011.

Upon information and belief, Keller Williams uses a pyramid-like business model whereby any realtor who recruits new realtors to Keller Williams receives a percentage of the profit received from that recruited realtor. Page 3, paragraph No. 13.

This was a line of reasoning they later abandoned since it could lead to a hard look at Deeds of Trust to stolen property marketed as an investment. Attorneys playing both sides of the street shy clear of opening the door to what could galvanize the attention of federal investigators. Corrupt attorneys become more focused on banking quid pro quo leverage than justice for any single client. The orchestrated dismissal was committed to; assigning no blame, post settlement.

Other lawyers have made the point that the Keller Williams business model tends to fuel unethical practices.[22] It dilutes what is owed to people down line.

---

[22] The Iowa Realty Company, Inc. case – Keller Williams, Golden Circle Real Estate Group, LLC; Des Moines Iowa. In this authors opinion, the bullying tactics that framed the push back from Keller Williams was extreme. The same assaultive, bullying and threatening tactics were used against me to perfect the illegal seizure of my home. See also, the Ryan Leonard Case, Superior Court, Pennsylvania. In this case, informing that Keller Williams indoctrinate agents to accept unethical business practices, the Keller Williams agent described his own unlawful behavior in the doublespeak confidence that he had done nothing wrong. The same posturing was used by Criminal Enterprise Appraiser, Larry Lane Billings in his defense to the State of Tennessee regarding the illegal appraisal history of my home. Crony corruption succeeding were justice fails the state of Tennessee were more invested in protecting criminals, concealing bank fraud and REO property flip schemes operating state-wide, than defending the public welfare.

As of the writing of this chapter it seems that no person responsible for hacking the Collins-Maury Prudential Realty computers lost their jobs. This outcome has shielded the perpetrators from federal attention. Collins-Maury would have had to agree that there would be no public record whereby Keller Williams – MEM 2, LLC accepted responsibility for the criminal infiltration of their company computers. Keller Williams devotes a lot of time to scrubbing complaints from the internet. I have seen complaints go up on various sites only to disappear a day later.

Showing a pattern of prior bad acts, if allowed due process, I would have informed the jury of the information technology (IT) expert confirmation that the Collins-Maury computers had been hacked: ***"internet protocol address 66.193.59.2, which is Keller Williams IP Address;"*** as noted on page-four of the November 10, 2011 filing (Case No.: CH-11-1860/Part-3) A fake g-mail account was set up in the name of a Collins-Maury executive and was additionally traced back to the same Keller Williams IP Address.

I firmly believe that the same people hacked my email account and interfered with receipt of select notices from the federal district court. The hope was that I would not read Magistrate Judge Vescovo's repeated slander of my claims and object within the limited time period allowed. This was among the first attempts to tank my Civil RICO Case at the *screening for merit* juncture with apparent full confidence that the possible interference with email delivery from a federal district court would never be investigated.

After Judge Vescovo noted that I had failed to file the exhibits, in a panic I rushed to comply. I always felt at a huge disadvantage; willing to accept that I had done something wrong. At this point I did not understand my rights. I did not understand how screening in the hands of a corrupt judge could abort my right to be heard before a jury of my peers. Among the exhibits I filed was a full text copy of the November 10, 2011, Collins-Maury filing; my Exhibit No.: 64. I had described the secret JP Morgan Chase Bank loan granted to the REO Fraudsters skimming equity from 65 Pinehurst Drive days after I listed my home for sale. When I later attempted to support this statement with additional proof it was refused by the Clerks Office. The exhibits were important to Judge Vescovo. And then they were not.

Looking back, it is shocking to consider that no bank helping to launder my property title, helping to establish the REO identity theft claims over my home, ever disclosed any of this information to me.

Never followed up verifying the imbedded fraud narrative fed into their own records. It is as if they were never trained to recognize and report suspected fraud. Intentional lack of disclosure to homeowners, has fueled these thefts and increased the victim pool from thousands to millions nation-wide.

There was no requirement that Judge Vescovo see these exhibits other than to report back on how much evidence I actually had. Again, this is because at the screening juncture all claims are to be accepted as true. Screening is not due process.

If I had an attorney the case would have bypassed screening and gone directly to be docketed for a first hearing. It is certainly the case that the defendants would have asked for an immediate dismissal, but I could not be allowed to get this far. At every juncture were a public record could inform the activities of the RICO Criminal Enterprise and arm any other victims to fight back, that right to be heard in a court of law needed to be sabotaged. This was the end-goal repeatedly accomplished... sadly all the way up to the Sixth Circuit Court of Appeals trailing into the failure of the Circuit Executive to address my complaints.

Memphis, Tennessee is a small town sort of city with a very particular culture. Segments of the population are very poor. There is a huge disparity between the broken public-school system and the many private schools in the area. Judge Vescovo complained that poverty led to too many meritless pro se cases. Her solution was to dispense quickly with these cases. She is a Memphis-gal. She knows how to play its ideocracies, tragedies, and foibles to best advantage.

If she would limit the exposure of the Financial Industry Defendant's and certain Memphis attorneys, Judge Vescovo could not allow the Collins-Maury Case to be linked in any way to my Civil RICO Case. Why? Because the pandora's box of crony corruptionism making so much money for Memphis professionals must stay sealed. All the bad-actors were in bed with each other. Pattern informs intent and in the corrupt culture of our times, justice may, in theory be blind but coincidence is neither blind nor random.

One degree of separation.

With the illegal seizure of my home the Boyd's lived around the corner and five homes away from the groups finance man, Max Jones. It was a short walk to the home of Jeffrey Kelley on Lewis Fairway acting as the chief operating officer. Vernon "Wayne" Boyd's sister, Lennie, lived with her husband Charles Kelley in the same county. The groups attorney and others were clustered close by. Planning meetings and theft progress reports, background of new targets profiled as unlikely to fight back could take place at these various homes leaving no record of comings and goings. Any questionable meeting could be characterized as a church fellowship gathering since many of these players attended the same church, not merely just connected by blood or marriage. There were small businesses through which profits could be laundered. Fayette County had been targeted by a parasitical group of con artists. Wherever these fraud schemes thrive unrecognized and almost never prosecuted each player is intentionally launched as a strategically positioned force imbedded into the communities they target.

Collins-Maury Prudential Realtors (Doug Collins) were represented by the Memphis law firm of Farris, Bobango PLC; (Farris-Bobango). As already stated they were the first of my three attorneys. They were the same law firm that briefly represented me during that crucial, forty-eight-hour window when the illegal seizure of my home going off without a hitch, hung in the balance. I had formerly worked at Christ United Methodist Church. I recalled Phil Mischke.[23] We were not friends. We had served on at least one church committee together. A mutual acquaintance held him in high regard telling me that he had a reputation for honestly. I called his office and explained my dilemma. An associate at his firm returned my call.

Farris-Bobango then communicated with my contact person at Bank of America. As it turned out Christopher Kohl,[24] was not, nor had he ever been a Bank of America employee. Farris-Bobango immediately recognized that they were talking with REO Fraudsters already named by them as defendants in the Collins-Maury Case.

---

[23] I tried to communicate with Phil. Though we talked and I wrote to him hoping to open a discourse I got nowhere. As the man of faith, he claimed to be I felt he should have crossed sides and worked to expose these crimes. He told me that he had his family to think of. He was not constrained by attorney client privilege if Doug Collins was truly and really the client. I'd like to think he felt ambivalence for the path he chose. Though perhaps the threat of what happened to Judge Oscar Carr overrode any better instinct.

[24] Christopher Kohl repeatedly identified himself as an employee of Bank of America. I traced his identity to one of three persons. He sold the bogus Bank of America new program for seniors with equity in their homes that in fact did not exist. Unlike some others like Michelle Brunk, Brian Michael Demma, Sherry Rupp, Joseph Daniel, aka, Joseph Fistula, and Muriel Adams his real identity remains a mystery.

They were talking with a lacky for the secret Note-Holders and not with the Making Home Affordable Department within Bank of America. Although I did not know it, the REO Fraudsters had been masquerading as Bank of America. They had told me I could sell my own home under the terms of a new Bank of America program, "for seniors with equity in their homes," that in fact did not exist. Thus, I was cruelly positioned to be shocked when I was told that a foreclosure had already taken place.

Keller Williams and Vernon "Wayne" Boyd had transferred the listing of my home to the criminal enterprise "muscle," ERA Chamberwood Realty Group per MLS No.: 3249765. Because Keller Williams agents held the note that identity could not be tied to the phony foreclosure of 65 Pinehurst Drive. The plan was for the Boyd's to purchase a home they already owned from the decoy realty company. In my case that was the Criminal Enterprise Muscle. Vernon "Wayne" Boyd and Sherry Boyd could then emerge, post-eviction, as the straw buyer for the Keller Williams REO Private Investor Group of fraudsters.

In a first meeting with Hattie Brawley and Loretta Martin (ERA Chamberwood Realty Group) I was told that a Fayette County judge had ordered my eviction. I had shared this with my Farris-Bobango attorney. Rather than fax that forged court order directly to my forty-eight-hour attorneys, ERA Chamberwood Realty Group elected to fax the "Vendor-Only" copy of the Core Logic Equator work order.[25]

Faxing a copy of the Core Logic work order from ERA Chamberwood Realty to my brief attorney served as, "hands off," marching orders. A particular hand written note told Farris-Bobango that their cooperation was needed. This intersect was a way to communicate that my home was secretly and illegally owned by their secret clients, not Doug Collins, but Keller Williams Memphis East acting as an operational arm of the RICO Criminal Enterprise. What I came later to call the Jones, Kelley, Boyd Perpetrator Nexus.

Based on what they read in these faxed pages, after speaking to Christopher Kohl and perhaps, Arnold Weiss as the Memphis eviction attorney, Farris-Bobango recognized that nothing I told them and

[25] The Core Logic Equator work order is described in more detail later in this book. This internet platform was important bridge evidence. It served to send and receive instructions, naming many of the key players engaged in the illegal eviction premised on the charade of the phony foreclosure.

believed was true, actually was true. This level of ignorance compounded to my exhausted emotional state was weighed to advantage.

The Core Logic Equator paperwork proposed that it was not me, a homeowner needing to be evicted but a fictional renter. The original fraud narrative that had established my home as being abandoned and derelict in 2009 needed to be preserved. Abandonment of secured property under a valid Deed of Trust served as the premise for acquisition and control over the Property Title and its first "flip" into a HUD program. Document fraud served the ongoing deception, over that three-year period. It had to because, start to finish, the REO Fraudsters had to appear to be in compliance with the terms of the HUD federal program they had illegally hijacked.

Arnold Weiss and Vernon "Wayne" Boyd (REO ID No. 00906148) instruct ERA Chamberwood Realty and their agent, Hattie Brawley to: ***Please obtain a copy of the Tenants lease ASAP.*** Of course, there is no lease. This is filling out paperwork in anticipation of a defense if needed. It serves only to posture compliance with a regulation, law, or act of required due diligence. Nothing more than a smokescreen. The document fraud you will uncover will be replete with these kinds of empty assertions used to grease the chain of theft; appearing to be in compliance, operating within the rule of law. This is fraud under, "color of law."

Farris-Bobango had a choice. I was their client. In that single Core Logic Equator work order they had the REO ID Number denoting the secret Note-Owner identity. I had lived in my home uninterrupted since purchasing it in 2005. The HUD REO Number told them that at one time my home was a HUD owned property. Farris-Bobango did not suggest that I verify that there really was a Fayette County Judges, "order of eviction" or read up on the eviction laws in my state. They did not refer me to another attorney. They did not tell me that the Hattie Brawley threat of the Fayette County Sheriff's Office waiting to put everything I owned on the street if I did not make immediate plans to leave my home did not comport with how the legal process actually worked.

I would like to have been a silent listener as Farris-Bobango players came together to decide how they could get rid of me with the least possible risk to the deep pocket pay off they anticipated for mitigating the Collins-Maury defense. While at the same time stringing Doug Collins along the track toward an unpublished settlement. The fact is, if they had continued on with me as a client, they would have had to disclose corporate espionage as prior bad acts and a telling pattern of ongoing criminal activity informing the operative national footprint of these crimes.

Take a deep breath and think about this for a moment. At that point in time, March 2012, Farris-Bobango had the same defendant in two cases. This would normally have made any honest lawyer ecstatic. My case provided leverage, informing motive, regarding why the Collins-Maury computers were hacked in the first place. Doug Collins and his case provided leverage to my case informing a pattern of prior bad acts. Looking this gift horse in the face, what appeared on the surface to be an inexplicable irrational decision, the solution was to drop me as a client, making no referral to another attorney.

After this I was daily bullied and harassed by the REO Criminal Enterprise, "muscle" ERA Chamberwood Realty Group and Hattie Brawley. When I write these words, I mean them in the true mafia context of that word picture. I was alone and helpless, exactly in that place that the REO Fraudsters need their victims to be.

To understand why crony-corrupt protection of a lucrative fraud scheme took priority over client-rights. Why, over and over again, three Memphis attorneys who owed me a fundamental standard of care, displayed the same pattern and intent to protect the deep-pocket shadow client(s), one would have to dig deeper into my case and the Collins-Maury case. They intersect on many levels and even touch on the timely death of a Memphis judge. This same culture of crony-corruptionism has detrimentally harmed many other clients of other Memphis law firms. And because these crimes have not been investigated and prosecuted, they have continued as a destructive pox up to today.

After I fired Webb Brewer I kept a short list by my computer of what I felt I needed to be on the lookout for. This included any other case involving Keller Williams Realty. Any lawsuit naming the principal members of the Jones, Kelley, Boyd Perpetrator Nexus and that operational team connected to them. This is how I discovered that Bank of America had once sued Lewis Garrison. Perhaps explaining why, he delegated to other law firms.

I discovered the Collins-Maury case during one of those random searches. I drove to down-town Memphis to acquire a copy. I was asked to sign a piece of paper stating why I wanted it. This felt wrong. Didn't I have the right to public information without my interest attracting the attention of dangerous people?

After getting a copy of the first filing and reading its content I phoned Doug Collins. I spoke to him on April 17, 2015. This is how my journal entry reads.

*Talked with Doug Collins – seemed to me his attorney (*Farris Bobango) *is managing him in the same way I was managed...* by Webb Brewer.

1. *They told him not to file a criminal complaint.*
2. *Not to contact the FBI.*
3. *They were not moving the case forward.*
4. *Not sharing communications.*
5. *Not identifying the defendants.*

Doug Collins had hired his attorneys and filed his case in 2009. The two case numbers are: CH-09-2341 and CH-11-1860. In April of 2015 he expressed ignorance of my case. Why wouldn't Farris-Bobango share what they knew of the defendants' prior history of crime, with their client. For the same reason that Webb Brewer did not tell me about the Collins-Maury Case. Straight from the justice sapping playbook enabled by layers of crony corruptionism, they were protecting the deep pocket RICO Criminal Enterprise operations.

In one of a very few conversations with Phil Mischke, he characterized David Osborn as someone to admire. When I wasn't buying this, he shifted gears to say that despite what one might think, David Osborn was not very smart. Taking offense that I wasn't buying this, he then broke composure to yell at me, *"Why don't you give up?"* I responded, *"Because these people are criminals!"* At the time I was sitting in a car as a good friend drove. We were on our way to have lunch with another friend who had moved to the Pickwick area. Startled at the change in tone she jumped veering slightly off course.

Three years after they had abandoned me to the theft agenda in 2012. Leaving me to believe the lie that a Fayette County Judge really had ordered my eviction, Phil offered me the names of three attorneys. Trust irrevocably broken, I did not call any of them. Third and last attorney, Katherine Maceri, would play the same game as that of Webb Brewer and Farris-Bobango, but with far more skill and finesse.

I was never the client. I was always the opposition. If there is a constitutional lawyer out there interested in representing me please get in touch. At some point we realize that the levels of corruption are so great that in fact... to quote again the Brad Pitt character, "they are the fuckers."

In April 2012 I put some things in storage and hurriedly sold others. A neighborhood wide garage sale was scheduled to take place and I asked if I could stay long enough to participate. This earned another bullying lecture from ERA Chamberwood Realty Group. The so called "Judge" would allow no delay. I packed for Memphis spring weather, believing that I would be returning to my home. When winter hit with no job and little money, I was ill prepared.

God went ahead of me. To quote King David, *"I saw the Lord always before me."* Unprompted, my friend Mary offered me a winter coat and some very nice clothes that got me through those winter months. Mary is a fashion aficionado. She would never leave her home not looking polished. I was out of uniform in a cashmere sweater with sparkle about the collar and other items, some of which still had their original tags. Then another friend (Joan and Penny) offered me a temporary job. Joan followed that up with other part time work. I then picked up some human resources contract work doing some writing for another friend (Nancy). Friends included me on Thanksgiving and Christmas. People did things for me over that first year away from 65 Pinehurst Drive that I was not capable of doing for myself.

In those first months from April to August 2012 I found myself literally unable to function. Brian Churchill was still alive at the time and would try to draw me into his plans for marketing the earlier prospectus I had written; making the Wood's End script into the film he felt passionate about directing. My mind made plans, but my body could not cooperate. I was very much in shock and I believe suffering the effects of a kind of breakdown. Living in a small apartment attached to the home of Nina and Mark Haines, Nina played a crucial role in those first months. I never asked for help. I vacillated between feeling numb and raw. At times like this we experience the altruistic kindness of others as healing. Each person, though many could not know how important they were, were God-sent.

What got me off that dead center, very dark place of inertia was a threat. Under the definition of what constitutes "racketeering activity" is predicate act Section: 1513. **Relating to retaliating against a witness, victim, or an informant.**

In August 2012 I sat at my computer and brought up that partial appraisal history of my home already described in a previous chapter. When it became clear that I was asking questions, one could not even say at this point that I was investigating anything, I was threatened by Sherry Boyd.

Concealment of her own crimes were on her mind. She accused me of what she was habitually guilty of many times over. She had stolen my home and was living in it, but now she accused me of breaking into 65 Pinehurst Drive and stealing a valuable piece of jewelry, a felony. Of entering 65 Pinehurst Drive after the eviction and in the company of my dog, breaking and entering. Her detailed description of my crimes included that Declan had defecated on the carpet. She had committed bank fraud, but now she accused me of stealing mail from her mail box, also a federal crime.

Then, of all things, paying her comcast bill. In anticipation of damage control, she was seeking to contradict the financial history of me being the occupant of record and paying utility bills over the prior three years that she and her husband simultaneously claimed to be the lawful occupants of what they told HUD was an abandoned and derelict property. As ludicrous as her rationale sounds the Comcast police were investigating me having paid these bills. She also sought to paint me as mentally unhinged. Should she need an order of protection, she claimed that I had randomly entered the premises when she was not there and done a load of laundry. By her characterization I was dangerous, an unreliable witness to how I had been defrauded. I was mentally unstable.

Upon learning that I had called Keller Williams Corporate in Dallas, Texas seeking the name of the appraiser she threatened to file a police report. Threats of retaliation must have worked well with other victims. The verbal assaults of Hattie Brawley, badgering and harassing me on an almost daily basis, though different in content, felt similar to the Sherry Boyd aggressive response.

Still knowing next to nothing I wondered, why she cared who I called? Unless of course there was something to hide. As a red flag, her response to me tracing the appraisal history of my home in August of 2012 at first seemed out of proportion. Unless one realized that she and her husband were illegally squatting in a home they did not actually own. Furthermore, there were many other victims, crimes and thefts skimming the surface of recognition.

I am somehow certain that there have been times in the past when these REO Fraudsters needed orders of protection filed against their victims. That was not me. I would focus on facts; on what I could prove. This had always been my default position. As a writer I enjoy research and a task list. Even before the Sherry Boyd threats, the Carole Ann Burns statement, "be very careful," and the August 2012 runaround from Keller Williams Corporate let me know there was something very wrong about the so called, "residential arms-length sale" of my home. "Property Flip Scheme," was not yet in my vocabulary. I had a huge learning curve. But, thanks to the Sherry Boyd threats, I had a reason to pull myself together. There were answers out there and, though obstructed at every turn, it became my job to find them.

I consulted with a retired attorney from my church and also with my Pastor about the Sherry Boyd threats to have me charged and arrested for crimes I did not commit. They each separately told me to ignore her. I took that advice, but I did not forget. The emails describing these threats were entered as exhibits with the Civil RICO Case. After perhaps two or three sleepless nights I decided that Sherry Boyd had far more to fear from any investigation than I ever would.

When I saw Sherry's photo on line I realized that she was the same person who had come to my home in 2011 during the period that I had my home listed for sale with Crye Leike Realty; MLS No.: 3223195. She had asked if she could come inside. I told her to call my realtor. I also told her that I had been pre-approved to apply for HAMP. But the fact is. Looking into her face and reading her body language my creep-antenna was sending off a strong current of alarm. Something felt decidedly off.

I will never forget her parting shot as she turned from my door irritated that I had not allowed her to step over the threshold of a home, that on paper, per title theft, she already claimed to own. The sarcastic, contempt laced, "good luck with that," at the mention of the HAMP program rang in my ear as it does today. Every HAMP application, every request for documentation and my compliance with those requests, all mail was funneled through the Bank of America Mail Clearing Center to the secret REO fraudsters who had no authority to process a HAMP Application. As one of five separate schemes I called this one The HAMP Fraud Scheme.

Sherry Boyd did not achieve entry on that day. But why bother? The Crye Leike Realty photos were on line. As you will read in more detail further along, Ann Jones, a member of the REO fraudster group was in and out of my home on a regular basis. If they wanted to know what the inside of 65 Pinehurst Drive looked like she could tell them. No! That was not it at all. These people wanted to see the victim they had exercised secret control of; not the interior of my home. There was a perverse risk laced thrill to be had in direct contact with targets of this theft scheme that any intelligent white-collar criminal would have avoided.

Under the pretense of being a buyer Vernon "Wayne" Boyd did gain entry. Accompanied by Ann Jones, so did Lennie Faye Kelley. Jeffrey Kelley contrived that I would meet him at the Ann and Max Jones' home. The thrill of courting danger was a piece of the incentive package. How else does one explain this? Each completely unnecessary contact with me and the subsequent escape from recognition reinforced the notion that the evil behavior is magically protected. There is a supernatural component to this. Some are fully aware and pay homage; testing, testing.

Once she moved into my home, the same Sherry Boyd conveyed a very odd invitation to me through a neighbor. She wanted me to come by and see the changes she had made. I could not get my brain around the disparity between threats to have me arrested on the one hand and now this very inappropriate invitation.

In the book, Channel Bonfire[26] author, Wendy Lawless wrote of the compulsive need for perpetrators to stay in physical proximity to victims. Telling her own story, she described, despite the risk and perhaps because of the rush a perp gets from risk, there is a need for continued access to what she called "the narcissistic supply."

My neighbors decided not to tell me about Sherry's invitation until later, waiting until I was stronger. Their answer to Sherry Boyd, *"Why should Alex do that? She knows what her house looks like."* And in regard to Declan, defecating on the carpet... *"Alex no longer had her dog."*

Gossip was floated out into the community. Some of it came back to me and was very hurtful to hear. Only once did I step back in time to confront opinions and gossip coming from a woman who attended my same church. I could not control what people thought or believed. I retreated into the investigation that loomed before me. The fledgling start was August of 2012. I am now endeavoring to complete this book before the 2019 last calendar page turns over to read 2020. I had no idea how long or how consuming the journey to expose these crimes would turn out to be. The thought of other victims who have no way to fight back has kept me going. This need to frame my experience by facts informing a body of truth evolved into a keenly felt moral responsibility to speak for past and future victims.

---

[26] Channel Bonfire, by Wendy Lawless; Gallery Books, Simon & Schuster, Inc.

CHAPTER THIRTEEN

"We cannot, by total reliance on law, escape the duty to judge right and wrong. There are good laws and there are occasionally bad laws, and it conforms to the highest tradition of a free society to offer resistance to bad laws and to disobey them." Alexander Bickel

Three attorneys, at separate times and working at Memphis law firms had undertaken the responsibility to represent me. Their commonality of purpose in explaining away evidence, failing to follow-up on evidence and, or, failing to disclose what they knew to be true denied me recognition that there was no real or valid foreclosure. Title theft predated the empty charade of foreclosure as a crime taking place under color of law. As long as they kept me focused on the premier nonissues, they were able to catch and kill my case. Each had the same shadow client whose interests superseded my own. A bribe is not always about money. A bribe can be the promise of future business or the forgiveness of debt. It can be the exchange of gifts and services where the bill never comes. Where what appears as a steady stream of quid quo pro outcomes corruption may even be rooted in coercion and blackmail.

In 2010 Fannie Mae recognized that REO Investor Fraud Groups were operating in specific areas of the country more than others. What opened the door was lots and lots of product created by the 2006-2010 subprime mortgage collapse. While this was devasting for those that lost their homes, it represented no more than a hiccup for banks. This tells us how important the mortgage industry is to the global financial markets. Securities backed with mortgages marketed world-wide is an industry that disregards entirely the right of homeowners to know who holds their debt. Banks knew these mortgages would not be paid back. As it turned out this bitter pill facilitated reformation into the Bank Theft Delivery System that we see in operation today. From the Fannie Mae Website. *Current analysis of these types of fraudulent transactions involving investment clubs and REO properties has identified some of the largest trend patterns occurring in the following geographic areas.* Among the areas listed: *Memphis, TN and Cordova, TN.*

In a 2008 Fannie Mae publication banks were advised to: *Follow the chain of title: Ensure that the seller holds the title, understand the property history and watch for pre-existing relationships between buyer and seller*. Fundamental due diligence. The very least that should be expected. Too bad these requirements are repeatedly ignored.

Those that decide to go back and look at how their homes may have been stolen and fed to The Bank Theft Delivery System described in this book need to look at the operational presence of Core Logic, Inc. One would also need to look at the Multiple Listing Service (MLS) history. And of course, any HUD-1 attached to any secret sale of your home falling within the theft time line. The theft time line that you develop will extend before and after the phony foreclosure as an empty exercise in deceit.

The MLS history of my home was acquired piece meal. REO private investor groups are required by law to list these homes for sale, offering them on a level playing field to the buying public. Doing so would of course defeat the theft agenda.

If your property title was flushed through The Bank Theft Delivery System and you are told that you have copies of every Multiple Listing Service (MLS) listing this may not be true. The MLS system is commonly hijacked by criminals. They help to conceal that flips of the property title are by no objective measure "arms-length transactions." Not only do you not know that REO Fraudsters have acquired control of your property title, but with a lot to hide some listings arbitrarily appear as "closed." To mean that the home is not offered or advertised to the buying public.

The MLS becomes part of the loan package. It conveys an aura of legitimacy to banks, failing to: *Follow the chain of title: Ensure that the seller holds the title, understand the property history and watch for pre-existing relationships between buyer and seller.* You can sue banks that helped to launder your chain of title. In doing so they assist in establishing the identity theft claims over your home predating the foreclosure charade. Add these banks to your defendant list. If the feds won't hold them accountable, perhaps a growing number of Civil RICO cases will inform a body of evidence empowering, *We The People*, to defend private property rights in America.

MLS listings that are never made public is another piece, rooted in the choke-hold over disclosure that disenfranchises homeowners from defending their homes. Realtors and appraisers operating as part of the theft network use the MLS system and Core Logic to posture validity in loans and transfers of authority over the digital property title that in fact does not exist.

You need the following:

1. Each HUD-1 connected to any Bank flip of your property title represented by any FHA insured loan skimming equity.
2. The complete listing history of your home both public and private. Get affirmation from the Multiple Listing Service that you do have a complete history. This allows you to recognize the forgeries that will not appear on that list. If they protect criminals add them to your defendant list. Look for altered and, or, omitted content under the same MLS Number. One number – different content. These are forgeries.
3. The Core Logic "Equator work order."

Core Logic and the Equator "work order."

Does the name Core Logic appear within those very limited documents dumped into the public land records? If so, what I came to call the Core Logic Equator work order will also exist. I adopted the "work order" term because it best describes how the Core Logic internet platform functions as a communication device sending, receiving, and checking off each task needing to be accomplished if physical seizure of your home will go off without a challenge.

This is a tricky juncture. Targets must be so deceived that they cooperate as assembly line judges blindly rubber stamp these thefts. A crime is a crime whether people are conned to cooperate or not. The best hoped for scenario is that homeowners will simply follow the coercive and bullying script laid down for them and walk away. If they do not the harassment and bullying tactics become far more threatening. The illegal seizure of your home takes place in blatant violation of the Fourth Amendment to the United States Constitution.

FARRIS-BOGANO and the Core Logic Equator Work Order

During this brief window, while the harassing build-up to the illegal seizure of my home transpired, Farris-Bobango had in their possession important bridge-evidence by way of the three-page, "Vendor-Only" Core Logic Equator work order. Forgetting everything they had been taught in law school ethics class Farris-Bobango cooperated with the directive of their shadow client; Keller Williams – MEM 2, LLC and David Osborn. Such behavior normalized as acceptable business practice stifles justice and sits like a plague over any legal community where it is allowed to thrive unchecked by any moral filter.

ERA Chamberwood Realty Group had faxed the Equator directive to Farris-Bobango on March 28, 2012. Writing: *"...this is the documents that Alex need to sign."* Revealing that more was faxed than the three pages in my possession since there was no place for my signature on these pages.

I had picked up the copy left by Hattie Brawley as she embarked on an unescorted "illegal search" of my home. In my depleted emotional state, made worse by the stranglehold over disclosure that had gone before, I could not have processed or understood its content. However, as crucial bridge evidence the Core Logic Equator work order was all that any attorney needed. It claimed to be evicting a fictional renter and gave the name of the Memphis eviction company perpetrating this piece of the fraud scheme. It gave the REO ID number; the REO designation informing the existence of a private investor and not, as claimed, a bank. This should have led to the HUD fraud. It gave the name of the secret Core Logic MERS interim lender who would remain secret over the MERS System. Rounding out the arm in arm coordination, keeping exposure to a minimum, Core Logic was a licensed mortgage company able to do business in the State of Tennessee.

By the time I got to my last attorney I understood how the Core Logic Equator work order was used as a communication device to accomplish the illegal seizure of my home and as an example, theft of other homes on a massive scale operating within a national footprint. The Jones, Kelley, Boyd Perpetrator Nexus, including David Osborn and Keller Williams Corporate needed my state case to be dismissed or withdrawn from Fayette County. As explained more further along selling me on Civil RICO and then tanking that option evolved as the next plan to deny any access to due process. That strategy failed in the hands of Kathryn Maceri but as of today has succeeded via the *Screening for Merit* blockade and failure of the appeals process to address my appeal questions; failure to address the Motion(s) for a Void Judgement, separation of my filings and other abuses described in previous chapters.

At this crucial juncture Farris-Bobango did not say: *Sorry Alex, but nothing that you believe to be true, is true.* They dropped me abruptly as a client making no referral to any other attorney; fully expecting that this would be the end of me. Webb Brewer, as my second attorney followed suit. It was his job to sell me on the smokescreen of the court ordered eviction and the foreclosure as real events; the only plausible explanation for what had taken place.

Two wasted years later I remembered that I had given Webb a copy. He claimed not to have it.[27] I had kept a copy, but was unable to find it among my documents. I was led to believe that what was faxed to Farris-Bobango on that day was the judges' order of eviction. It was upon this fictitious and forged so called "court order" that my home was successfully seized by the RICO Criminal Enterprise. I would not know that the Fayette County Judges Order of Eviction did not exist until July 2014.

Malcolm Futhey was the attorney that Farris-Bobango passed me off to when I first called their office asking for Phil Mischke. When it finally dawned on me that I should track down and read whatever it was that Chamberwood had faxed, Malcolm was no longer employed by Farris-Bobango. He sent my request directly to his former secretary. I did not have a fax machine. Therefore, at my request he had her send the Core Logic Equator work order, along with other pages I did not know I needed to see, to Webb Brewer's office.

Malcolm Futhey had co-authored the earlier Collins-Maury filing that I quote from in this book and which predates his brief representation of me. Meaning that he was the attorney of record for both me and also for Doug Collins. Informed by content within the Core Logic Equator work order he had the same Keller Williams – MEM 2, LLC defendants in both cases. Important information never shared with me. I could not be armed in any way to see the big picture. Look for this strategy in how your case may have been limited or tanked by any Memphis attorney you hired.

Obviously, I wasn't present, but this is how I imagine the catch and kill maneuvers were agreed to. Malcom had asked for, and I had given him permission in writing, a list of persons he wished to speak with on my behalf. This included Weiss Spicer Cash, PLLC, the local eviction company named in the Core Logic Equator work order. The Arnold Weiss name appeared in my later research; helping to perfect theft of other homes fed to The Bank Theft Delivery System.

This list also included Christopher Kohl whom I had been conned to believe was employed by Bank of America. Upon speaking

[27] Very little of what I gave him was returned. In hindsight I should have made a list of every piece of paper handed over to him that came from my own independent pursuit of information.

to these people Malcolm then found that the Collins-Maury Case and my case shared the same defendant in MEM 2, LLC; Keller Williams Memphis East. The REO number identifier appearing in the Equator communication tool linked Vernon "Wayne" Boyd to Keller Williams franchise owner, David Osborn. Upon realizing this, in those first hours Malcolm shared this information with his superiors. Running against all logic he was then told to drop me as a client making no referral to any other attorney. This risky act of omission informs that the real Farris-Bobango client was never me. Nor do I believe the real client was ever Doug Collins.

What did Malcolm think about this? Upon leaving his employ he would have been asked to sign a binding non-disclosure agreement. He left very nice offices with original art on the wall and a full staff at his disposal for a very small no conference room, two-man office in homeless-drug central, but within walking distance of the downtown court house. Clearly there is a back story.

Malcolm was already gone from Farris-Bobango when I decided two years later, in 2014, that I needed to see a copy of whatever it was that ERA Chamberwood Realty had faxed. I thought I would get back the Fayette County Judges order of eviction that I would soon discover never existed. If I had called Farris-Bobango directly I believe this information would have been claimed to be lost with the lapse of preserving an important client record laid at the doorstep of Malcolm Futhey. He would be the perfectly positioned scape-goat to whom Farris-Bobango could deflect accountability.

I would never have obtained and then been able to compare that Farris-Bobango faxed copy with the copy I later found in my own records if this had not gone down exactly as it did. If I were writing the script, I would characterize Malcolm as giving the finger to his former employer.

So... This is how I acquired valuable missing pages beyond the three picked up from my kitchen table in March 2012. As already stated, I later did find a copy of the original. I was then able to compare the Hattie Brawley – Chamberwood Realty copy with that of the Farris-Bobango copy faxed to Webb's Office.

What was strikingly different about the two copies? In an act of crony accommodation, the Weiss, Spicer, Cash PLLC name was redacted... by someone. Crony corrupt accommodation at work, this served to conceal the role of Arnold Weiss in perfecting the illegal seizure under the guise of evicting an unnamed renter on April 26, 2012. It read: *Eviction has been ordered* (ordered by REO ID No.: 00906148) *for the referenced property.* (65 Pinehurst Drive, Oakland, TN) *The Eviction Company is Weiss Spicer PLLC Sharon Hogan, 208 Adams Avenue, Memphis, Tennessee 38103.*

The pretense of evicting a renter preserved the fraud narrative that I had abandoned my home in 2009. This lie served to conceal from HUD how they had been used by the REO fraudsters to obtain control over property titles acquired by robbery.

Every person receiving and sending messages using that Core Logic Equator computer platform, printing and sending emails, as a conduit of instruction were committing a cybercrime. Each example is a, separate count of wire fraud and a RICO Predicate Act. At the time that I picked this form up from my kitchen table as ERA Chamberwood Realty Group were conducting the unescorted illegal search of my home[28] there were twenty emails noted in the body of this form. Persons named filled roles described as Asset Manager, Eviction Specialist, Vendor Manager, System Manager, and generally as Agent. Since the Core Logic Equator work order was routinely updated additional emails sent and received by these persons, would have been documented at least through April 26, 2012.

Any federal investigator or class action attorney could identify homes and victims simply by accumulating the Core Logic Equator work orders. Independent contractors greasing the chain of theft may provide a layer of distance, but are not always loyal. Approach the asset managers; some of whom may not be willing to fall on their swords; risking jail time. REO realtors have free reign use of this communication tool under the oversight of Core Logic "asset managers." Like the third-party mortgage servicer company, the asset manager could be working for anyone. I found that the Core Logic Equator platform was networked to the Keller Williams computer system out of Colorado. These thefts are not only lawyer heavy they are fueled by cybercrimes. To the extent possible a paperless system, reducing any public record footprint was developed by Keller Williams and Core Logic.

---

[28] This was illegal search and seizure under color of the forged Fayette County, Judges order of eviction.

Cybercrime is a computer-oriented crime. It involves a computer and a network. The computer may be used in the commission of a crime, or it may be the target. Cybercrimes can be defined as: "Offences that are committed against individual or groups of individuals with a criminal motive to intentionally harm the reputation of the victim or cause physical or mental harm, or financial loss to the victim directly or indirectly, using modern telecommunication networks such as internet and mobile phones." Issues surrounding these types of crimes have become high-profile, particularly these regarding hacking... Wikipedia

In the same vein as the Weiss Spicer redaction from the Core Logic Equator work order. Informing cover-up in anticipation of a defense. Webb wrote into a filing: *"Malcolm Futhey, who represented Ms. Clair in a divorce."* Upon belief that Farris-Bobango asked Webb to place this out of context bit of propaganda into the court record. Malcolm's connection to me needed to be explained away. Not least of all to foreclose any possibility that a federal investigator might look into The Bank Theft Delivery System tied to Keller Williams – MEM 2, LLC. Tied to REO ID No.: 00906148. Tied to HUD Fraud.

What observations were made regarding one of the three REO fraud groups merging out of the pattern example groupings I developed? A study of the addresses led me to believe that specific territory was agreed to; staying out of each other's way. Much in the same way that Mafia families divided up the northeastern seaboard before moving south and west. These criminals had not escaped prosecution for so long without planning ahead and anticipating where weaknesses lay.

Upon reading Webb's statement that Malcolm had been my divorce attorney when he knew that my only connection to Malcolm was through Farris-Bobango, I emailed back. *"No. I had no attorney in my divorce from Brett. I got copies from the court house... filled out the divorce papers myself and then filed them. The judge saw me in chambers and granted the divorce as written. Brett didn't show up and didn't contest."* Just as Webb protected Weiss Spicer Cash, PLLC he protected Farris-Bobango. In case you've missed it, this informs collusion and coordination.

Equator[29] is a Core Logic internet platform. Normally this vendor-only copy of the Core Logic Equator work order would be like receiving a winning lottery ticket. As important bridge evidence, tying all the pieces together, it was never cashed. The Equator internet platform is routinely used as a tool to perfect the illegal seizures of other homes. It documents the progress among co-conspirators. Each party whose name appears is tasked to perform a job. Or they lent their names and credentials to foster the impression of legitimacy without ever performing the job itself which was the case with the law firm of Arnold Weiss. A disclaimer and warning appear. Sending an aggressive message to those being defrauded by its use it reads:

"EQUATOR PROPRIETARY, CONFIDENTIAL, AND TRADE SECRET INFORMATION. This document contains proprietary and confidential information that is legally privileged. Any disclosure, copying, or distribution or use of any of the information contained herein that is not expressly permitted by Equator in writing IS STRICTLY PROHIBITED. This document additionally contains protected trade secret information of Equator..." etc.; well you get the picture.

Translation: YOU NEED THIS INFORMATION building recognition and proof of how you were targeted within a very specific chain of operation. I noticed that no laws were cited at the end of this threatening disclaimer. This is because stealing property is itself the crime. The assertive and bullying language, wherever you interpret it as over-kill and hyper-defensive is a red flag. You are on the right track. In all my

[29] Nationwide Foreclosed Home Listing Service; www.equator.com. Note past tense use of the term, "foreclosed." My home was presold in 2009 premised upon a forged Certificate of Abandonment. This event was withheld from the Registry of Deeds Office in Somerville, TN and from me. Theft perfecting events must be forward dated in the public record. This to disenfranchise any target of this scheme from current, real time information needed to defend their property rights at the time they are first assaulted, usually before the Assignment of the Deed of Trust is ever filed at the Registry of Deeds Office. Bank of America willingly and intentionally corrupted their own records. While the interim equity skimming portion of the scheme transpires homeowners are subjected to harassment in the form of a set of problems fitted to the circumstances of the homeowner and which turn out to be unfixable. By design and intent overwhelmed homeowners are invited to give up. Every entity complained to is biased to accept the bank created Private Investor claim of ownership. And especially were the HUD seal of approval is used to deflect recognition of outright theft.

dealings with the Criminal Enterprise there was a constant theme that ran throughout. For not cooperating with theft of my home, I was the one breaking the law. Then for branching out to investigate other thefts, I was an obsessed, "nut job."

When Farris-Bobango dropped me as a client they claimed to have a "conflict of interest." As I would later discover, that conflict of interest was not the Collins-Maury case. Both that case and mine shared the same defendant in Keller Williams – MEM 2, LLC. The conflict was the shadow client with deep pockets. It was multiple Keller Williams franchise owner David Osborn and REO ID No.: 00906148, a.k.a., the Jones, Kelley, Boyd Perpetrator Nexus – REO Investment Group.

The transfer of the "closed" listing of 65 Pinehurst Drive from one fraudster to another transformed MLS Listing No.: 3249765 into a fraud device. Once again, the REO secret Note-Holders needed to hide their identity, this time behind that of ERA Chamberwood Realty; the Criminal Enterprise "muscle." Chamberwood provided another layer of distance while making certain that 65 Pinehurst Drive was never offered to the buying public. Their role was to conceal same buyer, same seller, same realtor, same broker, same secret Note-Holder.

The Bank Theft Delivery System marshal select realtors to function as "eviction specialists." Hattie Brawley and Loretta Martin received this training in how to use the Bank Vendor System to perfect theft of private property. They did not identify the role they had been weaponized to play. Because they flashed the fictitious Fayette County Judges Order of Eviction, I thought they represented the authority behind this order.

A later document proved that Bank of America was carefully monitoring the REO progress regarding theft of my home and therefore as a pattern of practice, many others. The bank cannot have the REO Fraudsters deciding to keep too many of these homes for themselves. Every theft-asset needs to end up as part of an inflated, over-valued security bought and sold by the criminal banks to their investor depositors. The entire system is set up to feed rental property to the securities market, retuning long term profit back to the criminal banks while price fixing the rental market.

During the required HUD retention period, between 2009 and 2012, there were five known flips of my property title. In the Andrews theft example described in Part 111 of this book there were so many secret flips of their property title that MERS refused to number them. In your case there may be less. In all cases that I reviewed selected lenders just accepted what was presented by the REO Fraudsters. It was intentional, no accident, that Bank of America, JP Morgan Chase Bank, Evolve Bank & Trust, Bank of New York Mellon and HUD failed to... *Follow the chain of title: Ensure that the seller holds the title, understand the property history and watch for pre-existing relationships between buyer and seller.* If they had performed even a modicum of due diligence my home and the many others would not have been fed as fodder to the Bank Theft Delivery System described in this book.

Crony Corruptionism and smaller community banks.
Smaller banks are less restricted by federal regulations. Bank of Fayette County was used to launder assignment of rents in the Turner theft example described in Part 111 of this book. Red flags denoting fraud are not missed. They are blatantly ignored.

With deep roots in the community bank regulators trust that smaller banks will do a better job than larger banks in discerning the borrower's motives. This may be true, but they are also more susceptible to the practice of failing to apply fraud detection tools in selected instances. Tools they have been trained to apply to all loan applications are not equally applied.

The fraudsters must have the money laundering structure in place before they begin reaping the cash-rich benefits to the massive scale that I saw branching out from West Tennessee. There is the little problem of house payments that victims of this scheme believe are going to pay down a valid mortgage, but entered into the enterprise books disguised as something else. Banks that accept an assignment of rents in payment for home improvement loans, or any other loan that uses the theft asset as collateral, are laundering income. They are actively engaged in establishing the REO identity theft claims of ownership over a home acquired by robbery.

According to the IRS: ***The term "money laundering" refers to the activities and financial transactions that are undertaken specifically to hide the true source of the money. In most cases, the money involved is earned from illegal enterprise and the goal is to give that money the appearance of coming from a legitimate source.***

A skilled CPA is needed. Max Jones lived five doors down from me in the Fair Oaks neighborhood. It was his fulltime job to work for the RICO

Criminal Enterprise; David Osborn and Jeffrey L. Kelley among others of this cadre. Make a list of every lender noted in any filing Instrument. In particular, after you left your home, who next purchased your home and what bank perfected that loan? When did your home emerge as a rental? Who, were the loan officer(s) tied to each flip of the property title? How are they networked to the REO Fraudsters socially and professionally? Obtain a copy of the HUD-1. Was there a decoy HUD-1?

The REO Fraudsters might even have manipulated you into renting your own home. They do not tell you that per document fraud you have been a "renter" for a very long time. In this adaptation of the same basic fraud scheme they forward date that event that the mortgage was secretly assumed. This was a practice of the Blackstone Group, Inc.[30] Blackstone is a private equity firm that operated in many parts of the country in similar ways as Pretium Partners, LLC operated in Tennessee. Both used shell companies to conceal the Warranty Deed transfers and the operational connections to the local, boots on the ground, REO Investor Groups.

What I found is that some of these equity skimming loans were made by smaller banks. Using simpler tools, they generate fewer automated reports flowing forward to federal bank regulators who are more focused on the larger banks. For those homes that are undervalued it is clear to any loan officer or underwriter that the loan is fully collateralized.[31] When a home is overvalued, no problem. The

---

[30] The UN's housing advisor has accused private equity firms and one of the world's largest corporate residential landlords, Blackstone Group, of exploiting tenants, "wreaking havoc" in communities and helping to fuel a global housing crisis. May 2019, www.theguardian.com. "We remind all states that while gold is a commodity, housing is not, it's a human right." Mary Catherine Wellons.

[31] Your home may or may not have been pooled into and then purchased out of a HUD program. This does not mean you did not experience the same basic chain of theft; you are just omitting one element. Any home pooled into and then purchased out of a HUD program delude banks into blindly accepting the below market appraisal. The HUD presence predisposes the bank to accept claims of a property being derelict and in need of home improvement funds. This paints the REO criminals as doing the community a service by rehabbing and stabilizing home values. This is set up for lucrative home improvement loans that loan officers, anxious for a commission and perhaps a payoff on the back end, can sell to their superiors as fully collateralized by the undervalued theft asset. The loan funds are not used for the stated purpose. As attested to by the Crye Leike Realty photographs of my home taken on May 5, 2011, by Carole Ann Burns, these same photographs were later used to posture 100k of bogus improvements. Track down any so called before and after photographs of your home.

assignment of rents flow into and out of Criminal Enterprise trusts paying off the loans up to the point that the theft asset goes into default and the cycle starts anew.

Do not give smaller community banks the, benefit of the doubt simply because your friend works for them, likes the job, and these banks take part in local charity events. They are more prone to turn a blind eye to local players. They need deep pocket depositors and see the RICO Enterprise bad actors as business people. It is harder for local bank employees to pivot and see those they may go to church with or serve with on community based committees, in any light that informs the criminal nature and illegal source of funds.

Dedicated staff at small banks are not fully trained. When they see something that seems to indicate possible fraud, they are more likely to accept superficial explanations by higher ups. Federal regulators presume that smaller banks know their customers and will report fraud. Big mistake. The fraudsters know all this. Instruments related to the Turner theft, dropped into the public land records described in a later chapter demonstrates how completely the circle of corruption believe themselves insulated from federal oversight by crony corrupt infiltration and strategic development of community relationships.

ALERT. The Equator record produced by Core Logic is part of what closes out the HUD File at the end of the HUD retention period. Under HUD the REO Investors, i.e., the Jones, Kelley, Boyd Perpetrator Nexus were not allowed to sell my home for three years. The Core Logic Equator work order, claiming to evict a fictional renter, is instrumentality used to support the original fraud narrative that I had abandoned my home in 2009. It was used to commit bank fraud and in addition fraud upon a federal agency. Look for same or similar patterns of practice related to how you were targeted.

The Evolve Bank & Trust HUD-1 revealed a payment to Core Logic for "REO Servicing fees." Read any reference like this and know that REO equates to the existence of a private investor. Not the lender you think you have been working with. The Core Logic Equator work order identified the Note-Owner as REO ID No.: 00906148. Payments to co-conspirators come from the HUD-1 closing fees and conceal that the REO fraudsters are also the buyer. These are not arms-length transactions. Each HUD-1 exposes one loan of several that has served to launder your chain of title, establishing the identity theft claims over a home acquired by robbery.

More about how the Multiple Listing Service is used to conceal the illegal conflict of interest arm in arm transactions.

Even before Webb Brewer agreed to represent me. In August of 2012 when trying to track down the appraiser one of those I called was Norma Wood. She told me that the listing agent was "Wayne Boyd," also the buyer and seller of my home. Webb Brewer told me he would get a copy of this listing that would later turn out to be, MLS listing No.: 3249765. He repeatedly put me off finally saying the information was incorrect. Finally, getting me off topic telling me that it did not exist.

The reason that a complete MLS history is so important is because it helps you fix, the theft time line. You need a copy of every MLS listing that exists within the theft history of your home. The Norma Wood acknowledgment that "Wayne Boyd" was the listing agent, the buyer, and the seller predating the illegal seizure was huge. During the Evolve Bank & Trust flip of the property title, propped up by the ERA Chamberwood Realty listing, Vernon "Wayne" Boyd and Sherry Boyd were then able to emerge as innocent residential buyers having no prior claim over my home.

Despite what Webb told me, I continued to believe that what Norma Wood had disclosed in August of 2012 was accurate. Today she stands out as one of a very few that broke ranks with the crony corrupt attempts to shield criminals.

The theft history starts on that date that your home was first targeted by local white-collar criminals. It starts when your mortgage was offloaded by your lender to be assumed by the REO Private Investors whose sole intent is theft. Think of the end-date as somewhat fluid. The theft scheme ends when the goals of the Criminal Enterprise are achieved and not before. This takes you beyond foreclosure and beyond the illegal seizure to when the theft asset of your home emerged as a rental. When was the property title transferred by Warranty Deed or Quit Claim Deed to that entity that would pool your home into a Wall Street commodity? To thus, return long term profit back to the criminal banks that set this chain of theft in place. Each party perfecting some part of the fraud scheme were responsible to vet for fraud. Beginning with: *Follow the chain of title: Ensure that the seller holds the title, understand the property history and watch for pre-existing relationships between buyer and seller.*

I came to see my job as needing to obtain everything I could get my hands on that fell within that time line of Spring 2009 through the fall of 2012. Among the documents you seek out is a copy of every MLS Listing, private, public, or forged that exists and falls within the dates that your home was flushed through The Bank Theft Delivery System. You want to know the name of the secret Note Holder. You want to know the decoy realty firm they hide behind.

You are looking to document Enterprise Plus Relationship. Each individual function for the enablement of the Criminal Enterprise. Though different names appear, under the RICO Statutes, they are considered one entity. No individual that by their actions, no matter how small, greased the chain of theft can later say they were disconnected from the goals of the Criminal Enterprise.

What I learned when I was deposed by the REO Fraudster attorneys.

The extent to which I had been led to believe lies became evident to me during the deposition of May 6, 2014. On that day I sat at a conference table flanked by the attorneys for Keller Williams (Boyd's). ERA Chamberwood Realty Group (Loretta Martin and Hattie Brawley). And by the attorney singularly described as the attorney for Bank of America, but in fact representing the bank approved vendors, whose roles in theft of my home and many others I would not have a working grasp of until after this deposition. Understanding the role of the bank vendor system in reducing risk of exposure, let me finally see how start to finish these thefts were an inside job. This deposition not going as planned, ushered in a new era. Disjointed pieces, many questions I did not have answers for, suddenly made sense.

Webb Brewer, sat to my right. He did not invite the necessary clarity. I believe that he saw me as perfectly indoctrinated to the fraud narrative. At some point his growing dislike of me became harder to conceal as I brought him more questions and suggestions for information we needed to acquire; including the Evolve Bank & Trust HUD-1. In sending his associate into meetings he lost touch with how much what happened to other victims began to matter to me.

The deposition that I was told would last no more than a couple of hours went seven hours, because these attorneys were not getting into the transcript or on film what they had been led to believe would be a slam dunk. There are reasons why afterwards Webb held this client record hostage. He wanted me to pay him a thousand dollars. Money, he knew I did not have. Later the Boyd's law firm refused to disclose the name of the videographer or court reporter. My error was in not asking for business cards from everyone present, including the videographer and court reporter, before the deposition got underway. Trust had been eroding, frustration building, but it had still not occurred to me that I was not Webb's client. Big mistake! Call, me if you are out there and have *unedited* copies.

Only after I fired Webb Brewer did I find that correspondence was copied to Byron Rogers, First American Title Insurance Company, having nefariously asserted to Evolve Bank & Trust and others that the Boyd's were in possession of a clean chain of title. In failing to identify a crucial defendant Webb Brewer played his expected role to catch and kill my case. Because it is so necessary to the theft-step-process I write more about the role of the title insurance companies further along.

A month after the deposition I fired Webb Brewer on June 10, 2014. "You have done nothing," was a charge lodged at him from the Boyd's attorney, John "Bucky" Phillip, during this May 6, 2014 deposition.

Even without the video record, for me these were hours well spent. Going into it I worried that I might cry. As it turned out I did only briefly as I described the mafia-like bullying tactics, dredging up the visceral fear and helplessness in how I was treated by Hattie Brawley. Although it happens far less often, over the first two years I was ambushed by flashbacks. As I was questioned, Hattie Brawley sat behind me along the wall to my left. She was not within my view, but her positioning and presence was intentional. This was meant to be a painful reminder of what I'd been put through. I wanted to confront these people, but wanted to do so openly, face to face in a court of law before a jury of my peers presenting evidence and facts.

This made me think of a murder trial I had attended. At the time I worked at Memphis Union Mission. One of my jobs was over volunteer services. The daughter of one of our auxiliary members had been brutally murdered. Certain photographs had been excluded from evidence by the judge. The defense attorneys placed a lap top at the end of the table. At a key juncture in the testimony they brought up one of these gruesome photographs turned in the direction of where this mother was seated. They hoped an emotional breakdown would prejudice the jury leading to an appeal of the case they were clearly losing. It wasn't the same, but Hattie Brawley sitting just behind me throughout that deposition felt similarly strategic. They hoped I would lose composure.

In the same vein one of the attorney's had a stack of my blogs from a faith-based website that elaborated on some of the themes in my book, *Discerning Spirits: Visionary Gifts in Practice.* I believe they hoped to paint me as an out-there in crazy land religious zealot. I would not have managed four departments at a large Methodist church, allowed to write and teach as part of my job if this were the case.

What was really going on? There was an important piece of evidence that needed to be undermined. These very clever attorneys, having pigeonholed me, hoped to elicit comments on my friends openly gay relationship matched to my religious views. Why bother? Because, Affidavit *of Joshua A. Morgan,* was an objective firsthand account of how I'd been treated by the Criminal Enterprise Muscle. It was later filed as, Exhibit No.: 25 in my Civil RICO Case.

Josh had been staying with me for a few weeks as he prepared to move to another state. He was witness to ERA Chamberwood Realty's bullying and threatening behavior on that first day. The plan was to discredit Josh as a witness using words, they hoped to provoke from me. Words a jury might hear, if in fact, my state case and the Machiavellian endeavors to have it dismissed by a Fayette County Judge did not work out as planned.

Right now, Josh is sick. But upon investigation they knew he would make a strong, unshakable witness. He is factual, honest, compassionate and loyal. One of Webb's broken promises was that he would depose Josh and get a fuller account on video. Josh had picked up details that I was too ambushed in the moment to process and thereafter, trying to control the flashbacks, wished I could forget.

At the end of his affidavit. Speaking of Hattie Brawley Josh wrote: *This woman insisted to Alex's face that everything needed to be out of her house by the 26th of April or it would be "out on the street." I know that this entire interaction was painful and terrifying for Alexandra... I had never seen her so upset. I think we were both a bit in shock at this representative's behavior and that is the only reason I can find for myself not having spoken up more loudly and immediately in the realtor's presence. I also believe the stress and immediate terror as a result of the alarmist bullying rendered my friend Alexandra incapable of level-headed responsiveness I have grown to see as her intrinsic character... she was simply too traumatized. It was truly unbelievable.*

The Criminal Enterprise aggressive attacks are meant to paralyze people into shocked, deer in the headlights, inaction. It is one thing to watch such violent interaction in film and quite another to experience it. ERA Chamberwood Realty, as the criminal enterprise "muscle" came back to my home three times on that first day. This was followed by almost daily harassment through the end of April. Josh would leave on the following weekend, but he was a God-sent objective witness to a pattern of practice not at all limited to what I, as a, single victim experienced.

Josh's account of that day, on a very personal level, has assisted in the healing process. Though it happens far less often I can be snapped back in time. Rather than go there, I've learned to manage what in, the first two years I had little control over.

This deposition came to represent seismic shifts beginning deep underground and repositioning everything on the surface of my perceptions. After that day how I processed the proof in my possession was no longer filtered through Webb Brewer and his associate, Diedre Smith. My third and last attorney, Katheryn Maceri could not just pick up where Webb left off. A whole new strategy, but designed to accomplish the same goals were needed. I must not achieve due process. My evidence must not catch the attention of any federal investigator. It must not arm any other victim being played as I had been to fight back.

Don't they teach first year law students not to have client-lawyer conversations within the hearing of the opposition? In part here are takeaways from that deposition.

1. In a shock of realization, I understood why Webb Brewer wanted me to sign an agreement that admitted that I, as the plaintiff *"has no evidence to contradict the Boyd's affirmative defense statement in their answer that Boyd's are good faith purchaser for value without notice."* Webb asking me to sign this felt very, very, very wrong. Immediately following, in an April 2, 2014 email, I wrote to him: You wanted me... to *admit that the plaintiff has no evidence to contradict the Boyd's affirmative defense statement in their answer that Boyd's are a good faith purchaser for value without notice. What do they mean by, 'defense statement?' Did they send a defense statement and I haven't read it? I hate doing this last minute...* Last minute referring to how urgency was used to unsettle me, forcing compliance. This same tool was later used as a trigger just as effectively by the third and last attorney Kathryn Maceri. Webb failed to turn over the Boyd's "defense statement" after I fired him.

2. On June 3, 2014 *"Motion for Sanctions pursuant to Rule 11 of the Tennessee Rules of Civil Procedure"* was filed. This was the fruit of the, "You have done nothing" tactics. Moving my Fayette County state case toward dismissal took planning and coordination and was right out of the David Osborn, Keller Williams play book. If I had not fired Webb Brewer a month after the deposition, I am certain that a Fayette County Court would have delivered.
3. The out of context statement by John "Bucky" Philip to Webb Brewer, "you have done nothing," led me to question what had and had not been accomplished. Just before the deposition I had asked Webb if he had sent the Chamberwood interrogatories. He stated that he had. This was a lie.
4. The very odd, Bucky Philip statement to Webb appeared to distance the Boyd's attorney from collusion taking place behind the scenes. I believe that Bucky Philip was sending a self-serving disclaimer into the transcript. The deposition, not having gone as planned, these attorneys made sure I never had a copy.
5. During a break in the deposition I overheard a heated exchange between Hattie Brawley and her attorney. This led me to look deeper into the Keller Williams – ERA Chamberwood marriage.
6. At some point in the deposition I realized there was a concerted effort to deflect blame away from the Bank Theft Delivery System and local REO Fraudsters. These lawyers handed me an email from my former Crye Leike Realtor, Carole Ann Burns addressed to Christopherr Kohl at Bank of America. The same Christopher Kohl at Bank of America that Farris-Bobango communicated with in March 2012. In this email Carole Ann stated that she had a buyer for my home. I was still living in my home. This offer was never presented to me. A single, scapegoat perpetrator, as a not unimportant, but lesser piece of the big picture was being offered to me on a platter.

Adding to the Cybercrimes, what I believe is a false Bank of America email address was one that I too had communicated through. It was Christopher Kohl that sold me on the *"special Bank of America program"* for *"seniors with equity in their homes"* that in fact, did not exist. For all I know I may have been emailing back and forth directly with Vernon "Wayne" Boyd or some other of that cadre of con-artists.

These lawyers put on their running shoes and crossed a line. I've wondered if some attorneys, having to navigate a living within this culture of corruption and peer accommodation at the expense of their clients have felt a bit like Lot living in lawless Sodom.

From Keller Williams to Chamberwood – the MLS Listing that Webb Brewer first promised he would obtain, then claimed he could not get, and finally said did not exist.

I had listed my home for sale with Crye Leike Realty from 5/5/2011 thru 11/5/2011; MLS Number: 3223195; Civil RICO Exhibit No.: 23. Other homes around me sold during this period. I had no more than two showings. As already stated, eleven days later, on May 16, 2011, JP Morgan Chase Bank approved a loan for $100,000 to the REO Fraudsters. This added to the weight of document fraud that painted me as trying to sell a home I did not own. It also cemented the identity theft piece of the Property Flip – Title Theft Scheme since anyone would wrongly assume JP Morgan Chase Bank had done their due diligence and verified the Boyd's as true owners of the Property Title. JP Morgan Chase Bank failed to: *Follow the chain of title: Ensure that the seller holds the title, understand the property history and watch for pre-existing relationships between buyer and seller.*

The dual claim of REO ownership was in place to obstruct and kill any offer coming from the general public. No realtor would show a home where the property title was in dispute. This Crye Leike Realty listing of my home, complete with photographs on line and a sign in my yard was dead in the water on day one.

Hank Hogue was my realtor's broker. The day after the deposition I dropped in on him, not calling ahead. I told Hank that during this deposition it seemed clear that Chamberwood and Keller Williams were blame shifting to his firm. He stood up from his desk, walked out of the room, and a short time later came back with the mystery MLS that Norma Wood had described in August of 2012. This MLS documented transfer of the listing of my home from the secret REO Note Holder, Keller Williams and Vernon "Wayne" Boyd, to ERA Chamberwood Realty Group and Hattie Brawley. When I fired Webb Brewer on June 10, 2014 it was long overdue.

Did Hank Hogue say to my Crye Leike realtor, Carole Ann Burns, *We're, not going to try so hard to sell this home."* Did she really conceal from me a valid offer of sale? Did she or Hank Hogue know that 65 Pinehurst Drive was already claimed to be an REO Repossession? Making my Crye Leike Realty sales contract a fraud.

Same MLS Number – Different Content. How it ties together. Victims cannot recognize forgeries they do not have access to. MLS No.: 3249765 became my Civil RICO Exhibit No. 24. An altered and therefore forged copy of the same listing became Exhibit No 24-A. What was different about the two versions?

1. The altered version reads that it was prepared by Joe D. Pickering. It replaces the name of the Crye Leike Broker, Hank Hogue. Pickering's primary role is to serve the REO Industry helping institutional investors to liquidate their REO holdings. In this case, lending his name to a fraud device he closed out the HUD fraud.
2. The altered version replaced the selling agent name of "Wayne" Boyd with that of Hattie Brawley. The Jones, Kelley, Boyd REO Fraudsters cannot be seen to be buying a home they already own.
3. The altered version replaces the selling office name of Keller Williams Realty with that of ERA Chamberwood Realty Group. Chamberwood becomes the decoy selling office hiding the conflicts of interest. They also become the muscle, perfecting the illegal seizure in violation of the Fourth Amendment to the United States Constitution.
4. The "closed" MLS refers to a, lease to purchase agreement. To explain why Evolve Bank & Trust will cooperate in perfecting the last illegal flip of a Property Title acquired by robbery. This reinforces the lie that the REO Fraudsters have retained and lived at 65 Pinehurst Drive over the prior three years from 2009 through 2012. To posture the lie that they are in compliance with the hijacked HUD program.
5. On page-13 of the Boyd's, *Lease to Purchase Agreement,* the Boyd's claimed that they had been renting my home from the HUD-REO Private Investors over the prior three years leading up to the illegal seizure. If any party were doing their job these contradictions fitted to the theft time line could have been easily spotted.

There is an appalling lack of due diligence. The HUD email referenced earlier had referred to "Mr. Boyd's, portfolio of properties." How many ended up as rentals? How many ended up being fed to the securities market returning long term profit back to the criminal banks? And as a theme, how many are today managed by Sherry Boyd and that same cohort of bad actors?

You have noticed that this entire house of cards is premised on document fraud. Where fraud is involved everything else is tainted. None of this paper has the power to enforce. Each flip of the digital title amongst the same parties demonstrate that the REO Fraudsters are laundering title to stolen property. As a pattern of practice, every illegal transaction, puts a layer of distance between your Deed of Trust as a legal contract and their identity theft claims over your, home as an illegal contract.

As pathetic as this is there is no pushback from those that carry badges and, or, hold the public trust. Laws already on the books are not enforced. Bank regulations and fraud reporting requirements are ignored. Another line from another film: *Well who's gonna monitor the monitors of the monitors?"* Enemy of the State, screen writer, director: David Marconi.

In summary get a copy of every **HUD-1.** Get a copy of what will be claimed to be the complete **MLS history.** Altered content is adapted to the shifting needs of the theft goals; informing timeline. The MLS is commonly used as a theft device because on the surface, failing to verify the claims, it is superficially trusted. Get a copy of the **Core Logic Equator work order.** These three documents, along with what has been dumped into the land fill of the Registry of Deeds Office by **foreclosure mill attorneys**, discussed in Part 111, provides an excellent foundation. Proof that fleshes out this picture is waiting to be found. Don't give up. You may have to lay the groundwork; acquire evidence on your own, before a lawyer will help you.

The Deep State needs a population of renters because statistics show that renters are less likely to vote. The month to month life struggle means fewer Americans protesting deep state corruption, a trend that well-paying jobs and a vibrant economy impedes. There are reasons why the notion that draining the Washington swamp is fought against with the ferocity of an invading army. This isn't about liberal or conservative. It is about an agenda wanting global control. Let's be real. There are those that hate the United States Constitution, notions of equality and the Bill of Rights.

The Cash for keys bribe and the all barrels loaded death squad hustle.

I did not sign any of the documents aggressively forced on me by ERA Chamberwood Realty Group. Not because I was so smart that I knew better, but because I was so emotionally distraught that I was not in my right mind.

After completion of the HAMP Fraud Scheme I had been led into a false sense of security.[32] Christopher Kohl (whoever he is) had told me that I could sell my home under the safety of this Bank of America program for senior citizens, *"with equity in their homes."* I contacted my relator to relist my home. Vastly relieved I was sleeping well for the first time in two years. After months of contentious back and forth this made the sudden appearance of Loretta Martin and Hattie Brawley at my door two weeks later, wielding the fictional order of eviction as a, weapon all the more effective. The complete lack of ability to obtain answers or control an outcome, is assisted in the chokehold over institutional disclosure to homeowners carefully targeted and profiled. The see-saw timing of these two effects understood in context to how career con-artists operate to keep their victims unsettled and pliable to the fraud narrative is not coincidental. Look for these cruel and heartless maneuvers in how you were treated.

If you were offered this "cash for keys" payment, whether you accepted it or not, whether you signed the paperwork forced on you or not, you may safely conclude that there is a Core Logic Equator work order, functioning as a Criminal Enterprise communication tool. The Cash for Keys exchange of money implies that victims of this fraud scheme sold their right to later object and bring charges.

[32] HAMP was created pursuant to the Emergency Economic Stabilization Act, 12 U.S.C. § 5201. I was preapproved to apply for HAMP. Bank of America fielded that application though they had no authority to do so having already off loaded my home to the REO Fraudsters. From August 2011 thru February 2012 the third-party mortgage servicer company hired by the REO Fraudsters masqueraded as the Bank of America department processing my HAMP Application. In numerous conference calls with Bank of America and a nonprofit authorized by Treasury (Money Management International) to assist HAMP Applicants, Bank of America repeatedly lied so as to protect The Bank Theft Delivery System and the secret REO Note Holders.

This is what they want you to believe. In fact, this claim would not hold up in court.

In the third visit to my home on that first day Hattie Brawley stood over me with a, pen as I cried. Her bullying language was intentionally delivered to convey that there are no choices. To impede rational thought. In her obsessive determination to get these documents signed, documents I was in no state to read, she blocked my driveway so that I could not disappear into the garage. On one occasion she prevented me from entering my own home as she blocked entrance through my front door, publicly haranguing me. The deadline to receive this Cash for Keys money was repeatedly put off. Last chance became now and then tomorrow a new "now" deadline. The help of Farris-Bobango was elicited. Declan was no dummy. He came to recognize her approach and erupted in aggressive warning barks; once having found her peering in my window having navigated the rose bush thorns.

Among those documents I refused to sign was a release addressing anything I did not have time to pack. They wanted me to accept Cash for Keys, without bothering to pack; beginning by telling me I had forty-eight hours to be out. Everything I would leave behind became the property of the REO white collar criminals. Sherry Boyd later complained to neighbors that I had not left them the gas stove. I had sold some items for pennies on the dollar to finance moving my possessions into storage where they would stay for six long years. In the chaos many items simply disappeared. I had made a list of these losses for Webb Brewer and given that list to my last attorney Kathryn Maceri. Neither made any attempt to recoup these losses.

At the Cash for Keys juncture my refusal to sign away my legal rights and accept this "cash for keys" payment deeply offended Hattie Brawley. I was the troublemaker breaking the law, systemically bullied and harassed over the following weeks.

The "seller" at this juncture was proposed to alternately be Bank of New York Mellon, HUD, and REO ID No.: 00906148. Many red flags were ignored by those trained and required to report bank fraud. Evolve Bank & Trust were my very last opportunity that I could have remained in my home. I later found that the loan officer was linked to Loretta Martin at ERA Chamberwood Realty Group.

After the illegal seizure of April 2012, the theft-asset, a.k.a., 65 Pinehurst Drive, came full circle. As squatters the Keller Williams straw buyers, under a broken chain of title, via bank fraud, per forged and notarized paper, via a highway of fraud committed against several federal agencies moved into my home. Where, as of, this writing they remain today.

In the first year I felt that there were no circumstances by which I could be restored and healed. If I would go on with my life this lie needed to be dislodged from my thinking. Injustice named itself and by its own imperative cried out for exposure. That impetus carried me forward. I can say today that I did not choose this fight. Despite anything that I could have, would have, wished I could have done differently, this work chose me. The angst of emergence from turmoil is expressed in the following poem written some time in 2014, after I had fired Webb Brewer.

AMBIVALENT VICTOR

I could not go on.
An avalanche of minutes passed through blackest wood.
Splintered twig mercy to the tempest whim.
No foot fixed.
No life in compass.
I would not go on.
Until the hand that loosed, the comet on a path.
Throne to Spirit,
Spirit to heart, God spoke.
Ambivalent victor you shall be.
Go On!

CHAPTER FOURTEEN

"There is no neutral ground in the universe: every square inch, every split second is claimed by God and counter claimed by Satan." CS Lewis; Christianity and Culture.

Why had all three attorneys focused derailment of my case on protecting ERA Chamberwood Realty Group and the role they played in achieving eviction as one of the last pieces of the con-job? I had the obvious superficial answers, but not until I recognized that Bank of America had allowed criminals to assume my mortgage and could name them. Not until I recognized the HUD piece of the fraud scheme could I understand why everyone went to great lengths to conceal the Chamberwood exposure. The HUD piece of the fraud scheme offered banks the rationale for why these homes were undervalued. A conventional property flip scheme will usually see a home overvalued. The pattern I unearthed were homes undervalued, many by as much as 50% or more, leading to the cash heavy home improvement loans. Both scenarios represent bank fraud, a federal crime.

The role that Chamberwood played embodied a pattern of practice not just taking place in Fayette County, TN; but everywhere. While I was focused on the brutal way that I was treated, lawyers saw what they were trained to see. They saw actions, motive, and intent of a RICO Criminal Enterprise seated in the two documents carried into my home in March of 21012. Hattie Brawley and Loretta Martin were primary links between the local and the national chain of theft. They carried the instrumentality of the con-job into my home. One piece they left behind. The other was shown to me, overplaying their hand, so as to bully and intimidate me into compliance.

First... I somehow think that if you or I forged a court order and signed a judge's name to that order, granting permission to seize property worth six figures we would be in some kind of trouble. But not in Fayette County, TN. This was an explosive piece in the well-oiled chain of theft that could expose the big-picture operations.

Second... They carried the instrumentality of the communication device into my home. And left it behind; the Core Logic Equator work order.

When Hattie Brawley and Loretta Martin brandished that forged court order, they did so with the expectation that the power of the financial industry had their backs. That Fayette County corruption was so locked down that even if I did later investigate and find that no such order existed no one would take action.

The Chamberwood links in the chain of theft had to be protected. The peril of the instrumentality carried into my home on that day had to stay disconnected from the national scope of these crimes. Chamberwood was a leak in the dam of recognition begging for responses from law enforcement, regulators, and legislators. Many fires start with a tiny incendiary device so small it is hardly noticed. People like Marie McDonnell had been voices of warning crying into the yawning jaws of enablement, apathy, and inaction for many years. The degree to which property rights in America were under assault by the financial industry needed to stay buried.

I keep a journal. I don't write in it every day. My journal notes are not cohesive, but shift randomly from topic to trivia.

On September 13, 2013 I wrote: *Meeting with Webb. Tells me to settle with Chamberwood. They will testify against Boyd's. Felt bullied. Don't want to give us anything. God said, 'no.' Webb mad at me."*

In my journal notes a year later I wrote: *Kathryn pushing me to settle with Chamberwood. They are a distraction. Then call them to testify in the federal case."*

Kathryn Maceri had eloquently talked of the need to help other victims as a shared endeavor that we both felt passionate about. She too pushed Chamberwood to the margins. She suggested that it was only because I felt so emotionally hurt by them that I elevated their importance beyond what was realistic and helpful to my case.

Kathryn did one really good thing for me. On that very first day that we met. Before David Osborn, Keller Williams, and the extended Criminal Enterprise had any opportunity to interfere with the case, she instructed me to go up to the Fayette County Court House and verify that there really was a Fayette County Judges Order of Eviction issued any time before or after March 19, 2012. She was mystified that Webb Brewer had not confirmed the existence of this order. "Are you sure?" she asked.

She also instructed me to verify that the Sheriff's Department had a copy of that order that would have authorized them to put everything I owned out on the street. What I described did not comport with what she knew of how foreclosure and eviction functioned under Tennessee law.

I was shocked to learn that neither order existed. After that, Kathryn Maceri could not back-step foreclosure as a fictious event. But she could sell me on March 19, 2012 as the salient date that moving forward set the statute of limitations that I could bring a Civil RICO Case.

Kathryn was the exact opposite of Webb Brewer. She had listened to me describe the disputes that had set me afloat from his control and would play me with far more skill. Webb had pushed me away. She drew me in, appealing to my ego, telling me that she valued my research capabilities. It was Maceri who introduced the option of filing a Civil RICO Case in federal court. A journal entry of August 13, 2014 reads. *Kathryn had some tough things to say about the case. But she told me the truth and redirected me. So, I have some decisions to make.* Decisions about withdrawing the state case from Fayette County and letting her file the Civil RICO Case in federal court.

According to Kathryn, a federal judge would dismiss Chamberwood as a defendant because they entered the picture after the proposed March deadline. Like Webb she lined up the statute of limitations to begin at the Bank of America March foreclosure charade. This kept me from understanding that Bank of America had allowed criminals to assume my mortgage, no disclosure to me, three years before. Because of the instrumentality they had carried into my home, take Chamberwood operating as the Criminal Enterprise muscle, perfecting the physical acquisition of my home out of the Civil RICO equation and what you have is a vastly weakened case.

Kathryn had fixed the statute of limitations for RICO at three years. I wrote her lie into my journal: "*...the statute of limitations for Civil RICO is three years. Deadline March 19, 2015.*"

As already stated in a prior chapter the Civil RICO Statute of Limitations is four years. It does not begin at any foreclosure juncture. Nor at the illegal seizure juncture. Nor, if the REO Fraudsters can get it, upon "Deed of Trust in Lieu of Foreclosure" as the golden ticket. No! It begins on the day that the victim of any version of this scheme finally recognizes how they were defrauded.

I could not be allowed to see the illegal seizure of my home as a violation of the Fourth Amendment to the United States Constitution and the main event. In fact, there was no foreclosure. Foreclosure is the rabbit trail sending everyone down a wrong path. In contrast the illegal seizure is not a smokescreen. A primary goal of the Criminal Enterprise is not met until the physical seizure of the home takes place so that criminals can move in.

Contrary to what Kathryn Maceri told me, I could have pushed the RICO Deadline forward from the April seizure of my home to the start of my investigation, August 2012. Which additionally coincided with the post foreclosure final flip of the property title via Evolve Bank & Trust to the Keller Williams straw buyers and previous Note Holders, Vernon "Wayne" Boyd and Sherry Boyd. Same buyer, same seller, same broker, same appraiser... you get the picture.

If the crony corrupt conspiracy to deliver the outcome that I never get to stand before a jury of my, peers and present evidence of a RICO Criminal Enterprise and The Bank Theft Delivery System would succeed I had to be skillfully maneuvered to fall lock step back into line. I had signed our attorney/client agreement on July 22, 2014. Kathryn had first introduced Civil RICO in August. It was now November and I was dragging my feet. An immediate decision needed to be made because time was "running out" and she had a lot to do. She described needing to register with the federal district court as an attorney able to file the Civil RICO Case in a matter of weeks. We needed to withdraw the state case from Fayette County.

Expert con artists can also be lawyers. Sadly, it seems there are more of them out there than we might think. Although I could not know it, I was to meet with Kathryn Maceri for the last time on November 7, 2014. The goal of silencing me finally and forever had been set in motion and thought at last accomplished. Coercive persuasion and dissemination of the truth for immoral purposes are useful skills for any lawyer to have. Absent a moral compass it is a deadly combination. Maceri knew full well that there would never be a Civil RICO Case filed by her or by Claiborne Ferguson Law Firm, PA.

At the start of our interaction Kathryn told me that she had been cured of cancer. She described that battle, frequently bringing it up. She showed me photographs of her young son, telling me how grateful she was for each day she could be a mother. She also told me that she too, had once lost a home. She described how traumatic this had been for her family. Establishing common experiences and interests created a rapport and false bond leaving me more pliable to manipulation, more prone to rely on her judgment.

This is where today's skepticism kicks in. It was expected that I would conflate Kathryn's cancer scare with that of my good friend,

Brian Churchill. After the goal of withdrawing the state case had been achieved. After I was successfully pointed in the direction of Civil RICO a return of this possibly fatal cancer was revived as a manipulative fraud tool. This provided the excuse, sound familiar, for her to drop me abruptly as a client though she would be smarter than Farris-Bobango had been in setting up the needed exit.

Though I did not reciprocate by discussing him, Brian had been about the same age as Kathryn. At forty-three he had passed away far too young. A lot of people knew and loved Brian. His memorial service was standing room only. His wife had asked me to be among the speakers. Kathryn's descriptions of what she had suffered connected us beyond what would normally be the case between client and attorney. With an early background in nursing, I felt motherly and protective toward Brian. I could not help but feel the same toward Kathryn which of course was the point.

The end goal is always that the "mark" be maneuvered to dismiss red flags. Any con-artist sales person learns to anticipate questions and objections and get them dismissed on the front end. Victims feel foolish for having put critical thinking skills on the shelf and blame themselves for what happened. Feeling foolish afterwards far too many victims of skilled white-collar criminals then fail to report these crimes.

As soon as the goal of withdrawing the state case was met, Kathryn disappeared. She premised her departure by telling me that very suddenly her cancer had returned. She would be in Arkansas undergoing chemo treatments, but had already discussed the Civil RICO Case with a lawyer who had agreed to take over. But first we needed to secure Chamberwood as being willing to testify in the upcoming Civil RICO Case. Why? Because... "they were a distraction" and did not "meet RICO criteria."

Did Kathryn Maceri then or ever have cancer? Did she ever lose a home to foreclosure? I, don't know. Lies are better when peppered with bits of truth. As she talked, I naturally thought about Brian. I missed our long conversations. When he could not sleep, he would call me late at night. Long conversations about film and its' collaborative process. Wood's End had inspired his imagination. He believed he would someday direct that film. He had a gift for humor. On one occasion, following his instructions and pushing him in a wheel chair he deliberately got us lost on the wrong floor of a wing. He was exhausted and probably in pain but he laughed as we spun around retracing our path.

I don't need an answer as to whether Maceri experienced the health crisis she described. What I do know is that the expert manner by which my memories of what Brian suffered, conflated with what she described, came right out of the con-artist play book. The stranglehold over disclosure, my desperate need for legal representation, respect for the law and authority made me especially vulnerable.

In agreeing to let ERA Chamberwood Realty Group and Brawley/Martin off the hook I felt I had betrayed other victims. I had somehow been led to believe the new attorney, Brian Lynn, stepping in to replace Maceri was contingent on moving Chamberwood out of the defendant category. The degree to which I felt disadvantaged in not having an attorney was used as leverage to keep the con-game going. Feeling trapped I had tears in my eyes as I signed that Chamberwood agreement. I refuse to call it a settlement. The real settlement took place off stage and behind closed doors, enriching lawyers, "payment for services rendered." This was an Avenatti type scam. Finally, and taking far longer than expected it was payment from the shadow clients to lawyers for the criminal manner in which they worked to tank any possibility I would ever achieve due process.

On that last day, as we waited for Brian Lynn to show Maceri playacted her dismay that he had missed our meeting. There had to be a good reason, right? She made several calls to his office. Covering her bases, she needed to appear in compliance with the ethical standards of the legal profession. The fact is that this attorney had just been censored by the Bar Association and there was not a chance in hell he would touch any part of this conspiracy to protect a Criminal Enterprise. I think if he were called... maybe you can get him on the phone. He would say that he knew nothing about this.

At this point I was thought handled successively by three attorneys. I am somehow certain no one was counting the days. They were all convinced that the RICO bar introduced through Kathryn Maceri could not be achieved by someone like me. In their minds I had been effectively, if not ruthlessly thwarted (silenced) at every turn. Under the auspices of crony corruptionism and its criminal reach what was guaranteed to every American under the Bill of Rights was not worth the paper it was written on. More people could be defrauded, more homes fed through the pipeline of The Bank Theft Delivery System and the feds were not taking a second look at where many of these Tennessee homes ended up.

Immediately afterwards, that very next day, Maceri promptly disappeared. In my wildest dreams I would not have anticipated this. I could never again reach her by telephone. The law firm where she worked: The Claiborne Ferguson Law Firm, PA informed me that they did not have a copy of this agreement. They stated that Maceri was an "independent contractor" who merely "rents office space" from them. They had no idea where she was. Did not have a forwarding address. Had no current phone number. Utterly devasted I wrote in my notes: *"Kathryn's name is off the website.*

Took money and ran. Won't return my calls." I accepted a check for under 10K. Money to be used for research into the RICO collaboration. It was the Chamberwood behavior that I had most strongly experienced as violence. Even the Sherry Boyd threats to have me arrested had a layer of distance, coming by email. Giving what I had come to label the Criminal Enterprise muscle a pass... how did that protect other victims? I could feel myself breaking down. A single flashback I had not experienced for at least a year threatened a loss of composure. We agreed to meet on the following day. I would pick up the paperwork at that time. I drove away from her office feeling very conflicted. Never to speak with or see Kathryn Maceri again.

I believe today that there was a closed-door settlement that transpired current to our last meeting. She left and returned to the room multiple times. It reminded me of Webb pacing the room, looking at his cell phone and texting. Evolve Bank & Trust, Bank of America, JP Morgan Chase Bank, Bank of New York Mellon, Keller Williams Corporate, the David Osborn team, the Chamberwood crew... huge potential for a substantial pay out. If anyone is interested, as they say, follow the money. I could use some help to do this.

Although different, the Maceri sabotage felt similar to what Jeanine Hance proposed closing out her Case Manager responsibilities at the sixth circuit. Her assertion as to why the motion for a void judgment would never be presented to any panel of judges to thus, conceal administrative corruption, was that I had no right to file it in the first place. Her suggestion. Appeal to Supreme Court. Maceri' s plan, file a Civil RICO Case via her decoy, phantom replacement. Well that was equally considered a very safe, dead in the water, alternative.

The steady drip of coercive persuasion was expertly wielded as a weapon. I was trapped in what is normally a mutually beneficial and trustworthy association. Thinking otherwise is not reinforced by societal norms. If you have experienced these con-artist assaults do not blame yourself for not having recognized and responded as you wish you had in the moment.

I wrote in my journal on January 30, 2015, *"No lawyer – fasting praying if I should move forward."*

I have no proof of what I share next. I describe it only because the memory has stayed with me. On that last day I overhead angry voices coming from a closed meeting room; which was the room where Kathryn and I usually met. I was sure that one of those voices belonged to Webb Brewer who I believe would not allow any payout to take place without him getting his pound of flesh. I later excused myself and went to the ladies' room. There were now murmuring voices. I regret that I had not been bold enough to open that door and walk in.

There never was any plan to file a Civil RICO Case on my behalf. I was never the client of Farris-Bobango, Webb Brewer, or Kathryn Maceri. Retrieving my files after Maceri disappeared was like pulling teeth. Phone messages were ignored. I wrote several letters that were not answered. I was not allowed to pick up my files for a month. As with Webb Brewer selected items were missing. A box was not offered to put these files in. The outside street door was locked from the inside. When I finally did have my files precariously balanced in my arms there was a delay before the door was buzzed open. Much of what I had provided was out of the original jackets or the plastic sleeves. If I am anything I am organized and I was immediately alarmed by what I saw. It looked like many hands had sifted through this material and left it in a chaotic mess.

For this reason, I refused to sign the release as written that unequivocally stated that I had reviewed and been given back everything I had originally left in the custody of Maceri. Tensions ran high between myself and the Claiborne-Ferguson employee tasked with not letting me leave without signing that release. She had her arms over the stack. I had my hands on the same stack. I decided I would have to call the police. Suddenly Mr. Claiborne bounded down the stairs. In angry fashion he scribbled over the qualification I had written with: *"She refuses to look at her file."* File singular, a massive understatement. I'm pretty sure there were lots of cameras in that office and if an interior designer were describing the motif, would say, paranoia classic.

On this form dated December 9, 2014 the names of the Claiborne practice lawyers are listed. It reads on the letterhead in the left column: Claiborne H. Ferguson. Haden Lawyer, Kathryn Maceri, Eric Montierth. There is no disclaimer to say that these attorneys are independent contractors renting office space.

The criminal cohort believed that with Kathryn Maceri out of the picture I would never file a Civil RICO Case at the Federal District Court in Memphis, TN. Bias and prejudice told them that despite what the U.S. Constitution guarantees to every American citizen, in today's culture, this would be a bar too high for a seventy something senior citizen with no college degree. The system was rigged. Unchecked crony corruption and accommodation, obstructing access to due process, to the benefit of the privileged few had rigged it.

Feeling hopeless I returned from that last meeting with Maceri, crying and distraught. I immediately tried to phone Maceri. I needed to say that there could be no agreement with Chamberwood. What I did not know about their ties to the Jones, Kelley, Boyd Perpetrator Nexus, a label I had not yet coined, was a lot. There, would be no reply... Not then or ever.

As always Marj was there to inject her no-nonsense brand of pull it together, no frills logic. She reminded me of a phrase heard in Al-Anon rooms. A phrase that from that time forward rang in my mind each time a paralyzing sense of inertia threatened to derail the pursuit of justice. "Do *the indicated next right thing*." Goals are met in the accumulation of many small steps. Throughout human history God has used unlikely people to accomplish His purposes. A well-known New Testament verse reads: ***"My grace is sufficient for you, for power is perfected in weakness. Most gladly, therefore, I will boast about my weakness, so that the power of Christ may dwell in me."*** 2nd Corinthians 12: 9.

Free of my last corrupt Memphis attorney motivation to achieve justice took on a broader context. I saw the common features in how each victim was profiled as unlikely to fight back. Pieces of the back story were learned through the documents I read and the backgrounds I examined. Every property was fitted to some adaptation of the same Property Flip – Equity Skimming – Title Theft step-process. I was far from the sole victim that Magistrate Judge Vescovo would label me. Responsibility to address what others had suffered, arming them to fight back, took shape. The names and some of the stories will forever stay with me. I went to bed thinking about these people and I woke in the morning praying for them.

In 2008 the, famous mortgage debacle took place. Tax payers paid to fix a problem that today just wears a different skin. King Solomon said: *When a crime is not prosecuted people feel it is safe to do wrong (Ecclesiastes 8: 11).*

In accepting an academy award for his film, Inside Job, Charles Ferguson said:

"Forgive me, I must start by pointing out that three years after our horrific financial crisis caused by financial fraud, not a single financial executive has gone to jail, and that's wrong."

CHAPTER FIFTEEN

"We always see humanness as a variable quality. Sometimes we think not all have it. Some seem to have little of it. And who possess it, have varying degrees of it, are never constant in it and from time to time fail in it completely. Free will is the liberty to choose what is right according to God's law."
Malachi Martin

Some of the names I later traced from both the HUD-1 and the Core Logic Equator work order, like Michelle Brunk,[33] were linked to David Osborn; multiple Keller Williams franchise-owner. He drew in Keller Williams employees from outside the Memphis region. They were assigned titles and signing authority that were entirely bogus. This fraud scheme depends upon victims assuming that the documentation is legitimate. The Fraudsters do not expect that any victim of this scheme will check the backgrounds connecting these imposters to the Criminal Enterprise operations. Or that they will educate themselves on how to read these signed and notarized instruments. Start out believing almost nothing that is stated until proven otherwise.

The Evolve Bank & Trust HUD-1 and the decoy HUD-1 provided by the State of Tennessee revealed a wealth of information. Within the HUD closing documents, for their role in bullying, threatening, making false claims while presenting forged documentation to me, ERA Chamberwood Realty Group were paid $3,691.00. The secret REO note-owner, Keller Williams-MEM 2, LLC, as both the seller and the buyer paid themselves one of several kick-backs $5,724.00. These

[33] Michelle Brunk was the marketing director at the Florida "Citrus County Dream Team-Keller Williams" To minimize risk David Osborn used those under his leadership to act as signing agents. His powerful position and control over promotion and favor would have been leverage. Brunk signed in various contradictory roles within both the HUD-1 and the decoy HUD-1. She robo-signed blindly as a non-party to paperwork that functioned to perfect forgery and theft. Names like Michelle Brunk and Brian Demma, a.k.a., Michael Demma are tied to Keller Williams Corporate through David Osborn and the now deceased Michael Harlow.

two sums total $9,415.00.[34] Multiplied many times over in many other properties there are lots of creative ways to skim profits.

From the same seller funds, disclosed in one version of a HUD-1 and withheld from another version, Core Logic was paid: $1,908.00. This allocation of funds was described as "REO management fees." Given the known back ground of the Boyd's this should have been an immediate red flag to Evolve Bank & Trust. One must ask, what other loans they made to the Jones, Kelley, Boyd Perpetrator Nexus? The, signs were everywhere that these buyers were flipping a home they already owned. This money, converted from the seller funds at closing, paid for use of the fraud communication tool, the Core Logic Equator work order. As previously described, this internet platform kept everyone on the same page as the illegal seizure of private property was accomplished.

One of the mistakes I made was to read something that didn't make sense and then dismiss it as an innocent error. The accumulation of these errors later revealed various patterns; informing intent. Among the names associated with flips of my property title were James Wooldridge and Charles Stackhouse. You will find that some of the names you read appear to be entirely made up. Others are real people.

Once the fraud narrative is established it has to be born out in the spirit and in context to everything else that follows. This is why, in my case, the Core Logic Equator Work Order claimed to be evicting an unnamed renter in April of 2012. The two names, Charles Stackhouse and James Wooldridge surfaced as living in my home between 2009 and 2012. In perfecting the Evolve Bank & Trust loan (bank fraud) the Boyd's claimed that they also had been living in my home over those same three years. When you stumble upon names associated with your property address, some bleeding over from internet searches, document the names. Do not dismiss as an innocent error. You are building your case from multiple sources that eventually will form a completed puzzle picture.

---

[34] My Exhibit to the District Court No.: 12-D. Decoy HUD-1 "Total Commission" based on price; line-701, line-702, "Settlement Charges" page-2. Keller Williams straw buyers skimming equity from a property they have, per document fraud, owned for their cohort since 2009. There were two HUD-1's each proposing a different set of facts which is a common practice used to defraud the IRS. HUD never investigated. The failure of HUD to investigate how they were used. Failure to restore my home and others to their rightful owner. Failure to take action and reverse these thefts speaks to corruption within our federal institutions at toxic levels of corruption.

Examine every line from any HUD-1 attached to any loan you uncover. I saw that wire fees were paid from the seller funds. The question then becomes what was wired to the bank loan officer that caused this person to rubber stamp the theft? Was this a lazy person ineptly putting together what was needed for the required loan approval, failing to vet the information? Meaning that they need to be fired. Or, is this a loan officer being paid off to perfect bank fraud for the REO Private Investor Groups? Meaning that they need to be prosecuted.

When employees acting within the course of their employment break the law the employer is legally responsible for those actions. This is called: "Respondeat Superior." Keller Williams Corporate is responsible for the actions of David Osborn, Michelle Brunk, Vernon "Wayne" Boyd, Sherry Boyd and others. ERA Chamberwood Realty Group and Bank of America per the Bank of America eviction specialist training and use of approved bank vendors as a highway of operation were responsible for the actions of Loretta Martin and Hattie Brawley. Federal laws and regulations over banks make banks especially liable. Establish these links and consider including any bank that assisted in laundering the chain of title in any law suit you file.

When we hear that a bank loan has been approved, we assume that a rigorous process of oversight, complying with federal laws and regulations has been met. We know from the 2008 housing meltdown leading to a mega financial crisis that wiped out people's pension funds that banks deliberately made loans they knew would never be paid back. Do we really think they didn't know they would get these properties back? They, took possession of private property feeding residential homes to the securities industry. A bank loan is a point of contact between the criminal and the bank where these theft-schemes could be abruptly halted. Evolve Bank & Trust and JP Morgan Chase Bank, in just these two transactions alone, one year apart, netted a combined total of $290,000 to criminals using 65 Pinehurst Drive as collateral. This does not even include illegal funds derived from the short sale flip. Nor, as in other cases, house payments repurposed as assignment of rents. The fraud perfecting bank transactions are cash-heavy and formalize the following lies:

1. "Covenant" to say that the REO Fraudsters are the legal owners of the theft asset and can thus sell or take out a loan using your home as collateral.

2. Conceal that the sellers are, at the same time, buyers of the same residential property. No warning to you that your property title is under assault.
3. Each flip of the property titles is claimed to be an Arm's Length Transaction when everyone knows they are not. Banks that approve these loans are laundering the chain of title. It belies common sense that fraud reports may be filed with the federal government, but there is no warning to resident homeowners trapped within the scripted harassing and bullying chain of theft. The choke-hold over disclosure is an inside job.
4. By their actions all agree the prior vested interest in the property will NOT be reported. To thus let the bank off the hook, no Suspicious Activity Report (SAR) forwarded to bank regulators. Criminals escape prosecution.

Without these lies being stated and accepted as fact, foregoing all due diligence, there would be no loan. No price fixing per phony appraisals. Signed and notarized instruments seal these thefts. Many are false; bearing no resemblance to what is actually taking place. They are wired to and by complicit title companies; some set up by the foreclosure mill attorneys to contain risk and limit exposure. Filing instruments withheld from the public land records are secreted away in the MERS E-Registry System described in Chapter Nineteen. The notarized instruments like the newly minted Deed of Trust, stand on a foundation of fraud. Signed and notarized paper asserting lies are selectively mailed and, or, wired to the County Register of Deeds Office, to banks, to title companies, to and from the complicit title insurance companies. And, if HUD played a part in theft of your home, they close out the REO Private Investor HUD file that I found I could never gain access to. These signed and notarized endorsements, like the Core Logic Equator work order and the phony judge's order of eviction are instrumentality used to perfect theft of American homes.

Banks comply with the law when they report all potential crimes to the federal government. They are not allowed the option to delay these reports. The Office of the Comptroller of the Currency regulates banks. Under the Bank Secrecy Act banks are required to file a Suspicious Activity Report known as an "SAR." These reports assist the federal government in preventing financial crimes, embezzlement, money laundering, drug dealing, and yes, robbery of private property per any version of the Property Flip – Equity Skimming – Title Theft Schemes.

The lenders that make these thefts possible are not reporting these crimes. Just as the previous 2008-2010 financial disaster were the brain child of the financial industry so too, is this one. Just waiting to implode; making them richer and even more powerful.

Lennie Faye Kelley – 20 Lakewood Cove; Ellen Rita Snider, Hilda Cabrera and FREO TN, LLC, a.k.a., Pretium Partners and no SAR Report.

Among the many other properties morphed into a rental to be pooled into a Wall Street Security there is 20 Lakewood Cove, Oakland, TN. So as to confuse data retrieval, sometimes referred to in the train of document fraud as 20 Lakewood Drive. This home was subjected to the same chain of theft by the same Jones, Kelley, Boyd Perpetrator Nexus. I called and wrote the cooperating bank(s) a letter. I sent them proof of how they had been used to flip this home; laundering the chain of title. I alerted them to the HUD fraud used to perfect this particular theft. I named the elderly couple targeted as unlikely to fight back as well as the straw buyer.

This was a theft process that banks are trained to recognize and required by law to report. But when I attempted to provide proof of how certain banks had been used to launder the chain of title to homes acquired by robbery, as an example Patriot Bank became unreasonably defensive. Rather than be put off or intimidated because you are made to feel a fool think of this reaction as yet another red flag. Develop a thick skin and be encouraged. I happen to know that, after reading my letter and looking at the proof I sent, Patriot Bank and Federal Home Loan Bank of Cincinnati did not file the required Suspicious Activity Report (SAR) with the federal government. Nor does it appear that they reported title and identity theft using a hijacked HUD program.

Patriot Bank is part of a holding company; Security Bank of Tennessee, Inc. After making several phone calls I wrote a letter sent with attachments. I found that when I offered information of bank fraud the issue became not what I was reporting, but how did I happen to have this documentation. This was the case here. I was somehow breaking the law, invading privacy because I knew more than, I should have. I believe that the REO Fraudsters sell this scheme to cooperating bank employees as bullet proof. This becomes a piece of the inducement.

Loan officers and others are told, and it is mostly true, that carefully selected targets, will never know what hit them. 20 Lakewood Cove was among those homes flipped by the Jones, Kelley, Boyd Perpetrator Nexus and their cohort of bad actors.[35] Like my home, there was an application for HUD funds, though to a different HUD program.

David Hayes: President and CEO
Security Bank of Tennessee, Inc.
120 North Mill Avenue
Dyersburg, TN 38024

December 26, 2017

Dear Mr. Hayes:

I spoke today with Hal Johnson about a particular loan perfected by your bank that evidences a broader pattern of theft. I am enclosing a copy of Special Warranty Deed No.: 09005052 which references Patriot Bank, Collierville and the first page of Warranty Deed No.: 14002230. Please excuse my notes on these copies. In the interest of protecting your bank from being an instrument of fraud you should examine all the instruments on file connected to this property. Courts,

---

[35] The straw buyer applying for the loan was claimed to be *"a very low – or low – or moderate-income household as defined in the applicable Federal Housing Finance Agency regulations for the AHP in which case the retention period ends..."* The HUD Retention period over my home was three years. Per this loan it was five years. The rehab funds were skimmed as cash to the fraudsters, following pattern, secured by an appraisal that undervalued the property by almost 50%. When income could no longer be skimmed from this theft asset, the home was transferred by Warranty Deed, per Straw Buyer, Hilda Cabrera, to FREO Tennessee, LLC, "a Delaware Limited Liability Company." Actually, a shell company for Pretium Partners, LLC. This is the Jones, Kelley, Boyd Perpetrator Nexus and the financial industry feeding another rental property to the Wall Street Securities Market. Found in the Fayette County Registry of Deeds is Exhibit A, Special Warranty Deed, Instrument No.: 09005052. And, Warranty Deed, Instrument No.: 14002230. The original owners of this home fit the profile of those targeted; both elderly and sick. It is possible that their heirs did not inherit this home as they should have. A Power of Attorney not found is referenced. It appears that Ellen Rita Snider and Joseph Herman Snider bought the home in 2004 from Lynmore Homes, LLC for $134,000. It was acquired as an REO Repossession in 2009 for $77,639. We again see First American Title Insurance Company this time as both the underwriter and the Trustee. Is that legal? Keeping the circle of risk tight, (everyone in bed with everyone else) Mark Rosser is a Manager at First American; Trustee No.: 06010486.

have ruled that these filing instruments carry the weight of a contract. Document Fraud, standard operating procedure for this particular chain of theft, fraud within, makes each null and void.

Rather than quote the entire letter which is perhaps longer than it needed to be here are a few excepts; written in italics below.

As is the case with this loan and other properties in my pattern groupings, fraudulent use of HUD Programs meant to benefit the poor is a feature of the fraud step process used by an Association in Fact Criminal Group. You will note Exhibit A, "Federal Home Loan Bank of Cincinnati / Retention Language for projects that receive 'Welcome Home funds.'"

I described the chain of theft. *As is the case with all my pattern examples, at some point, this property was undervalued ($77,639.) appearing fully collateralized. This invites a loan officer to fail in basic due diligence; failing to verify the transfer, sale, assign history of the property by which the scheme can be recognized.*

And... *The Property Title(s) are "flipped" through various financial transactions. This is laundering the chain of Property Title for the same purposes that drug money is laundered accomplishing the same clandestine goals.*

And... *My intention in calling and speaking with Mr. Johnson was not to incur his anger, but to offer you this information...*

...From what I've read in bank-fraud deterrence and training publications, the scheme I described is not something that should elicit an incredulous response from anyone at Mr. Johnson's level of responsibility. My purpose in calling today was to inform. Hijacking tax dollars meant to benefit the poor has significant, long range socio-economic consequences for this country and is, of course, a significant federal crime. Reporting crime is a requirement of your charter. To adopt the attitude that this could not possibly happen is counter-productive.

...Start to finish this is price fixing; REO Owned properties never offered to the buying public. Evidenced in where, as one of two tracts, these properties (after equity is skimmed) end up, with Pretium Partners, a.k.a., FREO TN, LLC.

... My hope is that your bank will investigate this transaction and report any crime(s) to HUD. Of course, any investigation would have to include the MERS secret assigns of temporary authority amongst fraud collaborators, transfer(s), and sale history; to include missing documents routinely withheld from the Registry of Deeds Office.

... A question for your bank to consider is: What parties/entity actually had control over this property from 2004 up until the point that the Property Title was transferred to Pretium Partners, LLC, a.k.a., FREO TN, LLC? It is very likely that Patriot Bank will appear associated with other flipping transactions. Currying favor at the local level is a necessary feature of the REO fraud partners. What is not in doubt is that Patriot Bank, as connected to this property (pattern example) was used to accomplish "Theft by Deception."

I closed out this letter by writing*: This property represents a bridge-example exposing the broader picture as isolated from one of the pattern groupings.*

And... There are most probably other suspect loans, made for the same criminal purposes I've described. In the interest of the public welfare my hope is that these crime(s) will be, at some point, vigorously investigated by those with the power to deliver legal consequences. Feel free to call me with any questions.

Thank you for your attention to this matter. I hope for the best and feel there is less and less generalized collective tolerance for widespread corruption in our country's institutions and especially the financial industry.

I then signed this letter and copied it to*: Charles Ennis: Patriot Bank.* I did not waste time and effort by sending a copy to Hal Johnson who berated me for sharing with him proof of theft he felt I was not entitled to have. This was the same reaction of Larry Lane Billings regarding his series of phony appraisals reported to and then ignored by HUD and the State of Tennessee. Here is a news flash. Those that grease the chain of theft for a RICO Criminal Enterprise are not the victims. It is not they, that need protection.

Hilda Cabrera was the straw buyer.[36] When her usefulness was up regarding this property address, it appears that Lennie Faye Kelley

---

[36] It appears that Hilda Cabrera was a first or second generation, immigrant from Cuba. Coming from despotic regimes Immigrants are less likely to trust the authorities and report crime. To intimidate a neighbor the Boyd's' parked a vehicle outside her home that bore a sign identifying the vehicle as belonging to the United States Immigration Service. In a panic she went searching for her birth certificate and proof that she was indeed an American citizen. The knock on her door never came, but the scripted anxiety was inflicted to wear her down. The goal of these bullying tactics is to impede rational thought and critical thinking skills. When victims do fight back, they are aggressively attacked and slandered.

moved her to another property in Germantown also flipped per a version of the same fraud scheme. Did Hilda know how she was being used? Did she realize that bank fraud was being committed in her name? Did she know that her identity was used to conceal the true REO Note-Holder identity? I have no idea. In attempting to draw attention to these crimes I had no clout and no ability to investigate except as a private citizen. Too bad, We The People, "basket of deplorables" are not listened to.

I am told that the FBI routinely screen certain categories of cases for ties to actual and possible fields of investigation. After I had a meeting with IRS Agent, Marguerite Howard on January 23, 2015. Having prepared a three-ring binder with some of the key bits of evidence. Allowing her to copy any other document she chose. Not hearing anything, I followed up with a phone call. At which point Ms. Howard informed me that the evidence I had provided had been forwarded to the FBI; *"they are taking over your case."* Hearing this I was elated only to be, not for the first time, cruelly let down.

Though I attempted to communicate with them, the FBI Memphis Field Office would not meet with me. One might think they would be interested in a Criminal Enterprise operating within a national framework. That within its creative adaptations defrauded the Securities and Exchange Commission (SEC[37]) The United States Department of the Treasury. The United States Department of Housing and Urban Development (HUD). The Internal Revenue Service (IRS).

---

[37] The Securities and Exchange Commission (SEC). Using my home as an example. The first illegal appraisal undervalued my home by 134K at the start of the flipping sequence. The investors in the securitized trust managed by fully engaged and complicit Bank of New York Mellon, also lost money. If efforts to sell my own home had not been interfered with (Tortious Interference) by the secret, dual claim of ownership corrupting the chain of title these investors would have fully recouped their investment. When one multiplies my loss by millions so as to artificially feed the securities market with more product, the loss to American investors is staggering to consider. By intent of how the Securities Fraud is structured, the repackaging of the former CWALT securities siphons profits and dilute returns. It additionally means a complete loss to some. The REO fraudsters secretly paid off Bank of New York Mellon at a loss before start of the HAMP Fraud Scheme, August 2011. These transactions take place with no disclosure to homeowners, nor to investors that the predatory exchange of mortgages leads to long term societal harm including homelessness.

Free of my last corrupt attorney my knowledge of these crimes grew over time. I had to shed myself of the double-speak interpretations coming from lawyers fully invested in keeping me confused. Not until I saw the role played by HUD did, I understand that theft of my home began in 2009.

HUD stood as a barrier to the truth. I would ask one question and they would answer another unrelated question; often repeating the fraud narrative coming from their own records. This happened so often that I could no longer give HUD the benefit of the doubt. All Americans want to believe that employees of the federal government care about the public welfare and are invested in the truth. In one very disappointing response from HUD. Which I interpreted as: *Stop bothering us, we are not interested in uncovering fraud within our own agency...*"

On May 29, 2017, losing patience with the near-constant deflection and apparent scripted run-around I wrote back to: Mark E. Malec. U.S. Department of Housing and Urban Development, Office of the Assistant Secretary of Housing; Federal Housing Commissioner, Washington, DC 20410-8000.

Topic: Financial Fraud. "I received your letter. You write: ... *you do not have a Federal Housing Administration Loan (FHA) mortgage, which are the only ones in which HUD can directly intercede on a mortgagor's behalf...*" I replied: "I was not, nor have I ever, asked HUD to intercede on behalf of a mortgage. You entirely miss the point. My home was targeted for theft by an REO Investor group that failed to comply with REO Investor HUD requirements and have repeatedly used HUD to misrepresent targeted properties as distressed and, or, abandoned so they can acquire these homes, per fabricated-forced defaults, with a minimal public records footprint."

Further quoting from this same letter to Mr. Malec. "Per a corrupt HUD-1, that HUD evidently has no interest in seeing, HUD claimed to be the "seller" of my property. White collar criminals devalued my home by $134,000, claimed to have purchased my home, which was fictitiously styled as an abandoned and derelict property from HUD. Are you seriously telling me that your office is not interested in fraud schemes that carry a national footprint of operations misusing the HUD System to steal property; much of it from senior citizens? And that in defense of the HUD mandate, having this knowledge of crime, there is no referral forthcoming for investigation?"

This letter went on to include a step by step excel document that documented the slowly escalating appraisals as red flags before the Property Title could emerge out from under the secrecy of the MERS data base and back into the public land records. I detailed how much money was skimmed per bank loans that helped to launder the chain of title, which in turn established the identity theft claims over my home as a single example of many.

HUD had made a significant contribution to the chokehold over disclosure. They had failed to file the however brief HUD ownership premised on a fraud narrative of an abandoned and derelict property at the Registry of Deeds Office in 2009 where I or other victims could have access. With this information, where a HUD program is hijacked by criminals, targets of these theft scheme would be armed to recognize title theft right out of the gate. While still in their homes. HUD certainly did not feature in every example making its way into my pattern example groupings. They did feature in enough to know that HUD has been used many times over to steal private property that ended up as rentals morphed into a security, bought and sold through investors. Enriching the financial industry. This is as far removed from its original mandate as one can get.

All elite structures, coalesced around wealth and power devolve toward corruption. This is a trend well documented. For this reason alone, guarding the welfare of American citizens that become victims of special interests molding government to work for them and against the welfare of the common good cannot be allowed to continue. HUD demonstrated a callous disregard for me and thus, I must conclude for many other victims whose homes were lost via criminal use of HUD programs. I am pretty convinced that Dr. Ben Carson is not up to the task of draining the swamp at the United States Department of Housing and Urban Development.

The improperly and poorly regulated globalist financial network, having access to corrupt government programs, is not to assist democratic structures, but to bring its citizens and its lands more completely into subjection.

Must we really wonder what is behind the effort to keep a Churchillian president, committed to the United States Constitution off the next ballot. Sending a message to any of that ilk who may come after that any fight is not worth the effort.

CHAPTER SIXTEEN

"I always go in with an open mind... I don't even believe what the police tell me. They always try to tell you a story. I let the evidence speak for itself; otherwise, you can overlook exculpatory evidence."
Dr. Henry C. Lee – September 2010.

Murder by Suicide?

A judge can voluntarily recuse from any case without stating the reason. This option is intended to preserve fairness and does not reflect one way or another upon a judge's reasoning. Three months after Judge Oscar Carr was assigned and then recused himself from the Collins-Maury Case he died a tragic death.[38] According to news reports, seated in his car in the parking lot of the Memphis Country Club he took his life. One of his former legal partners expressed dismay, sharing that Judge Carr was looking forward to a new chapter in his life. As I began to work on an outline for this book, I spoke to his son. I asked if he were at all suspicious about the circumstances surrounding his father's death. He told me that he was not. His father had a history of depression.

It takes energy to run against the grain of those ethical standards one is by law and profession sworn to uphold. Oscar Carr the judge, far more than Oscar Carr the lawyer, would have been required to mask and internally negotiate character-eroding levels of corruption. Perhaps he spoke to his better self, saying something along the lines of, *"enough is enough!"* The Collins-Maury Case posed a question. What kind of judge would he be? Saturated levels of corruption normalized into any culture results in a kind of agnosticized lack of self-checking awareness. Did demands dictated by crony corruptionism imagine they will always run the show? Before he was ever sworn in, this judge was already in the line of fire to experience such pressures.

I've asked myself a lot of questions. Judge Carr's former law group, Glankler Brown, PLLC is connected to FREO Tennessee, LLC, a shell company for Pretium Partners. They are also connected to SunTurst Bank brokerage arm pooling these homes, morphed into rental properties into marketable securities. Clients are connected to

[38] Order of Recusal and Transfer to Part 1; Case No. CH-11-1860 Part 111; Chancery Court of Shelby County, TN; thirteenth judicial district at Memphis.

the Jones, Kelley, Boyd Perpetrator Nexus – REO Investment Group. The REO Investment Group includes Keller Williams – MEM 2, LLC and therefore David Osborn, multiple Keller Williams franchise owner. The Collins-Maury Case names Keller Williams – MEM 2, LLC as a defendant. Additionally, there was the little problem of an attorney from his law practice representing Keller Williams in this corporate espionage, computer hacking case.

It is not much of a leap to consider that when he made the right choice to recuse himself from the Collins-Maury Case he may have incurred anger from those who thought they could leverage the power of his new position. The mafia-like way that ERA Chamberwood Realty Group had been unleashed upon me, mirrored in the same aggressiveness launched against Iowa Realty, represents a pattern of practice. Upon belief that this Criminal Enterprise has pretty much regarded themselves as untouchable. And so far, it seems they are. After the recusal, did some of these people question Judge Carr's willingness to keep their secrets? They had a lot to hide and he had a first-row view of corrupt entanglements scripting illegal outcomes via misuse of position and power.

Judge Carr did espouse the Christian faith. Taking him at his word he is today part of that great cloud of witnesses described in Hebrews chapter twelve.[39] He knows and can see events taking place here on planet earth. Scripture tells us that blood violently shed cries out for justice. This would include those pushed to take their own lives. People drawn into the scope of operations described in this book grew to be fearful of how income or position could be impacted. They opted for passivity seated in the kind of life-stealing cowardice that demoralizes ones' human spirit. These feelings were expressed by two people I spoke to.

Did the over-stretched Memphis Police Department prematurely close a cursory investigation into his death? Did anyone determine if Judge Carr had met anyone earlier at that club? Was the scene staged?

---

[39] *"Therefore, since we are surrounded by such a great cloud of witnesses..." (Hebrews 12: 1a).* Regarding these witnesses, among them loved ones that have died and gone on to heaven before us... *"But you have come to Mount Zion and to the city of the living God, the heavenly Jerusalem, and the myriads of angels, to the general assembly and the church of the first born who are enrolled in heaven, and to God the Judge of all, and to the spirits of righteous men made perfect" (Hebrews 12: 22, 23).*

Did cameras catch other parties in the vicinity? Did anyone bother to look? What did the toxicology report show? Did the autopsy produce evidence of bruising or defensive wounds? Was there finally going to be any investigation by the white-collar crime unit of the FBI or any other federal agency that occupies a field office serving Western Tennessee? I can only say that the lock-down over information raises questions.

While I had no trouble obtaining the police report from Colleyville, Texas documenting the earlier death of Michael Harlow and names of those investigators at the scene, I was blocked from obtaining that same information on Carr's death in Memphis. One cannot understand the death of Judge Oscar Carr unless one views it in context to the RICO Criminal Enterprise that personally and professionally invited so many needed professions into the West Tennessee web of corruption.

The RICO Criminal Enterprise bad actors contrived that I was never heard. They could bury my complaints at the Circuit Executive. It is alarming indeed that displaying no inclination to preserve the appearance of fairness another judge with a conflict of interest was assigned to oversee those complaints that I filed with the Circuit Executive; which may inform why they have never been addressed and why I have never been contacted about them.[40] Judge Carr was another matter entirely. I had no power, no lawyer, no money. I was easily slandered and pushed to the margins. But if Judge Carr decided to report these crimes he could not be so easily dismissed as I and other marginalized victims had been. His every word would have been hung on. As long as he was alive, the proof he offered could not be so easily buried. I believe that Judge Carr was pushed too far toward the inevitable self-hatred and disgust.

The carefully laid fraud narrative has always included out of context disparagement that blame shifts to victims. Attacks on the integrity of victims is built very early on into the fraud narrative corrupting official records. Suicide fits the pattern and is equally convenient. In death Judge Carr could be colored as temporarily mentally ill. Suicide brings

[40] Judge Alice M. Batchelder was assigned to oversee the complaints I filed with the Office of Circuit Executive at the United States Court of Appeals for the sixth circuit. My letter of December 6, 2018 objected to her having control over the direction of these complaints and is published in a prior chapter. There was no reply to this letter leading me to conclude that a year later, still hearing nothing these complaints are going nowhere. If anyone cares: Complaint(s) of Judicial Misconduct No.: 06-18-90103 / 104 / 105 / 106 / 107 / 108.

up the script that invites shutting down any subsequent look into the facts. Why would a man who seemingly had everything to live for take his own life? He must have been mentally ill. End of story, case closed. His son would know if he had been depressed. He said so, and I believed him. But Judge Carr may also have been searching for a way out. He was not mentally ill.

I believe that the death of Judge Carr pierced the arrogant assumptions of those who have enabled, partnered, financially benefited and gotten away with these crimes for far too long. Insulated by the cesspool of peer corruption, conned by con-artists to believe that the "fix" was permanently "in" to the extent that there would never come a day that any entity or person would be held accountable. Nor, that the Criminal Enterprise machine would ever turn on one of their own. Think again!

It is my conviction that those that have enabled and fostered theft of private property interpreted the death of Judge Carr in very different terms other than the spin of suicide. Right or wrong, they saw it as a warning and took it as a threat. If you don't think so, bury your head a little deeper in the sand and binge watch the Sopranos.[41] Read the chapter that addresses the Ann Jones reaction to the death of Michael Harlow. When criminality becomes organized into a pseudo military, cult-like, assaultive structure everything it seeks to control devolves in that same direction. History has shown us that some will go to any length to avoid exposure, prosecution, and imprisonment. To think otherwise is reckless and damaging to the public welfare.

How this toxic Criminal Enterprise does business in West Tennessee is a microcosm of a far wider and broader scope of operations. As these crimes most intimately impact victims, that reach begins at the local level with the profiling of likely victims. The goal is to feed as many homes as possible to the yawning jaws of the securities industry.

Homeowners must not ever have enough information that they can fight back. At the local level justice was stymied by the Sheriff's Office located in the county seat of Somerville, Tennessee. The Sheriff's office refused to take a police report. They had a protected interest not to do so. Their authority was habitually co-opted as a

---

[41] The Sopranos 1999 – 2007, HBO television series. Described by critics as an accurate depiction of mob-life.

tool to accomplish some of these property thefts. Some knew that this authority was being misused by powerfully positioned persons operating within the old-boy-gal politically charged infrastructure of Fayette County. As long as no one drew attention to the utter failure to protect the public welfare no need to internally take steps to dislodge the stranglehold of white-collar crime normalized as acceptable business practice.

When I did research on what properties were served eviction papers by the Sheriff's Office, I found that some of these families had already been forced from their homes at the time of service. Timing is everything. This made the act of serving notice entirely redundant supporting the fraud narrative that a property had been abandoned while foreclosing any opportunity of victims to fight back.

Victims forced from their homes before the eviction papers were served is right out of the con-artist playbook. What these criminals need is a minimal public records footprint. Filling out a form is not the same as complying with the requirements of any policy or legal process. This timing serves up the requirement that there is no opportunity to defend property because targets of this scheme, as we shall see with the Andrews example (Chapter Twenty-Six) were safely gone from the premises before notice of a pending legal action was claimed to be served by the Fayette County Sheriff's Office.

The illegal seizures take place when the REO Fraudsters decide they can no longer safely skim equity from a single property. Or when the harassed and conned homeowners, having no idea with whom they are communicating with at any given time, give up dealing with the harassing build up and stop making house payments. When house payments are no longer flowing into the coffers of the Criminal Enterprise profitability is diminished. Time for the tricky juncture of illegal seizure to play out doing an end run around state laws and those rights accorded every citizen under the United States Constitution.

Delay of serving eviction papers informs a disturbing degree of coordination amongst Fayette County departments. If the homeowner is not gone, as was the case with me, the claim that a Fayette County Judge had ordered my eviction per a forged court order served quite well. Even this charge by me never got the attention of any federal agency. Nor of the Mayor or the State of Tennessee.

The legal principal is that no person or entity can give or sell what they do not own. Title theft and fraud in the conveyance of stolen properties invalidates every subsequent action that claims a vested interest in the property.

Obtaining an assignment through fraudulent means invalidates the assignment. Fraud destroys the validity of everything into which it enters. It vitiates the most solemn contracts, documents, and even judgments. Walker v. Rich, 70 Cal. App. 139 (Cal.App.1926).

I arrived at the Sheriff's Office with proof in hand. Among those carefully organized papers, showing the chain of theft, was the: Tennessee Residential Condition Exemption Notification Form. This form was signed by Keller Williams straw buyers Vernon "Wayne" Boyd and Sherry Boyd on June 21, 2012. The Sheriff's Office refused to read or listen to me explain the significance of this form. They did the same regarding other hard evidence through which the chain of theft could be recognized. Whatever state you happen to live in, if HUD is involved, there will be some version of this form. It was submitted to Evolve Bank & Trust and to HUD.

Having a completed form in hand that appears to comply with federal regulations is not the same as vetting for fraud. When I first spoke to her, in 2013 one of the first questions Marie McDonnell asked was, "did you file a police report?" It is never too late to document crime that has an ongoing scope of operations. In fact, this is your civic duty.

The, selected assertion reads: **"This is a transfer of any property where the owner** [Alexandra Clair] **has not resided on the property at any time within three (3) years prior to the date of the transfer" Line 91.**

If they had been willing to listen to me, I was prepared to use 15 Rachel Cove as another example, showing a Fayette County Sheriff's detective that 15 Rachel Cove and 65 Pinehurst Drive were just the tip of the iceberg. 15 Rachel Cove appears to have started out as a builder buy out scheme purchased by Boyd's daughter, Amy C. Boyd, directly from the builder, T & A Construction. The Rachel Cove property was then flushed through the same Property Flip sequence. Following pattern, on 2/23/2006 it was claimed to be an **REO Resale / "Arm's Length Transaction" acquired from Bank of America...** sold back to the same Jones, Kelley, Boyd Perpetrator Nexus – REO Investment Group. Again, following pattern, it was then transferred by Warranty Deed No.: 14004539, August 2014, from Amy C. Boyd to FREO TN, LLC – shell company for Pretium Partners, LLC. Between 2006 and 2014 equity was skimmed via various fraud schemes.

In paperwork that assisted the theft of my home, "Wayne" Boyd falsely claimed that he had moved to my home from his former residence of 15 Rachel Cove in 2009. The actual family home in 2009 was located in Germantown, Tennessee. He was fostering the impression that he was just an average residential buyer purchasing up and into a better neighborhood. In fact, he was balancing different stories. First the HUD fraud, purchase by an REO institutional investor upon claims that my home was abandoned and in derelict condition. Then the, interim secret flips of the property title taking place during the HUD retention period.

Banks repeatedly bought the legitimacy of these flips failing to: *Follow the chain of title: Ensure that the seller holds the title, understand the property history and watch for pre-existing relationships between buyer and seller.* At the very least they should have verified occupancy and condition separate from what the REO Fraudsters were selling them. As a best practice banks are required to: *Compare elements of the final title policy to the original title commitment and with other closing documents (e.g., HUD-1). Periodically conduct physical verification of the location and condition of selected subject properties and comparables.* Steeped in crony corrupt enablement banks are not: *monitoring systems for appraisers that exhibit suspect practices.*

In keeping with a Ponzi Scheme some of these interim loans are paid off with proceeds from other loans from other properties. It is in the interest of the REO Fraudsters not to overtly defraud banks whose ongoing services they will need. Conspiracy via the Bank Vendor System (Chapter Twenty) is described later in this book. Cooperating loan officers and underwriters ignore document fraud in the signed and notarized endorsements. Some of these interim loans are so obviously premised on document fraud that one must conclude quid pro quo payment for services rendered. Feeding another home to the rental backed, price fixed, securities market destined at some future date to implode from within. Stick with me to see how banks compensate for losses while concealing the crimes they fail to report.

I explained to the Fayette County Sheriff's office, offering them proof, that following pattern and keeping the circle tight, all the same bad actors were attached to flips associated with 15 Rachel Cove and others in one of three pattern example groupings. The Sheriff's Office were aggressively opposed to hearing that 65 Pinehurst Drive, evidenced by many other theft examples, fit a very specific pattern. I had already looked at their records and knew that there was no record that claimed I had been served eviction papers. Why were they so committed not to hear anything about white-collar theft schemes operating under their noses? I explained that Keller Williams straw buyers were squatting on property they did not own. That there was a forged Fayette County Judges order of eviction. That I had been threatened with the prospect of the Sheriff's Office poised to put everything I owned on the street when in fact, no such order existed. If they would continue to allow their authority to be used as a tool to perfect these thefts to thus, maintain the status quo of crony-corruptionism operating as a stranglehold over justice. Well... I had to be gotten rid of as quickly as possible. There could not be any record of my charges.

Just before I left Fayette County, I had an opportunity to vote in the local elections. Though he was re-elected, needless to say, I did not vote for Sheriff Bobby Riles. The trouble in bringing an outsider Sheriff into line, not quite with the program and with an independence of spirit might have posed serious problems counterproductive to the ongoing need for containment and cover-up.

Armed with proof I made two attempts to file a police report. The first on January 29 and the second on February 1, 2018. I was not invited to sit. I was cut off each time I attempted to speak. I was told that I had gotten my information from the internet to say that I did not know what I was talking about. They had been prepped by someone when they made the claim that foreclosure of my home had taken place in 2014 (two years after the illegal seizure). All my prior research into many other stolen properties in Fayette County meant nothing. The hard proof I offered was treated as if tainted with a deadly virus.

Unbelievably I was told that unless the Assistant District Attorney whose office was located in Somerville, Tennessee as the county seat gave her permission, they would not take a police report. When I said that I had over 200 exhibits I could provide copies of. That these exhibits proved that other Fayette County Properties had been targeted for the same chain of theft the tone became accusatory. Once again, I was the criminal. I was in possession of documents that I had no legal right to possess.

In the same vein the HUD Atlanta Office changed the date range of one of my FOIA requests so as to avoid, once again, implicating the REO Fraudsters they had enabled and were actively protecting. They could not deny that this happened. I was therefore told that editing a FOIA request to "make compliance easier," was common practice. Changing the date range so as to sabotage the response I was entitled to was not simple editing of a FOIA request.

I was repeatedly expected to accept illogical excuses. I cannot be the only American citizen having experienced this. More and more of us are going to have to combat corruption wherever we encounter it in our government. "**We the People,"** our treatment, concerns, and pleas for help have become the dispensable problem to be quashed and silenced. At the end of my journal notes of January 29th I wrote: *Pretty sure my civil rights were just violated. I wonder how many people they've driven away who could have informed these crimes."*

I believe that the Sheriff's Office had been coached on how to handle complaints like mine. By whom? The Sheriff's Office were fully on board that property theft or claims that mafia-like tactics were used to achieve illegal seizure of private property in violation of the Fourth Amendment to the United States Constitution could not be found within their records. The solution... no police report.

I was also told that theft of my home as a white-collar crime was a civil matter. The irrational thought process followed. Thus, I could not file a police report. I pointed out that if I were reporting a stolen car and not a stolen house, both requiring proof of title, they would not hesitate to document and investigate. My experience of standing at the counter that day, asking to be heard, the purpose of my visit formally documented did not include physical force and yet I felt ganged up on. The scripted pushback was intended to intimidate.

Before those first two attempts to file a police report I had asked for verification of notice served of pending eviction and court actions regarding a select group of Fayette County properties from one of three research groups. It took two requests and two visits before I got the printout. Thus, I believe they were ready for me. Someone had provided an explanation, a rationale. If such an attempt to forward-date the charade of foreclosure of my home from March 2012 to some nebulous date in 2014 existed **(perhaps the date it was transferred to Pretium Partners, LLC)** I never saw it. What I do know is that the Fayette County Sheriff's Office were adamantly opposed to hearing the truth. They were groomed NOT to listen. They arbitrarily chose NOT to accept my offer of evidence that might have been passed upline to a superior outside the Fayette County conclave. The single goal was to get rid of me as efficiently as possible. Doing so, having achieved the goal, that no record of my visit appeared in any retrievable record.

There have been times when I have been frightened. Other times, as when I was told by a certain attorney that if I did not give up trying to expose these crimes I'd be sued and lose everything I owned. This was intended as a warning, but I was amused. I had already survived the loss of pretty much "everything I owned." I welcomed any opportunity to present my evidence to any judge under any circumstances in any venue that included a jury.

The message was unmistakable. I left feeling intimidated and chastened, but I also planned to return and try again. I do not believe any law-abiding citizen, seeking to report crime, should ever leave a police station feeling afraid. In this internet age every police station is equipped to take a report that documents any claim of white-collar theft. I had a civic duty to report crime and they had a fundamental duty to document my claims and enter those claims into the data system. They were primed and biased to buy hook, line, and sinker that I was the problem. What I had to report, supported by documentation, would have flowed beyond the geographical strictures of Fayette County. Investigated or not the raw information would have been coded into some category under white-collar crime where it could inform reports coming from other Tennessee citizens. That wasn't happening. Not in Fayette County.

I determined that I would return to the Sheriff's Office and try again. But not before I made a trip to ADA Chandlers Office. The claim that I needed her permission before I could file a police report was ludicrous. This was a transparent ploy to get rid of me, but one that other victims might not see through. I wondered how had this same ploy been used against other victims? How did use of her powerful position inform the degree to which at almost every level state government were containing recognition of these crimes? I wondered if ADA Chandler would cooperate with obstruction of justice. Would she also lie to me? This was worth testing.

The ADA's office was located in the courthouse on the square and the justice center was located about two miles toward the outskirts of town. I drove the short distance, parked and walked upstairs. The hallway to her office was dark and the office door was locked. What a surprise.

My second attempt to file a police report went no better. The same rationale was offered. They would not take my report without the permission of ADA Chandler. Why? This was a civil matter, not a criminal matter. To say that keeping the peace, protecting and serving the public welfare did not include white collar-crime. These tactics and infiltration of federal and state services came right out of the Jones, Kelley, Boyd Perpetrator playbook. The clever reasoning served to absolve the Sherriff's Office of responsibility per the well-worn strategy, commonly known as PASSING THE BUCK. Standing my ground. I stated yet again that I was there to file a police report concerning white-collar theft of my home. I stated that it was my duty to report crime and their duty to document crime.

I wrote in my journal notes of February 1, 2018: *Told me* (again) *this was a civil case and I could not file a police report. I asked. If I were reporting a stolen car would they take a police report (*both a house and a car requiring proof of title.) --- *told them there was no foreclosure. Criminals squatting on property they didn't own. Held the door for me to leave.*

Informing how I felt in that moment. Speaking to the tense atmosphere. Treated as if I were the criminal, I concluded my notes of that day writing: *I may get arrested because I'm going back tomorrow. Said I had a right to file a police report and the Sheriff's Office has a duty to investigate crime and take a report.*

The statement that I needed the permission of Assistant District Attorney Chandler was repeated. Maybe, just maybe she would accept the proof that the Sheriff's Office, after a cursory flip through the pages had refused to take possession of. I left the Sheriff's Office and again drove over to her office located on the second floor of the old court house. I believe they were warned that I was coming. I wrote in my journal. *Went back up to the Court House. Spoke with Tracy and asked if Fannon* [Chandler] *– ADA – has clarified for the Sheriff's Office that I did not need her permission to file a police report.*

Her assistant, Tracy, defensively informed me that not only would Ms. Chandler not meet with me. When I attempted to leave the documentation, it was adamantly refused. When I referred to Ms. Chandler by her first name, in elitist condescension Tracy contradicted me, putting me in my place with, "ADA Chandler." The office of David

Kustoff, followed suit. Crony acquiescence and accommodation, was so pervasive that there was no clear line of demarcation between right and wrong, good and evil, a real crime and a non-crime. I was referred to people fully invested in protecting the status quo no matter how corrupt.

In dealing with the Sheriff's Office and with the strategically twice-absent ADA Chandler, her assistant, the mayor, and other Fayette County employees I was reminded of the film Pleasantville.[42] In this film the townspeople, with few exceptions, are stuck in the alternate reality of an artificially created milieu. They are mind-controlled to a level of complacency that disabled common-sense and independent thought. Thinking for oneself, forming reasonable conclusions based on fact and deductive reasoning was a radical and dangerous prospect. Where evil is not recognized it proliferates. Those who felt they had a duty to the image of Fayette County superseding the reality needed to take the blinders off.

As a side note the new justice center is named after a former Fayette County Sheriff who in turn is related to Jeffrey L. Kelley.

As it turned out I did not make a third trip to the Fayette County Sheriff's Office. My brother was out of the country and wanted me to wait until he returned. He thought that if I went back, I needed a witness who could not be coerced to remember things different from how they actually transpired. He told me that if I were arrested, I needed someone to bail me out of jail. I'm not sure what the charges would have been, but his willingness to drive from Iowa to Tennessee was touching. I'd like to think that the shut-down of my right to file a police report would not have gone that far, but Marj, big on common sense and many times proved right in her advice, agreed with my brother. Then coming in with a snow storm and impassable ice-covered country roads I became quite sick. I had to cancel a meeting with the Oakland mayor and the city attorney. I was out of commission for over a week. I took all this as a sign.

I did however report the refusal to take a police report as a violation of my civil rights to the pre-Barr, first term Trump Justice Department. I had already been attempting to bring the HUD fraud and the Vescovo conflicts of interest to their attention to no avail. I followed up with the

---

[42] 1998 Oscar winning film Pleasantville written and directed by Gary Ross.

Justice Department per a phone call on May 8, 2018. I had received a second confirmation letter. Now suddenly there was a different number assigned to my complaint. I asked why. I was told that the first complaint was closed, no explanation as to why. Another had been forwarded to the "EOUSA." I had to look this up. The Executive Office of the United States Attorney.

I've come to believe that telling American citizens that complaints have been referred to some other federal agency means nothing. Because these crimes were ongoing, I felt urgency in having them recognized by those with the authority and the power to protect those who were utterly and completely disenfranchised from being able to defend themselves and their homes. I therefore kept reporting these crimes.

As a ploy to limit exposure I was characterized as a crackpot and a nuisance. I felt the brunt of this attitude in how I was summarily dismissed. I would be a broken record, until someone would take steps to proactively clean up the corruption that had been providing free license for The Bank Theft Delivery System networked to the local REO Investment Groups to operate unimpeded across this country. Complaints by American citizens who have no political clout and therefore, unless there is some political advantage; told that federal agencies are looking into what they have no plans to look twice at, on a deeper level means that bureaucratic injustice as an established and unelected cabal no longer functions for the welfare of ordinary Americans.

It is good to be reminded of what "**We the People**" actually refers to. As I've fought this battle the United States Constitution and Bill of Rights has become very dear to me. The introduction to the United States Constitution reads: ***We the People of the United States, in Order to form a more perfect Union, establish Justice, ensure domestic Tranquility, provide for the common defense, promote the general Welfare, and secure the Blessings of Liberty to ourselves and our Posterity, do ordain and establish this Constitution of the United States of America.***

CHAPTER SEVENTEEN

"Every person remembers some moment in their life when they witnessed some injustice, big or small, and looked away because the consequences of intervening seemed too intimidating. But there's a limit to the amount of incivility, inequality and inhumanity that each individual can tolerate. I crossed that line. And I'm not alone." Edward Snowden

The Collins-Maury Case was filed November 24, 2009. No mention of corporate espionage in the description of the case at this time or anywhere else on the docket at any time whatsoever. Sound familiar?

There was also no mention of David Osborn or Keller Williams Corporate. One would have to intuit that internet hacking as a federal crime was the mystery crux of this case. This informs the chase for leverage by limiting exposure and outcome of data searches. Regarding the case I filed with the Memphis district court the heading "Civil RICO," was replaced with a dishonest, misdirecting label that implied a mere foreclosure dispute.

Concealing topic appropriate descriptions from the public record is common practice allowed by our courts. These accommodations serve to obstruct searches by federal agencies that review certain categories of cases. It also obstructs searches by other victims and plaintiff attorneys. In the Collins-Maury Case no mention of internet hacking served to limit recognition of corporate spying by Keller Williams Realty.

The first set of, *Request For Production of Documents*. The *First Set Of Request For Admissions. First Set of Interrogatories;* Docket No.: CH-09-2341 were not filed until, October 17, 2017. The quite unbelievable eight-year delay was a necessary consequence. It delivered no record that could reflect on the ongoing operations of a RICO Criminal Enterprise. To thus constrain the possibility that any criminal charges by an empowered prosecutor could follow. If the Jones, Kelley, Boyd Perpetrator Nexus and their cohort would continue to operate unimpeded by law enforcement my case and the Collins-Maury case could not be linked. Delay also served the sabotage of due process ending with derailment of the appeal by the corrupt sixth circuit Clerk's Office.

Both Iowa Realty and Collins-Maury experienced an interim period that the recruited Keller Williams broker knew they were leaving, but stayed on as did some of the other realtors secretly recruited to leave with them. This pattern fit precisely how the high-pressure Keller Williams performance scripts function. Regarding Iowa Realty: *"Attempted clandestine efforts of Keller Williams to recruit Iowa Realty agent to act as a 'mole;'"* (read footnote below.) The daughter of the newly recruited Keller Williams broker, heading a new office and breaking ground into the Des Moines market stayed on at the Iowa Realty West Des Moines office.

How newly recruited and then departing brokers and realtors are coached to make the most of that interim period was articulated in a news article explaining why Keller Williams suddenly dropped their law suit against Iowa Realty.[43] Reading: *"Corporate Espionage normal operating procedure. In one of these examples the mother signed on to work for KW* (Keller Williams) *and the daughter continued to work for Iowa Realty at their West Des Moines office feeding computer / company-proprietary information to the mother who passed this information along to the Keller Williams Franchise owner. That's where this law suit was heading and in part informed why KW* (Keller Williams) *dropped the law suit. An uncharacteristic move for them."*

In addition to Collins-Maury I also named the Iowa Realty Case as one of three examples that demonstrated a pattern of prior bad acts with the threat of ongoing criminal activity. RICO criteria require that we establish these connections. When I wrote to the District Court

---

[43] Board sides with Iowa Realty in Keller Williams Dispute. *"Sanders, the board chairwoman, is listed in Iowa Realty's lawsuit. She did not comment on the proposed rule change. The lawsuit accuses Sanders, a former Iowa Realty agent, of breaching a contract by, 'secretly working' for Keller Williams."* (Des Moines Register story.) Also: Real Estate Cat Fight in Des Moines, Iowa: Why Real Estate Brokerages Guard Turf Like Fort Knox. Selected content reads: *"damaging and unwanted recruiting efforts." "Attempted clandestine efforts of Keller Williams to recruit Iowa Realty agent to act as a 'mole.'"* Also: *"Corporate Espionage normal operating procedure. In one of these examples the mother signed on to work for KW and the daughter continued to work for Iowa Realty at their West Des Moines office feeding computer / company-proprietary information to the mother who passed this information along to the Keller Williams Franchise owner. That's where this law suit was heading and in part informed why KW dropped the law suit. An uncharacteristic move for them. Defense included extortion and bullying tactics to force shared commissions."* (candydirt.com/2013/09/04). The actual law suit filings are worth reading. Fifteen Iowa Realty agents left with Sanders to join Keller Williams. *"The number is actually higher. Fifteen is merely the number that stayed with Keller Williams."* The intent was not to compete with the main regional competitor, it was to decimate the main competitor.

objecting to the failure of email delivery, I cited the Collins-Maury Case as evidence of hacking computers by the same people. In the interest of preserving the integrity of a federal court, this needed to be investigated. It wasn't.

Magistrate Judge Vescovo stripped any mention of the Collins-Maury Case from her conclusions to dismiss. She was undermining my RICO claims. She assumed that given the huge imbalance of power no one would bother to read what I actually wrote. And she was right. Farris-Bobango failed to reference any other cases. I sent Doug Collins a copy of the Iowa Realty filings and news clippings because they were so strikingly familiar to what he experienced. There was no reply.

Ross E Webster, Glankler Brown PLLC, Judge Carr's former law practice are noted as: *Attorney's for Defendant Keller Williams Realty.* Judge Carr's former law practice were representing Keller Williams as stated in: ***Complaint For Injunctive Relief and Monetary Damages*; 11/11/2011.**

Protecting criminals via manipulation of the docket and dumbing down a case was in sharp contrast to the Ryan Leonard Case. Farris-Bobango recognized the David Osborn role which was very clear from a conversation I had with Phil Mischke. It was a carefully weighed choice not to name him. How did that omission serve the defense offered to Doug Collins? In fact, it did not. Attorney, Ryan Leonard successfully sued and settled with, among the defendants named, Keller Williams International.

Upon belief that Keller Williams must conceal the pyramid like business model that places undue pressure on brokers to produce and recruit other realtors. Upon belief that what is described as a personality test is actually a means to select high earners willing to skirt and cross lines of legality to accomplish the goals of a RICO Criminal Enterprise.

Screening for merit hijacked in the huge imbalance of power, as a legal framework to silence me, foreclosing all access to due process was the course of action already committed to. It is nearly impossible to believe that the federal District Court did not require a read receipt. Breaches of procedural due process achieved via administrative corruption impacts far more Americans than we might think.

Rusty Allen, owner of TechAnywhere, Inc., reviewed the assertion that the selected emails were delivered to my inbox. Blame shifting to me, the district court asserted that I had not read them. TechAnywhere, Inc.

confirmed: ***I reviewed Ms. Clair's Microsoft Outlook account on 7/22/2016. The four emails in question (from the court) are not present in her email history; nor were they present in trash, or any other included folders that were searched.***

And ... ***I was assisted in this review by James Boomer the owner of Brickwall Security. He and myself have assisted government agencies in the retrieval of forensic data.***

And ... ***if the court wanted to prove the mail was sent to Ms. Clair's email, they could have simply sent it with a read receipt, which in this case was not done.***

The TechAnywhere conclusions became my RICO Exhibit No.: 179. The onus of responsibility to clear up what presented at best as a mistake and at worst as administrative corruption should not have fallen on, me, the pro se litigant to investigate and clarify for the District Court. The Core Logic Equator Internet platform used to commit theft of my home and the failure of email delivery as a pattern of practice could have proved helpful to other cases. The stranglehold of crony corruptionism operating unchecked in West Tennessee smothered such connections from recognition.

The Collins-Maury Case filings tell us a lot about how these people operate. Patterns that are repeated inform intent carried over to other cases. Quotes written in italics below come directly from: Collins-Maury, Inc., d/b/a Prudential Collins-Maury Inc., Realtors vs MEM 2, LLC d/b/a Keller Williams Realty, a/k/a Keller Williams Realty Memphis, East; Docket No.: CH 11-1860; November 10, 2011. When quoting from one of the 2017 filings, filed six years later, that is noted. When comparing the two sets of filings it seems clear that the Keller Williams part of the settlement, letting them off the hook as a back-door accommodation, deflecting from the criminality of their actions, by the time we get to 2017, is now in the bag.

Denise Martin[44] was a former Collins-Maury real estate agent. She joined Keller Williams purchasing her position as broker. I was never

---

[44] My Civil RICO Exhibit No. 64-A provides an on line promotional sales description to the unsuspecting public. It reads: *Welcome to Keller Williams – and the Denise Martin Team. Denise Martin and our team are committed to continually educating ourselves to provide world class service and advice to help our clients and our community to make the best real estate decision. We provide the most innovative tools, ethical advice, positive energy, leadership, communication, marketing and community support.*

able to verify if Denise Martin was related to Loretta Martin either by blood or marriage. I do know that they are connected to Keller Williams Memphis East and therefore to Vernon "Wayne" Boyd.

A person named Lynn Martin is purported to have lived at the location where Michael Harlow died; his death written of further along. But, not sitting in his kitchen at his home as Ann Jones described, but at another location that according to www.rehold.com was occupied by Lynn Martin and Kelvin Martin. Is Lynn Martin an alias for Loretta Martin? Now that I've shared the "Rehold" information watch for Keller Williams Corporate to bully "Rehold" into taking that information off their site. The two locations between the commercial address and the Harlow home is a mere five-minute drive.

Farris-Bobango used the initials PCM to mean: Prudential Collins-Maury. I'm sticking with Collins-Maury; both interchangeable to mean the same. We read: ***Martin and Keller Williams had a substantial interest in recruiting realtors from PCM to join Keller Williams;*** Paragraph No.: 14, page 3.

Under pressure to perform, if she would make maximum profit from the work of others, paying residuals to Keller Williams Corporate, Denise Martin needed to recruit other real estate agents to join her team.

In hacking the Collins-Maury computers Keller Williams was not just in search of leads. Competition for properties fed to the securities market per use of The Bank Theft Delivery System was fierce. My Civil RICO case tied to the Collins-Maury hack informed the broader motives. Presumably HUD would not always extend lack of enforcement of the anti-flipping regulations, which have allowed these crimes to proliferate. One Facebook exchange amongst these bad actors celebrated when it was realized regulations already on the books would be ignored for another year. It is my belief that Keller Williams – MEM 2, LLC were in search of more victims fed to this same chain of theft. One has to wonder what other realty firms have been hacked.

At least thirty-months went by before Doug Collins realized his firm had unwanted electronic company of the spying variety. ***As part of the duties of Ms. Martin, and for which she had the opportunity to be compensated, she recruited realtors for Keller Williams. Denise Martin accessed PCM's email accounts from her office at Keller Williams. She used the Keller Williams IP address to access the PCM email accounts.***

Interrogatory No 6, Response, page 3, from First Set of Interrogatories; October 19, 2017.

It speaks to a proficient skill set that Keller Williams were able to bypass those fire walls without any detection measures alerting to other files, emails, and proprietary information accessed and downloaded. Upon belief, passed along to other David Osborn controlled Keller Williams agencies. I have been told that this is a special skill set of Vernon "Wayne" Boyd.

When defendant Martin left PCM* (Prudential Collins-Maury), on *November 14, 2008, she began working for PCM's competitor, Keller Williams; Page-3, Paragraph No. 11.

The Keller Williams hacker decided to humiliate Collins-Maury leadership. In doing so they exposed that hacking was not a one time, nor a recent event. Discrediting the Collins-Maury leadership might lead to more recruited Keller Williams realtors, but on the other hand, huge risk with no measurable reward implies unchecked impulsivity. This characteristic makes any white-collar criminal all the more dangerous. Fleshed out further along, although I could not recognize it at the time, Jeffrey Kelley and Max Jones handed me a compass and a road map for the momentary pleasure of lording their power over me, as a single victim. The arrogant god-like conviction that they were far smarter than any victim or any federal investigator was tested and affirmed each time they skated on consequences.

I am not a psychologist, but I believe this speaks to the particular compulsive need of the Jones, Kelley, Boyd Perpetrator Nexus to maintain proximity to victims before they even know they have been targeted. In a parody of intimacy there is a thrill to be had in pushing the limits of exposure and escaping recognition.

One only need look at this crime in a superficial context to realize that if Collins-Maury had not fully investigated the source of this breach the designated fall-guy, Marla Pennington, would have been blamed and fired. Was this the plan? There is a back story here and we don't exactly know it.

I do not believe this was the work of a single person. Neither did the company hired to investigate the hack.

***Interrogatory No. 2:* Please identify all experts you have retained and/or intend to call as a witness at trial...** Page-2.
***Response:* PCM identifies Jeff Wilkinson... operations**

manager for Sekweta, a company that provides PCM with information/technology support. He is familiar with information-technology support; he is familiar with information-technology, computer security systems, and the means by which the hacker accessed PCM's computer system. PCM reserves the right to supplement this response as appropriate pursuant to the Tennessee Rules of Civil Procedure. See LogicForce report heretofore produced. Page-2

Why has Denise Martin never been fired by Keller Williams? Why has she never been interviewed by any federal investigator? Corporate espionage is, of course, a federal crime. ***Upon information and belief, Martin had an understanding of the PCM remote webmail system, including initial passwords and login ID's provided to realtors upon joining PCM***. Paragraph No.: 10, page-3.

So how did Keller Williams – MEM 2, LLC get caught?

Denise Martin was a principal broker with Keller Williams – MEM 2, LLC. David Osborn oversaw this Keller Williams franchise and was the registered agent in 2011 when these crimes occurred. Denise Martin left Collins-Maury to join Keller Williams in November 2008. ***PCM revoked any and all authority Martin may have had to access any part of PCM's computers, servers, or webmail when Martin ended her association/employment with PCM.*** Paragraph No. 12, page-3.

The Keller Williams attorneys, including Glankler-Brown, wanted Doug Collins to agree that Denise Martin acted on her own. To say that while at Collins-Maury she was an independent contractor. Denise Martin had her own attorney separate from that of Keller Williams. I hope they truly did put her interests first. Past behavior a good predictor of future behavior, it seems to me she should sever all ties with Keller Williams and verify any conflicts of interest her attorney may have had. Of course, I would like her to report what she knows. In defense of her behavior she could start with inflated promises and the Keller Williams pressure to recklessly produce. She could inform how this opened the door to inciting actions that normalized by indoctrination the criminal behavior. I'd like to know if by blood or marriage she is related to Loretta Martin.

The following quotes come from: **"First Set Of Requests For Admissions," October 10, 2017.** The conspirators were now certain that the fix was in at the district court and the sixth circuit. They were safe to parody the mutually arrived at dismissal in the public record. They felt certain that at this point I would never have an opportunity to stand before a jury of my peers and talk about the Collins-Maury hack as Keller Williams accepted operating procedure spilling over to impact theft of my home and obstruction of district court email delivery.

Request No. 1: ***Admit that Denise Martin was never an "employee" of PCM.***
Response: ***Denied. As a manager at PCM, Denise Martin was an employee of PCM.*** Page-2

Request No. 2.: ***Admit that Denise Martin was, at all relevant times, an independent contractor with PCM.***
Response: ***Denied.*** Page-2

Farris-Bobango would file this suit on behalf of a client they would betray in a failure of morality and ethics. They set in motion the interminable delays that would lead to the agreed upon dismissal favoring their shadow client in the delicate balance of playing both ends against the middle. Hiding the terms of any actual settlement and therefore limiting the public record exposure; sealed by nondisclosure agreements.

Eric Hudson was the Chief Financial Officer (CFO.) Marla Pennington was a real estate agent; not part of the PCM (Collins-Maury) management team.

The following is quoted from the 2011 filing: Paragraph No.: 15 thru 21; page-3 thru page-5.

[15] Around 3:30 p.m. on or about October 7, 2009, PCM's CFO, Eric Hudson, sent a confidential email regarding PCM's business policies to nine managers at PCM, Inc., which included John Stamps.

[16] Marla Pennington, a real estate agent with PCM, was not an original recipient of Eric Hudson's email.

[17] However, around 5:34 p.m. on or about October 7, 2009, Eric Hudson's email was forwarded with certain words and phrases emboldened to all email addresses at PCM from Marla Pennington's email address.

[18] Marla Pennington herself did not forward Eric Hudson's email.

[19] An investigation conducted by an information technology (IT) expert contracted by PCM revealed that the email forwarded from Marla Pennington's email address originated from a computer with the internet protocol address ("IP address") 66.193.59.2, which is Keller William's IP address.

[20] The investigation showed further that Marla Pennington's email account was accessed from the Keller Williams computer via PCM's remote webmail from an embedded link on the Facebook webpage; http://www.facebook.com/denisemartinrealtor.

[21] Upon information and belief, the noted Facebook webpage is Martin's.

Let's stop to consider. Marla Pennington was positioned to be left holding the bag. She was selected to be the source of that email chain meant strictly for senior leadership? Had she ever had any conflicts or successes that offended Sherry Boyd and or, her husband? I pose this question because Sherry Boyd was aggressive about threatening me. She aggressively harassed a particular neighbor merely because she perceived that this person was continuing to communicate with me in the years that followed the illegal seizure of my home. Ann Jones had called Sherry, "dangerous." Marla Pennington was the designated scapegoat. Why? It was not enough that Keller Williams had already read and accessed the proprietary information. They did not need to send that email chain to every Collins-Maury Realtor. They did so for no purpose other than to cause harm inflicting maximum damage with no measurable financial reward. This must have been a moment in time that was extremely difficult, even scary for Marla Pennington.

According to Wikipedia an internet troll is: **"...a person who starts quarrels or upsets people on the internet to distract and sow discord by posting inflammatory and digressive, extraneous, or off-topic messages in an online community with the intent of provoking readers into displaying emotional responses and normalizing tangential discussion, whether for the troll's amusement or a specific gain."**

Interrogatory No.: 10:* *Please state, with particularity, which trade secret you contend this Defendant misappropriated.
Page 5

Response: ***PCM refers Defendant to e-mail sent from Eric Hudson to PCM's managers around 3:30 p.m. on or about October 7, 2009. The e-mail contained business strategy available only to and reviewable only by PCM's managers. Other information contained in the e-mail was available only to PCM employees. Denise Martin also had the PCM commission schedule.***

PCM's IT personnel also discovered that when Eric Hudson's email was originally sent to John Stamps, the email was forwarded to the Gmail account jestampscollinsmaury@gmail.com (the "noted Gmail Account"). Paragraph No.: 22, page-4.

Quoted below from Paragraph No.: 23 thru 25; page-4.

[23] An inspection of John Stamp's PCM email account revealed that a message forwarding utility automatically forwarded all emails sent to John Stamp's PCM account to the noted Gmail account.

[24] John Stamp's did not create the noted Gmail account or know that the message forwarding utility had been applied to his PCM account.

[25] Records subpoenaed from Google reflect that the noted Gmail account was created on June 1, 2009, from the IP address 66.193.59.2, which is Keller William's IP address.

This experience would have been disconcerting for John Stamps. Even when one is innocent it is easy to be tarnished with misplaced blame. Some must have wondered if they could have recognized sooner the hacking operation. With the email forwarding feature installed I'm wondering how many emails never arrived in email inboxes. How much potential business; how many follow-up opportunities were picked up by Keller Williams and lost to Collins-Maury because they never read forwarded and deleted emails.

Collins-Maury was not targeted just because Denise Martin started working for Keller Williams. They were targeted as a competitor per the actions of expert hackers. Upon belief that Collins-Maury cannot be the only company impacted by similar illegal dirty tricks.

Concurring with my belief that Denise Martin was not the only person pilfering whatever useful information could be harvested from the Keller

Williams hack of the Collins-Maury computers the following, reads: **Martin and, or/other employees and/or agents of Keller Williams.**

Upon information and belief, Martin and/or other employees and/or agents of Keller Williams used Martin's knowledge of PCM's initial password to access John Stamp's and Marla Pennington's PCM email accounts, created the noted Gmail account; applied the message forwarding utility to John Stamp's PCM email account; wrongly accessed Eric Hudson's email of October 7, 2009, and forwarded Eric Hudson's email to everyone at PCM through Marla Pennington's PCM email account. Paragraph No.: 27, page-4.

Eric Hudson is the Chief Financial Officer. He prepares the profit and loss statements. It is interesting that the attorneys for Keller Williams asked for these statements which they would have likely compared with earlier copies acquired by fraud via the long and entangled infiltration of the Collins-Maury Computers.

Valuable financial data was on the Eric Hudson computer. Freely accessed over those many months Keller Williams knew everything they needed to know to inflict maximum damage upon a competitor. If they can access the computer of the CFO, they could access any of the leadership team including Doug Collins himself and presumably even his personal email exchanges. It is no stretch to consider that they also interfered with emails from the District Court which they hoped would be the end of me. I believe that intimidation practices in the form of blackmail and extortionist threats are in the play book of these Keller Williams fraudsters.

At all times pertinent hereto, Martin has been employed by and/or served as Principal Broker for Keller Williams, and all of the acts complained of herein occurred while Martin was acting in those capacities, in the course and scope of her employment with Keller Williams, and on information and belief, with knowledge and assistance of Keller Williams. Paragraph No. 33, page-5.

Documented descriptions of corporate hacking and other crimes described in the November 11, 2011 filing were written and submitted by Farris-Bobango attorneys, Robert F. Miller and Malcolm B. Futhey 111; Docket No.: CH 11-1860. The Core Logic Equator work order was faxed by ERA Chamberwood Realty Group to Malcolm Futhey four months later in March 2012. Thus, everything Farris-Bobango had written and charged within this Collins-Maury filing were fresh in everyone's mind. This was an important case worth lots of money. At some point Malcolm Futhey left his employ at Farris-Bobango. Farris-Bobango cited a "conflict of interest" and summarily dumped me as a client. They failed to make a, referral to any other attorney. Doing so they would have had to disclose to any new attorney that the Fayette County Judge's "order of eviction" did not exist. That there was no foreclosure. And just for starters, that my home was owned and being flipped by the same Farris-Bobango defendants named in the Collins-Maury Case that they themselves had filed against Keller Williams Memphis East. Privilege does not matter where it is already broken and the goal is to further the interests of a RICO Criminal Enterprise.

It was a year after Judge Carr's tragic death, in the same month, that I filed the Civil RICO Case with the Federal District Court on April 20, 2016. I am told that Judge Carr had socialized with Magistrate Judge Vescovo and Judge Lipman. Did his death strike them as alarming for reasons other than the natural compassion one would feel for an acquaintance, a colleague, or a friend?

On the face of it, it may seem coincidental that another person more intimately tied to the Jones, Kelley, Boyd Perpetrator Nexus also died by gunshot wound. I had interacted with Oscar Carr, met with and spoken to him, but did not know him as a friend or a colleague. At the time he was not yet a judge. On the other hand, I never met Michael Harlow who at some point had also threatened, or put in danger, the ongoing viability of these same fraud schemes. Though my information about him came second hand, it came from an insider intimately tied to these property crimes.

The untimely death of Michael Harlow was by no means the sole topic of my conversations and interactions with Ann Jones. It was no coincidence that she was in my life, building the pretense of a neighborly friendship, from the start of the Property Flip sequence in 2009 up to the charade of the phony foreclosure and illegal seizure of my home in 2012. When Michael Harlow died, I was merely a convenient good listener and Ann needed someone to talk to. She wasn't looking for feedback, but an outlet; a safe way to hear her own thoughts as she vented alarmist feelings of ambivalence and fear.

Recognition of these property theft schemes is vigilantly impeded by a complete lack of legally required disclosure to homeowners. This is proven in the uninterrupted success of these schemes. It was fortunate for me that Ann Jones, wife to Max Jones, the REO Private Investor Group's accountant was assigned to spy on me. Ann considered me safe. Experience had shown her that I would follow the con-artist delivered script and never learn enough that I could connect anything she told me with the Property Flip – Equity Skimming – Title Theft of my home. Nor would I recognize that the illegal seizure of my home to which she and her husband were intimately involved was premised on document fraud. As it turned out, much of what she told me later proved invaluable to my investigation.

Ann's circle of acquaintance was limited to those that were connected to the Jones, Kelley, Boyd Perpetrator Nexus inner circle and the legalistic church she attended. Cult-like groups require conformity, secrecy, and concealment. In talking with me beyond the strictures of what was allowed Ann let me hear the name, Michael Harlow not once, but many times over. I thus, became the recipient of confidences that in 2010 I would not begin to recognize as significant until four-years later.

At the time of these confidences in 2010 I was the totally deceived mark who had not yet begun to throw up roadblocks. I had not yet listed my home for sale.[45] That listing presented a monumental threat since as a matter of public record it contradicted the phony claims of REO Ownership, valuation, condition, and occupancy of 65 Pinehurst Drive. Though I was thwarted from doing so I was not yet making plans to file Chapter 13 asking a bankruptcy judge to protect the equity; allowing

[45] Crye-Leike, Inc., Realtors; MLS No.: 3223195. This was a six-month listing 5/5/2011 thru 11/5/2011. Sale price in the depressed market of 2011, 234k. Photographs posted on line overtly contradicted REO claims of a derelict and abandoned property needing to be rehabbed at the expense of 100k per the JP Morgan Chase Bank Loan also granted in May. May 16, 2011 but forward-dated in the fraud riddled Evolve Bank & Trust HUD-1 by one year. Bank Fraud put 100k of pure profit into the pockets of the RICO Criminal Network including: Keller Williams Realty / Jones, Kelley, Boyd Perpetrator Nexus – REO Investment Group. Multiply that neat trick (skimming equity) thousands upon thousands of times and you have the greed fueled motive and intent for undervaluing these homes at the start of the Property Flip Sequence since any complicit loan officer can see that the property is fully collateralized by the theft asset. You have an explanation for the risks taken as the property title is then illegally laundered through phony and secret sales, assigns, and transfers amongst the same bad actors with the illegal seesawing value matched to whatever fraud narrative is initiating the current flip.

me to sell my own home. At this early juncture in 2010 Ann's almost involuntary need to talk overcame any wiser inclination to keep silent.

I came to the opinion that Ann believed Michael Harlow had been murdered. When in 2015, I read about the death of Judge Oscar Carr, I had a far more fleshed out picture of how dangerous and toxic these people were. My first thought was that he too, had been murdered. I certainly do believe that at minimum, if such a word can be used in conjunction with such a tragedy, he was driven to take his own life. Murder by hand or proxy interrupts the destiny of a soul. Even if no one else was paying attention as far as I was concerned blood had been wrongly shed on the altar, of protecting the ongoing criminal reach of very dangerous individuals.

Judge Oscar Carr and Michael Harlow were two very different men, but they had far more in common than the instrument of their death. Posthumously and via what Ann confided, I formed a picture of Michael Harlow. His death represented a significant unsettled loss. Not until I read his name in several trust documents filed in Shelby County and Fayette County did I make any connection to the RICO Criminal Enterprise operations.[46] He had been a trusted executive in the successful execution of these crimes.

Ann was not normally careless. In all interactions that I had occasion to observe, between herself and others, what I wrongly interpreted as a kind of shyness was, with very good reason, the need to be guarded.

During this same time period, 2009 and 2010, Ann and her cohort had already acquired control of my mortgage. The well-worn con-artist trap that establishes commonalities between the mark and the white-collar criminal were expertly and coldly built on the exploitive pretense of friendship. If I had asked Ann if she thought Michael Harlow's death was murder her confidences would have come to an abrupt end. Today I believe that God wanted her to talk. He wanted me to listen

---

[46] The Lennie Faye Kelley Living Trust(s); The Charles L. Kelley, Sr. Living Trust(s). To say that if Lennie Faye Kelley or Charles Kelley, Sr. are unable to serve... ***"Michael W. Harlow shall serve as successor Co-Trustees."*** At minimum, three trusts were used to park stolen property until it was safe for them to emerge back into the public land records. The trusts function in part, in the same capacity as MERS to conceal Note-Owner identity. Filed with the District Court as Exhibit No.: 8 and Exhibits No. 9 and 9-A. There are very likely other Trust vehicles that I never found, used to accept and disperse income; filed also in Florida, Arizona, and Texas.

and remember. Upon belief that with the death of Michael Harlow Ann experienced the fear of time running out. Of an out of control Criminal Enterprise taking greater and greater risks. When faced with rebellion within the ranks she suspected that these people had resorted to murder. It was after this too that Ann began to talk about moving out of the Fair Oaks neighborhood.

I wish I could have talked with Memphis detective(s) that had been present at the scene of Judge Carr's death. I would have asked questions that I believe, especially in death he deserves to have raised. Did anything raise the hackles of suspicion? Was there ever a time that someone attempted to abort the investigation upon expression of consideration for a grieving family? Or to preserve the legacy of a so called upstanding Memphis judge? Or in crony consideration of his former law firm?

After refusing me a copy of the police report I met with two Memphis police detections. Unlike the Fayette County Sheriff's office, they brought me into a room, talked with me, and took possession of what I offered them. Though they told me they were not authorized to release the police report. Why not? During that interview I was told that the investigating Memphis detective was retired and for some reason unreachable. I was told that the three-month interim period between Judge Carr's decision to immediately recuse himself from the Collins-Maury case on January 12, 2015 and his untimely and tragic death on April 6, 2015 indicated "no cause and effect."

This absurd statement challenges common-sense. Three months is just enough time for paranoid people with a lot to hide to construe or overthink and, or, reading too much into a decision that challenged the reach of their influence and authority. This RICO Criminal Enterprise has not operationally survived as long as it has by leaving much to chance.

CHAPTER EIGHTEEN

"I know for certain, that before I was humbled, I was a stone lying in deep mire. ...I do not know for whom I should lament more; for those who were killed, or for those who were physically enslaved or those, instead, that the Devil himself has ensnared so terribly."
The Confession of Saint Patrick. Early 400AD

Among the pieces of information, you need is that approximate date that the complicit bank allowed the fraudsters to assume your mortgage. That event can be informed by the date that the county in which you live allowed a RICO Criminal Enterprise to pay your property taxes with dirty money. Doing so with no effective fraud detection practices in place. No warning that your property title is under possible attack. Ask yourself, who does it serve not to close these theft perfecting loopholes?

There is a chicken or the egg question that for far too long occupied my thoughts. At some point I decided it was a waste of my emotional energy to feel I had to have every answer. There were too many possible avenues of investigation. The immediate group that targeted me branched out to include satellite partners. Each group were connected by their methods and in the services, they relied upon. Some properties piqued my interest more than others. There were many times that I wished I had the funds to hire a skilled private investigator. I had to limit my investigation to what branched out from 65 Pinehurst Drive.

I've always wanted to know, where did my ordeal begin? With Bank of America or with the Jones, Kelley, Boyd REO Investment Group of local operatives? Did it start over a weekly canasta game where a person who routinely fed leads to the local group of bad actors, for a commission, and another whose son was working with this group report that Brett had left me; had relapsed into drugs and alcohol.

Loss and situational turmoil, was the precursor to many of the properties fed to The Bank Theft Delivery System. These people were tracking obituaries, rehabilitation and nursing home admissions.[47] Any temporary absence from the home attracted the razor-like predatory instincts of these white-collar criminals.

---

[47] This is not outside the pale to consider. In his book: CULTS INSIDE OUT, Rick Allen Ross describes how his grandmothers nursing home was targeted by a group that implanted a network of operatives into that facility.

The question is, did Bank of America say to their partner co-conspirator REO Investors, "here is a property we want fed to the securities market? Western Tennessee is your assigned region. Go to work." Or far more likely. Did these boots on the ground REO Investor Groups jumpstart the very successful and well-worn chain of theft by profiling victims and then targeting those selected mortgages to The Bank Theft Delivery System.

In every case I looked at, including those that appeared to have started out as a Builder-Buy-Out Scheme the same Property Flip sequence takes place. Builder-Buy-Out Schemes are a twist on the same con-operation. Builder-Buy-Out Schemes occur when contractors cannot sell homes fast enough to pay off short-term construction loans. These homes are illegally moved off the books when loan applications are fabricated to straw buyers. The plan is for these homes to go into default. REO Investors network with builders and straw buyers with the end-goal of feeding these properties for the eventual slide into the securities market.

Some of the homes in my pattern example groupings appeared to have started out as Builder-Buy-Out Schemes with the default as set up for the first lucrative home improvement loans. This included 430 Ridgecrest Drive, Arlington, TN. This property was flipped amongst the REO conspirators, to my count, fifteen times. It started where it ended with Jeffrey L. Kelley and Ronald Lee Gintz. Bank theft at minimum: 500k.

The mere suspicion of bank fraud requires that a Suspicious Activity Report (SAR) be filed. A bank complies with the law when they report suspected fraud. Suspicion is the threshold. Proof of fraud is not a requirement.

If the fraudsters cannot posture that they have a vested financial interest in these homes they cannot take out interim loans skimming equity. The requisite paperwork must be presented to loan officers. A piece of this paperwork is a receipt from the county trustee; stamped taxes "paid in full." Forced placed insurance will usually follow. Why should the fraudsters pay for what they can extort from their victims?

It is not that the insurance and the taxes are not paid. It is that they are no longer paid out of escrow funds, by the original lender on behalf of the homeowner. That account is closed so as to distance the bank from having off-loaded your mortgage to criminals. An escrow receipt is used as another identity theft document. There are no fraud detection mechanisms in place at the county or state level that track the source of these funds requiring affirmation that the money is clean. Paid in full escrow receipts are common fraud tools submitted to banks as part of a loan package.

Fraudsters paying taxes on property they do not own feed the travesty centered on broken chain of title. There is no excuse for this. At least in Fayette County it is approximately two dozen steps to cross the hallway and walk through the door of the Registry of Deeds Office to verify a few facts. Who does this serve? An arm of county government helps to establish the claim of having a vested interest, and therefore fictitious authority, over stolen property. The property tax receipt will be built on as an important piece of what will grow into layers of document fraud. Much of it dumped into the land fill of the Registry of Deeds Office by foreclosure mill attorneys.

Property taxes accepted by the county and marked paid in full on behalf of the criminal identity is among the first steps in establishing the Criminal Enterprise proxy ownership. Counties that accept money in reckless disregard of the source of those funds are committing a financial crime. They are working against the welfare and rightful ownership claims of the homeowner.

In most cases the Deed of Trust is a legally binding contract that hold the bank responsible to pay the taxes out of the escrow funds. Once, the original lender under the Deed of Trust has allowed the REO Fraudsters groups to assume the mortgage they pay the taxes. This allows the REO Fraudsters to divert escrow funds. Property taxes are no longer paid to the county on behalf of the actual homeowner under the terms of the original Deed of Trust. They are paid in the name of the REO Fraudsters and, or, a proxy that is in effect a shell company. The goal is to extinguish the property owner rights under a mountain of document fraud. This is among the first steps.

After a breathing period that tell the REO Fraudsters that no one is paying attention equity is skimmed. Authority to do so is premised in part on the claim of taxes paid by the theft entity. Not only do targets of this theft scheme not know that a predatory criminal enterprise whose sole intent is theft has stepped in to pay the property taxes, but homeowners are further disenfranchised because the county blindly accept this dirty money.

Most bureaucratic structures are resistant to change. It is long past time that with fresh eyes and clean hands plans are implemented whereby, in an electronic age, county government will function proactively to protect property rights.[48] We are seeing today that some systems are so corrupt that current leadership needs to be voted out of office.

Under the terms of the majority of mortgage loans taxes and insurance are factored into the house payments. The money goes into an Escrow Account managed by the bank or an agent of the bank. When taxes and insurance are due the bank releases these funds. Any history of the bank claiming unpaid taxes or forced placed insurance or an arbitrary rise in your house payment and, or, unexplained ancillary fees is a screaming in your face red flag that should send you running to the county trustee with some hard questions and demands that they investigate who has been paying the property taxes on behalf of what entity. If they give you a superficial explanation tell them you suspect title theft and demand that they launch an investigation. Using escrow funds as a tool to establish a phony claim of ownership or authority over a home targeted for theft is, just for starters, a financial crime(s).

Homeowners are slandered within the bank records as delinquent on their taxes long before this surfaces as an issue of dispute. Not knowing what is going on behind the scenes victims are disenfranchised from the ability to fight back. They are positioned not to recognize the changes because in all prior years and into the expected future, per contractual agreement, taxes are most often paid by the bank, on behalf of the homeowner, from the bank-controlled escrow funds.

The fraud narrative says that taxes are not paid. The county records show property taxes as paid. **This is a distinction with a huge difference that any victim of these theft schemes will need**

[48] Seattle invited Marie McDonnell Property Analytics in to do an audit of their property recordation system. Shocked by what she reported they then decided they would not publish the report paid for with tax dollars. Fortunately, citizens aware of and, or, defrauded by these schemes did not allow the cover-up. Any claim that Fayette County has had an audit to say that all is in full compliance with the law would be a snow job. This would be akin to the oncology doctor finding widespread evidence of cancer infiltrating every vital organ except the brain, giving that limited diagnosis, and sending the victim on their way to mislead that every other part of the body is healthy. Corruption is so great that Fayette County is not capable of policing itself. Upon belief that cover up and containment would lead to more abuse of the public trust.

to track back. To do this the proactive cooperation of a municipality interested in ethics, integrity, and guarding against administrative corruption to commit crimes must be mutually committed to. The question is who paid the taxes? The first superficial answer will be wrong. The homeowner is delinquent in the bank records, but the secret private investor Note-Holder/Note-Owner is not because the county has documented the taxes, due on a home just acquired by fraud, as paid in full. We do NOT hire and elect officials to assist theft of private property. Further along we will look at another Memphis case (REO Holdings) with a slightly different twist on the same scam.

Regarding my home and others in my research groups Fayette County performed no due diligence as to the source, intent, and circumstances by which dirty money was accepted from a RICO Criminal Enterprise. It matters in this country under the rule of law that the source of money is NOT derived from mafia-like criminal activity. Let that sink in. Just as bank employees are required to report suspected fraud county employees should be equipped and trained to do the same. The overwhelming success of these crimes is proof that criminal theft of private property is fully assisted by antiquated laws and outdated practices that in our electronic age is systemically reckless and inherently lazy.

Proof that the REO Investor Group(s) and, or, the shell company have paid the taxes and that this money was accepted communicates to future lenders the fiction that there was a fraud free exchange of funds. The Fayette County stamp, *taxes paid in full*, means that fictitious authority is granted over to the fraudsters as the source of these funds. Verification of property taxes paid in full will become part of any future loan package using stolen property as collateral, skimming equity as the property flip sequence gets underway. The REO theft-agents allowed to pay the taxes absent all due diligence as to the source and intent of those funds serve to distance the original lender from the part, they have played in off-loading the mortgage to criminals with no disclosure to homeowners.

Administrative Corruption is the tool that obstructs access to information of vital importance to homeowners. It requires cooperation from the bureaucratic system having forgotten that their first priority is to the public welfare. Such failures are violations of the fiduciary responsibility owed to tax payers. Not to banks and their partners in crime, but to property owners.

Lack of disclosure at multiple levels is a necessary piece of the Bank Theft Delivery System assault on private property rights in America. Homeowners are deliberately and methodically positioned not to know a problem exists until the groundwork has been laid. The point at which counties accept money from criminals and assign those funds to payment of property taxes, offering up an important piece of the identity fraud is a lost opportunity that these theft-schemes can be stopped in their tracks.

Payment of property taxes by an entity whose sole intent is theft predates the filing of an, *Assignment of Deed of Trust*, at the Registry of Deeds Office. We discuss the *Assignment of the Deed of Trust* functioning as the Breeder Document in a later chapter. I would propose that the "Property Tax Receipt(s)" sent from the county trustee on county letterhead back to the RICO Criminal Enterprise qualifies as an even earlier Breeder Document. Both are used to retitle a property in the name of white-collar criminals. Both are used to commit bank fraud. The Property Tax Receipt plays an important role in jump starting Title Theft. Thus, the county property tax receipt is an even earlier, though no less important, Breeder Document.

When the County Trustee accepts this dirty-money they are in effect stripping authority under the original Deed of Trust from the homeowner. As happens victims are never, thereafter able to reverse the fraud narrative. They are actively prevented from challenging the authority of an REO Private Investor Group whose identity rarely, if ever, seeps into the public record. A substantial down payment meant that the value of my home exceeded the loan amount. Therefore, I paid my own taxes and insurance. Only because of this, upon going up to pay my property taxes in 2009, I was told by a county employee that they had already been paid. Very little information was given to me. No help was offered despite the fact that this represented a significant red flag denoting the title theft feature of the fraud scheme that was now being validated via the passive assistance of county government. An appropriate fraud detection process should have been generated.

It is likely that the Jones, Kelley, Boyd Perpetrator Nexus did not know that I paid my own taxes. They expected this layer of the title theft validation to slip by unrecognized. And most often it does. They immediately set to work on damage control. And as usual they did so via links with the corrupt Memphis legal system.

I later found that the 2009 taxes were paid by the REO Investment Group through a third-party entity that I traced to California. This third party turned out to be an arm of Bank of America tied to REO ID No.: 00906148, who per the HUD fraud were required to pay the taxes. In a letter dated July 13, 2009 I asked for the identity of the person or entity that paid my taxes. In the minutia of mounting coincidence, I noted that letter copied to Oscar Carr, at Glankler-Brown.

Oscar Carr had represented me in another matter when my car was rear-ended at a red light. After Judge Vescovo complained that I had not filed exhibits this letter was entered as Exhibit No.: 65-A. This to expose the very common property tax piece of the fraud scheme and its subsequent cover-up by Bank of America and the REO Fraudsters. As with all other evidence that reflected upon Memphis attorneys greasing the chain of theft, it was ignored by Magistrate Judge Vescovo.

Intent to commit a crime is not a factor in charging those whose actions contribute to accomplishing the goals of a RICO Criminal Enterprise. A claim of ignorance may mitigate sentencing, but under RICO it does not let any party off the hook. Certain departments within government act as fiduciary for the tax payers. Accepting funds to accomplish a task, where the source of those funds is derived from the activities of a RICO Criminal Enterprise is, if you're keeping track, another RICO Predicate Act. Predicate means foundation. This makes Fayette County, TN where my home and most of the other homes featured in the pattern examples that I developed fully complicit in perfecting these crimes. Too bad I was denied due process, silenced at every turn.

The implications of an unknown entity stepping in to pay taxes is huge. When the new and secret REO Investor pay taxes on a Note they have secretly just acquired control over this allows the complicit bank to add a layer of confirmation over the fraud narrative already corrupting their records. The county trustee that accepts the payments contribute to building authority that does not exist. Documentation from the County Trustee that asserts the taxes stamped, "paid in full," are submitted to lenders as the property title is flipped; skimming equity from the theft asset. Get the picture? It takes a village to perfect these crimes. A lot of people have decided and, or, are manipulated not to perform their jobs. Described in an FFIEC White Paper.[49] **Fraud Narrative: "Bank files contain notices**

[49] Federal Financial Institutions Examination Council (FFIEC).

that the property taxes are delinquent under the terms;" *(under the terms of the original mortgage).* It isn't that they are not paid. They are just paid by white collar criminals. Lies come from multiple sources and coalesce to disenfranchise the property rights of ordinary Americans.

The engineered claim of delinquent taxes shifts blame, from the bank and REO Investors to the homeowner. One has to dig past the proxy shell company or that partner that is claiming to manage the portfolio of at risk mortgages/properties before getting to the criminal identity that will be posturing to the IRS at year end that they are the taxpayer of record; submitting write-offs as expenses over properties they do not actually own.

It should be the job of county trustee's offices to close loopholes centered on the very common tax feature of these fraud schemes. They will need full access to the MERS E-Registry System (Chapter Nineteen) at least until MERS is called a shell company whose sole purpose is to obstruct justice; placing an electronic fence around disclosure. Suspicion of fraud, not proof of fraud, the threshold that generates a report to homeowners and to the investigative arms of state and federal government.

Bank of America tracked the theft trajectory of 65 Pinehurst Drive. Their doing so is documented among my exhibits. They did the same with all other properties fed to the Bank Theft Delivery System. They had an end-goal. A vested financial interest in the outcome. Among the exhibits I filed with the District Court were depositions from former Bank of America employees.[50] One of these depositions came from Ms. Theresa Terrelonge.[51] Paragraph-16 of her deposition

---

[50] I quoted from some of the following depositions (Bank of America brave former employees) in my Civil RICO Case; all context ignored by Judge Vescovo. Obtain copies from the United States District Court, Massachusetts. Bank of America Contract Litigation. William E. Wilson, Jr., Theresa Terrelonge, Steven Cupples, Recorda Simon, Erika Brown, Bert Sheets. My Exhibit Numbers 36 thru 44. Though this refers to HAMP and HAMP is no longer a federal program administered by Treasury, as quoted by the judge "independent of HAMP" the illegal theft practices are still being utilized to perfect the schemes described in this book.

[51] Filed in the United States District Court for the District of Massachusetts. Re: Bank of America HAMP Contract Litigation. Honorable Rya W. Zobel. MDL No.: 2193. Case No.: 1:10-md-02193; filed 06/07/2013; page 2 of 8. "Under RICO past illegal acts support the current claims. They show that the illegal past conduct has projected into the future, continues as a practice independent of HAMP. That these practices are ongoing. Repetition of these practices are harming other victims up to today. The illegal practices have facilitated ongoing theft of private property, did not end, but has continued indefinitely and will do so until stopped."

reads: ***I witnessed employees and managers change and falsify information in the system of records, and remove documents from homeowners' files to make the account appear ineligible for a loan modification...***

The practice that Ms. Terrelonge describes did not end with HAMP. As a practice it had an ongoing application for other schemes adding weight to the Civil and Criminal RICO criteria that there is an ongoing threat to the public welfare. HAMP Fraud is no longer a conduit of operation. It has been replaced by The Bank Theft Delivery System achieving the same goals described in this book.

Eventually I got around to asking. Where did the tax money go that I reimbursed Bank of America in 2009? As they say, follow the money. If the wall of deception would hold up over the following two years, Bank of America could not disclose that they were no longer the Note-Owner, Note-Holder, or the Servicer of my loan. Since the Bank of America record showed my home as abandoned and sold to REO Private Investors why would I be paying taxes? As a dereliction of duty no one looked into the forged Certificate of Abandonment. These are not grab and run crimes. The success of these theft schemes, required that I and all other targets, remain oblivious. Unfixable problems, confusing excuses, failed promises as the harassment kicks in is set up for the phony foreclosure, followed by illegal seizure of the theft asset. Start tracking all the many instances where you were lied to.

The funds I sent to Bank of America to reimburse taxes in 2009 may have passed through Bank of America into the pockets of the REO secret Note-Holders. Or funneled forward to Bank of New York Mellon. Or failing to tell me that they no longer owned or serviced my mortgage Bank of America just kept the, money.

The amount showed up as a miscellaneous sum on a Bank of America statement. I entered this statement as an exhibit in my Civil RICO Case. Like all other evidence that did not comport with the predetermined intent to deny due process at the *screening for merit* blockade, it was ignored by Magistrate Judge Vescovo.

Look for the same pattern of forward dating assumption of your mortgage. In my case I had to be obstructed from recognizing the year-2009 tied to the predatory private investor taking over the mortgage, pooling my home into a HUD program, and paying my property taxes. The date of record had to move forward three years to 2012. In your case, because the HUD fraud may not have been a feature, this interim period between assumption of the mortgage and the foreclosure fiction is shorter. The interim period is lucrative. The secret REO Note Holders will extend this period between secret assumption of the mortgage[52] and the charade of foreclosure as long as house payments can be laundered or some other financial benefit exists.

The date that REO Fraudsters first stepped in to pay your property taxes can be aligned with when they assumed your mortgage; taking control as the new secret Note-Holder for the sole purpose of driving your mortgage into default. You need to generally fix this date. The county trustee records are a back door way to fix your time line. Was the money wired? (wire fraud). Was a check mailed? (mail fraud.) As they say, follow the money. Tracking the money will take you from the county trustee to the comptroller for the state in which you live.

The practice of forward dating the assumption-date serves to distance the complicit bank from the theft. It serves to hide the fact that the actual theft took place long before the illegal seizure. This means that foreclosure is an entirely redundant and fictitious event existing only to deceive homeowners, heirs, courts, and judges.

The county that accepted these funds should be fully on board helping you while at the same time demanding answers that undergirds commitment to protect the public welfare. Obtain an acknowledgment that your county officials will fully share information, holding nothing back. Some will want to protect the stranglehold of crony corruptionism. Resistant to accountability and change they are impeding justice and revealing their true colors. Take your complaints public. Be a broken record and don't give up.

It goes without saying that mortgages should be off-limits as an investment vehicle. Bank of New York Mellon, as trustee, have been managing the large group of securitized mortgages acquired by Bank of

---

[52] "A **deed of trust** to secure **assumption** is a document that creates a second lien on a piece of property, explains Legalzoom." The second lien gives the secret REO Note Holders the right to take back the property (foreclose) upon claim that the phony loan, never disclosed to the homeowner, is not paid. The REO Fraudsters I looked at used phony loans and fictitious liens to establish their authority over homes they did not own. Assuming the mortgages they then drove those mortgages into default using the Bank Theft Delivery highway of operation described in this book.

America when Countywide failed. They play an important role in these thefts. It is not just homeowners that are defrauded. The investors in the CWALT Trust(s) have been considered collateral damage. The former Countrywide securitized mortgages dwindled as the original homeowners died off or properties were sold. The goal to retain profits led to the growth of mortgage backed securities as price fixed rental properties. Buying and selling via the same unchecked, and for all intents and purposes, unregulated securities structure.

The investors in the CWALT Trusts should be filing more law suits because the contrived losses they experienced were used to build The Bank Theft Delivery System that we see today.[53] Spilling over from the Bank of New York Mellon/Bank of America collaboration to other banks.

The theft-step-process is thought to be so layered and complex that no homeowner, federal agent, or investor in the CWALT trusts, after the fact or during can recognize, defend against, or prosecute these property crimes. All along investors and homeowners knew that something was wrong. This subliminal discernment has led to some pushback, but not enough. We must defend against the criminality of banks wherever we find it.

At the start and the end of the continuum no one really cares about the personal stories of those families whose single most important tangible asset is robotically fed to The Bank Theft Delivery System. The feds might file charges, but this doesn't mean you will ever get your home back. This is unacceptable.

Those that lend their professional expertise to perfecting these thefts are performing a task for which they are paid. It is far too easy to see the sitting duck of the homeowner, deprived of all legally required disclosures, or in the case of elderly victims their heirs, as somehow bringing this massive fraud scheme upon themselves. For those in the middle, who trade their professional credentials for

[53] CWALT, Inc., Alternate Loan Trust Certificates Investor Law Suit. Plaintiff alleges violations of the Securities Act of 1933. Omitted material information in violation of Sections 11, 12(a)(2) and 15 of the Securities Act. There is no full disclose as to how the new investment practices involving these repackaged CWALT original securities dilute profits and inflate value premised on fraud and theft perpetrated upon American citizens.

a piece of the action, the victims become an abstract. The bait and switch big picture only slowly disclosed. No one says, *"you there... we need your professional credentials to perfect a property theft scheme that defrauds several federal agencies. Tears apart and destabilizes families. That includes bank fraud and forgery while breaking countless state and federal laws."*

The RICO Criminal Enterprise focus on the end-goal. This is the objective that requires a steady stream of homes as product fed to the artificially created securities market. Many of these homes end up over-valued. Who verifies the stated value of these securities? There is no objective measure that these tangible assets are worth what they are claimed to be worth.

It appeared that some of the same property addresses, and especially those in more stable neighborhoods, feature in multiple investment pools. What entity actually goes out into the field and to any objective measure will confirm value? How many pension funds have been invested in these securities?

If you have invested in these pools of rental property get a list of the addresses claimed to be in the pool(s) that you supposedly own pieces of. At the very least go to google maps and take a look at those homes and others around it. Rents have to stay high to back the securities over sold; standing on a foundation of theft. Thus, price fixing of rental property is a big piece of this theft structure. Criminal banks operate under the learned expectation that when all this implodes our elected officials will yet again declare them too big to fail. And that elected officials, expecting donations to reelection campaigns or some other quid pro quo exchange will be pressured to bail them out with American tax dollars.

PRICE FIXING: From the Federal Trade Commission... means when competitors agree to restrict competition, the result is often higher prices. Accordingly, price fixing is a major concern of government antitrust enforcement. A plain agreement among competitors to fix prices is almost always illegal; whether prices are fixed at a minimum, maximum, or within some pre-agreed to range.

There is no middle class like that in America. Predatory criminals have invested in the disenfranchisement of the American dream upon which a healthy democracy depends. People are at their best when they can be independent. Not dependent upon government, not debt ridden, able to have a safe abode in which to raise their children. Get rid of a vibrant free-thinking middle class and you have a population whose children or grandchildren will become anarchists leading to despots putting down insurrections, leaping to ever corrosive controls by government.

CHAPTER NINETEEN

"MERS and its partners made the decision to create and operate under a business model that was designed in large part to avoid the requirements of the traditional mortgage recordation process. This Court does not accept the argument that because MERS may be involved with 50% of all residential mortgages (trending upwards of 90% today) in the country, that is reason enough to turn a blind eye to the fact that this process does not comply with the law."
Judge Robert E. Grossman, Eastern District of New York

Information bled over to and from other county-seats. I concentrated my research on Western, TN. The majority of the suspected fraud examples did not make it into my pattern example groupings. The chain of theft appeared to be the same, but these homes were only peripherally connected by commonly used services such as the same title insurance company linked to the same foreclosure mill attorneys linked to specific clients, a.k.a., REO Private Investors, having hired these servicers. Any federal investigator or class action attorney could put together a cluster of homes fed to the securities industry after first being acquired by fraud. Then being morphed into a security backed by the price fixed rental market. And hopefully returning some of these homes to their rightful owners or heirs.

Occasionally I met others who appeared to be researching a title history. I volunteered that despite what they had been misled to believe not everything is filed at the Registry of Deeds Office. In order to facilitate theft of private property banks and their partners needed to break the credibility of the Registry of Deeds system across this country. They have done so with almost no push back from the judiciary, from state legislators, from states attorney general, or from counties across this country having lost billions of dollars in stolen filing fees that might otherwise have gone to law enforcement, education, beautification of parks, fire and rescue services.

The legal right to foreclose, seize, sell, or transfer a home can only be proved per an unbroken chain of notarized paper. These instruments are generally referred to as endorsements. Many are no longer filed with the Registry of Deeds Office. The theft required fraud narrative is supported by the incomplete record at the Registry of Deeds Office whose employees are not empowered to vet for fraud; nor are they able to report fraud to any outcome that informs fraud checking statistics. This means that any random white-collar criminal can make a false claim of ownership without challenge. When making a ruling, judges should require that a complete record of "endorsements" are presented. This would be all the signed and notarized paper that step by step lay out the entire title history as proof that the home is not being stolen. That an affidavit signed by the foreclosing party and, or, the foreclosure mill attorneys affirm that nothing has been withheld from the public record or from any court. Not some nebulous, "to the best of my knowledge" but a definitive affirmation that due diligence has been applied and what the court has before them, and what victims have access to, includes the entire MERS record. At least until MERS can be shut down.

When transferring ownership over a car proof of title is required. When cars are stolen police reports are generated. Charges follow. Today no such common sense barrier to wholesale theft of private property by the financial industry is in place to protect American consumers. What was formerly a trustworthy recordation system, that in some states require that every Deed and every transfer of the Deed be recorded, no longer functions as it once did.

Karen A. Yarbrough, Cook County, Illinois Recorder of Deeds is quoted as saying: ***...because County Recorders are not authorized by law to review the legal claims made in documents before recording them, every homeowner in Cook County is vulnerable to this crime.***[54]

When viewing an obviously forged document this is to say that Registry of Deeds employees who view thousands of these filings and are perfectly positioned to start the ball rolling against wholesale theft of private property are rendered no more than paper shufflers. They are strategically impeded from reporting patterns of fraud, suspected forgeries, and even are blindly expected to file whatever is presented by foreclosure mill attorneys no questions asked. These levels of negligence make a mockery of consumer rights.

The former strength of the land recordation system lay in that confident American citizens could trust it. That rich and poor alike can investigate title history to their homes without having to hire an

[54] Karen A. Yarbrough article: http://cookrecorder.com/property-fraud-arrest

attorney or a title company to do this work for them. The standard long held to, in principal, but no longer in practice, is this. It is fair, just, and moral that there should be no price tag attached to establishing proof of property rights in a free society.

A forensic accountant and treasury agent had the following quote on his phone. From the start of his career he kept it handy as a kind of touchstone. **There are two modes of invading private property, the first, by which the poor plunder the rich...sudden and violent; the second, by which the rich plunder the poor, slow and legal. John Taylor, *An inquiry into Principals and Policy of the Government of the United States (1814).***

Theft perfecting filings are routinely withheld from the public land recordation system and hidden away in the MERS E-Registry System. MERS provides a big piece of the very specific and needed theft structure. Equality of access is precisely what The Bank Theft Delivery System needed to shut down. Criminal banks needed to launder the chain of title secretly buying, selling, transferring, and assigning theft perfecting authority to third parties making no disclosure to homeowners.

How is this possible? One word. MERS. The MERS E-Registry System, MERSCorp Holdings, Inc., and the Mortgage Electronic Systems, Inc., are collectively known as MERS. When reading their name in any instrument think: FRAUD. The doublespeak definition of a MERS Loan is: a loan for which MERS is the mortgagee, beneficiary, or grantee when in fact MERS is not allowed to own anything. The intrusive introduction of the MERS name into any filing, instrument, or endorsement serves only to hide the name of the MERS member driving the Property Flip sequence while claiming beneficial ownership or authority over homes acquired by robbery.

It would be well worth the time of any attorney or judge to get copies of the earlier MERS Rules of Membership, content of which are replete with Orwellian double-speak. Language is crafted to contradict former or subsequent statements. Isolated pieces can be raised in a court of law to offer a defense while another part says something entirely different. The earlier copies of the rules are more overtly and transparently devious and malleable. They are written by a pass-through shell company fully aware that their practices enable theft and illegal seizure of private property while disenfranchising the American public from any means of defense.

Because of MERS homeowners never know who is actually foreclosing on their property. Due process rights say that we have the right to confront that actual entity or person attempting to steal our homes under cover of law. With full disclosure homeowners would be armed to fight back. Thus, the chokehold over disclosure.

States attorney generals were slow to act on nicotine addiction as a public health crisis even though the repercussions over many generations were obvious. Slow to respond to the opioid crisis despite millions of casualties, something that no parent of a dead young person missed. It is well beyond that time that prosecutors turn their attention to the role played by MERS in helping to prefect theft of millions of American homes, disenfranchising victims from information needed to fight back.

It is not that legislators have not learned from the past. It is that the financial industry commits heavily to supporting the campaigns of politicians that supply legislative protection to these and other financial crimes. Many of these crimes take place in blatant disregard of laws already on the books.

An early attempt to level the playing field for ordinary Americans came from the Commonwealth of Kentucky. The Obama era bailout of banks, the *"banks are too big to fail"* mantra had a lot to do with the fact that this law suit went, essentially nowhere. Meaning that MERS is still in business enabling theft of private property with no real or credible push back from those that carry badges. Obtain a copy of this law suit. Read and quote from it.

***Commonwealth of Kentucky ex rel JACK CONWAY, Attorney General v. MERSCORP Holdings, Inc. a Delaware Corporation.* Filed January 23, 2013. Franklin Circuit Court, Division I, Civil Action No.: 13-CI-00060.**

Right out of the gate former Attorney General Conway got it right. **The Plaintiff, the Commonwealth of Kentucky, by and through its undersigned Attorney General, brings this action against Defendants, who created the mortgage registration and foreclosure enterprise known as the Mortgage Electronic Registration System (MERS).** Paragraph 1, page-1.

Conway went on to state: **The MERS System effectively eliminated homeowners' and the public's ability to track**

the purchase and sale of properties through the traditional public records system. Information that was once readily available in the public land records is now stored in a private database maintained by MERS. However, the MERS database is unreliable and inaccurate. Paragraph No. 10, page 3.

By design of The Bank Theft Delivery System you will not read the identity of that person or private investor group that has secretly assumed control of your mortgage in any public records. The term, "Beneficial Ownership" refers to that person or entity without actually naming them.

It is not that enforcement has not caught up with laws already on the books. It is that enforcement at every level where it could make a difference has failed. In the hands of corrupt bureaucrats' enforcement is arbitrary and trending toward preservation of deep state agendas. President Trump's message that proclaimed a forgotten America resonated across party lines because it was true. Enter MERS. Information is power. At every step the answers you need are concealed; coalesced around intent to undermine the authority of the United States Constitution. Criminal banks have counted on the fact that American homeowners are effectively disenfranchised by MERS.

Banks have rigged due diligence to appear compliant. They do not vet against administrative corruption in their own record keeping. With the end game in mind they willfully decide that they will not see the "flips" of the property title amongst members of the same group of private investors for the red flags that bank employees, from loan officers to underwriters, have been extensively trained to interpret as fraud. They ignore the Bank Secrecy Act.[55] Disclosure is shielded by MERS. Deception and dissemination built into the MERS scope of practice shows utter contempt for federal compliance. And therefore, for American tax payers.

Each digital and secret flip of the property title takes place over the MERS System. The secret Note-Owner/Note-Holder is replacing your name with theirs. The truth too long ignored is this: **MERS is THE DATA BASE DEPOSITORY FOR IDENTITY THEFT.** This is because the original Deed of Trust must be buried, building the fraud narrative that overwhelms and slanders the truth. The intent is

[55] What is the Bank Secrecy Act and Why Does it Exist by, Julie Stackhouse. **www.stlouisfed.org/on-the-economy/2018/april/what-bank-secrecy-act-why-exist**

to render homeowners defenseless. Doing so with the help of states attorney generals that have passively allowed MERS to corrupt County Register of Deeds data bases. That have allowed MERS to usurp and corrupt what property owners have relied upon since John Adams was a circuit riding judge in Massachusetts.

It is no accident that nearly every entity name read in those documents selectively filed at the Registry of Deeds Office is a MERS-Member. All those named are on the same page and thus, where fraud is proven in any single endorsement that greased the chain of theft each MERS Member named is culpable to one degree or another. REO agents serving the long-term goal of the banks can piggy back on another MERS Member access to use the MERS system. The Bank Theft Delivery System plan to grow rental property as a marketable commodity needs a lot of product.

MERSCorp is owned by many of the most significant stakeholders in the mortgage industry, including mortgage originating and servicing companies (e.g., Bank of America, CitiMortgage, Inc., GMAC Residential Funding Corporation, and Wells Fargo Bank, N.A., government sponsored entities (e.g., Fannie Mae and Freddie Mac), mortgage insurance companies and title companies (e.g., First American Title Insurance Company Corporation and PMI Mortgage Insurance Company), and the Mortgage Bankers Association. Paragraph No. 6, page-2.

Others are shareholders including foreign entities. Other than the limited list above, appearing over and over again in my pattern examples, were SunTrust Mortgage, Inc. and its affiliates. Core Logic and its affiliates including the Equator communication platform. Stewart Title Guaranty Company. The MERS-member third-party mortgage servicer companies have the power to levy fees and other charges that assist in driving a mortgage into default. You need to know who hired them. Expect that you will be lied to. Document the record of lies.

Nearly every profession and professional licensure needed to lend an aura of honesty and authority to these theft schemes, working to deceive a compliant judiciary, are all MERS Members. When homeowners push back and show up in court with the few documents available to them judges have been groomed to rubber stamp the foreclosure. Very rarely do they stand up to the cohort of criminals and require that all the notarized paper is presented and made immediately available to targeted homeowners. The onus of authority to foreclose by design and intent goes unproven.

You may read this chapter, go up to your Registry of Deeds Office, copy everything on file connected to your name and property address. Include those filings post foreclosure. Finding repeated use of the MERS name, hiding the name of the actual REO Note Holder you recognize one piece of how you were deceived.

The MERS Signing Agent. MERS allows almost anyone to be a MERS signing officer. They do not reveal at whose direction or under whose employ the theft perfecting trail of document fraud is signed. Though the entire property flip history is open to them, banks robotically accept what the Title Insurance Companies, hired by the REO secret Note-Holders sell them. They fail to do their own due diligence. And thus, they imagine that they are off the hook for perfecting theft of your home.

Mortgage Fraud includes that role of Title Insurance Companies perfecting theft for white collar criminals. **Mortgage Fraud is defined as a material misstatement, misrepresentation, or omission of information relied upon by an underwriter or lender to fund, purchase, or insure a loan. Mortgage fraud can be classified into two general categories: fraud for housing and fraud for profit. Source: FBI Financial Crimes Section, Financial Institution Fraud Unit, Mortgage Fraud: A Guide for Investigators, 2003.**

It is necessary to the success of these theft schemes that homeowners believe they are still working with a, trustworthy lender. Or with a third-party mortgage servicing company hired by the original lender. The bank that off-loaded your mortgage to criminal partners, need MERS to cover for them. MERS help out allowing persons working with the REO Investment Groups to be the signing agent of record; hiding behind the MERS name. You may read the name of your original lender. This leads you to believe the lie that nothing has changed. The unnamed secret Note-Holder has control over the chain of theft because they have already established their identity theft claims over the digital property title. When homeowners seek answers, they are in all effect, speaking to a brick wall; deceived as to whom they are communicating with at any given time. It is the secret REO Note-Holder that has control, driving the mortgage into default, while at the same time skimming equity.

If you read that MERS is the signing agent for your original lender or any lender, think FRAUD until proven otherwise. Look to see if MERS is claiming to be the signing agent in any documents appearing at the Registry of Deeds Office. More about this in Part 111.

Any judge that fails to issue a court order for the full title history with or without you having formally requested it is failing in a fundamental care of duty. Judges have the power to force compliance. They must demand a full chain of title, all the actual paper by which forgeries and repurposed, fill in the blank endorsements can be recognized.

As the build up to the foreclosure unfolds the MERS name will appear in key instruments as the nominee (proxy name) for the actual entity that is foreclosing. Homeowners are helpless because start to finish they are deceived as to what entity is bringing the foreclosing action. Courts are too quick to give the benefit of the doubt to the very powerful financial industry. Judges may read MERS or a major bank name and do not ask, who is the real owner of this mortgage? Has this property already been transferred into a REMIC Trust? When, was the mortgage assumed and by whom? What entity is the MERS name concealing and why is secrecy and deflection necessary? When were the investors in the securitized trust paid off? Just how sophisticated is the unrepresented or under-represented victim standing before the bench? Does this beleaguered person even know enough to ask the right questions? This does not absolve a judge from rubber stamping theft of private property under color of law. Do I have before me and does the foreclosing party assert as a matter of record that nothing is withheld that informs a clean and complete chain of title viewed per the endorsements, i.e., the signed and notarized paper?

MERS plays a very necessary role in deceiving judges and courts. MERS is the shell company that is perfecting title theft as the precursor to the foreclosure charade.

A Shell Company is by definition, a ghost. It does not have any significant assets or operations of its own. It does not make anything or collect money for having made it. "It's generally used as a 'pass through' to allow another company

or business to smoothly move financial assets from one place to another." Dirty Money: CBS News

And this is exactly what MERS does. They secretly move (launder) your property title from one entity to another; no disclosure to you. Having control over the mortgage, the REO Private Investors hire a third-party Mortgage Servicer Company that is also a MERS Member. This is how they manage to receive your house payments and begin laundering income; often as assignment of rents wired into the trust entity. In the process of establishing the engineered default under the original Deed of Trust the MERS transfers of authority make theft and illegal seizure of private property possible. If you knew any of this was taking place in real time as the theft-step process unfolded you would fight back. You are strategically and heartlessly positioned not to do so.

Eventually the property title will reemerge out from under the operative MERS umbrella. This very important event is preceded by filing the, Assignment of The Deed of Trust in the public land records. The Assignment of the Deed of Trust is another Breeder Document. It is set up for the secret Note-Holders to publicly appear as the owners after it is understood that homeowners are gone and cannot fight back.

When courts fail to put the onus on the foreclosing party to prove they have the authority to foreclose they are failing the United States Constitution. When they allow foreclosure mill attorneys to skate on producing the secret note-holder making a physical appearance they are depriving you of your civil right to confront the person or entity bringing the charge of foreclosure. This is a violation of due process rights. Demand that this person, group, or entity who from inception to completion has hidden their identity, actually show their faces.

It is not for the beleaguered homeowner to produce all the signed and notarized paper (endorsements) that show a complete title history. This is the responsibility of the foreclosing party. Go to court and demand this paper. Never ignore any summons. Ask for a postponement giving you time to review what is supplied. From reading the MERS Rules of Membership you already know that MERS frequently and uniformly will not comply with any court order. Make this clear to the judge.

You might say something like: *"Your Honor. Foreclosure fraud by MERS Members is well known. Before you grant this foreclosure and what I believe will be an illegal seizure of my home in violation of the Fourth Amendment to the United States Constitution. I am respectfully asking that by court order you require MERS to produce the name of the Note Owner, any Note Holder, Interim Funder, and Permanent Investor. Every electronic documentation of any transfers, sales and assigns of authority to any other MERS Member. The physical mailing address and email of any destination receiving and sending communications over the MERS E-Registry System. Including the full mortgage servicer record, and the name of the Title Insurance Company. The HUD-1 attached to any sale of my home during the time that I was still living in my home. I am asking for documentation of every assign, transfer, and sale of my mortgage between* (state the start date) *the time that I first took possession of my home under a valid and legal Deed of Trust up to today* (state the end-date). *In other words, a complete title history. And please Your Honor, may I also have a postponement of this matter giving time for MERS to respond and me adequate time to examine these records."* Ask for a six-month delay.

The MERS System has made it even more difficult to ascertain whether a foreclosing party actually owns or holds the note with proper endorsements. Without this knowledge it is difficult, if not impossible, for a homeowner to determine whether the foreclosing party has standing to initiate the suit. (the foreclosure) Paragraph No. 15, page-5.

The Property Flip sequence requires that the electronic title to your home be secretly transferred, bought and sold amongst the same bad actors. Each transfer, sale and assign are represented by a formally signed and notarized instrument (endorsement) that is intentionally withheld from the Registry of Deeds Office and concealed in the MERS System. Broken chain of title is a big piece of the Property Flip theft-step sequence. Some of these sales and transfers are to family members or REO Group members. This pattern of practice (laundering the chain of title) is well known to courts and bank regulators and when you bring it up is reason enough as to why a court should grant you full access to the complete record. This is an inside job in that those connected to the RICO Criminal Enterprise by blood, marriage or some other tie will keep their mouths shut. If your investigation should widen look for repeat straw buyers surfacing in the portfolio of REO owned homes.

Look into each identity that surfaces; establishing enterprise plus relationship. The Boyd's shamelessly used and drew their daughter, Amy into these schemes.

When judges fail to vet the title history, they are falling in line with, The Bank Theft Delivery System. Demand the full MERS history and the full history produced by any Title Insurance Company that greased the chain of theft. Demand the actual paper by which forgeries and fill in the blanks, repurposed endorsements can be recognized. Limited filings, telling the fraud narrative, filed in any county Registrar of Deeds Office would include the required, "Assignment of the Deed of Trust." As a fraud device the Assignment of the Deed of Trust will forward date when the actual title theft took place. Take this document in hand and demand everything that went before that is concealed in the MERS data base.

Here is a word picture. To rely on the public filings is like counting the dots on the "Sunday Afternoon" Georges Seurat painting. These theft schemes render victims and courts unable to see the forest for the trees. These skilled con-artist banks, foreclosure mill attorneys, and REO private investor groups are selling courts on colorfully merged clusters of dots, each cluster a limited story and by omission of the complete title history and Note-Owner/Note-Holder identity a set of lies.

MRES are not beholden or paid by tax dollars. They could care less about the public interest. Being in contempt of court means nothing to MERS. In the end, if the foreclosure and illegal seizure goes forward and the judge has given MERS and the foreclosure mill attorneys a pass you have grounds for an appeal. Do not leave your home until all issues have been resolved. The criminals do not have the physical property fully under their control until after the illegal seizure.

If you run into trouble with a judge who seems to be bending over backwards for the smartly dressed lawyers pitching for the Criminal Enterprise ask if these securities feature in pension funds or any personal portfolio of investments. Refusal to answer is not the point. You've raised the issue and gotten possible conflict of interest as a concern on record. Most judges care passionately about protecting the integrity of the court, the justice system in general and any appearance of bias. They should equally care that some of their company are corrupt.

The MERS system effectively eliminated homeowners' and the public's ability to track the purchase and sale of properties through the traditional public records system. Information

that was once readily available in the public land records is now stored in a private data base maintained by MERS. However, the MERS database is unreliable and inaccurate. Paragraph No. 10, page-3.

There are no consumer protection laws in any state that would allow this behavior and yet they do allow it. This informs the state and federal bureaucratic protection syndicate that has built up around theft of private property. If we link secret assumption of mortgages with no disclosure to homeowners and call that a financial crime. And... given recognition of the long game we call that violations of the Truth in Lending Act of 1968 which is a federal law that requires informed disclosure regarding use of consumer credit... your mortgage falls under this federal law. The seriousness of these crimes is further exposed by extortionist debt collection practices supporting your RICO Claims.

After the illegal seizure of my home the Jones, Kelley, Boyd Criminal Enterprise then sold my so called "debt" to a debt collection agency that claimed to be acting for Bank of America. This is yet, another creative means to skim additional funds from properties acquired by robbery via extortionist debt collection practices over homes acquired by robbery. Insist that any debt collector produce the complete title history, who hired them, a copy of any contract, and exactly what entity sold them this debt. Turn any assault back on them by chasing back the source of all paper at every opportunity. When I did this, I was taken off the call list. The law firm later lost a class action law suit regarding collection of debts they could not prove were real.

The time between notice of the upcoming foreclosure and the illegal seizure is streamlined, fast tracking the physical acquisition of the property before homeowners can mount a defense. Thus, you will read in the Conway quote below, *"and shorten foreclosure times."* You will read, *"rapid sale(s)"* informing the ambush; no process that alerts homeowners that the digital, electronic title has already been flipped amongst the same bad actors many times over and pre-dating the foreclosure charade.

MERS mislead targets of these theft schemes into thinking they are the entity that is foreclosing. While you chase this lie, digging past the smokescreen, courts rubber stamp, the foreclosure charade. The Kentucky case makes the point that MERS is a *shell company*. You read that MERS is the *"nominee"* and *"mortgagee."* They are not the foreclosing party. They do not own or hold the mortgage. This is the MERS white-collar theft role of concealing that entity that has hired the foreclosure mill attorney(s) and ordered the foreclosure before homeowners can learn enough that they can mount a credible defense. In reading this book you will go into court with a list of what is needed before any foreclosure can be deemed valid.

MERS remain the mortgagee of record until it is safe for the REO investor to step out of the shadows. In my case this happened with the Evolve Bank & Trust Loan to the Boyd's taking place four months after the illegal seizure. Followed by the Warranty Deed transfer to Pretium Partners, LLC returning long term profit back to the banks that set the Bank Theft Delivery System in place.

The mortgage industry created MERS to enable financial institutions to evade county recording fees, avoid publicly recording mortgage transfers, facilitate the rapid sale and securitization of mortgages en masse, and shorten foreclosure times. In the MERS System, MERS Members purportedly log all of their mortgage transactions in a private electronic registry, instead of publicly recording the transfer in the local county clerk's office. Financial Institutions attempted to avoid having to record these transactions by designating MERS, Inc. – a shell company with no economic interest in any mortgage loan – as the nominal "mortgagee" of the loan in the public records. The basic theory behind MERS is that, because MERS, Inc., serves as a "nominee" (or agent) for most major lenders, it remains the "mortgagee" in the public records, regardless of how often the loan is sold or transferred among MERS members. Paragraph No. 9, page-3.

Quoting again from Cook County Registrar, Karen A. Yarbrough. "***I like to tell people that it's easier to steal a house than it is to steal a car," said Yarborough. "To steal a car, you have to make sure nobody is around, pry open a door or break a window, if there is no alarm, find a way to get it started, which isn't easy with anti-theft technology today. To steal a house, a thief only needs some public information found easily online, ten minutes Photoshopping a fake deed, and a trip to one our offices to record their false ownership."***

"...some are content to carefully and quietly select their victims, with a preference for elderly persons who have paid off their mortgages. When the victim passes away or leaves the home for an extended period of time, their families may discover after it's too late that the fraudster has sold the home or taken out a mortgage."

Under the Civil RICO statute of limitations there is no "too late" caveat on what is proposed in any instrument tainted by fraud, propped up by forgery and utilized as a device to accomplish outright theft. Quoting again... **Obtaining an assignment through fraudulent means invalidates the assignment. Fraud destroys the validity of everything into which it enters. It vitiates the most solemn contracts, documents, and even judgments. Walker v. Rich, 70 Cal. App. 139 (Cal.App.1926).**

When it was perceived that I was spending too much time researching title histories other than my own I was accused of being a sovereign citizen. On one occasion I was yelled at and threatened with the Somerville city attorney because I did not choose to answer questions about what I was researching. I was making too many people nervous and cross-checking too much information.

This treatment was the exception. More often, if I asked for help it was freely given. County employees are public servants. It is a travesty that they lack the training to report the document fraud they are routinely confronted with. I believe many already recognize, to one degree or another, how their positions have been dumbed down and leveraged by white collar criminals to perfect these thefts. It is a, gross dereliction of duty that they are not authorized to generate reports. Nor is any data collection system in place by which patterns of practice by foreclosure mill attorneys is informing these crimes; forwarding reports to those with the power to investigate followed by criminal referral to States Attorney Generals.

No homeowner in this country should ever be prevented, obstructed, and deceived from knowing who is the Note-Owner, the Note-Holder, the Servicer, the Sub-Servicer, or any secret interim funder or investor. They should know when their mortgage is entered into any REMIC Trust. Each instance that their mortgage is pooled into a security; bought and sold, recklessly traded and commoditized beyond their control. Members can be kicked out of the MERS system if they are found to have committed robbery, larceny, embezzlement, fraudulent conversion, forgery, misappropriation of funds or other dishonest acts. These are all crimes that feature as part of the Bank Theft Delivery System. They should appear as "counts" in any law suit you file. MERS members do not experience real consequences. Thus, they consider themselves untouchable.

To write about MERS would be another book. Some judges have tolerated MERS more than others. The Financial Crimes Enforcement Network (FinCEN) is a department of the United States Treasury. This is the bureau that is mandated by law to enforce the Bank Secrecy Act. Content of what follows drips contempt for the rule of law and for federal enforcement.

When laundering money derived from stolen assets it is common practice to hide behind a number-identifier. One has to pay taxes on at least some of this income. There is a paper trail evinced on the self-reporting side. It is not just HUD that uses a number ID system. MERS does too. When challenged to reveal the operational identity behind these numbers MERS will go to extraordinary lengths to prevent victims of foreclosure fraud, illegal seizure, and outright theft, their attorneys and even judges from having the **NPPI** list of names and numbers.

The **NPPI** is the MERS **"non-public personally identifiable" number** of that entity laundering the chain of title. That identity behind each flip of stolen property, controlling the "electronic Note" and flushing it per use of the MERS E-Registry System through the Bank Theft Delivery System. This is an important piece of how you can connect the banks to the local boots on the ground cabal of theft partners. Wire fraud on a massive scale. You need this identity. It is thus, fiercely guarded. Take this demand before any judge. Establish a record of requests for what you need. Keep asking MERS for this number and the identity behind these numbers.

If the MERS Entities are required (by any government authority) to disclose a Member's NPPI information pursuant to a subpoena or court order or request of a regulator, the MERS Entities shall promptly notify the Member in advance of such disclosure and shall cooperate with the Member to resist, limit or delay such disclosure of such NPPI Information to the maximum extent of the law.

Rule 9; Use and Ownership of Information; Section (2) my copy: page-33; March 18, 2013.

Quote MERS speaking in their own words to any judge you stand before. Don't wait for the *resist, limit, delay strategy* to surface. Proclaim it as modus operandi. Most already know that MERS has a history of thumbing their noses at court orders. If you cannot find a copy of this March 2013 "rule" I'll send you a copy. MERS is not regulated as Banks are and yet they are an arm of the banking industry. The Bank Secrecy Act does not apply to MERS because special interests have shielded them. And legislators have stepped lock-step into line helping to make these thefts possible.

The consumer fraud perpetrated by MERS is so pervasive and common that there should be a large and prominent sign in every Registry of Deeds Office across this country. To alert in bold letters that despite what citizens are misled to believe additional filings are routinely withheld from public access and scrutiny; concealed in the MERS E-Registry System. Register of Deeds Offices should be responsible to fill in the gaps since it is their incomplete system of filings that routinely mislead judges, courts, consumers, and targets of these theft schemes. Because many targeted are elderly it must be remembered that rightful heirs of estates are commonly deprived of property they should have rightfully inherited. Those already in debt to extortionist credit practices or having some tragedy draining their savings are commonly targeted because it is assumed that they cannot hire an attorney.

The Orwellian point of the MERS shell company is to avoid any straight answer showing utter contempt for private property rights, courts, and the rule of law. For example, any attempt to find the identity of the permanent investor tied to when the mortgage was first assumed any person might be fed the name of the interim funder. MERS makes a distinction between the Note-Holder and Note-Owner. While we could say that Vernon "Wayne" Boyd was the Note-Holder the actual Note-Owner was the larger investor group including Max Jones, Jeffrey L. Kelley, David Osborn and others. They would be the Note-Owner only until homeowners are dealt with and it is finally safe enough to transfer another theft asset, per Warranty Deed or Quit Claim Deed, to a company like Pretium Partners, LLC.

While a request for information may seem clear, MERS will find a way to parse the words appearing in any subpoena or any question asked during any deposition. The MERS dissemination means that every response must be tested. The propensity to lie is deeply imbedded into the DNA of an obdurate culture that for survival must depend upon concealment. When writing any subpoena get the MERS and Core Logic glossary of terms. Compare them to the Marie McDonnell glossary of terms. Let these be your guide as you anticipate the ***resist, limit or delay*** tactics designed to protect the operational theft structure of these financial crimes of which MERS play a key role.

The point at which the electronic note can no longer be safely flipped, skimming equity, Core Logic steps up to the plate. The Core Logic Equator computer platform helps to perfect the illegal seizure, assigning duties and keeping track of progress. Core Logic and MERS are two muscle groups streamlined to operate in tandem. **The MERS electronic operations launder the chain of title to stolen property as set up for the foreclosure and illegal seizure ambush assisted by Core Logic. One and the, same in purpose, goals, and outcome. All linked by relationship.** In RICO terms: enterprise plus relationship.

If not for the role played by MERS these crimes could not transpire as they do. When using the "MERS" abbreviation in conversation, although I was corrected at the May 6, 2015 deposition whose transcript and video record, I was aggressively prevented from having, I prefer the disease pronunciation. The MERS system operates as a petri dish for contagion.

CHAPTER TWENTY

"Let me tell you about coincidences. I don't believe in them." Judge Judith Sheindlin

Robosigning practices, forgeries, absent endorsements and replacement instruments are routinely walked into courts across this country. This takes place with almost no push back from judges. Nor from legislators, or federal enforcement.

Each time a judge allows a foreclosure without demanding a full chain of title they are chipping away at private property rights. They are assisting the agenda that fills to capacity the price fixed rental complexes built by mega corporations and foreign investment. They are doing so at the will of those that claim to hold the paper (the note) absent any proof that they have the right to foreclose. It isn't that it should be easier to foreclose which was the scripted sales pitch that has dumbed down enforcement. It is that it should be harder to foreclose.

Distilled to motive and outcome this was the toxic manifesto of the colonist in Ireland, Africa and everywhere else across this globe that has experienced the tyranny of absentee landlords; those with no loyalty to anything but greed. Because of the Second Amendment there can be no conventional invasion by foreign powers achieving outright theft of American resources. It is not an invading army wearing the recognized uniform of an enemy country that has needed open borders that undermine our sovereignty. It is the globalist financial network laundering money for drug cartels. They have been empowered on multiple fronts, including the stealthful acquisition of American land. Today nearly thirty million acres of American farm land is owned by foreign interests holding no loyalty to this country. Stop reading just for a moment and let that sink in.

At the height of the Irish Potato famine the English were shipping Irelands grain out of that small isle to feed its other colonies. Two million people died. It will not be Great Britain, but do we really imagine that our country and its resources are not jealously coveted and that some sort of invasion on multiple fronts is not already taking place? This is largely due to unchecked corruption. Espoused globalists, the Clinton machine handed over twenty percent of America's Uranium supply owned by the American people in exchange for $120 million dollars granted to the Clinton Foundation.

Those behind the Bank Theft Delivery System described in this book hold globalist allegiance to a borderless world order that practice disdain for democratic systems of government. What happened to me began in small town Tennessee. But as a single example had a corrupt reach that traveled all the way up to the second highest court in our land. As a mere single example this is the fulfillment of how enemies of human rights have structured the great American land grab with a reach that undermines those constitutional protections upon which a free and vibrant population depend for survival.

Nothing since the subprime mortgage collapse of 2006-2010 had curtailed these crimes. They are alive and flourishing. These markets are still being manipulated passing along profits to borderless global investors. Americans still do not know who owns their mortgage. This disconnect is intentional. It means that we are slow to connect the local theft assault of American citizens and their homes to the big picture globalist agenda enabled by courts and legislators.

The artificially created mortgage backed securities, much of it founded on theft and illegal debt collection practices; each tangible asset of a single home having an average value in excess of 200k. Criminal banksters do not care if this market implodes. Absent intervention, reform, and prosecutions these theft schemes will be recreated in preparation for the next cyclical market adjustment that weeds out the dead wood of lesser, expendable competition. Reaping more and more product while condensing competition until it is entirely eliminated.

The Victorians had a word of phrase for how they saw themselves as colonist intruders in foreign lands. They rode through the streets of India and retreated back to their palaces of splendor calling that bigoted subjection squalor. Inequalities' between splendor and squalor have led to countless wars all down the long march of time. When that dichotomy of the larger populace dominated by a political, economic, and social elite reaches the point where it can no longer be tolerated God always raises up restorative confluences seated in the individualism of a Mother Teresa, a Robert Emmet, a Martin Luther King, a Nelson Mandela, a Mahatma Gandhi, a Saul (Paul) of Tarsus, a George Washington, a Donald Trump, etc... We recognize these imperfect people, many of whom never gain notoriety, because they are unreasonably and preternaturally hated by the entrenched and corrupt status quo they offend.

At the center of all these conflicts is the fight for land, its' resources, and control over the soul of a populace. America is a young country. For as long as WE THE PEOPLE still matter without having to holster weapons, we must work to reaffirm private property rights in America. We must make foreign purchase of American farmland illegal. There are multi-pronged, ever-encroaching globalist agendas to monetize and bring under subjection every strata of American existence.[56]

Criminal banksters have profited from the blank check of the *"banks too big to fail"* legacy fully empowered by lack of consequences. It is not just that at every turn those targeted for theft of a home are disenfranchised from a defense. It is that some judges and most legislators are sold on the notion that these homes cannot be backed out of the securities they are pooled into without our country facing another financial disaster. This is economic blackmail.

It is my belief that the actions of Magistrate Judge Diane Vescovo, rubber stamped by district court Judge Sheryl Lipman, rationalized that they were not only holding the line against the Civil RICO alternative for lawyerless average Americans as a slap in the face for why the RICO Statutes were created in the first place. But that Judge Vescovo deliberately slandered my RICO claims at the *screening for merit* blockade because she thought she was holding that same crony corrupt line of defense for those reaping huge profit from these crimes.

Backing homes out of these securities. Returning them to victims is not at all an impossible feat. It is simply put a process of restitution that would shed long overdue light on predatory theft of American homes. When applications for mortgages and terms are presented the buying public must have the option to reject securitization of these mortgages on the front end. Doing so without fear of being rejected for home loans that people are prequalified to receive. When banks reject these applicants on grounds that put every mortgage holder at risk, this must be prosecutable as a civil rights violation. WE THE PEOPLE must take back powers and protections already granted to us. There must be

---

[56] Debt as tyranny exists in any area where it seeks to imprison a populace via the actions of the corporate and policy elites. Academia has placed higher education beyond the reach of most American citizens. They seduce young people into debt, encumbering families over the first twenty years of their working lives to pay for higher education costs; neither a coincidence nor an accident.

a few activist attorneys willing to join ranks and bring some of these civil rights violations into court rooms across this country.

The leopard could not change its spots. It merely regrouped. Under the revised theft model that we see today the securities industry does not accept title to stolen property... transferred usually via Warranty Deeds from the boots on the ground REO Investment Groups **until after the property title had been fenced through the Bank Theft Delivery System.** This is a, very important distinction to get your head around; to gain verbal and intellectual command over. In laundering the chain of title, the electronic title to stolen property is being, for all intents and purposes, fenced by a revised theft structure. Under this more layered theft model **the unpredictable human factor is neutralized on the front end.** There are far fewer outraged victims knowing enough to shout loud and clear that they were set up for foreclosure **scripted into an adapted theft model contrived by the same financial services industry.**

The Bank Theft Delivery system of today has set in place, degrees of separation through partnerships with select bank vendors. The sitting duck of the homeowner under today's theft structure remains shot, dying, and muzzled so that parodies of justice, can leave victims out of any settlement. So that due process as a necessary casualty precludes any victim from getting their homes back leading to recognition and alarm.

Though they are proportionally few in number, I am happy to report that some judges could not be so easily swayed to accept the sloppily created, forged, and incomplete title histories carried into courtrooms by criminal enterprise attorneys.

In JP Morgan Chase v. Butler, "Chase" could not produce the original Note or the Mortgage. They claimed that they had a legal right to insert themselves into this case after the failed Washington Mutual went bankrupt. Chase expected to cash in on FHA insurance (funded by tax dollars). They also expected to cash in on another home fed as a rental to the Wall Street securities industry. Just as REO Private Investor Groups target and profile local victims, bank lawyers also troll for random foreclosure actions they can take control of for the sole purpose of extorting money, expecting the judiciary to cooperate.

It is my contention that in presenting themselves before judges in cases where Banks know full well that they cannot prove they actually have the right to foreclose, the expectation is that theft of private property will be normalized. It is not just about hit and miss finding the right lazy or complicit judge. It is about generally wearing down the judiciary trending our courts toward lower standards.

The judge presiding over JP Morgan v. Butler cared about the constitution and the rule of law. Judge Arthur M. Schack[57] concluded: *Chase, the improper plaintiff, engaging in bad faith is "a waste of judicial resources."*

*It is clear that Chase's representations that it was the plaintiff in the instant action "is [*12] completely without merit in law" and "asserts material factual statements that are false."*

The JP Morgan Chase lawyers believed the judge could easily be manipulated to accept re-created forged documents. Why not? Regulators were asleep and law makers were indebted to special interests and campaign funds coming from the key racketeering players.

"... it appears to the Court that the delay by Chase in producing the subject Butler Note was to give (its lawyers) *ample time to temporarily borrow the Butler Note from Fannie Mae for its May 2, 2011 presentation to the court."*

And... *"This court cannot, and will not, countenance a lack of good faith in the proceedings that are brought before it, especially where blatant and repeated misrepresentations of fact are advanced, neither will it permit equitable relief to lie in favor of one who so flagrantly demonstrates such obvious bad faith."*[58]

After the dust settled on the former foreclosure and subprime mortgage debacle it became too risky for banks to produce and order

---

[57] This was not the only case where Justice Arthur Schack (a former school teacher) stood in the gap for helpless Americans coming up against the power of the financial industry. He made a name for himself tossing out banks' attempts to foreclose on many Brooklyn homeowners during the 2008 housing crisis. He died at age 71. Lawyer Chuck Otey said of him, "Artie was a dynamic presence, and the most honest person who simply thought the courts were for the people." The wise prophet said: *The value of a good name is to be chosen rather than great riches, loving favor rather than silver and gold (Proverbs 22: 1).*

[58] Read JPMadoff: The Unholy Alliance Between America's Biggest Bank and America's Biggest Crook. By, Helen Davis Chaitman and Lance Gotthoffer. From the Bernie Madoff Ponzi Scheme this book looks at the criminal activity of banks and various whistle blower cases including in part, the bank created mortgage crisis and the failure of our federal government to hold criminal banksters accountable; not weeding out federal employees that fail their oaths of office.

up the needed forged documentation themselves. Today that is the job of the boots on the ground REO Private Investor Groups working through the Foreclosure Mill Attorneys. These operational changes created degrees of separation from the banks that engineered and put in place the Bank Theft Delivery System. Think of this as a conveyer belt. As the Property Flip – Equity Skimming – Title Theft features progress along the path of operation banks are shielded. Vendor partnerships take the hits that are costed into budgets off set by huge profits. This rigged system provides degrees of separation and broader reach to build the syndicate relationships feeding homes to the securities market. One of these days that overvalued, price fixed securities market will implode and we'll ask yet again. Why did bank regulators and the SEC stand back and watch?

Title Insurance, Mail Fraud, and the Bank Vendor System

It is unlawful for banks to approve loans where there is no clean chain of title. The REO Fraudsters flipping the property must prove they have a beneficial interest in the mortgage. The answer to banks foregoing due diligence, streamlining theft of American homes, is title insurance. Stolen properties cannot be flipped (laundered) through various sales, transfers, and assigns of authority amongst conspirators without title insurance.

This is not that homeowners' insurance taken out against wind, fire, and flood. An insurer-grantor who is also in on the scam is needed. Broken chain of title and identity theft holding sway over mortgages acquired by robbery is obvious to everyone. Thus, an approved bank vendor will cover for the REO Fraudsters. Title insurance provides, the dog ate my homework, rationale to underwriters and loan officers who willfully decide they will not perform their own due diligence. The bank vendor of the title insurance company has agreed to take the hit if banks are sued for their part in perfecting theft of American homes.

Keller Williams Realtors, Vernon "Wayne" Boyd and Sherry Boyd knew just what company they should buy this insurance from regarding 15 Rachel Cove, 65 Pinehurst Drive, 35 Lewis Fairway Circle and many other homes in the REO portfolio, all destined to be fed to the yawning jaws of the securities market. The SEC might actually have to wake from the Bernie Madoff type self-imposed coma they are in.

Before companies like Pretium Partners, LLC can absorb these homes. Before temporary authority can be assigned to on board foreclosure trustees and the foreclosure mill attorneys. Backed by title insurance everyone agrees that approved bank vendors functioning as racketeering partners will take the hit in order to keep the billion-dollar Bank Theft Delivery System operational.

Banks are thumbing their noses at the Bank Secrecy Act and the purposes for which regulators are mandated to enforce it. I experienced this first hand when a Treasury Investigation looking into my home and others was abruptly shut down. Each lender that fail to do their own due diligence, superficially accepting the title insurance claims, are rubber stamping the, chain of theft. What's more they know it. They are allowing title to stolen property to be laundered through their banks. Last time I checked money laundering was a crime punishable by jail time.

As we shall see in Part 111 of this book, the Andrews chain of title (Chapter Twenty-Six) did not pass the laugh test let alone the smell test. The REO Note-Holder and the foreclosure mill attorneys were required to do a lot of back stepping before the illegal foreclosure charade could take place. This required committing a fraud upon the Fayette County Court to which, in my opinion, the judge was fully complicit.

Setting the operational standard, First American Title Insurance Company acknowledges that, *private investors could claim to own a property and yet have no proof of ownership.* The doublespeak Orwellian logic excuses how they function to make these crimes possible. In context to the fraud schemes described in this book Title Insurance puts forth an opinion that each flip of stolen property premised on forged documentation is free and clear of fraud. The title insurance company needs to be named in any Civil RICO Case you file.

Fraud jumps from the page via what is filed in the MERS E-Registry System; withheld from the public land records. You need these records. Complicit banks perform no independent review of the actual status, occupancy, condition, and appraisal claims of the REO secret Note-Holders. They fail to require proof of when the mortgage was first assumed by criminals. They do not require a full record of what is claimed over industry only websites with what is filed in the Registry of Deeds Office and in context to what the MERS E Registry System conceals.

Use of select bank approved vendors shuts out competition and limits exposure. First American Title Insurance Company claims: **"If an insurance company (First American) is comfortable**

with all the title evidence it reviews, it will assume the risk of defects that may not be disclosed in the public records, spreading that risk among its many premium payers. Obtaining title insurance can be more expensive than obtaining a lawyer's opinion, but its comprehensiveness makes it preferred by most investors and lenders, and it is required for mortgages trading in the secondary markets."

Which of course is the point since trading mortgages like poker chips over the secondary markets is itself the crime. It is well past time that we call it what it is.

Only after I fired Webb Brewer and got my hands on a very limited bit of his correspondence (I was entitled to all of it) did I notice that both he and the crony conspirators had been copying Byron Rogers, First American Title Insurance Company on correspondence. Look for payment to the title insurance company showing up in any HUD-1 adding to the list of federal crimes routinely committed with full expectation that there will be no consequences.

Just as you can fix the approximate date that your mortgage was off-loaded to criminals by looking at when county taxes were paid by the RICO Criminal Enterprise look also at the title insurance history. When was this title insurance first taken out? By what entity or individual? Who has been paying the premiums? Are the payments wired or mailed? What are the protocols that were ignored by the title insurance bank-vendor selling this title insurance to criminals, failing in their own due diligence, violating their founding charters while trashing state and federal insurance laws?

We could say that the start of the Title Insurance in the name of these white-collar criminals, or a proxy, is another kind of Breeder Document that serves to establish ongoing identity theft authority over stolen property titles. Like the, "paid in full" county tax receipt, proof of title insurance, is needed if income will be laundered and if the costs associated with running a, mafia like criminal enterprise can be submitted to the IRS as write offs at year-end.

Like the paid in full receipt from the county trustee, title insurance postures the fiction that a fraud free exchange of funds took place. Along with the fraud dealing Multiple Listing Service (MLS) certain documents are submitted to complicit lenders, adding to the loan package. Title Insurance with First American was taken out by the REO Fraudster secret note holders, Vernon "Wayne" Boyd and Sherry Boyd.

1. While I still lived in my home.
2. Upon lies that my home was abandoned and in derelict condition
3. To then indemnify corporate robbery of private property.
4. To normalize this highway of operation in that it is not investigated and no one is held accountable.

First American claims that information available to them is even more comprehensive than what can be unearthed in the public records. Criminals are further insulated because MERS will alert all those involved before they release any information even to federal agencies and prosecutors. They will, **"resist, limit, delay"** compliance with any subpoena or court order giving time for The Bank Theft Delivery System to cover their tracts while thumbing their noses at the rule of law.

First American Title Insurance Company is a subsidiary of First American Corporation. They induce underwriters and loan officers to look the other way telling them that they have done the work for them. Byron Rogers knew that First American Title Insurance Company was being used to feed an interim pay-off, a bribe to the boots on the ground REO Fraudsters for flushing these homes through The Bank Theft Delivery System. In failing to identify a defendant Webb Brewer was protecting his shadow clients, constraining and limiting the reach of my law suit, and more importantly my knowledge and recognition of the existence of a Bank Vendor System greasing the chain of theft.

Despite Webb Brewer's consistent efforts to keep me in the dark, after I fired him, I found the Byron Rogers name in a letter traded amongst Webb Brewer and the Defendants. After telling me I could not obtain the HUD-1 I found: *Title insurer – underwriter fees. Underwriters portion of the total title insurance premium... Memphis title* ***for*** *First American; First American Corporation*: $1,674.95.

Payments are often broken up to be less conspicuous under different lines. As an aside, the Core Logic Management fees paid from the closing funds were: $1,908.00. Core Logic and Equator, like first American Title Insurance Company are all subsidiaries of First American Corporation. This one Bank of America vendor provided services on four fronts. Name the title insurance company in any law suit you file. Always verify the parent company. Investigate the role of any subsidiaries.

Mail and Wire Fraud. Stewart Lender Services, Inc., is another Bank of America approved vendor. They are a wholly owned subsidiary of Stewart Information Services Corporation. They controlled the flow of information. They subverted every HAMP Application. In conversations with me they identified themselves as the Bank of America Mail Clearing Center. This positioned me and countless other victims to believe the lie that Bank of America was still the servicer and Note-Holder when in fact, they would have already paid off the investors in the securitized trusts, also being defrauded. The name may be different, but there will be a mail clearing center in the theft history of your property. Mail and wire fraud feature in most RICO cases.

Stewart Lender Services, Inc., sent selected mail addressed to myself and my ex-husband in another state. Doing so at the direction of the REO secret Note-Holders that hired them. Returned mail or mail not responded to is commonly used to support the fraud narrative that by design, at every juncture possible, will assign blame to homeowner targets of these schemes. The, Jones, Kelley, Boyd REO Fraudsters knew and capitalized on Brett's seriously diminished condition. Brett's condition and circumstances fit the pattern of profiling and targeting victims unable to fight back.

Many inconsistencies peppered official records that no one with the responsibility to do so actually investigated or reported as red flags. One such inconsistency on the self-reporting side was that the Boyd's were living in my home while balancing another lie that they had rented my home to one, Charles Stackhouse.[59] And then later establishing another flip of the property title, skimming even more equity, another mystery person, one James Wooldridge, also a resident. I think I would have noticed if I were living with complete strangers from start of the Title Theft in 2009 up to the foreclosure charade and illegal seizure of 2012. The Stackhouse name appeared as a straw buyer in other instances within my pattern example groupings. And though a somewhat limited

[59] Charles Stackhouse real or not had a local phone number, fielding calls from potential buyers whose interest in any property controlled by the REO Investment Groups were subverted and killed. That number was: 901-466-0170. Was he a real person, a made-up identity, or an example of identity theft?

connection the Wooldridge name was tied to Jeffrey L. Kelley. Proxy names fit the pattern in other examples. Some like Jerry Lee Lewis were entirely made up.

Investigate the source of mailings. Pay careful attention to any solicitation(s) sent to your address, but naming a person whose name you do not recognize. This red flag slips by when retirees seasonally vacation out of state or there is a physical rehabilitation stay or any other prolonged absence from the home. Given the current culture of corruption and the protectionist syndicate that exists regarding these types of crime, adult children of elderly parents would be wise to be watching for red flags while periodically checking the title history over homes they expect to inherit.

Stewart Lender Services and the shamelessly titled Home Retention Group, were approved Bank of America vendors. The mail clearing center(s) as independent contractors and approved bank vendors will forward your house payments to the entity that has hired them. They have no loyalty to you. Some victims are given the identity of the third-party mortgage servicer company. Unlike me, Linda Howard knew what servicer she was dealing with.

About the Linda Howard Case; 1247 Trotters Cove, Cordova, TN. Fred and Linda Howard are senior citizens who made all their house payments. Their street was targeted. It helps for management of rental property to have homes contained within a certain area. Thus, the fair oaks, Oakland, TN neighborhood was targeted. As were two other areas by different groups connected to the Jones, Kelley, Boyd Group of operatives. Did they have a meeting and decide that to avoid conflict they would stay out of each, others way? I think they did.

First Tennessee Bank sold the Howard Mortgage (the Note) to Private Investors based on a ridiculously low appraisal; never verified. The Private Investor changed the Mortgage Servicer from FI Mortgage Company, d.b.a., Tennessee Mortgage Company to Nationstar Mortgage Company on 10/2/2014. This change of the Mortgage Servicer Company is a crucial step in execution of these types of crime. The change should always be regarded as a red flag until proven otherwise. The change serves to distance the original lender from complicity in the fraud scheme. Nationstar had gone through several prior reformations. If you suspect any third-party mortgage servicer company of fraud, making or implying threats, refusing to reveal in writing who hired them take the offensive. Demand a change. Investigate your title history. Document your requests.

The Howard's mortgage was intentionally maneuvered into default per bogus fees that suddenly materialized. The planned harassment began; no problem being fixable, promises made, nothing changes. One should not under estimate the effects of frustration and helplessness building over time upon victims by this planned harassment. The unpaid fees placed the mortgage in default while slandering the Howard's credit history and character.

Nationstar Mortgage Company used the unpaid fees as the pretext to suddenly refuse the Howard's house payments sending them back. This to forward date assumption of the mortgage which in fact had already taken place predating the engineered default. Once REO Fraudsters became the secret Note-Holders. No warning to victims. From that point on. For as long as the Howard house payments were accepted, they did not go to pay down a mortgage. They were funneled into the coffers of the REO Private Investors. As we shall see in Part 111, in one example these house payments were mislabeled in IRS filings as, "assignment of rents."

It is my opinion that the Howard's got a tepid, very limited defense. Still far more than I ever got, which was no defense at all. Upon belief that some Memphis area attorneys have offered a proxy defense to select clients so that they can later point to those efforts to say that they were not part of the crony corrupt theft of West Tennessee Homes.

The fraud narrative in my case was that I had abandoned my home in 2009. As you will see in Part 111, the Andrews theft centered on a fictitious lien, identity theft, and a forged Power of Attorney. In the Howard case it was unpaid fees. Abandoned property, unpaid fees, the phony lien, each establishes the "Fraud Narrative" as the premise for the phony foreclosure charade. Which in every case predates when criminal banks first off-loaded mortgages to their boots on the ground REO, partners in crime.

The Howards were carefully profiled and selected as unlikely to fight back. Elderly victims experiencing a health crisis were common. Both were senior citizens and Fred Howard had been sick. The REO scam artists underestimated Linda Howard. I've already suggested you create a perp wall as a powerful visual that keeps the investigation on track. These thefts require very specific professional credentials. Identify the roles needed and pin that label to your perp wall. Then match these roles with the names that fit. Look for same people filling more than one role.

For me it was:

1. The mail clearing center; Stewart Lender Services.
2. The insurer grantor claiming no fraud in the title history; First American Title Insurance Company.
3. A money manager was needed. Max Jones, CPA.
4. A HUD licensed appraiser who is also licensed by your state to thus limit exposure keeping the circle tight and lean. In my case it was Larry Lane Billings; possible alias for Jeffrey L. Kelley. The Broker Price Opinions were provided by Keller Williams broker, straw buyer, and secret Note-Holder, Vernon "Wayne" Boyd.
5. At least two Real Estate companies. (Keller Williams – MEM 2, LLC and ERA Chamberwood Realty Group). The decoy realtor will be paid from the seller funds noted on the HUD-1. The first and prior listing, Keller Williams Realty, carried the secret REO MLS Listing not made public. The other is the decoy public face of the listing; ERA Chamberwood Realty Group. This partnership contrived that no random member of the public could purchase what has been a theft asset for a very long time. Two MLS listings conceal the arm in arm criminal collusion that price fixes any apparent sale while flipping the theft asset back to the same REO Investor Group.
6. Production of forged endorsements are needed. A foreclosure mill attorney firm is hired by the secret REO Investors. In effect they function as a vendor arm of the Criminal Enterprise. This role is explored in Part 111, of this book.
7. Other lawyers are needed. A lawyer is usually found as an inner circle member of the REO Perpetrator Nexus. Some will oversee the bundling of theft-asset homes into pools of securities outsourcing to brokers.

The Gintz brothers were banned from selling pools of rental property as securities in the State of Washington. Ronald Gintz tied to Jeffrey L. Kelley.

Pretium Partners, "Types of Clients" include REO Institutional Investment Groups feeding homes to this securities market. Quoted from Part 2A of Form ADV: 2017 Firm Brochure. Pretium Mortgage Credit Management, LLC (PMCM); page-9 Item-7. *"The minimum capital commitment for investing in the fund is 2 (two) million, which minimum may be waived by the Fund's General Partner.*

"Investing in the fund," is code for investing in a fraud scheme, able to leverage the bank vendor system. Link the vendor racketeering partners to the core group of local players. Link all that to the goals of the Criminal Enterprise. Choose a name for your group that evokes a word picture. It took time before I could recognize and write about what emerged as the Bank Theft Delivery System. I could not do so without recognizing how the local players shielded and provided distance to the criminal activities of the banking industry. And how this reciprocity operated through approved bank vendors shielding recognition of the national footprint of these crimes. I settled on titles: *Jones, Kelley, Boyd Perpetrator Nexus – REO Investor Group.* I settled on: *Bank Theft Delivery System.*

The executive branch of government has the power to enforce the criminal laws of this country. The Clinton-Bush-Obama legacy of insider politics has repeatedly let criminal banksters and their boardroom hucksters off the hook. Whether in Fayette County, TN or Washington, D.C., corruption cannot survive without there being control of the public record, a stranglehold over disclosure, corrupt civil servants, and a double standard of enforcement.

CHAPTER TWENTY-ONE

"The question goes, do we support a free market system that supports the middle class or will we continue to turn our backs on capitalistic ventures that suck the life out of the middle class." J.D. Vance.

I had socially crossed paths with the locally situated group of bad-actors. Not only do I believe that Fayette County was targeted, but my specific neighborhood where some of these people set up residence, was targeted. The Andrews property[60] and mine where targeted to the REO Group via the Fair Oaks social connections. I played a weekly canasta game with at least two of this number. In a recent conversation with a former neighbor he listed which homes were now rentals. It is no coincidence that the neighborhood association was disbanded since it functioned as an impediment to the neighborhood being converted from private ownership to rentals.

Coinciding with when Bank of America off-loaded my mortgage to the local fraudsters, one of them, Ann Jones, befriended me. She attended a neighborhood Bible Study that I taught. This so that she could keep tabs and report back on how well the wall of deception was holding up. If I wasn't too worried, I must still have no idea that premised on a forged Certificate of Abandonment my property title had been effectively stolen. Having this assurance, skimming equity could proceed.

So, yes. This was personal. Today I know that I should never have left my home and that those who advised me to do so were part of the group think operating within a culture of corruption.

Scales fell from my eyes when I could finally shed the interpretations of my corrupt attorneys and come to grips with the backstory emerging from my research. Research into other properties let me see how many other Tennessee citizens had been targeted and harmed. There were no bleeding wounds and need for sutures. But there was need for healing. What happened to me and others was every bit as violent as a series of physical assaults. White collar crime is insidious, the impact of which is far too often dismissed and minimized. There is something

[60] The Andrews theft is profiled in Part 111; Chapter Twenty-Six, 35 Lewis Fairway Circle, Oakland, TN.

about having suffered these levels of injustice normalized as acceptable business practices that makes the "get over it" script a ludicrous in the extreme panacea.

While behavior can be predicted it cannot be guaranteed. Thus, the chain of theft includes local REO operatives keeping track of victims. Doing so from inception up to the charade of foreclosure and the upcoming illegal seizures. Proximity is needed. Max and Ann Jones, Jeffrey Kelley, and others lived in the Fair Oaks subdivision. After I was strong armed to leave my home, Vernon "Wayne" Boyd and wife Sherry were added to that number.

Over the length of time that I stayed in the Oakland and Somerville area odd little bursts of hostility came from people I did not know. At a Wood's End book signing, at the bank, at least half a dozen times from strangers at the grocery store. Whether on behalf of themselves or because they knew one or more of the criminals, it became clear to me that I was marked out as a trouble maker. I needed to be labeled in keeping with bias that blame shifts to victims.

I found some encounters deeply disturbing. It seems cowardly to deliver such a zinger as "whack job." To then walk haughtily off, I guess feeling some satisfaction at having defended the down-trodden and misunderstood white-collar criminals. As my fight for recognition of these crimes became more public the, local operatives and their cohort could not quite grasp that I was fighting back. I was an affront to an ego that had scripted the victimology. They wanted me to move away from where my research needed to be centered.

I never lost sight of, could not talk myself out of, could not rationalize away the deep and profound injustice that had intersected my life and the lives of many other innocent senior citizens and families. One day I sat in the smaller chapel at The Church of the Incarnation in Collierville. The purpose for being there had been ambushed by unkind words. Words I more easily ignored in other circumstances, but not so much on that day in that location. I could not stop crying. One of the lay priests leaned over to ask, "can I help?" My spirit was struck in that moment with the conviction that God had already gifted me with the answer. I needed to change how and what I prayed for. A divine order had gone out from His throne and angels had their marching orders. In His very great love of my enemies there was a trajectory, winds and tides, that had nothing to do with me. After that the literal admonition to pray for our enemies became less and less a forced task of obedience.

Daily existence became easier. What happened in that chapel was like gazing at the stars or long over the ocean expanse and finding in that smallness of me as a single individual a shift in the spiritual weight of proportion.

I would eventually move away. Not because I was threatened to do so, but when God told me it was time. Others came to that same conclusion at that same fork in the path ahead. Their concurrence alleviated me from the guilt I might have felt at abandoning what had been for me, ground zero. That said, from 2012 forward I have never felt completely safe. I was vigilant about my surroundings. Marj and Ray Piece were among those to whom I will always be grateful. For a short time, Ray had been Brett's recovery sponsor. Another friend came along with a temporary job just when I most needed it. It was important to the investigation and for me personally to disengage from Brett. Al-anon meetings and certain people helped me grieve the loss of all I had envisioned of a future that was not to be.

On the day that I arrived at Deerwood, Marj had set up a table for my computer that looked out over a beautifully tended garden. I woke to birds singing and went to sleep with moonlight streaming through the window. Marj cooked healthy meals and for four years the three of us ate as a family each evening.

One by one God closed every avenue that stood in the way of my full attention being focused on the operational reach of these crimes. I cannot count the number of times that I went to bed with a headache from reading the small print in documents I did not understand. Only to wake the following morning with a clear idea or understanding. There were periods that I dreamt in numbers that connected to my investigation.[61] As the enormity of these theft schemes took shape out of the accumulated hard evidence I stopped seeing my "job" as a burden. Burden morphed into purpose. Purpose became its own incentive.

Kathryn Maceri had made the mistake of talking about RICO as if it were the answer to helping other victims of these crimes. She appealed

[61] ***I will bless the Lord who has counseled me; indeed my mind instructs me in the night (Psalm 16: 7).***

to the strong desire I had to see other homeowners and past victims armed with knowledge; equipped to fight back. The mistake she made was in overselling Civil RICO as a higher goal. In the same catch and kill agenda of Webb Brewer this was a promise that was never intended to materialize.

Kathryn was never going to return my calls. The attorney she had selected to take over while she was, "*undergoing chemo therapy*," was a complete fiction. I had been skillfully played in her office on that last day... yet again. My treatment was symptomatic of how widespread corruption had eroded ethics and any thought of the law as a higher calling to serve the greater good. It was not that I could not give up. It was that God did not want me to give up.

The closed door, *Avernatti type negotiations,* were in all effect an extortionist plot. Payoff for having secretly served the real and actual deep pocket clients. Upon belief, to then launder that income through the settlement structure made in my name, but never disclosed to me. These lawyers were in all effect hired by the Criminal Enterprise to silence my evidence from ever being heard in any venue that could leave a record. Some must have celebrated when I walked out of the Claiborne Ferguson law offices on that day. Once again, I was thought handled to the extent that they could all breath a collective sigh of relief.

To extort is to use information or threat of violence to acquire cash or something else. Extortion is a classic shakedown, a gouge, a squeeze. Usually it's money someone is after if they're going to extort you for it. www.vocabulary.com.

Shortly after this I ran into a woman from the Fair Oaks card group. She greeted me with a big smile and the words: "I heard you got a big settlement." My expression caused her smile to evaporate very quickly. I'm still waiting for the help God promised He would send. Where are you?

I was just one person. When people come to me with a list of what I could have, should have done, I can only say that I had a huge learning curve probably greater than any reader of this book. I had to pick and choose my battles. I prepared to file the Civil RICO Case. Farris-Bobango, Webb Brewer, and Kathryn Maceri would be named as defendants.

I gradually began to grasp how Civil RICO was intended to function for any American citizen empowered to act as a citizen-prosecutor. Only those rigging the system want common sense laws twisted so that certain crimes can continue to flourish. I had approximately eight months. The four-year statute of limitations clock did not start ticking with the sales pitch date of the foreclosure charade that both Webb Brewer and Kathryn Maceri attempted to legitimize; searing it into my brain. It began when the goals of the criminal enterprise were met and not before.

I do well with deadlines and goals. April 25, 2016 became that for me. I could have pushed the statute of limitations start date further off. I decided to stick with the date of the illegal seizure. I filed the Civil RICO Case with the federal district court with five days to spare on April 20, 2016. It was very clear that I was not an attorney. But I had researched RICO criteria and ticked all the boxes as I named defendants and established enterprise plus relationship with ongoing threat to other victims.

The United States Constitution is a document that a population driven to powerlessness must not know the import of. I would get a copy and refer to it often and especially after being denied due process at the *screening for merit,* blockade. I kept a copy nearby as I wrote the Pro Se Appellant's Brief that, as it turned out, no judge at the sixth circuit would ever read. If any say they did they must explain why the appeal questions were never addressed, replaced by a clerk authored proxy question I never raised. Could I have done a better job? Not without an attorney. But then, courts do not exist for lawyers and power brokers, but for WE THE PEOPLE.

I knew that my fourth and fourteenth amendment rights had been trampled upon. I was not so easily sold on the Vescovo/Lipman/Hance Orwellian logic that though my objections had not been addressed at the lower court. And then my appeal questions had not been addressed at the sixth circuit. Somehow magically and inexplicably they had been addressed. Intimidated by the huge imbalance of power quashing justice I should therefore abandon all logic, follow the pro se script laid down for me, echoed in the words of the Farris-Bobango attorney, "why don't you give up!"

Kathryn Maceri lied to me when she said the statute of limitations was three years. This lie was tied to her abrupt departure leaving me to conclude that I was out of time with no path forward. She lied when she told me that a federal judge would throw ERA Chamberwood Realty Group out as defendants because they did not fit under the RICO umbrella of offenses otherwise known as Predicate Acts.

Both she and Webb Brewer needed me to believe that the foreclosure was the salient event. I must never learn that it was a complete hoax proposed in the public record to deflect from the pre-foreclosure assumption of mortgages. In fixing any defense on the foreclosure charade as the single watershed date fraudsters are protecting and deflecting from the Bank Theft Delivery System.

It was not just my story that needed to be silenced. I had amassed three pattern groupings of other homes, most located in Fayette County. Those stories jumping from the spread sheets, specific addresses, names of victims, names of straw buyers, commonalties of practice amid forged documentation would be entered into evidence to become a permanent public record. It seems a kind of poetic justice that I was led to RICO, introduced to it by criminal attorneys whose bias told them that filing a Civil RICO Case was a bar too high for average, lawyer-less Americans.

I am told that federal regulators and investigators scan Civil RICO Cases. Smaller cases often lead to wider, broader prosecutions. My case was prejudiced on the day it was filed. It was mislabeled by the federal district court as a mere foreclosure dispute. Any data search under Civil RICO would throw my case out of any search results. Do not imagine for a single moment that this was a coincidence.

RICO: 18 U.S.C. § 1962(c): It shall be unlawful for any person employed by or associated with any enterprise engaged in, or the activities of which affect, interstate or foreign commerce, to conduct or participate, directly or indirectly, in the conduct of such enterprise affairs through a pattern of racketeering activity or collection of unlawful debt.

Under RICO, **"Enterprise," means individuals, legal entities, and illegal entities, including partnerships, corporations, associations and unions Id. § 1961(4).**

These thefts must take place under the pretense of being lawful. They must appear as legitimate transactions, at least upon a superficial inspection of what is publicly available. It is hoped that the incomplete public filings representing broken chain of the title, will be as far as any investigation will go. This is among the goals of the Criminal Enterprise theft model.[62]

Real estate companies operating as an arm of the local groups make more money on the back end, providing, *"REO management services to the Fund."* They are managing groups of homes. This is why you will find many clustered in specific areas. The Pretium Partners model is not to accept stolen property until after the title is laundered and fenced through the Bank Theft Delivery System. At this point the local REO scam artists become *"servicer affiliates"* managing the pool of stolen properties for the "Fund." The "Fund" is the group of securities, backed up by stolen property that is being marketed by Banks to their investor-depositors.

The Pretium Partners section on: **Code of Ethics, Participation or interests in Client Transactions and Personal Trading**[63] reads like here is the standard everyone acknowledges to be right, moral, and lawful. At the same time, in practice, explaining how the rule of law can be skirted. The conflicts of interest among the servicer affiliates explain why my realtor and Crye Leike Realty, at the time I had my home listed for sale, failed to tell me that the listing was dead in the water before the photographs ever appeared on line. My home was already an REO Owned property. What happened to me has happened to countless other American homeowners. Seen as a whole, this is a gangster conclave acting like a small country, flaunting their power in the face of numerous federal agencies including Treasury and the Securities and Exchange Commission.

---

[62] Pretium Partners, "Types of Clients" include REO Institutional Investment Groups feeding homes to this securities market. Quoted from Part 2A of Form ADV: 2017 Firm Brochure. Pretium Mortgage Credit Management, LLC (PMCM); page-9 Item-7. *"The minimum capital commitment for investing in the fund is 2 (two) million, which minimum may be waived by the Fund's General Partner. The minimum capital commitment for opening a managed account, if applicable, shall be described in the written investment management agreement entered into by and between PMCM and the managed account client, and is subject to negotiation." And from page-4 Item 4 – Advisory Business. "The Fund invests principally in the United States residential housing credit market though purchases of pools consisting of nonperforming, reperforming, and subperforming residential mortgage loans and, from time to time,* ***residential real property (REO)."*** *And: "PMCM has entered into side letters or other writings with* ***individual investors,*** *which have had the effect of establishing rights under, or altering or supplementing the terms of, the limited partnership agreement."* Individual Investors, aka, the needed boots on the ground REO Investment Groups. My limited investigation identified three groups operating in my geographical area. Perfection of the theft scheme described in this book is lawyer heavy.

[63] From: Form ADV Part 2A Brochure / 2017.

Keeping the circle of exposure tight, Pretium Mortgage Credit Management, LLC – *"...due to the nature of its strategies, PMCM does not generally trade in public securities and, therefore does not generally utilize broker-dealers for transactions contemplated by this section."* Let me interpret. Due to the illegal theft practices (strategies). Limiting exposure of a mafia like Criminal Enterprise... we do not generally trade in public. There is the local Ponzi scheme, with Deeds of Trust invested in before the same theft asset is transferred to the Pretium Partners model to be sold globally many times over. The local investment in Deeds of Trust are a kind of Ponzi scheme since the local investment is lost and profits are diluted. Only the local REO Investment tight circle retain profits.

Look at the transactions that took place post-eviction. In West Tennessee, after equity was skimmed, targeted properties were transferred per Warranty Deed into the Pretium Partners shell company of FREO Tennessee, LLC; operating by different names in different states. Shell companies limit exposure of the national scope of these crimes.[64] They are also used to launder income. At year-end Pretium Partners would have provided statements and residuals to their boots on the ground co-conspirators.

Civil RICO, empowers average Americans to act as citizen prosecutors under the RICO statutes. Its purpose was clearly stated.

RICO / Public Law 91-452. *Be it enacted by the Senate and House of Representatives of the United States of America in Congress assembled, that this Act may be cited as the "Organized Crime Control Act of 1970." The Congress finds that (1) organized crime in the United States is a highly sophisticated, diversified, and widespread activity that annually drains billions of dollars from America's economy;*

[64] Pretium Partners uses shell companies registered by different names doing business in different states. This limits recognition of the RICO Enterprise and national footprint of these crimes. In Tennessee, FREO Tennessee, LLC. A branch of a Tennessee foreign liability company; number: 000727687. Incorporated: August 5, 2013 in Delaware. Registered Address: 2015: 7500 N. Dobson Road, STE 300, Scottsdale, AZ 85256-2727. Agent Name: Corporation Service Company. One of the founders of Pretium Partners, LLC resides in Arizona. Many of the Tennessee phony foreclosures were notarized in Arizona. Also sharing the same New York address as that building that houses Bank of New York Mellon; defrauding the investors in the securitized trusts.

(2) organized crime derives a major portion of its power through money obtained from such illegal endeavors as.... theft and fencing of property.

(3) this money and power are increasingly used to infiltrate and corrupt legitimate business and labor unions and to subvert and corrupt the democratic processes.

It is the purpose of this Act to seek the eradication of organized crime in the United States by strengthening the legal tools in the evidence gathering process, by establishing new penal prohibitions, and by providing enhanced sanctions and new remedies to deal with unlawful activities of those engaged in organized crime.

A "fence" is a person who knowingly buys or temporarily takes possession of stolen property. In the electronic age of today, those that launder the property title to stolen homes do so over the MERS data base. MERS is acting as the booster crew, in the fencing of stolen property capacity. There is not a pawn shop in the picture. In an electronic age there is instead the MERS data base. The property title has to be periodically parked. Think of this as parked in the back room display case of a corrupt pawn shop. When police come calling the stolen property is out of sight.

The property title is conveyed (fenced) per a theft perfecting conveyance document to those that will launder (fence) the chain of title. This may include an assignment of authority granted to another party like the third-party mortgage servicer company. Proceeds are turned over quickly and used to finance theft of other homes. This scheme is cash-rich. Thus, house payments become assignment of rents. Laundered income is off-set by claims of exaggerated and phony expenses. This money is traceable; as they say, "follow the money."

The difference between 1970, when RICO was enacted into law and today, is that the financial industry has so corrupted government and infiltrated themselves into policy decisions that the fleecing of an American populace is normalized.

In chapter nine titled: *"A Roadmap for Reform."* Helen Davies Chaitman and Lance Gotthoffer wrote: *"Glass Steagall was enacted in 1933, at the height of the Great Depression. It prohibited banks whose deposits are insured by the federal government – that is, by the taxpayers – from engaging in investment banking activities whereby money owned by depositors was used for speculative business activity on which the profits are inured 100 percent to the banks." From their book: JP Madoff.*

RICO Violations (predicate acts) are specific and clear. Here is a partial list. Download the complete list and think about what applies to theft of your home.

1. "Racketeering activity" means
   (A) any act or threat involving murder, kidnapping, gambling, arson, **robbery,** bribery, extortion, dealing in obscene matter, or dealing in a controlled substance or listed chemical...
   (B) any act which is indictable under any of the following provisions of Title 18, United States Code: 201 relating to...

What follows is an incomplete list. Some will be applicable to you and some may not be. You only need two.

- Relating to Racketeering, section 1952
- Relating to extortionate credit transactions, section 1028.
- Relating to fraud and related to activity in connection with identification documents, section 1029.
- Relating to fraud and related activity in connection with access devices, section 1084 An access device is any card, plate, code, account number or other means of account access that can be used alone or in conjunction with another access device, to obtain money, goods, (property like a house), or services or any other thing of value, or that can be used to initiate a transfer of funds or property (other than a transfer that originates solely by paper instrument. This would include almost everything filed over the MERS system initiating a transfer of your home to thus launder the theft asset, replacing your name with the identity theft moniker of the fraudsters.
- Read also 1994 US Code title 18: (Fraud and Related Activity in Connection with Access Devices, 1028, 1028A, 1029.)
- Relating to mail fraud, section 1343.
- Relating to wire fraud, section 1344.
- Bank Fraud, section 1344.
- Relating to financial institution fraud, section 1425.

- Relating to obstruction of justice, section 1510.
- Relating to obstruction of criminal investigations, section 1511.
- Relating to the obstruction of state and local law enforcement, section 1512.
- Relating to tampering with a witness, victim, or an informant, section 1513.
- Relating to retaliating against a witness, victim or an informant, section 1542.
- Relating to the laundering of monetary instruments, section 1956, 1957.
- Relating to engaging in monetary transactions in property derived from specified unlawful activity, section 1958.
- Also, fraud in the sale (price fixing) of securities as a monetary instrument.
- False statements on a credit or loan application, section 1014.
- Destruction, alteration, or falsification of Records; 1517, 1519.
- Also, under Title 11 any interference of the criminal enterprise to obstruct your right to apply for bankruptcy, protecting your home and allowing you to sell it yourself.

There is no complete picture without identifying the local fraudsters. Sadly, you will find that some of these people were in your immediate orbit of relationships.

Enterprise plus Relationship. Imagine two wheels side by side. Using my home as an example, Bank of America sits in the center as the hub of the first wheel. Spokes branch out to draw in those other corporate entities like MERS, First American Title Insurance Company, Core Logic Services, ReconTrust Company, and the third-party mortgage servicer company etc. The REO Fraudsters and the Bank also need a mail clearing center. A way to subvert communications and money. Stewart Lender Services, Inc. and in Orwellian doublespeak another moniker; Home Retention Group. **Every cog in the wheel is a Bank vendor and a MERS member. This is the link to establishing Enterprise Plus Relationship.** As the theft asset (your home) moves along the vendor conveyer belt each plays their part. This first wheel is a visual of what makes up the national scope of practice. Insert the names that fit your investigation.

The dangerous Jones, Kelley, Boyd Perpetrator Nexus – REO Investment Group formed the HUB of my second wheel. These local Enterprise-Relationships operate within the community footprint researching, targeting, and selecting likely victims.

They also freely use the MERS System. The groups I looked at had bought into Pretium Partners or a brokerage arm of Sun Trust Bank. Your investigation may produce other names, other banks and bank vendors. The local groups may end up managing their own portfolio of rentals, selling and reselling these commodities; propped up and sustained by theft, fraud, and the price fixing of the rental market. Thus, they hide their identity behind proxy bank-names and interim lenders that have allowed them to skim equity pre-foreclosure charade from homes acquired by robbery.

These local groups of operatives are not a regulated industry with a board of directors holding rogue CEO's to a standard of care. These are thugs running a kind of Ponzi scheme drawing in and inducing an army of dupes into feeding more and more leads to their attention.

Other creative methods have surfaced. Any sudden rise in taxes over a specific geographic area where the demographics include an aging population. People with few resources including immigrants buying into the American dream of home ownership. Who was bribed to help carve out that area, making it ripe for title theft under cover of law because of this sudden rise in property taxes? Whose connections have influenced career civil servants to set the ground work for a strategic land grab?

I added David Osborn, Keller Williams, and others as my investigation progressed. Of particular interest to you are the local title companies and lawyers that have falsified those documents on file with the Registry of Deeds Office and with MERSCorp Holdings, Inc.

Make a trip to the local office supply store. Invest in plastic page sheets, file folders, labels, and two large three ring binders. There were some documents that I repeatedly referred to. I kept copies of these documents in an elbow accessed smaller binder. Certain paper that hovered over the trash receptacle by my computer, though I could not anticipate its usefulness, later proved very helpful and I was glad I'd drawn my hand back. Stick to the maxim, when in doubt save, label, and file. There were times that I saved something and later did not recall why. I learned to attach a note that explained my reasoning. Only recently have I purged some of that paper.

I found it very helpful to read other Civil RICO Cases. Especially those where a district court judge had rejected a Civil RICO Case on the grounds that it did not meet RICO criteria and then had that decision reversed on appeal.[65] The Kalitta Air case was filed in the Eastern District of Michigan alleging Civil RICO claims as well as state offenses. This case centered on money stolen from an escrow fund.[66] This escrow fund was set up to provide jet fuel for international flights. Escrow funds, like pension funds are attractive targets of financial crimes. This should sound familiar.

Kalitta Air, LLC Plaintiff-Appellant v. GSBD & Associates, et, al., Defendant-Appellees. United States Court of Appeals for the Sixth Circuit. Case No.: 14-1027. Not Recommendation for Full-Text Publication: File No.: 14a0847n.06.

Why the heck not! *"Not recommended for full text publication."* Or, *"Not recommended for publication"* translates to the court censoring access. In light of today's skepticism, I read statements like this and conclude that the court is concealing a poorly crafted decision that would not receive passing marks from a law school professor. To say that it was crafted by someone that lacked skill and knowledge. Someone other than an actual judge. The lesser standard of care described in my complaint(s) of judicial misconduct represented and opened the door for administrative corruption at the sixth circuit.[67]

The value in reading other RICO cases is that you come to recognize the very many commonalties they all share. The plot and drama are different. But the bones of what makes the story a RICO story is the

---

[65] Kalitta Air, LLC Plaintiff-Appellant v. GSBD & Associates, et al, Defendants-Appellees. On appeal from the United States District Court for the Eastern District of Michigan. Case No. 14-1027. "Because we conclude that the district court erred in dismissing Kalitta's federal RICO claims against both the defaulted and non-defaulted defendants, it abused its discretion in declining supplemental jurisdiction under 28 U.S.C. § 1367(c)(3), which applies only if the court has "dismissed all claims over which it has original jurisdiction."

[66] At the point that the REO Fraudsters assume the mortgage the question is, how are escrow funds converted to private use by the Criminal Enterprise? Escrow funds like Pension funds are frequently targeted by white collar criminals.

[67] Des Moines Register. "Iowa judge admits hundreds of his rulings were ghost-written by attorneys, raising a host of ethical and fairness concerns." By, Clark Kauffman; ckauffman@dmreg.com.

same. In the Kalitta Air Case the RICO Predicate Acts alleged were, in part wire fraud, mail fraud, and money laundering. Over a thirty-two-month period $4.7 million dollars was stolen from the Kalitta Air escrow account. Some of this stolen money was used to refinance a mortgage. The lower court's decision to dismiss this case was coincidentally overturned at the Sixth Circuit Court of Appeals. In comparison my appeal was assigned no care at all in that the appeal questions were never addressed.

Kalitta Air does work for the United States military. It was alleged that GSBD & Associates presented an ongoing threat to future victims because they were continuing to operate. Some other of the counts cited were: common-law conversion, fraud and fraudulent inducement, breach of contract, breach of fiduciary duty, conspiracy, and concert of action. Reading other cases, what was charged, what survived after a challenge, and what was reversed on appeal was not only entertaining, but it served as a kind of rudimentary education. One of the defendants, First International posed as a bank. Through them the escrow funds were stolen. The stories can be pretty fascinating. But distilled to what they achieve the practices are banal, repetitive, and not that hard to recognize. Take it one step at a time. Do not be intimidated.

Under the False Claims Act the United States has a cause of action when it is defrauded. How are decisions made? Some crimes are considered hot topics of redress while others are less important. Bias of the judiciary to think no lawyer no case. To imagine that Civil RICO in the hands of armatures sets a dangerous precedence. These elitist assumptions codified into action cut the legs out from what is guaranteed to every American under the United States Constitution.

Confirmation-bias is any preconceived stance, outlook, conclusion that will not be dislodged by facts or objective evidence. An example of confirmation-bias would be that untenable stance taken by holocaust deniers. To say that the extermination of six million Jewish men, women, and children by Nazi-Germany during World War 11, despite absolute historical evidence augmented by first-hand accounts and the Nuremberg trials is a fiction. Confirmation bias can also be quite subtle. In confronting these crimes and raising awareness of how they operate we need to push back against the insidious rationale that home owners are solely responsible for what happens to them.

I talked with Doug Kalitta. He did not fully appreciate his companies and lawyers contribution in strengthening the civil RICO statutes for ordinary Americans in the very corrupt culture of our times. The Sixth Circuit recommended that this case not be published. Its content could therefore, not strengthen the position of other victims filing Civil RICO cases. The intent may have been to shield the lower courts failure to rule according to the law. There is yet another damaging ancillary outcome in censoring public access to certain cases. We must look at whether some appeals courts are more prone to employ censorship and what types of decisions, written by whom, informs a pattern of bias. Fully intentional or not the questions become, what judges are more prone than others to recklessly abdicate their responsibility to clerks and staff attorneys, rubber stamping the Deep State need to undermine equal access and delivery of Constitutional protections seated in due process and the right to be heard.

RICO more reasonably addresses that criminal organizations and their ruthless activities take time to uncover. Under Civil RICO, and not elsewhere, there is a very present opportunity for average citizens to appear before a jury when otherwise the cost of a trial would be prohibitive. Anyone who meets the requirements can apply for pauper status.

Whether they agree to appoint you an attorney or not, after the *screening for merit,* impediment to due process is overcome the government will carry these costs. It is in the spirit of the Civil RICO statutes that exposure of such crimes was thought important to preserve. In contrast, as a lazy hypothesis, bias tells an elite class that no lawyer uniformly equates to no case. This mindset filters down to corrupt the thinking of federal employees. There was a time in our history when income did not dictate access to Due Process. When access to a fair judge was defended and valiantly upheld.

Learn your way around the law library at the local university. If you can afford it there are people there you can hire to do research for you. If not do it yourself. I found that the University of Memphis (Cecil C. Humphreys School of Law) employees were helpful even when I asked the same question several times over.

Courts do make mistakes. They have in the past bowed to political-societal-economic pressures. One infamous example was the Dred Scott Decision that is even today a, blot on our justice system. This decision declared that even in free states Dred Scott, as a black person, was still a slave. To thus, set a dastardly legal precedent that human beings deemed chattel should be returned to their masters.

The Alan Dershowitz remark: "**Judges are the weakest link in our system of justice and they are also the most protected**" is informative. Despite objective evidence that Magistrate Judge Vescovo had slandered my claims, Judge Lipman rubber stamped those decisions, ignoring my objections, allowing slander to stand as an official record. The nature of bias is that we do not always recognize it working through us.

Confirmation-bias worked against me. It was assumed that I would not have read the United States Constitution and Bill of Rights. I could be coerced by the huge imbalance of power, the information gaps, and administrative corruption to accept my fate. *Screening for Merit* is not Due Process. Clerks willfully doing an end run around the right to have appeal questions recognized and addressed is an actual crime.

The Caperton Case is an example of that deadly confluence of confirmation-bias and a corrupt judge protected by an enabling judiciary. This judge was convinced that his office placed him above the law. This case is well worth reading and if you run into trouble, quoting from.

"Caperton v. A.T. Massey Coal Co., 556 U.S. 868 (2009), is a case in which the United States Supreme Court held that the Due Process clause of the Fourteenth Amendment requires a judge to recuse himself not only when actual bias has been demonstrated or when the judge has an economic interest in the outcome of the case, but when "extreme facts" create a "probability of bias."

Caperton was the plaintiff bringing this case. They were awarded $50 million in damages by the lower court. The state appeals court overturned the lower court decision. Knowing that the West Virginia Supreme Court would consider this appeal Massey decided to stack the deck in their favor. Don Blankenship, Massey's chairman and principal officer supported the election campaign of a particular judge they wanted assigned to hear appeal of this $50 million-dollar judgement that had gone against them. Solution: set up and buy off a judge. Judge Brent Benjamin was the recipient of a three million-dollar campaign donation.

Benjamin then won by fewer than 50,000 votes making this donation a significant factor in tilting the outcome of that election. He then upheld the reversal meaning that the injured party, Caperton, lost the 50-million settlement awarded to them by the lower court. Caperton then moved to disqualify justice Brent Benjamin based on the conflict of interest arising from that campaign donation. Justice Benjamin refused to recuse himself despite two requests to do so. He held on to any outcome with an iron grip. Magistrate Judge Vescovo, enabled by Judge Lipman did the same.

Unlike Judge Oscar Carr in the Collins-Maury Case, Justice Benjamin did not look at the defendant list and voluntarily excuse himself at the outset. He did not care how his behavior reflected badly upon the court. Nor how that behavior spilled over to breed distrust of those honest and good judges that endeavor each day to embrace duty as a privileged calling. Although a court may not deliver the outcome we want Americans must be able to trust that judges are not corrupt. Both Magistrate Judge Vescovo and Justice Benjamin put a dent in how judges are perceived.

Unable or unwilling to admit even the possibility of bias, four months later Justice Benjamin went so far as to file an opinion, affirming his own decision, defending the failure to recuse despite overwhelming evidence that there were conflicts of interest. To quote an astute and discerning observer of human nature, William Shakespeare: *Methinks thou dost protest too much.*[68]

Like Kalitta Air, we can thank Caperton for pursuing its right to a fair and unbiased judge. They performed a service to every American that values the United States Constitution and Bill of Rights as the premier law, above all other laws.

They appealed to the United States Supreme Court. Massey Coal Company must have weighed the odds and believed the Supreme Court would never accept this case since so few are selected to be heard at the highest court in our land. This must have also been on the mind of Case Manager Hance when, offended that I had filed a motion for a void judgement, she told me to appeal instead to the United States Supreme Court.

---

[68] William Shakespeare, Hamlet Act 3, Scene 2: "The lady doth protest too much, methinks."

There were many junctures that the Criminal Enterprise thought they held absolute sway over obstruction of my Constitutional Right to be heard. Don Blankenship, Massey's chairman, thought he had won. The Jones, Kelley, Boyd Perpetrator Nexus and the Bank Theft Delivery System thought too that it was over. Each had positioned a corrupt judge to deliver the outcome they needed. We can easily imagine that the Massey attorneys told their clients they were off the hook to pay this money and would never be held accountable for in effect, contriving to put a judge biased to deliver a corrupt outcome, on the bench.

As it turned out the Supreme Court did agree to hear the Caperton case. This informs that they felt clarity was needed over an issue that they perhaps saw as trending away from the rule of law and the public welfare. The Supreme Court ruled on points of law, in part, centered on conflict of interest and judicial recusal.

Repeating they ruled that: ***The Due Process clause of the Fourteenth Amendment requires a judge to recuse himself not only when actual bias has been demonstrated or when the judge has an economic interest in the outcome of the case, but when "extreme facts" create a "probability of bias."***

There must be safety in admitting mistakes. Stubborn refusal to do so speaks to a defect of character. To say that we are human is not the death of ego, but a greater grace. Admitting mistakes does not diminish a judiciary it strengthens and builds public confidence for the judiciary. We say that justice is blind to say that the *"Judge or Judiciary makes decisions based upon the evidence presented without outside influence or predisposition and upon the appropriate law;" (Wikipedia).*

I am still waiting for my complaints of judicial misconduct to be addressed. I am still waiting for my motion for a void judgement to be ruled on. That is... if what I submitted still exists and was not long ago fed to a paper shredder.

CHAPTER TWENTY-TWO

"Government has coddled, accepted, and ignored white collar crime for too long. It is time the nation woke up and realized it's not the armed robbers or drug dealers who cause the most economic harm, it's the white-collar criminals living in the most expensive homes who have the most impressive resumes who harm us the most. They steal our pensions, bankrupt our companies, and destroy thousands of jobs, ruining countless lives." Harry Markopolos *...and we wonder why an outsider populist president was elected and the efforts to impeach him failed.*

I became very curious about what makes a career con-artist. How do these people manage to blend so seamlessly into the communities they target? In looking for answers I took a go-to book from my bookcase; PEOPLE OF THE LIE by, the late M. Scott Peck. While at Christ United Methodist Church I wrote and taught a lesson series on the complex relationship between King Ahab and Queen Jezebel juxtaposed with Pecks description of evil and the interventionist actions of the Prophet Elijah in breaking the authority of that deadly partnership.[69] Only then could a land and its people begin to heal.

Peck did not discuss evil in the context of obvious stereotypes. As a psychiatrist Peck makes the point that those committed to a life-time of doing harm are deserving of our compassion even as we take steps to protect against them. He believed that evil was a distinct type of personality disorder. Dr. Phil McGraw has done a lot to raise awareness about the impact of neurological deficits upon behavior. Peck agreed with Erich Fromm that evil, left to its own devices becomes, more, evil meaning that the trajectory and reach of evil requires intervention. On the other end of that continuum goodness as a life-commitment evolves into greater good reflecting that kind of life journey actualized via the spirit of truth working through us.

[69] PEOPLE OF THE LIE: The Hope For Healing Human Evil. Simon & Schuster, Inc.; Copyright 1983, by M. Scott Peck, MD. First Touchstone Edition, 1985. First Kings Chapter 18, Chapter 19.

I would add that evil has a preternatural-manifested malevolence that intelligently seeks to flood any breach, deficit, or impairment.[70] Once a foothold is achieved that satanic realized malevolence is crack addict on steroids against any attempt of its prisoners to heal and change. While deliverance from what entraps us may be a burning bush kind of experience that instantly frees us, more often it comes as a multi-faceted process followed by a life commitment to walk out those changes.

According to Peck evil is recognized by the following consistently applied behaviors. Consistent being the salient word. The fact is that we are all situationally tempted at times to engage these behaviors. Most of us learn very early in life that such behaviors do not make for a happy life.

(a) consistent destructive, scapegoating behavior, which may often be quite subtle.
(b) Excessive, albeit usually covert, intolerance for criticism and other forms of narcissistic injury.
(c) Pronounced concern with a public image and self-image of respectability, contributing to a stability of life-style but also to pretentiousness and denial of hateful feelings and vengeful motives.
(d) Intellectual deviousness, with an increased likelihood of a mild schizophrenic-like disturbance of thinking at times of stress.

It took far more time and investigation for me to recognize the local players. They were well hidden and remained so concealing their identity in numerous documents behind that of Bank of America, HUD, MERS, and Bank of New York Mellon. The Bank Theft Delivery System was the unreachable, big picture shielded by power, influence, and money. In contrast, my neighbor and someone I had called a friend, Ann Jones, was another matter entirely. Along with wondering how career con-artists blend into their environment, I punished myself

---

[70] If you are interested in this topic read: DISCERNING SPIRITS: Visionary Gifts in Practice. Alexandra Clair; ISBN No.: 9780984705900. This book looks at three manifestations of demonic possession pictured in the Biblical Old and New Testament accounts.

wondering what I missed about what turned out to be a practiced and predatory intrusion into my life.

It is very likely that like me, you may look back and realize you could have named these local bad actors long before you recognized how they zeroed in on you and your home as a vulnerable theft target.

Many a pyramid scheme involves securities fraud. Just as there is the big picture securities fraud there is the local securities fraud having little to do with what is traded on Wall Street or the NASDAQ. Read the 1934 Securities and Exchange rule. Securities fraud include: *"any plan or operation for the* ***sale or distribution of property****, services, or any other thing of value wherein a person, for consideration is offered an opportunity to obtain a benefit which is based in whole or in part on the inducement, by himself or herself or by others, of additional persons to purchase the same or similar opportunity."* Partial description of securities fraud quoted from: State of Delaware v. (Keller Williams Realtor) David Attarian; I.D. No. 1303009480. Defendants Motion to Dismiss – DENIED.

A pyramid scheme based on promissory notes that read like Deeds of Trust, coming with an investment sales pitch meets the criteria of securities fraud. When others have stated that the Keller Williams business model resembles a pyramid scheme, they have not delved deeply enough into the way that the franchises feed homes to The Bank Theft Delivery System promising residuals that flow up, diluting returns down line until they are negligible and nothing like what was initially promised. At the end of the flipping cycle many of these homes go into default and are transferred by Warranty Deed or Quit Claim Deed to companies like Pretium Partners, LLC while the interim investors suffer losses.

The fanatic requirement to produce, colored by group think, cross the line into cult like structures that induce people to break the law. I was struck by a transcript in which a Pennsylvania Keller Williams Realtor[71] described under questioning how he contrived that a certain property was never legitimately offered to the public. What struck me was the lack of awareness. It seemed to me that he had been inoculated by

[71] Ryan Leonard Case, Superior Court, Pennsylvania. Ryan Leonard was an attorney who tried to buy a bank owned property and was prevented by The Bank Theft Delivery System and the Keller Williams listing agent from doing so. He also turned out to be a lawyer who recognized that laws were broken. It was no accident that he lost out on a "good deal." Among the defendants named by him was: Keller Williams International.

group-think against the realization that in not entertaining a legitimate offer of purchase, keeping the property in the price fixing title flip structure, he had committed several crimes both state and federal. I wondered what the judge thought as he heard this testimony.

Those that invest in these endeavors devote time, energy, and funds. This commitment requires one to rationalize continuing with bad behavior. This is reinforced by coercive group think. It becomes harder and harder to pivot back to critical thinking skills. A fence of secrecy and misplaced loyalties build up around the activities. Local bad actors watched what was happening to me. The fraud narrative was out. Some smiled and greeted me knowing that my mortgage had been assumed by predatory criminals long before I had a clue that anything was wrong. They said nothing.

I applied the term, "perpetrator nexus" in countless letters trying to garner help and recognition of these crimes. A lot of others, including those promised residuals that never materialized danced around this same perpetrator-orbit.

The working summary below is an account of the local connections. Though I established this in the Civil RICO Case I wrote this summary for myself. It helped me stay on track as other evidence tempted me into broader fields of investigation. I listed the names sequentially to inform when they intersected my life. David Osborn as the multiple Keller Williams franchise owner is not named in the Jones, Kelley, Boyd heading. As a kingpin he was only recognized later informed by ongoing research.

The chain of theft is embodied in the phrase: *Property Flip – Equity Skimming Scheme* coined by federal investigators and well known to courts of law. I've added *Title Theft as a goal established in the steady drip of identity fraud.* Title theft is accomplished when the fraudsters replace that name that appears in the original Deed of Trust, as the source document, with the fraudster identity in countless trailing documents. The golden ticket that starts the identity theft ball rolling is achieved at the state and local level when county trustees, performing no due diligence, stamp the tax receipt paid in full. One cannot skim equity, no disclosure to homeowners, until the fraudster identity buries that name appearing on the original Deed of Trust.

I kept a short elbow file close by. This was made up of key evidence frequently referred to. I created a time line of key events. This saved me from digging into my boxes of files each time I needed to retrieve a date. I copied much of my evidence and as a duplicate record stored it in a safe place. What follows in italics are the relationship connections. Write something like this so that when you talk about or write letters to those with the power to do something about these crimes you make the same points using the same words. Simplistic repetition of language already in use raises awareness that might otherwise be lost. Thus, perpetrator nexus, and Property Flip Scheme.

Ann Jones is married to Max Jones. They lived five homes away from me, our homes linked by a short walk along the path that encircles the Fair Oaks golf course. Max Jones served as the Certified Public Accountant for the Jones, Kelley, Boyd Perpetrator Nexus – REO Investment Group. Another associate of the group lived in the neighborhood; acting as attorney. Lewis Garrison had been previously sued for defrauding Bank of America. This may explain why he networked and delegated to other law firms.[72] *He kept a very low profile within the neighborhood. Lewis Garrison activities regarding other suspect neighborhood properties are tied to the law firm of Glankler-Brown at which Judge Oscar Carr had been employed while also interfacing and advising as needed, with the core group of local operatives.*

The name Max Jones appears as serving on the audit committee for Preferred Auto Insurance Company owned in part by, Jeffrey L. Kelley and Lennie Faye (Boyd) Kelley.[73] *My RICO Exhibits*

[72] General Sessions Court, Shelby County, Tennessee; September 19, 2002. Bank of America v. Lewis K. Garrison. Case ID: 915989. Judgement for plaintive September 11, 2002 in the amount of: $10,321.76 plus court costs. Shelby County Register of Deeds; Instrument No.: 02168654. Lewis Garrison lived in the same Fair Oaks Neighborhood as does his ex-wife. See also: Warranty Deed in Lieu of Foreclosure, Instrument No.: 10007010. See Special Warranty Deed, Instrument No. 11001483. Lewis Garrison, Glankler Brown, PLLC tied to Judge Oscar Carr, 111.

[73] RICO Case Exhibit No.: 61. State of TN Department of Commerce and Insurance Report on Examination of Preferred Auto Insurance Company, Inc., December 31, 2012; NAIC No.: 10223. Note page-5, Audit Committee; Max Jones. Page-17, quid-pro-quo incentive "Custodial agreement" with Bank of Fayette County appearing to launder income derived from stolen property. Civil RICO, Exhibit No. 117. Also Exhibit 61-A, Preferred Auto organizational chart. This and all other related evidence treated by Judge Vescovo as if it did not exist. Failing to accept my claims as true, as required at the screening juncture, she functioned like an aggressive defense attorney even citing information I did not have and would not have had until discovery. Screening is not due process. It is my prayer that I will someday stand in a courtroom and present the accumulation of hard evidence to a jury of my peers. There is no statute of limitations on a void judgement.

No.: 61; also informed by Exhibit No.:117. Vernon "Wayne" Boyd's sister is Lennie Faye (Boyd) Kelley. The local nucleus of criminals that targeted me included other bad-actors who traded their professional expertise to, for a fee or for the promise of investment residuals perfect these thefts.

The inner circle "relationships" that directly targeted me were: Max and Ann Jones, Jeffrey L. Kelley. Lennie Faye (Boyd) Kelley. Multiple Keller Williams Franchise owner, David Osborn. Vernon "Wayne" Boyd and wife Sherry Boyd (Keller Williams Realty). Hattie Brawley and Loretta Martin operated under the umbrella of the decoy listing agency; ERA Chamberwood Realty Group acting as the Criminal Enterprise "muscle."

Most are associated in business and additionally by blood, marriage, church ties and, or, the long history of criminality stretching back to the Gintz brothers/Kelley frauds operating in Tennessee and in Washington State. Real and pseudo familiar loyalties undergirded the delusion that as a group, no member would break ranks. Immune from detection because powerful financial industry players, even judges, had their backs. It remains to be seen if this Criminal Enterprise is above the law.

The Jones, Kelley, Boyd Perpetrator Nexus, included Keller Williams – MEM 2, LLC. Ongoing patterns of criminality is informed by the Collins Maury Case of internet hacking and corporate espionage. Further by interference of emails coming from the District Court to me. David Osborn and links to securities fraud can be tied to the common theft goals of the greater enterprise informed by where these properties end up. White collar criminals can be traced through their victims, informed by three pattern examples groupings.

It was no coincidence that Ann Jones befriended me in 2009 when my mortgage was assumed from Bank of America premised on the fraud narrative that I had abandoned my home only to be pooled and repurchased out of a HUD program. Ann's job was to act as spy informing on how well the wall of deception was holding up. She exited the field when the HUD fraud came full circle.

The chain of theft is documented by numerous exhibits. Even after they had off-loaded my mortgage premised upon the forged Certificate of Abandonment, Bank of America continued to track the chain of theft to completion. They did so to monitor the ultimate destination of where these homes end up. As evidenced by one of the three pattern example groupings all thirty-two homes transferred by Warranty Deed to Pretium Partners, LLC; shell company FREO Tennessee, LLC. To thus, return long term profit back to the banks networked to the REO Private Investor Groups. Banks then market these securities to their investor-depositors. This is a market founded upon theft and sustained by illegal seizure of private property absent due process in violation of the Fourth Amendment to the United States Constitution.

You may have kept some of the bank correspondence. Read the fine print found at the top or bottom of letters and documents. Look for dates imbedded into a series of numbers. I once worked for a large furniture company. The lowest price we could negotiate without calling in the manager was embedded in a number sequence on the back of every price tag. Messages are sent amongst conspirators using the same principal. Decipher these internal codes. Making sense of them told me when my mortgage was illegally transferred, i.e., off-loaded to the third-party mortgage servicer company by the REO Investment Group with no disclosure to me. Per this coding system I learned when Bank of New York Mellon was paid off at the fabricated loss so as to distance them from the HAMP Fraud Scheme. These deductions were later proved right as my ongoing investigation proceeded.

Bank of New York Mellon failed in their fiduciary duty as trustee over the CWALT trusts; containing the Countrywide mortgages assumed by Bank of America. They conspired with Bank of America to sustain the profit margins realized from a Property Flip Scheme as kickback to the REO Investment Groups for services rendered. Raiding the CWALT mortgage trusts were like organized crime raiding the pension funds of unions. Like legislators raiding social security funds. At first the role played by Bank of New York Mellon was merely a suspicion. That suspicion was later substantiated by other evidence provided by Marie McDonell; McDonnell Property Analytics.

As my investigation progressed something I cannot name chipped itself off the core of who I was and how I filtered life events. I cannot say today if the loss of this something was good or bad. I can only say that I was changed by its going. My faith told me that my stay on planet earth was temporary, but mattered enormously. There were times when I felt helpless and overwhelmed by the greater temporal power of those defending the operational sphere and reach of these crimes. It isn't that we just say to ourselves, "everything happens for a reason." It is that out of that reasoning we play the role of change-maker and defender to the best of our ability and by which, to the nourishment of our souls, we extract meaning from loss; silver from dross.

It was no coincidence that Ann was in my life from the 2009 start of the Property Flip Sequence up to the 2012 illegal seizure. It was her job to act as spy. It is my belief that she took selected mail out of my mail box and papers off my desk. She cultivated the pretense of friendship, reporting back to the criminal cohort on every plan I made to defend my property.

When I stumbled upon news of Judge Carr's death I immediately thought about another person who had died by gunshot wound. The death of Michael Harlow was more intimately connected to the REO Investment Group. I knew more about the circumstances of his death than I was ever intended to know. Ann had talked with me about it. Not extensively, but repeatedly.

When I listed my home for sale in May 2011 this must have sent a current of alarm through the Jones, Kelley, Boyd group of white-collar criminals. They had the note to my mortgage. They had corrupted the property title. They were successfully skimming equity. Would Crye Leike Realty who had listed my home tell me what was going on behind the scenes? Crony corruptionism extends into every area where these crimes have taken hold with no push back from law enforcement.

Over the six months that I had my home listed for sale I had no more than two showings.[74] On the face of what was selectively out there in the ether of the industry only domain(s) I was construed as the criminal trying to sell a home that on paper I no longer owned. No

[74] MLS No.: 3223195; May 5, 2011 thru November 5, 2011. Priced to sell in the depressed market of 2012: $234,000. The illegal JP Morgan Chase Bank loan tied to REO ID No.: 00906148 skimmed 100k of equity; May 16, 2011. This transaction needed to be forward dated in the fraud riddled HUD-1 by one year. This to conceal the presale of my home under the Bank of America forged Certificate of Abandonment and the HUD transfer to the same REO Investors buying my home now three years later. Look for the same pattern of forward dating key events. Other dates may be back dated. Both conceal the chain of theft.

one confronted me with this. This is because any degree of scrutiny would have exposed the real and true criminals. If this fraud scheme is to work the designated mark must remain entirely oblivious to what is taking place. Interested in other aspects of my life Ann never asked how sale of my home was going? She knew that within the crony corrupt culture of criminal enablement it was destined to go nowhere.

Crye Leike Realty started out as a family owned Memphis Company. In true crony corrupt allegiance, they failed to inform me of what they knew to be true. My listing was dead in the water before the photos and accompanying MLS (Multiple Listing Service) information ever went public. As anyone would I brought up the lack of showings. My realtor failed to see this as a red flag that should have led to a responsible level of due diligence followed by the disclosure that my home was claimed to be REO-owned. Having this information while I was still in my home would have made all the difference. As it was the unraveling process did not start until August 2012. Taking off in earnest only after I fired Webb Brewer only to be abandoned by Kathryn Maceri.

As it turned out I was a lot of work. The push back to perfect the theft of my home left a public records footprint. The footprint you are after may incorporate other details, but it is out there for you to find. If Ann had not been in and out of my home over the HUD required retention period of three years there is a lot about this criminal cohort of bad actors that I otherwise would not be able to write about today.

When and if victims of this scheme learn enough that they can speak out they are contradicted by the fraud narrative corrupting official records. They are neither listened to nor believed. Banks with a lot to hide are always ready with a lie for which paper can be produced so as to deter those investigators that actually carry badges. Official records don't lie? Right? Destruction, alteration, or falsification of records is another RICO Predicate Act; 18 U.S.C. § 1519.

With my HAMP Application Bank of America was forced overtly back into assisting the secret REO Note-Owners in bringing the HUD fraud to completion. Bank of America left behind a record of lies documented in the Money Management International (MMI) Call Notes acquired by me in 2012, after I'd been gone from my home. Just as Webb Brewer ignored the overwhelming significance of the Core Logic Equator work order he ignored the MMI record of phone calls.

While I was on the hunt for more and more understanding, he was busy limiting, controlling, and constraining that evidence.[75]

These call notes as a record of calls between myself, Bank of America, and various MMI representatives was at first difficult to acquire. Never give up asking for what you need. The fate of my home and my efforts to protect it was the subject of these calls, but claiming privacy I was repeatedly put off. No entity has the right to protect criminals. In doing so they become complicit in the racketeering operations. I became a broken record. Calendar the ask and send another letter. Be that persistent thorn in the side that produces results.

The MMI call log was entered with my RICO Case as Exhibit No.: 85. MMI was a nonprofit hired by Treasury to assist with communication between HAMP Applicants and the Banks. They certified me as eligible to apply. Fighting with Bank of America for that right forced Bank of America into the risky position of hiding the fact that they had already sold my home to REO Fraudsters who in turn, had pooled my home into a HUD program, only to turn around and purchase it out of that program so as to prop up the fraud narrative that my home was abandoned and in derelict condition. I guess more than anything else criminal use of a federal program meant to benefit the poor deeply offends my sensibilities.

MMI employees "escalated" my case on three separate occasions to Treasury for suspected fraud. At the very least they recognized that Title Theft had occurred, though they failed to tell me. This explains why they were so resistant to sending me the call notes. These were facts omitted by Magistrate Judge Vescovo who stripped the existence of the MMI Call Notes from her conclusions. Not accepting my claims as true she concealed key evidence. This informs that her primary goal was to obstruct due process at the *screening for merit* blockade. During the period of the HAMP Fraud Scheme MMI representatives realized that Bank of America

---

[75] I did not just randomly stumble upon Webb Brewer. The Tennessee Department of Financial Institutions proved so adversarial that I wrote a letter of complaint to Senator Lamar Alexander. His office did contact me. After that Michael Igney, Assistant Commissioner Compliance Division and Joseph A. Schmidt were, I believe, tasked with appeasing me, i.e., getting rid of me. These two men failed to refer the corruption of my property title in preparation of theft and illegal seizure for investigation. Patterns of practice by which many other Tennessee homes were then and still are today being seized in violation of the Fourth Amendment to the United States Constitution. I did not record the date, but it was during a conference call with the financial institutions compliance division that Webb Brewer was recommended to me as an attorney. It would be another book to write about the complicit apathy of the State of Tennessee as I sought recognition of these crimes.

was no longer the Note-Owner, Note-Holder, or Servicer of my loan. Every conference call entered into between me, the MMI representative, and Bank of America was a phony exercise designed to keep me in the dark. The existence of a private investor is referenced in the call notes only because this was one passage someone forgot to redact. Sadly, I did not acquire these call-notes until after the April 25, 2012 illegal seizure of my home.

What happened here can only be understood when it is realized that our federal government has repeatedly shielded powerful criminal banks from the crimes they commit against hardworking Americans. The Deep State shadow government is a parasite attached to a host. It is not just about getting rid of a duly elected president or continuing to weaponize cooperative bureaucrats. Unchecked corruption follows a historically proven trajectory leading to treasonous activity in the flagrant, intentional destabilization of trust in democratic institutions.

I have to remind myself that Ann and I were never friends. She does not deserve my protection. What passed for sincerity as we supposedly got to know one another was merely what was needed to achieve success over that job that she was tasked to perform. Over the three years that she was in my life I misinterpreted key pieces of information. I was blinded in part by a growing concern for her welfare. True or not she confided that she believed Max was addicted to prescription, pain killers. This confidence established common ground between us. A shared experience that allowed her to quiz me about Brett. It was not at all that she cared about Brett's struggle with addiction or how that had robbed us of a future together. She was tasked to keep tabs on what level of trouble he might cause if finally, clean and sober we repaired our relationship and got back together.

Ann opened conversations about Brett by telling me that she liked him. Most of my friends were so mad at him that there was no sharing my ambivalence and wish that our marriage be restored. Brett was just the kind of uncontrollable quotient that could derail any fraud scheme. His name was on the mortgage when in 2009 the forged Certificate of Abandonment was first presented to Bank of America. And then to HUD. He would not transfer ownership to me via a Quit Claim Deed until I filed for divorce. I know today that Bank of America never forwarded a copy of this Quit Claim Deed to the Jones, Kelley, Boyd Perpetrator Nexus. A certain amount of behind the scenes cover-up and backstepping was required. This timing made Brett a party to any legal action. It was not just me they were keeping tabs on it was Brett as well.

At the time I had begun attending Al-Anon meetings. This helped me navigate what no spouse or parent should have to deal with alone while living in close proximity to a spiraling out of control addict. As Ann talked about Max, I shared with her those recovery principals that were helping me.

While a sane person would limit exposure of what could send them to jail Ann introduced me to the core group. She let me put names to faces. It is difficult for someone like me to reconcile the motives in taking such risks. I wish there were more research out there on what makes a successful white collar con-artist group of operatives. Loner violent criminals are easily recognized. Not so the covert expertise seen in the devious behaviors that some adopt as a life-long operating commitment. My work in Christian ministry had made me aware of cults. I had read the first edition of the book Snapping which left a lasting impression on me. The current edition: *Snapping: America's Epidemic of Sudden Personality Change by Flo Conway and Jim Siegelman.*

I came to see that the Jones, Kelley, Boyd Perpetrator Nexus operated as a kind of cult. They sought to limit critical thinking skills. They required absolute conformity to the group-goals and profit driven agenda. If an exit threatened the group or upset the dynamics of power those with a lot to protect reacted aggressively. I came to believe that while greed was part of the picture it was by no means the entire picture.

Cult structures isolate people. Ann had no friend who was not engaged in these thefts and, or, part of the legalistic church she attended which discouraged and, or, prohibited women from wearing make-up and trousers. Knowing Max and the tight sphere of control he exercised I cannot see the church affiliation, which came from his religious background and not hers, as random. She was an abused spouse. She was also an abused spouse with growing antipathy for those around her. Blind allegiance to group-think was about to be unsettled by an event that struck her as profoundly alarming. And as sad as this event was I became the recipient of valuable information.

Ann's observations about those she talked of later proved accurate. The expressed desire to put distance between herself and some of these people, given what I know today, was healthy. In my presence, even out of context to the situation, Max belittled and humiliated Ann. I could not let this pass without comment though nothing I said had any change effect whatsoever in how he treated her in my company.

Over those three years I had no inkling that I had been profiled and targeted by skilled con-artists. I was therefore a long way from being able to recognize Ann for who she really was. She broached the subject of wanting to change her circumstances. It wasn't that she trusted me. It was more that I was a good listener, convenient and present. It seemed touchingly sad to me that the simple act of being listened to without bullying attempts to interrupt and criticize was a luxury she was starved for. I believe that there was value in hearing herself talk. This freed her to slide a wish for escape into the realm of possibility. Though I lacked context I went so far as to talk with a friend about getting her an interview with an abused women's shelter if it came to that. Clearly, I was not seeing the forest for the trees.

Accident or Murder?

Just as the death of Judge Oscar Carr sent a message, so did the death of Michael Harlow. It was obvious to me that his sudden death unsettled Ann. What I did not understand at the time was that it likely brought home that she could suffer a similar fate. Again, I was the convenient listening ear. She found a way to express her feelings absent most of the accurate context. His death unseated the topic of her marriage. It, unseated talk of two near death experiences she had survived one being a near fatal car accident in which she described being bedridden for months and feared most of all being left alone at night. I knew that she had suffered a significant physical injury. This was true. Today I know that the context of what she told me was usually fabricated. Carefully built walls of fictional context allowed her to express her fears without betraying the Jones, Kelley, Boyd Perpetrator Nexus. She described the manner of Michael Harlow's accidental shooting in morbid repetitive detail.

Upon getting the police report the only part of Ann's story that turned out to be true, was that Michael Harlow had, indeed, died by gunshot wound. Lies spun a place of safety behind which very genuine angst, pain, threat, and fear achieved an outlet. I do not entirely fault Ann for this. Having been threatened by these same people I can appreciate how incessant proximity to the threatening and bullying tactics on a daily basis wore her down and limited her choices. Ann had found a way to survive within a micro culture that conveyed a sneering kind of "got ya" satisfaction designed to bring every better instinct to heel. Sadistic obsessive control is what evil seeks and relishes above money. Power realized in the death of individuality and the God-given autonomy that allows healthy people to choose a course of action is what cult structures must kill to survive.

On the day, hour, minute that the illegal seizure was achieved other than running into her randomly on three occasions at the grocery store our lopsided relationship came to an abrupt end. There was only one other time that we had anything like a real conversation and that was when Webb Brewer filed the state case in Fayette County. Her value to the cult was in building and maintaining certain relationships and feeding needed intelligence back to the criminal cohort.

Over those three years I interpreted almost everything Ann disclosed simplistically in light of the spousal abuse I witnessed. I would not identify the REO Group of bad actors in the roles they performed until after the April 2012 illegal seizure of my home. I can only be grateful that Ann took risks that made this a far easier task than it otherwise would have been.

By the time our contact ended Ann had introduced me to the key players operating in her immediate orbit. Not only had I met them, but more importantly I had insight into her opinion of them. Over confidence and inflated arrogance told the Jones, Kelley, Boyd perpetrators that they were so skilled at choosing their victims that no one would learn enough that they could fight back. Ann's disclosures seemed voluntary. But, in the hindsight of today I see much of what she recklessly shared as involuntary.[76] On the one hand she was a fully functioning operative within the Criminal Enterprise. On the other she was resistant; passive aggressive in some of the survival strategies she had adopted. Therefore, in my mind and up to today, I believe there is hope for Ann. Was she trapped within that criminal organization merely because she had the bad-luck to marry Max Jones? It cannot be that simple. I have wanted to understand more about the thrall-like attachment to what is lethal, dangerous, and peace-stealing.

---

[76] I wrote the Dr. Phil show several times. If these crimes could be exposed there might be answers for some of the deeper questions about entrapment within the group dynamics. Not in context to religiosity, but in context to a RICO Criminal Enterprise. Because I genuinely cared about Ann her choices, capability and willingness to escape her circumstances has continued to occupy my thoughts. She was deployed as a predatory asset into my life. My failure to recognize her motives and question her intentions were a factor in the success of this white-collar criminal group of operatives. What could I have done differently? How could others be warned?

Looking back, I believe that Ann was already having doubts when I met her. I tried to build her self-esteem. I made efforts to broaden her circle of acquaintance which she resisted. I wanted her to see that the steady drip of bullying assault by Max, along with controlling religiosity in the form of indoctrination was undermining autonomy. If I had aggressively argued with her, I would have lost her. At the time, I saw very little of what I can write about today after a years-long investigation. I did not know that this group were sabotaging every effort I made to save the equity in my home. I had no idea that every piece of mail was fabricated to deceive me into thinking that Bank of America was still the note-owner and servicer of my mortgage.

Truth is its own imperative. There is a spiritual impetus by which truth will emerge. Even those who are very clever and practiced at deception cannot forever hide. A steady stream of disjointed disclosures came to me from Ann and accumulated like snow on a roof top. It took time, but at last that roof collapsed. Bits and pieces formed the cohesive picture that someone like me, a bit of a work-alcoholic, liking details and organization needs for stability. Much of what Ann told me would come back to haunt the tightly formed cohort of local criminals.

CHAPTER TWENTY-THREE

"Everything I did in my life that was worthwhile, I caught hell for." Justice Earl Warren. In landmark rulings he elevated the Bill of Rights over secondary state and federal laws.

HUD regulations required that my home be retained by the REO criminals for three years. They were stuck with me up until the phony foreclosure, illegal seizure and the August 2012 Evolve Bank & Trust Flip back to the Keller Williams straw buyers. I learned that Ann hoped to put distance between herself, her husband, and others whom she named. In particular Sherry Boyd. Only because she told me that Sherry was dangerous did that name jump out at me when I read some of the last filings that perfected the last flips of 65 Pinehurst Drive, dumped into the land fill of the Fayette County Register of Deeds Office.

Ann was forced into acquaintance with Sherry Boyd. She had little choice over who was and was not in her life. Her usage of the word "dangerous" lodged itself in my memory. Later I would have reason to decide that this characterization was entirely apropos.

Ann and Max invited me into their home where I met Jeffrey Kelley. Why would they take that risk? The simplistic explanation is that they saw this testing of a delusional conviction that they would always escape consequences; a kind of power trip they got off on. Only because I met Jeffrey Kelley and formed an impression of him was I later able to tie his name to the Gintz brothers' fraud operating out of the state of Washington as well as Shelby County, TN. The difference being that the State of Washington prosecuted securities fraud and Tennessee elected not to do so.[77]

My research produced evidence that Jeffrey Kelley assisted Ronald Lee Gintz in concealing assets from the state of Washington as they exercised what appears to have been a builder buyout scheme[78] putting $500,000 of needed cash siphoned from loan funds into the pockets

---

[77] State of Washington, Department of Financial Institutions, Securities Division; Order No.: S-11-0620-13-SCO1. "Cease and desist from selling pooled residential real estate." Memphis REO fraudsters, Judge Carr's former law practice Glankler Brown, PLLC assisted with the pooling of securities.

[78] Builder Buy Out Scheme showing prior bad acts; my RICO Exhibit No.: 118 and which connected another key player to the ongoing activities of a RICO Criminal Enterprise. Does the Memphis District Court still have my RICO exhibits? And if they do is anything missing? These are not unreasonable questions.

of the conspirators. Doing so at a time when certain assets had been frozen by the State of Washington. I've wondered if this money went to pay the Gintz brother's attorney's in that action filed by the State of Washington; Department of Financial Institutions.

Only because Ann brought Lennie Faye Kelley into my home under the pretext of watching the Wood's End pre-production trailer, though the link was accessible over You-Tube, did I eventually start looking at everything filed under the Kelley name in three counties.[79]

The name Michael Harlow appeared in both the Lennie Faye Kelley and the Charles L. Kelley Revocable Trust(s). "*If Charles L. Kelley, Sr. is for any reason unable or unwilling to serve or to continue to serve as the Trustee, then Michael W Harlow shall serve.*"

Trusts[80] were used as vehicles in which to park the illegally acquired properties until it was deemed safe, after equity was skimmed, to sell them and, or, transfer them to companies like Pretium Partners, LLC. The fraud vehicle of a trust-entity retains the right to amend, revoke, or terminate the trust(s) at any time. If a particular property is being investigated the paper can be refiled under the same name, given a later start date, and given a different Registry of Deeds instrument filing number. Just as any financial audit would look for interruptions in check numbers any investigator would have to look for disappearing

[79] Twelve minutes of film produced in part, and directed by Brian Churchill in hopes of raising the funds needed to produce an independent Christian film. Screen play based on my book; Wood's End. I look back on that book and feel that parts were almost prophetic; the Holy Spirt preparing me for what was coming. Among the friends of Woods End listed in the credits. Those who helped out in some way by feeding the crew etc., Ann's name appears. Brian Churchill passed away from cancer far too young, before we could realize our dream of seeing Wood's End translated through the medium of film.

[80] Shelby County Register of Deeds Office; Book D792-page-713; Book D792-page-713; page-717. Also filed in Fayette County, TN and perhaps elsewhere. Assertive language to discourage those investigating theft of their homes to convey that victims have no right to pursue information needed to defend their property rights; in part: "*Full power to deal with real estate without the approval of any court, joinder of beneficiary and without disclosing any beneficiary of the TRUST;" Page-2. Also see: Deed of Trust Fayette County Instrument No.: 12007679. Transfer of real property to The Lennie Faye Kelley Living Trust from Jeffrey L. Kelley and Carrie M. Kelley coinciding with threat of a law suit. Ties Jeffrey L. Kelley and to his sister-in-law Lennie Faye (Boyd) Kelley. Lennie Faye Kelley self-described, "best friend" of Ann Jones. Lennie Faye (Boyd) Kelley sister to Vernon "Wayne" Boyd. Sister-in-law to Sherry Boyd. Max Jones serving on the Kelley owned Preferred Auto Insurance Company audit committee; accountant for the larger group. By design of this configuration it is thought that no one will break ranks, crack under pressure, and report these crimes.*

instrument numbers removed from, and then plugged back into the Registry of Deeds system or any other public record.

Ending and then reforming the trust under the same name serves to establish a later start date. This to claim ignorance and innocence when superficially challenged. Later Trust entities may omit properties already transferred or under threat of a property title dispute or under investigation. This practice serves to deceive investigators and plaintiff attorneys as to timing. In addition, they mislead any investigator seeking to connect theft of a specific property by date to the group of REO-Fraudsters controlling the trust vehicle.

If a subpoena goes out for information the question is which trust? Formed and filed and, or, not filed at all in the public land records? Filed in what county? The practice of burying any troublesome document in the wrong county is a, fraud concealing strategy. We also see the practice of lifting documents from other states, altering the content to serve the theft agenda. The language of any subpoena needs to be inclusive of the possibilities.

The flexible series of past, present and retooled revocable trusts are highly effective at concealing the chain of theft as well as the true Note Owner or Note Holder identity. The fraudsters retain the right to direct the distribution of income and principal out of the trusts. This made the roles played by Max Jones functioning as the Certified Public Accountant and that of Michael Harlow as a kind of financial officer and liaison between David Osborn and Keller Williams Corporate vital to the ongoing operations of the Criminal Enterprise. If either man should assess the risk of any possible investigation and decide that they would break ranks, life span might be cut short. Though she described an accidental self-inflicted gunshot wound I am convinced that Ann believed that Michael Harlow was murdered.

The names Sherry Boyd and Michael Harlow surfacing in my later investigation and catching my attention only did so because Ann had talked about them. In true double-speak Ann equated the sudden death of Michael Harlow with that of a near drowning accident, a traumatic event from her own childhood. A life and death kind of struggle. One that she survived, but Harlow did not survive.

I do not want Oscar Carr or Michael Harlow to be forgotten. I want someone with a badge to fully investigate the circumstances of how they each met a tragic end while being linked to the same Criminal Enterprise. By design of this tight, cult-like group of bad-actors I do not believe they would have been allowed to live if in any way they threatened the ongoing viability of these crimes.

Long before I was rid of the last corrupt attorney, Ann had provided the bread crumbs that after the brutal eviction, over time, led me down a path that exposed the network of bad actors and corporate entities that made up the RICO Criminal Enterprise. After the Harlow "accident," one year into the Property Flip – Equity Skimming portion of the fraud scheme, Ann's demeanor took on a more obvious taint of fear. I misread the reasons for this, thinking it had everything to do with escalating spousal abuse.

History had shown Ann that "marks" like me, deprived of all legally required information, were helpless to fight back. In Ann's mind I was in that category of targets thought safe. I was someone to whom she could fling her emotional baggage, in speak out of context to what was really going on. The true nature of any dangerous cult being what it is, no one is ever truly safe.

Michael Harlow died on May 6, 2010. This is one year before the transfer of my Property title from Bank of America, dropped into the HUD Pool, and then re-purchased out of that pool by the same REO criminal network in 2009. It is one year after the JP Morgan Chase Bank Loan that transferred 100K of my money into the coffers of the same RICO Criminal Enterprise; May 2011. Michael Harlow died five years before Oscar Carr who died on April 6, 2015. Both died in familiar places. There may have been reasons why Michael Harlow posed a threat to the ongoing viability of the criminal network. I was never able to verify this information.

When Michael Harlow's widow moved from Texas to Tennessee Ann was given a new assignment. One that she resented. I did not see as much of her since the new task shifted from babysitting me to keeping tabs on the widow.[81] Now on her way to go shopping with Darlene Harlow as they pulled together the décor of Mrs. Harlow's new home, Ann talked about the pressing need for Max to buy her a home

[81] Sharon "Darlene" Harlow, moved from 4616 Dartmoore Lane, Colleyville Texas to 225 Ridgewood Drive, Collierville, TN after the death of her husband, Michael Harlow. Doing so the Jones, Kelley, Boyd Perpetrator Nexus – REO Investment Group had removed her from any lingering questions that Tarrant County, Texas law enforcement might in future, want to pursue. Another fraudster acting in different capacities as needed was tied to Terrant County, Texas, David Osborn, Michael Harlow and Keller Williams Realty straw buyers, Vernon "Wayne" Boyd and wife, Sherry Boyd.

that would be titled in her name alone. Foolishly I credited myself with helping to make Ann stronger. Able to stand up for herself. Like most women in impossible situations, she had learned to run an end game around her circumstances. She lamented, if only she could persuade Max to put the Oakland home on the market which they eventually did. Upon belief, only after given permission to do so.

Ann had strong feelings about Sherry Boyd. She told me that under no circumstances would Sherry get the listing of their home. It was during one of these conversations that she told me Sherry Boyd was dangerous. Even before the death of Michael Harlow Ann was searching for a way to extricate herself from group control. After his death she was searching for an alternate, less obvious survival-strategy. Upon belief that fear had snapped her back into compliance. As long as she was willing to be used as a spy, she was a useful deployable asset proving her value to the Criminal Enterprise. This concept is better expressed by the following: ***This requires that he*** (she) ***participate actively in the manipulation of others, as well as in the endless round of betrayals and self-betrayals which are required.*** *Robbins and Zablocki, Misunderstanding Cults: Searching for Objectivity in a Controversial Field, 181-193.*

The harm flowed both ways. Outward to people like me, and inward to those that abdicate personal responsibility resulting in soul destroying enmeshment to the will and goals of an abusive hierarchy.

True or not, Ann told me that Darlene Harlow had decided to remarry. Ann did not approve the choice of a former high school boyfriend reconnected with over Facebook. The fact is, I do not really know what it was that Ann disapproved of. Not even if there was any decision to remarry so soon after her husband's death. I can only say that Ann was resentful during this time and as usual vented her feelings in coded language considered safe. If at any time she was aggressively questioned or challenge by the mafia like criminal cohort she could lie with a straight face and most likely be believed.

In moving Darlene from Colleyville, Texas to Collierville, Tennessee the Jones Kelley Boyd Perpetrator Nexus had her within their sphere of influence during that tricky period that the estate was settled. Some of that money would be flowing to Darlene from the group funds. What seems clear is that the Criminal Enterprise got Darlene out of Dodge pretty fast. The move ushered her under "group" influence and control;

money such a thorny topic and especially when there is so much to hide. It was no coincidence that realigning priorities Ann was suddenly babysitting Darlene and spending less time keeping tabs on me. None of this made its way into my diary accounts. I had enough to deal with and remained strategically ignorant of what was taking place behind the scenes.

After I was rid of my last attorney, I was no longer viewing coincidence as random. The willingness to give others the benefit of the doubt is a trait that career white-collar criminals consider a weakness, look for, profile and prey upon. There are parallels between Judge Oscar Carr and Michael Harlow. How they died, both by gunshot wound, is incidental to the Enterprise-Relationship connections.

What Ann described was robotically unchanged. What did change was body language and facial expression. Angst seeped past the measured words leaving me in little doubt that Ann had been very unsettled by the death of Michael Harlow. The story went like this. Michael Harlow sat at his kitchen table cleaning a gun. I asked her if he had been a hunter and she replied that yes, he was. Unknown to him the gun was still loaded. It went off. The wound was fatal. According to Ann, his wife was out doing errands, not at home when this accident occurred. She returned and discovered her husband slumped over the kitchen table where he had, "sat cleaning his gun."

Michael Harlow did not die at home as Ann described. He did not die early morning as his wife, Darlene, was out shopping for groceries evoking the word picture I was left with. The location of his death, Veranda Lane, is a five-minute drive from what appears to have been the Dartmoore Lane actual residence. Michael Harlow was not already dead when Darlene arrived at the scene. She did not find him slumped over the kitchen table. He was still alive. The call for help did not come from Darlene. That call came from someone else. How that person may have been connected. If they were connected was omitted from the police report. Obviously, I cannot phone Ann and ask her to verify what I remember of her account.

Ann described this in such a way that I had an explanation for a fairly straightforward tragic "accident." There was no doubt in my mind that she grieved this death. Or, in hindsight, that the death of a man who was in on the ground floor Criminal Enterprise operations generated enough fear that she would back off from and rethink her plans for escape. If not for his death, I'd like to think she may have put on her running shoes and left Oakland far sooner than she did. I'd like to think she might have told me the truth. But this is giving her too much credit for levels of autonomy she may not have been free to exercise.

Much of the police report is redacted. It reads in part: "*On Thursday, May 6, 2010 at 1305 hours, I Officer R. McFadden 069 responded to a report of an accidental gunshot at 44 Veranda Lane, along with the fire department. The caller advised dispatch that a man had ran out of the house at this location, told his wife that had shot himself, and then ran back into the residence.*"

At the time I had other things on my mind. I was emotionally exhausted as I navigated the disintegration of my marriage. I was grief stricken over Brett's steady decline into drugs and alcohol after thirteen years of sobriety. In 2010 he had a near fatal car accident in which he suffered a brain injury. Brett was in the hospital for a good ten days before he could say who he was. When I saw him for the first time his face was still so swollen that I hardly recognized him. In and out of consciousness he wavered between telling me he was sorry, thinking I was his sister, and conversing with a mythical drug dealer. Though he was under the influence at the scene he was never ticketed; no one expected him to survive. I took him home to nurse him taking him to doctor appointments as he awaited an upcoming surgery.

Ann had visited me in the trauma unit waiting room, bringing me a gift of bottled water and snacks in an attractive basket. At a later time, she even asked her Pastor to call and pray with me over the phone. I saw this as evidence of her compassion. Today I see it as just another task. Brett's condition needed to be monitored. Not least of all because at this point mail on Bank of America letterhead, addressed to both of us, was being sent to his address in Mississippi. What if he thought to tell me? What if he sent me to retrieve his mail? Mail addressed to both of us and sent to his address in another state served to substantiate the HUD and Bank of America fraud narrative that I too had abandoned 65 Pinehurst Drive. This served to prop up the validity of the 2009 forged Certificate of Abandonment needed before the title theft could jump start the property flip sequence. And of course, this was mail fraud each instance a separate RICO Predicate Act.

Not surprisingly, during that time before I recognized that he had relapsed, Brett had messed up our taxes. Any claim of the IRS over any home fed to The Bank Theft Delivery System needed to be aggressively and immediately neutralized. I can only conclude that Ann saw some of this correspondence. A tax lien on the equity to my home (it didn't get that far) threatened the entire house of cards.

As a Certified Public Accountant, Max Jones was a private citizen who was required to report financial crimes and money laundering. Not doing so he risked losing his license and possible jail time.

From the article: ***Bank Secrecy Act Basics*** **by, Julie Stackhouse**: *"To meet the law's objectives, the BSA assigned requirements for record keeping and reporting by private individuals, banks and other institutions involved in the money transfer business. These records provide evidence used by the law enforcement agencies in prosecuting money laundering and other financial crimes."*

The previous transfer of my home into a HUD Pool of derelict and abandoned homes, seen in the context of what the IRS already knew, was independent proof of the Jones, Kelley, Boyd Perpetrator Nexus defrauding another federal agency. The threat of IRS oversight had to be handled and handled quickly. My correspondence with the IRS at this time demonstrated that I had no idea that my home was claimed to be abandoned and off-loaded to white collar criminals. Unlike HUD the IRS would have no reason to keep this information from me.

I'm a journal keeper. Although I didn't intend it and was not thinking in these terms some of what I journaled allowed me to create a time-time.[82] I did not record the following conversation with Ann. But I remember how it started. I was standing at the butcher block in the center of my kitchen, the perfect height for kneading bread and frosting a cake. The cake sat on its rotating platform. I had made fondant daisy's that were laid out on wax paper; ready to apply along the base after drawing up steep peaks of boiled frosting over the top. My former boss at Christ United Methodist Church was coming for dinner with his wife Nancy. I was excited about having them.

---

[82] I also kept a more impersonal call log of my conversations between myself and Bank of America during the period of the HAMP Fraud Scheme. When my later investigation began, I was able to trace some of the phone numbers. Phone numbers linked the planned harassment by the third-party Mortgage Servicer Company, masquerading as Bank of America, under orders from the Jones, Kelley, Boyd Perpetrator Nexus. This pass-through Servicer Company, AMS Servicing, Inc., after two reformations is now Nationstar Mortgage. Just as there never was a foreclosure, there never was a HAMP Application ever submitted to standard HAMP protocols.

Watching me, Ann asked: "Do you do your own taxes, Alex?" Skilled con-artists never push. I did not immediately bite.

On another day, soon after, "Max wants to help you."

I had another friend who was also a CPA. He had agreed to advise me on the IRS correspondence. What I did not know was if Brett had actually made a mistake. I felt I needed an, objective opinion. At this point there were times, weeks on end, that Brett just disappeared. I was sleeping on the couch with tin cans balanced on the door knobs. Even if I had been able to talk with Brett, I could not rely on his recollections.

A week or so later... "Did you find someone to help with your taxes?" And later still. Expressing that she knew I was worried, "Max and I would like to do this for you as a gift." I was so exhausted that whatever seemed easiest at this point was attractive. Max was a certified public accountant. I could not ask for better help; or so I thought. Although Max did not sign the return, his hand-written notation appears in red ink on a copy that I can only assume he did not intend for me to have.

Max Jones filed a 2008 amended return and did my 2009 taxes in 2010. In this way he gained access to all necessary personal data. He also gained access to what was most needed at the time. This was the address where Brett was residing in Mississippi. This allowed the criminal cohort to begin sending mail to both of us at that address to thus lend further weight to the HUD and Bank of America documented lies that I had abandoned 65 Pinehurst Drive and lived with Brett in another state.

All information was acquired under false pretenses, in violation of the code of ethics of Max's profession. The intent was to subvert the IRS dispute that might have exposed the secret, dual claims of ownership. In the end Max not only "fixed" this problem, but he got me an IRS refund, something I never expected. Was I lawfully entitled to this refund? I have no idea. This refund guaranteed that I would thereafter not be communicating with the IRS. More significant, still, they would not be communicating with me.

There came a watershed encounter with the Jones, Kelley, Boyd Perpetrator Nexus. Ann invited me into her home for dinner. I had been in her home many times before. But this was different. The invitation was last minute. I recall standing in my closet trying to decide what to wear. Thoughts swirled through my mind. I had visited Ann's church on two occasions and had been concerned about the chaotic manner in which so many people spoke in tongues. I am not against the spiritual gift of tongues. I have Christian friends that have this gift. But this was something quite different. I knew without being told that none of the women in the Jones home on that evening would be wearing make-up. Hair would be tied back or up. All would be wearing clothing of neutral color. All would be deferential to their husbands meaning that conversations would be stilted and one sided.

I opted to wear a skirt. I was hoping to see Ann helped. That was never going to happen if I took a stand on what was superficial. How I dressed was not by any measure the important crux of those issues by which I saw her as someone unduly controlled and constrained by legalism, bullying tactics, and religiosity. I did not want anyone telling her I was someone she should not be friends with. I need not have worried. She was in my life to spy on me and the people I met in her home that evening had ruthlessly deployed her as a weapon. It was on this occasion that I met Jeffrey Kelley and his wife Carrie.

What can be discerned from a single meeting? I am not psychic. I had no thought of him and multiple Keller Williams franchise owner, David Osborn as kingpins behind the fraud schemes that would later come to light. Upon meeting Jeffrey Kelley, I only knew that the sense of him was immediate and visceral. Wrapped in a shroud of superiority he sat back and appeared to scrutinize those around him in the vein of, "I am monarch of all that I survey.[83]" In the vernacular of today, he creeped me out. Both in the moment and then later, informed by evidence that bolstered those first impressions, and to use the word Ann assigned to Sherry Boyd, I understood that he was a dangerous personality.

Ann had been secretive about Max's job. After meeting Jeffrey Kelley, because of the deference that seemed to dance around him, I asked if he were Max's boss. Ann skillfully deflected the question, but doing so in a way that told me he was Max's superior. Stemming from that one evening I had the core and local group of those most directly tied to theft of my home. Lennie Faye (Boyd) Kelley was not there, but thanks to Ann I had already met her. This was again the risk laden, unwise, and perhaps involuntary need to stand face to face with the target. The only gain could be the addicts' rush of satisfaction and

[83] "I am monarch of all I survey. My right there is none to dispute... Better dwell in the midst of alarms, than in this horrible place." Poet William Cowper; 1731-1800.

affirming superiority for having escaped recognition and therefore consequences. Doing so to reinforce the supernatural, magical sense of invincibility; always a lie of Satan.

There had been an encounter with Vernon "Wayne" Boyd. I would meet Sherry Boyd for the first time on a day that she came to my home under the pretense of being a prospective buyer after I had listed my home for sale. Later, after a random encounter with her daughter, Amy, at a Community Bible Study I attended Sherry made an appearance. As she circled the room her gaze stayed on me, rarely shifting to look elsewhere. If she expected to provoke a scene, she was disappointed.

After the illegal seizure I chose not to return to the Fair Oaks Neighborhood unless there was a specific purpose for being there as witnessed by others. This contributed to my isolation since there were friendships I valued. I was not yet using such terminology and did not yet have the conceptual picture in my mind, but after that evening in Ann's home I had what comprised the bones of the Jones, Kelley, Boyd Perpetrator Nexus.

At some point I stopped giving any entity or person whose name I saw over and over again on fraud perfecting instruments the benefit of imagining this was mere coincidence. When lies break down and the elaborate façade of normalcy shatters to reveal the exploitive heartless greed fueled Title Theft Schemes...

Let me just say. If I fail to show up for any future hearing it will be because I was never served. And... To state this as strongly as I can, I am neither suicidal nor am I likely to have any "accident" involving a gun. Any "accident" will not be what it seems.

PART III

CHAPTER TWENTY-FOUR

"[Banks are] the biggest single cause of rising inequality, distortion of public policy, and generation of collective economic pain and anger." Bill Emmott – Former Editor; The Economist

These last chapters look at what specific filings found at the Registry of Deeds Office greased the chain of theft over two Fayette County homes. The same extended company of white-collar criminals are attached to these crimes. The fraudsters rely on the same infrastructure made up of those services and professional credentials delivering some part of the chain of theft.

I cannot comment on any innocent person that may have been caught up in perfecting these crimes. I certainly believe that one could perform a service and not know the illegal and, or, toxic outcome that follows. I chose these two properties from the many I could have selected, not because of the persons targeted, but because of the arrogant overreach and mistakes that were made followed by efforts to back step and cover up these crimes. It is not just judges' that rubber stamp these thefts, holding the line for powerful financial industry players, requiring no clean complete chain of title, but underwriters, loan officers, and banks in general do the same. In the Turner example we see how a small bank, in a quid pro quo exchange launder income for the local fraudsters. All these frauds rely heavily on document fraud.

Documentation fraud occurs when any document relied upon by the financial institution to make a credit decision, is forged, falsified, or altered. Fraud can also occur if proper due diligence and verification practices are not consistently applied. Similarly, obtaining documents to satisfy a checklist is not the same as having verified the authenticity of the document. From: Detection and Deterrence of Mortgage Fraud Against Financial Institutions: A White Paper.

Ignoring red flags indicate a bank operating environment open to fraud. The fraud perfecting endorsements are usually created by the foreclosure mill attorneys hired by the secret REO Note-Holders, sometimes called Institutional investors. Just as banks are required to maintain a suspect watch list of unreliable, even suspect licensed appraisers' they should compile a similar watch list of foreclosure mill attorneys whose documents are submitted as part of the loan package; flipping and laundering the chains of title.

I had no resources other than the ability to use the internet and pore over filings. I had no budget. Often my last twenty dollars went for filing copies. God took care of me in ways that let me know that I was not to give up. I never lacked for any necessity. It seemed almost a miracle that my car, with over 250,000 miles, kept trudging along taking me to and from places I needed to be in pursuit of other documents and other parts of my investigation.

All this to say that after reading this book you will not face the uphill battle that I faced. You will know exactly where to start; at the local Registry of Deeds Office in your county. Then to nail down what entity had been paying the property taxes. Doggedly following that train of investigation to the escrow funds, through the cooperative machinations of approved bank vendors and on from there...

I talked with Diane Andrews and Candace Turner whose documents we will look at as single examples that highlight the easily recognized chain of theft. I explained that what happened was not their fault. Title theft of these two homes had taken place before they could know they were in trouble. By design and intent of the Bank Theft Delivery System they had been systematically stripped of all information needed to launch a defense.

Sometimes I experienced a kind of let's kill the messenger sort of reaction. Other times people were wary and after what they'd experienced justifiably suspicious. The trauma of what was experienced is a kind of psychological torture too painful for some to, revisit. A lot of victims were dead by the time I read their names since they were targeted precisely because they were sick or infirm. I wish I could have gone deeper into some of the frauds that appeared to rob adult children of deceased loved ones. If I add any addendum to this book it would be to tell one of those stories.

The mix of response was difficult to reconcile since I would have been so appreciative if any one had knocked on my door and provided any insight into what was going on behind the scenes. There is an insidious and peace stealing dynamic when we encounter people that function as career pretenders. We wonder why they were not recognized though we meet them in safe predictable environments out of context to the masks they wear. There is a degree of helplessness associated with white-collar crime all the more difficult to deal with during that period that there are no facts undergirding the firm ground we rely upon for stability. There is power in fighting back. There is healing when we can ascribe meaning and purpose to suffering changing any future outcome for any that come after us.

Both Diane Andrews and Candace Turner suspected fraud. Like me neither had the needed information that armed them to fight back in real time as the chain of theft operated behind the scenes. Diane Andrews moved away. Candace Turner stayed on in that environment of cover up, concealment, and corruption. I wish them both well. My prayer is that this book finds them in a far stronger place. And that nothing I have shared will harm them any more than they have already been hurt.

No citizen today can rely solely on what is filed in the county land records. Municipalities must stop the criminal reach of the bank created MERS operations. They can and should claim damages and redress for billions of dollars in lost filing fees nationwide. In direct correlation to how the MERS E-Registry System, MERS business model operates, white collar theft of American homes has exploded.

Those in positions to do something about this have failed to act to protect the public welfare. Luke 10: 30-37 comes to mind.

CHAPTER TWENTY-FIVE

"This will be the path forward (w/public outrage) to jail many so-called 'untouchables.' You, THE PEOPLE, have the POWER." Q-ANON

Before we look at the two property thefts revealed through the chain of signed and notarized paper filed in the public land records, we are going to look at another property theft scheme and the Civil RICO Case that it produced. This case shows creative adaptations with many of the same elements that some will relate to more than others. We also see that not every REO investment endeavor is criminal in nature. Many people invest in and rehab abandoned and foreclosed properties without breaking any law.

This case is: REO Family Trust Services, LLC and Billy Gregory as the parties bringing the suit filed against Defendant, REO Holdings, LLC; Charles E. Walker; Jon Paul Johnson; Julie Coone; and Merdan Ibrahim, Defendants. Filed by the Nashville law firm of: Leader, Bulso & Nolan, PLC.

Tennessee Chancery Court for the Twentieth Judicial District at Nashville: Case No.: 15-780. 1V. Reading: ***...to recover injunctive and declaratory relief, compensatory and punitive damages, and other appropriate relief, as a result of defendants' fraud, conspiracy to commit fraud, racketeering, violation of the Racketeering Influenced and Corrupt Organization Act, (RICO) 18 U.S.C. § 1964, and violation of other statutory and common law rights of plaintiff's and members of the putative class, all arising out of Defendants' operation of a criminal enterprise in connection with property tax sales across the State of Tennessee over a period of at least 5 (five) years.***

As indicated by this case these crimes are a mere drop in the bucket. They succeed because comatose Registry of Deeds Offices in Tennessee are not looking for fraud, are induced to ignore fraud, and are not required to report fraud. Until MERS is dealt with and fundamental reforms take place this will be the generalized culture at almost any Registry of Deeds Office across these United States.

Most people, upon seeing that a document is notarized assume that laws and professional criteria were followed. That certain fundamental standards are in place to protect against administrative corruption and out right theft. That all parties with a stated interest in the property were physically present. That each person signed. That the identity of each signer was verified by the notary. The particulars of the signed and notarized transaction, is then, carefully recorded in the notary book as an independent record that should comport with what is postured in any filing Instrument. The notary book is kept in possession of the notary who upon request will produce it.

In Tennessee corrupt attorneys can register a signature that is no more than a scrawl. An example would be the registered scrawl of Memphis Attorney, Mark Miesse. Illegible signatures with no further identification are red flags. You have the right to know the identity of any person whose actions have facilitated theft of your home. Track down the identity behind these signatures.

Forged notary stamps were what drew the attention of the lawyers that brought the RICO charges against REO Holdings. It was also what drew my attention to a batch of Assignment(s) of the Deed(s) of Trust, including my own home, the Turner and Andrews properties as well as others within that batch where the notary seals and signatures were photocopied and affixed to these assignments by the same corrupt Memphis law firm that filed them.

I am quoting directly from this case in bold italics. In gathering everything filed in the public domain pertaining to your property look for some of the same features and practices having been used to perfect theft of your home. This was a more simplistic theft structure, also seen operating in Fayette County.

The lawyers for REO Family Trust Services asserted that REO Holdings had, ***"created false deeds and appended, applied, forged signatures and forged notary acknowledgments to fraud perfecting instruments."***

Just as the Jones, Kelley, Boyd Perpetrator Nexus – REO Investment Group carefully selected their victims, REO Holdings, identified and targeted, ***"absentee owners or owners otherwise unlikely to investigate or assert their interests;"*** Page-3; Paragraph-4.

As a pattern of practice forged notary signatures and stamps are common and one of the first things any investigator should look for. Page-4; Paragraph-8 reads: ***One out-of-state notary was so appalled at the flagrancy of the Defendants' fraud that, when presented with the Defendants' instrument purporting to bear her stamp and signature, she immediately contacted the Davidson County District Attorney.***

Did that office follow through picking up the threads of these crimes so blatant, obvious, and frequent that one could not help but stumble over them even if deaf, blind, and mentally challenged. It does not appear so. The dynamic here seems to be that when colleagues or those in positions of authority are making a lot of money it is hard to pivot and call the source of that income a fraud scheme with a national footprint of operation. The stranglehold of corruption has placed such property crimes low on any agenda. Too many people are just making too much money.

The case reads that REO Holdings, Inc., ***...have operated a criminal enterprise directed at obtaining title to real property and obtaining money in exchange for real property or upon mortgage of real property, based upon forged and pretended deeds and other muniments of title;*** Page-3; Paragraph-2.

(Introduction). ***...upon information and belief, the criminal enterprise described herein extends far beyond the specific cases described.*** And in paragraph 102, page-26 they assert: ***The Defendants enterprise entails ongoing unlawful conduct affecting unwitting victims across the State.***

Was any state or federal agency given the green light to investigate what is proposed in what I consider a bell weather important case? The answer is that they did not. The system-wide stranglehold of crony corruptionism has subverted justice many times over for many years. Theft of private property is in all effect a protected income producing industry. Tennessee has a new governor. Though I was told at various points that the Justice Department and Marguerite Howard with the IRS referred my case for investigation nothing has come of that. I've given up on HUD who is far more interested in protecting theft enabling practices of the REO industry than restoring integrity to that agency. They are sitting with absolute proof that my home and others were stolen and yet have worked diligently at obstruction, concealment, and cover-up making no attempt to restore these homes to their rightful owners or heirs. Although I can admire him, it cannot be that Dr. Ben

Carson is the right person to be draining the swamp at the Department of Housing and Urban Development.

Of the eight property examples and plaintiffs named in the REO Holdings class action Civil RICO Case, I found the Gomez-Martin example most interesting. This is because what is described was eerily familiar. Rightful heirs of estates in West Tennessee were defrauded by the same criminal practices. Phony claims of ownership rights, where none exist, perfected the Fayette County thefts of homes that should have rightfully gone to children and families of the deceased.

Once the property was identified as a vulnerable target the REO fraudsters dug into the background of that property and those persons named in the Deed of Trust. In this example they read the last will and testament of Manuel Martin. They were looking for any hook upon which to hang the fraud narrative. A story that would seem reasonable and thus, support the upcoming phony redemption claims of REO Holdings. The fraudsters found that Mr. Martin had disinherited a daughter.

Upon a little investigation here was a person who would likely never show up to point out how her identity was used to create a phony claim over the family home. The common tool of identity theft conveyed the home to REO Holdings. The hook was a daughter whose relationship with her parents was so broken that she had been disinherited. Thus, it followed that she likely had no communication with any other member of her family. Game on!

The Case reads: ***"Mr. Martin's will expressly disinherits a daughter named Clarice Gomez."*** The phony Affidavit and Quitclaim Deed in the name of Clarisa Gomez was presented to the Maury County Register of Deeds for recording. Once recorded REO Holdings had established their ownership and phony redemption claims. Note the misspelling of the name. This is entirely intentional. Misspellings or alterations of the actual names, as seen in theft of the Andrews home, described in Chapter Twenty-Six, are common features in how these thefts operate. Any data search will not connect the actual legal name to the theft. This reduces the likelihood that any one will show up and charge REO Holdings or the Jones, Kelley, Boyd Perpetrator Nexus and their criminal cohort with identity theft.

I saw Fayette County examples where I was fairly certain rightful heirs were utterly and completely disenfranchised and defrauded by prior false claims over real property. With these crimes going unchecked there was no chance that the intentions of loved ones would be honored. Nor that rightful heirs could exercise their legal right to live in and, or, rehab and sell the home they had inherited. A few of these examples, only because I could tie them to my group of REO bad actors made their way into my pattern example groupings. I've always been sad that I had to exclude others that did not quite fit the criteria I'd established to maximize limited time and resources.

These are equal opportunity offenders. Greed has no conscience. Someone needs to put crime-scene tape around the Fayette County Register of Deeds Office and convene a grand jury.

The Gomez-Martin example lays out how bits of information, taken out of context to circumvent the law pepper the phony redemption claims.

Paragraph-65 reads in part: ***The Gomez Quitclaim and Gomez Affidavits are forgeries. Clarissa Gomez, if such a person exist, is not Clarice Gomez, the daughter of Manuel Martin, and did not sign the Gomez Quitclaim or the Gomez Affidavit in any event.*** And... ***in an attempt to practice a fraud upon, inter alia, the court of Maury County, the heirs of Manel Martin, and the tax sale purchaser.***

Some combination of the same practices is utilized to perfect all these thefts. Notary stamps were copied via photostatic or electronic means. People were claimed to have knowledge of certain transactions that in reality had no knowledge of. Victims are, as always, carefully profiled as unlikely to fight back. Key assertions made within the filings were fictitious upon belief that the crony corrupt chokehold over disclosure meant that no one would notice until after the fraud had been perfected. These fraudsters stand on possession alone when the principal under law is that no one can give what they do not own. Forgetting that illegal seizure of private property absent due process is a violation of the higher law, above any secondary state or federal law, stands the Bill of Rights; The Fourth Amendment to the United States Constitution.

Some identities were entirely made up. Addressing the Burns/ Booher theft example, Paragraph No.-72 and Paragraph-73 reads: ***The Booker Affidavit is false and fraudulent several times over. First, the son of Betty Burns was not named Allen Booker, but was instead named Allen Booher: the Booker Affidavit is thus false as to its principal contention, that the affiant***

is the son of Betty Burns. Second, no one by either name, Allen Booker or Allen Booher, resides at 102 Park Avenue, Piscataway, New Jersey, 08854: indeed, no one resides at this address, which is a vacant lot.

Paragraph 73 continues: ***Third, even Allen Booker did not sign the Booker Affidavit: his signature was electronically or photostatically copied from a 1992 deed of record with Middlesex County, New Jersey, County Clerk at Book 3974, Page 824.***

In the Pattern Example Groupings that I developed I could see that some signatures were clearly *"electronically or photostatically copied"* from other filings. Others might look different like that of the MERS Signing officer in a batch of Breeder Documents. But upon examination I found that two signatures purporting to be the same MERS Signing Officer were randomly appearing and yet both were copied and forged from two other separate instruments which is why a few appeared different from others.

As lay persons we will always be invited to discount our first impressions. When I realized that I needed to connect the Michelle Brunk identity signing the fraud riddled HUD-1's related to theft of my home I got her signature samples from public records in Florida. In this way I was able to verify that she was the same Michelle Brunk working for Keller Williams and David Osborn in Florida. Michelle Brunk is named as a defendant in the Civil RICO Case I filed.

I learned to trust my instincts. Upon investigation I was sometimes proved wrong, but more often as I pressed deeper, I was proved right. Signatures looked the same, but lines were slightly off as to how deeply the pen seemed to be pressed into the paper (size and width). The lawyers[84] having filed the case against REO Holding provide an explanation. Regarding the forged signature of the fictitious Allen Booker (page-20). And the forged signature of New Jersey Notary, Mary Simms (page-21) they write: T***he task of making the lines on the signatures thinner or thicker can be learned and performed in Photoshop by anyone who devotes three minutes of researching the technique with an internet search engine***. Page-21; Paragraph No.-77.

---

[84] The REO Holdings Case was submitted by: Leader, Bulso & Nolan, PLC; Nashville, TN. Attorneys of record were: Eugene N. Bulso, Jr. and Paul J. Krog.

They then write in the following paragraph: ***REO relied upon them*** (forged instruments) ***to claim an interest in the Burns Property and commenced a redemption of the Burns Property on that basis on June 12, 2015.***

These property crimes both forward-date and back-date fraud perfecting events within the instruments that are filed. There is a story to tell that requires concealing the date that the mortgage was hijacked. Criminal REO Investors do not necessary specialize in anything except how to best churn out a steady stream of document fraud upon belief that no one will challenge them. That antiquated systems within Registry of Deeds Offices have not kept up with assaults by career criminals.

This important case and others like it equipped and informed my investigation. Given the corruption that I experienced I have to wonder if Leader, Bulso & Nolan, PLC experienced any push-back to limit their case. I believe it took courage for them to go against the grain and bring these crimes to light. In doing so they performed a service. It is true of life that we do not always recognize what events, choices, and commitments in life are the most impactful.

The lawyers bringing the case against REO Holdings drew a disturbing, but frequently articulated argument/distinction between class action cases and attempts of "individuals" with no muscle or legal expertise running point to bring suit against powerfully situated and mafia-like criminals. ***The likelihood of individual class members prosecuting their own respective claims is remote; even if every Class member could afford individual litigation, the court system would be unduly burdened by individual litigation of these cases;*** Page-27; Paragraph No.-102.

This statement negates what the United States Constitution protects. It puts forth an insidiously dangerous rationale that allowed a corrupt clerk's office, protecting a corrupt judge, to contrive that those questions I raised on appeal at the sixth circuit would go unrecognized via the separation of filings, outright forgery, and other sabotaging maneuvers. To say that the federal system is unduly burdened and therefore have an excuse to do an end-run around civil rights and constitutional protections for "less than" citizens and their complaints.

The answer to unchecked corruption cannot be that courts are "unduly burdened." Courts are not to selectively fulfill what they are mandated by law to provide on an equal footing to all litigants. The alarming statement made over and over again in class action litigation,

"the court system would be unduly burdened by individual litigation of these cases" ... impedes ordinary Americans from unfettered delivery and access to due process.

The United States Constitution was not written for an elite political, attorney, or corporate class of individuals. It was written with the rights of every American in mind. That a federal publication calling Pro Se Litigants a headache could pass any filter is deeply disturbing. Bias actualized into strategy, legitimizing administrative corruption, impeding the rights of average Americans may function under cover of being systemically acceptable, but is still, by any standard, a civil rights violation.

In too many class-action suits there is the concession that the lawyers bringing the suit will not use that same evidence to expand and bring any other case. This means that Federal Prosecutors must pick up were civil litigation is limited. Individual litigation on an equal footing with all other cases is the bedrock of our democracy. Only in recent history has a culture of bias against individual litigation by poor persons or average Americans tilted justice to the benefit of criminals.

Except for one plaintiff the other seven did not recognize that they had been defrauded. This speaks to a systemic failure of the Registry of Deeds and Property Tax Systems state-wide. Employees are already uniquely situated to recognize patterns of suspect behavior calling that behavior or that filing a red flag. Some have been in their positions for many years and could probably expand on how they feel each time they are required to assign a formal instrument number to a filing that is improper or even a day glow, screaming in one's face fraud device.[85] In effect their hands are tied. They are impeded from warning against or even reporting these crimes. In today's electronic age and culture of corruption this is like sending infantry into the heat of battle deprived of all weapons.

Who does it serve when common sense, critical thinking skills are not accorded a voice? Too many are under the boot print of a

[85] In the Asher/Turner theft we look at a Power of Attorney, used many times over in multiple states and with notary seals and signatures blacked out to posture authority that does not exist in appointing the Foreclosure Mill Attorneys as the resubstituted trustee. Fayette County Instrument No.: 11004022.

politically sanctioned system needing a bucket of bleach and the light of exposure. Though some are agitating for change it must be that property records systems no longer function at the behest of criminal lawyers and their clients seeking to institutionalize theft of private property.

I am grateful for the lawyers that took on the REO Holdings Case and also the Kalitta Air RICO Appeal that pushed back against the lower court's decision; obviously biased against RICO working for business owners and citizens. I am especially grateful for the Caperton Appeal going all the way up to the United States Supreme Court. I am grateful that Iowa Realty stood their ground against the bullying tactics of Keller Williams. That story was picked up by the press with past Keller Williams behavior expanded upon by journalists.

I found all this personally encouraging since it was far too easy for me to see the actions of Farris-Bobango, Webb Brewer, and Kathryn Maceri reflecting on all lawyers. There were some cases that I read many times over. They provided context, a sort of mini education, and even, dare I say, incentive and encouragement to persevere for exposure of these crimes.

In laying out the RICO Claims, **Count Vlll: Trespass and Ejectment** should be of vital interest to those fighting the battle to recover stolen property. Count VIII reads: ***As a result of the Defendants' enterprise, scheme, and artifice, they have obtained and presently retain possession of real property belonging to the Plaintiffs and to absent members of the Plaintiff Classes.*** Page-37; Paragraph No.-165.

The RICO clock starts ticking forward four years from when the crimes are recognized by those defrauded. Not when they actually occur.

As a consequence, the Plaintiffs and the absent members of the Plaintiff Classes have suffered damages and are entitled to reclaim possession of their respective lands. Page-37; Paragraph No.-166.

The police report I attempted to file with the Fayette County Sheriff's Office was important. I came armed with information neatly compiled in a binder that I wanted to leave with them. That they refused to file a police report. Refused to document my claims was a violation of my civil rights. No matter how much time has gone by file a police report. Document any push-back you experience.

It is interesting to me that one of the principal defendants in the REO Holding case, lawyer Charles Edward Walker, later violated a court order and attempted another fraud; using funds derived from another stolen property to pay his bankruptcy attorney.[86] *"The willful disobedience of a lawful court order is punishable as criminal contempt."* The old adage, don't believe everything you hear applies equally to, if you suspect fraud, believe almost nothing that you read.

[86] Court of Appeals of Tennessee at Nashville; September 5, 2017 Session; Case No: M2016-02524-COA-R3-CV.

CHAPTER TWENTY-SIX

"It's all about the thrill... High dollar criminals describe their machinations as having a "kick." They feel as if they're playing a game, and it's the game of their lives... Imagine the emotional charge to the "player" when the games power is combined with money as a generalized reinforcer, and both of these factors are playing out with real people and settings. This dealmaker is racing through a thicket of reinforcements, and the greater the risk – financial, legal, personal – the greater the thrill." From the book, Why They Do It: Inside the mind of the white-collar criminal by, Eugene Soltes

THIRTY-FIVE LEWIS FAIRWAY CIRCLE
The Andrews Property

This property was stolen by the same cohort of REO Fraudsters that stole my home. In what is described below, when you read Note Holder or Note Owner think Jones, Kelley, Boyd Perpetrator Nexus. This group additionally includes Keller Williams, David Osborn and the company of local enablers and investors.

There is a lot to learn from this property address as an example of how theft and illegal seizure of private property is accomplished. What we see in this example is that default was ultimately achieved via a fictitious loan and a fictitious lien. This was centered on the duplicate sale of the lot. This gave the Jones, Kelley, Boyd Perpetrator Nexus a beneficial interest in the mortgage. Very quickly house payments became assignment of rents.

As you examine those filings related to your property address pay careful attention to when any filing is claimed to be signed and notarized compared to when it was physically filed in your county Register of Deeds Office. Is any transaction event, back-dated or forward-dated? Do you read that your name is misspelled or in any way altered? Verify the notary stamps and signatures. Is the notary in one state but the parties signing, are in another state? These fraudsters go far afield to look for matching notary seals and signatures that they hope will never be investigated. How is any signing officer connected to the local group of operatives that you identify?

Gaps in the timeline between what is filed at the Registry of Deeds Office telling a limited story and what is concealed in the MERS E-Registry System with shadow documents fleshing out the truth will be needed. Establish a record of requests for this information in the back and forth between you and MERS (Chapter Nineteen). Sadly, there is a long road ahead in dealing with MERS.

Start at the local level and work up from there. As always, we look at taxes. You will want to get a print out of all tax payments coming from your mortgage holder and flowing through any other entity into state or county coffers. This should be a complete record going back to the start of your mortgage.

Just as mail and wire fraud feature in nearly all RICO Cases the criminal enterprise requirement to step in and pay taxes, usually followed by forced place insurance, must be seen as a conduit to establishing the identity theft authority over your property title.

When asking for the tax history your county and state will not be accustomed to meeting these requests. Few have any fraud detection practices in place that go beyond the superficial pretense of saying that they do. If they did, they would be catching and reporting these crimes on the front end. In today's electronic age these failures provide an open door to white-collar criminals. Come prepared with a list of what you need in writing.

Just as banks are required to investigate the source of funds and report illegal activity it is well past time that the source of tax payments is treated with the same level of due diligence. The history should be transparent and going beyond a superficial acknowledgment that taxes are indeed paid. How, what method, by whom should be vetted as accurate. I cannot watch the Tom Selleck commercials endorsing reverse mortgages. This is yet another conduit used to steal private property from elderly victims and by extension their heirs. Adult children should monitor the title history of any home they expect to inherit.

When investigating possible fraud you should not be charged for information needed in the course of your investigation. Search and copying fees can mount up. These fees disenfranchise segments of the population. Your expectation is that the county and state government will be a cooperating advocate. The integrity of any public office supported by tax dollars is on them to protect.

How your requests are complied with or not complied with tells you a lot. Not only whether inept or resistant bureaucrats are working against the public welfare, but any lack of transparency that inadvertently conceals fraud. You are a legal party to any act that impacts your property rights. You have the legal right to monitor how well your lender is upholding their end of the contract that is your Deed of Trust. States should not be controlled by greed fueled criminal agendas exercising undue sway over the outcome of any citizens right to full disclosure.

We start with the Andrews PROPERTY RECORD CARD. Your state may call this something different. It is usually found in the accessor's office.

Upon belief that the Fayette County local fraudsters have access to influence how details related to the theft of any home appears. This was apparent in the inconsistent use of the comment "Notes" section and what source document appears or selectively does not appear in the Property Record Cards I examined.

The Fayette County Property Record Card is meant to be a kind of overview. Regarding theft of the Andrews property it proposes only one Deed of Trust. This is misleading. Especially if this is as far as any citizen investigator will decide to dig; exactly the point. Not understanding how the recordation system works any lay person could be stopped at this juncture.

The REO Fraudsters needed the Property Record Card to reflect one Deed of Trust and not three. Three Deeds of Trust perfected on the same day, shortly after or before, should strike anyone as a red flag. This would trigger a deep dive into the records filed across the hallway at the Registrar of Deeds Office. There is the Countrywide Deed of Trust. Then there are the other two that function as fraud devices. They are falsely labeled, *Deed of Trust,* to convey a set of lies. The first Deed of Trust indicated by the MERS MIN Number (discussed further along) is the actual source document upon which everything else builds. It was either never filed or it is buried in the system under another name. Or it was filed and removed.

Stated on what Fayette County has titled: *Assessor of Property – Property Record Card*; 35 Lewis Fairway Circle was appraised in 2017 at: $211,100. James and Diane Andrews purchased their home in 2006 directly from the builder. The builder was Faxon Gillis one of two builders constructing and selling homes in the planned development of Fair Oaks. Brett and I purchased our home in 2005 from the other builder, Vintage Homes.

Diane Andrews was my neighbor. I met her for the first time walking my dog, Declan. That first conversation probably centered on her rescue dogs. Diane has a big heart. She loves animals. I got to know her better over a weekly card game played with other women in the neighborhood. I met her husband perhaps no more than two or three times. Unknown to us a Criminal Enterprise had moved in and created the fertile ground needed to operate undetected. Some had purchased homes and lived in close proximity to victims. Diane Andrews and I, as well as other neighbors targeted for this scheme were almost immediately in the weaponizing-sites of the Jones, Kelley, Boyd Perpetrator Nexus and their cohort of enablers.

It would be an interesting study for someone other than myself to determine just how many homes in Oakland, Tennessee from the year 2000 forward, have moved from private ownership to rentals controlled by the actions of one of three REO Private Investor Groups. All tied by relationship to those professionals and lenders that have enabled, and thus partnered in these thefts. There are anti-flipping laws on the books. HUD and the FHA have repeatedly suspended these laws to speed up REO Sales. This has exacerbated and empowered REO thefts of private property. At least one of the law firms with whom Judge Vescovo has a conflict of interest via a, family member, established a Washington lobbying group.

As a teaching tool, in sequential order of when filed, we will look at what signed and notarized instruments appear in the Fayette County Register of Deeds Office. These Instruments tell us a lot about the theft of 35 Lewis Fairway Circle. Unlike the chain of theft impacting 65 Pinehurst Drive far, more information was dumped into the Fayette County Registry of Deeds Office than would otherwise appear. This is because the Jones, Kelley, Boyd Perpetrator Nexus – Note Holders were challenged and being challenged the normally streamlined conveyer belt of theft was interrupted. Quite a bit of repair was needed; including help from a corrupt and, or, totally inept Fayette County Judge. The fraudsters had to back-step identity theft.

The Note-Holder holds all the marbles. Having gotten this far with the book you already know that they have established illegal authority to launder the chain of title. In preparation for the foreclosure charade the REO Fraudster – secret Note Holders must move title to stolen property, i.e., the electronic note out from under the MERS umbrella and back into the public land records.

When you download and read what is filed at your Registry of Deeds Office just know that they paint an incomplete picture. Only what the fraudsters need told so as to conceal the prior theft of the property title. Incomplete filings with no push back from states, serve to legitimize broken chain of title. The new normal that courts and lazy, complicit, or inept robo-judges are invited to rubber stamp. Before you vote to elect any regional judge question whether it has been or will be their practice to require a full chain of title, verifying any right of any party to foreclose.

In the Andrews example the Countrywide Deed of Trust did not appear. This tells us that unlike some others, this home was a theft-asset from the very beginning. House payments never went to pay down a traditional mortgage. If this Countrywide Deed of Trust should suddenly show up, I can only say that when I looked for it, asked help to find it, it did not appear. Read whatever you choose into that statement.

Print three copies of what is filed under your name and address starting with the original Deed of Trust. Keep one copy of each signed and notarized endorsement pristine. Another that you can highlight, write in margins, affix sticky notes... The third will carry an exhibit sticker. If you haven't already done so, start an exhibit file. The fraud perfecting filings in my case, and most cases is at minimum distilled to the first three listed below. Just because the transfer by Warranty Deed to a company like Pretium Partners does not show up does not mean it did not take place. Pretium Partners, LLC assumption of mortgages into the shell company of FREO Tennessee, LLC was not linked to many of the title histories as it should have been. That you cannot find this link at the Registry of Deeds Office does not mean your home was not transferred into a shell company that functions much like Pretium Partners, LLC.

The minimum that you will find regarding foreclosure is:

1. The **Assignment of the Deed of Trust, a.k.a., The Breeder Document** This document assigns the preexisting rights to real property from the original beneficiary to another entity. This step retitles the property in the name of the REO Fraudsters.
2. **Appointment of a Substitute Trustee.** This endorsement tells you what entity will conduct the Trustee Sale of the home. Where fraud is involved the first Trustee tied to the

original Deed of Trust needs to be replaced. Communicate with any Trustee and ask for the full title history upon which their authority depends. It is not the job of any trustee to perfect a fraud upon the court or a theft of private property under a repurposed Deed of Trust.

3. **The Substitute Trustee's Deed.** The replacement trustee flips the property back to the REO secret Note Holders. They are full partners in perfecting the last stages of the Property Flip – Equity Skimming – Title Theft of your home. They may even be the actual Foreclosure Mill Attorneys that have fabricated forged and robosigned endorsements. Depending on how many prior flips of the property title have taken place (concealed in the MERS E-Registry System) there may even be a third – Resubstituted Trustee. Look into the background of any Trustee. Request of any court an unbiased Trustee with no conflict of interest, revealing to you the full title history upon which their authority to act as they do must rightfully depend.
4. The foreclosure charade is usually followed by a flip to straw buyers post illegal eviction.

After the foreclosure charade the theft asset is usually flipped to a straw buyer. Identify the straw buyers in the post-foreclosure filings. Link these people to the Criminal Enterprise. When the coast is clear this last step will be followed by transfer of the theft asset, by Warranty Deed or Quit Claim Deed to a corporation or a company like Pretium Partners, LLC. What companies are operating in your area?

Enterprise plus Relationship. Link and establish same buyer, same seller, same appraiser, same broker, same realty firm(s), commonly used foreclosure mill attorneys, all tied to the same REO Private Investor Group. Each is an example of illegal, arm in arm, conflict of interest, price fixing measures operating within the Property Flip – Equity Skimming – Title Theft structure.

As you will read, a Fayette County judge, the Fayette County Register of Deeds Office, and the Sheriff's Office delivered the needed outcome that Diane and James Andrews were obstructed from their Constitutional right of access to Due Process. As with me, and other victims, there were multiple other violations of their civil rights.

WARRANTY DEED No.: 06004794
Signed May 10, 2006. Filed May 30, 2006

The missing Countrywide Deed of Trust is the quintessential source document. This Warranty Deed pretends to be the source document upon which everything that is subsequently dumped into the land fill of the Fayette County Register of Deeds Office claims to take its authority. Every instrument filed after this Warranty Deed is unenforceable. Going unchallenged, even by a judge, it stands as a blot on the justice system. Affirmed by a robo-judge it informs the extent that crony corruptionism has infiltrated Fayette County, stifled justice, and given a green light to criminal theft of private property.

This Warranty Deed gifts a valuable piece of real estate, an, empty lot, to James Andrews for the sum of ten-dollars. Too good to be true? You are right.

This is the first instrument filed in the Fayette County Register of Deeds Office. It is not the first that exists.

This Warranty Deed proposes an agreement between two people, but the party of the second part, James Andrews, did not sign it. Any valid contract requires that an offer be made. There must be consideration of that offer. There must then be acceptance of that offer proven by signature of all parties. When the Fayette County Registry of Deeds Office accepts an unsigned and thus, void fraud tool, assigning it an Instrument Number they are helping to perfect a crime. They are misleading the public whom they claim to serve.

Affixed are two notary signatures and seals. One appears to have been lifted from another document unrelated to this instrument.

What is the point of this useless, one party, unsigned piece of paper? These are not grab and run criminals. They are laying the groundwork for a long game to play out so as to maximum every possible penny skimmed from the theft-asset of this home. Nevertheless, they are constrained by state and federal laws. They must appear to be committing theft and illegal seizure under pretense of following the laws they are breaking; under "color of law."

Under Color of Law. The deprivation of rights under color of law is a federal offense which occurs when any person,

under color of law, statute, ordinance, regulation, or custom, willfully subjects any person on any U.S. territory or possession to the deprivation of any rights, privileges, or immunities secured or protected by the Constitution or laws of the United States, or to different punishments, pains, or penalties, on account of such person being an alien, or by reason of his color, or race, than are prescribed for the punishment of citizens (18 U.S.C. § 242).

1. Under color of law this Warranty Deed will be used to claim authority that does not exist in the following two filings. As a fraud device it trails forward to taint every signed and notarized document (endorsement) that comes after.
2. Under color of law the lot, severed from the physical build of the house, will be used as an asset rental.
3. The asset rental of the lot, temporarily "gifted" to James Andrews will be used to establish a fictious lien over 35 Lewis Fairway Circle.
4. Because he does not know this debt exists (and if he did, he would sue) James Andrews will not appear to be making payments. This is the point. Illegal interest and fees accumulate unchallenged.
5. This phantom unpaid debt, illegal fees and interest wait in the wings until they can surface as the pretext to assert a stake in the outcome of the future phony Foreclosure and Trustee Sale.
6. Under color of law the REO Fraudsters then seize the physical premises in violation of the Fourth Amendment to the United States Constitution. Yet again, they are buying (flipping) the property back to themselves.

In the fraud context the Warranty Deed or, similarly, any Quit Claim Deed are common tools used to perfect illegal seizure of private property. Going unchallenged they establish a fake claim of authority by which subsequent filings are created.

Quit Claim and Warranty Deeds may be used by someone who is transferring the Property title, but is not the owner or the owners' representative. The purpose of such a transaction is to sell the property outright or to refinance

the debt in a cash-out transaction to collect loan proceeds. <u>A fake Power of Attorney</u> may be used as authorizing the deed transfer. [87]

Diane Andrews was not present when the closing took place. She had signed a Power of Attorney giving permission for James to sign her name. The first Countrywide Deed of Trust was signed "Leslie" in keeping with how the Power of Attorney read. Leslie Diane Andrews is the birth name and official signature. When I spoke with Diane and also with the notary both confirmed "Leslie." This is the actual first instrument that does not appear in the public land records. Its absence shows the intent to steal this home from the very beginning, before the ink was even dry.

Having only heard "Diane" spoken in the neighborhood the Jones, Kelley, Boyd Perpetrator Nexus thought it safe to use "Diane" omitting "Leslie." As a successful fraud tool, this sows confusion into the digital footprint. It serves to bury the original Countrywide Dead of Trust. The Family Trust Services, LLC case against REO Holdings, LLC describe alterations of names so as to impede any federal investigator or citizen from recognizing how the property was stolen out from under them. Showing this pattern of practice examples cited included:

"Mr. Martin's will expressly disinherits a daughter named Clarice Gomez." The phony Affidavit and Quitclaim Deed in the name of Clarisa Gomez was presented to the Maury County Register of Deeds for recording. ...Thus, the Gomez Quitclaim and the Gomez Affidavits are forgeries. Clarissa Gomez, if such a person exists, is not Clarice Gomez, daughter of Manuel Martin. **(Read Part 5; starting at page-16.)**

First, the son of Betty Burns was not named Allen Booker, but was instead named Allen Booher: the Booker Affidavit is thus false as to its principal contention, that the affiant is the son of Betty Burns. **(From Paragraph no.: 73, page-19.)** My Chapter Twenty-Five.

---

[87] The Detection and Deterrence of Mortgage Fraud Against Financial Institutions: A White Paper. FFIEC Fraud Investigations Symposium; page 36. <u>http://www.ffiec.gov</u> Subsequent definitions in bold come from the same source.

A question in my mind will always be, just how corrupt is the Fayette County Register of Deeds Office? How far have they gone? We already know that cyber-crimes are in the tool-box of the Jones, Kelley, Boyd – Keller Williams – REO Investor Group.[88] Given that history it seems entirely within the scope of reason that they could have removed one filing from the data base and replaced it with a proxy Deed of Trust.

This void unsigned Warranty Deed is cited as legal authority for creation of two Deeds of Trust that follow. Both are fraud devices. One of them is referenced in the Property Record Card. It seeks to replace the original Countrywide Deed of Trust; addressing the duplicate sale of the lot. The second takes back the lot gifted to James Andrews. Neither are true Deeds of Trust.

Joan Zinser Topp notarized this Warranty Deed that falsely names James Andrews as a legal party to what is claimed within. Ms. Topp describes herself as a loan closer at Realty Title.[89] It was her job to gather the necessary paperwork and shop the loan package to prospective lenders.

In a sane world the Fayette County Register of Deeds Office, in an act of minimal due diligence, should have scanned the particulars and recognized that the Warranty Deed, as a red flag denoting possible fraud, was unsigned by James Andrews. At the very least why didn't they return the Warranty Deed to the law firm that prepared it?[90] Upon belief that employees at the Fayette County Registrar of Deeds Office have been groomed to accept and facilitate wholesale theft of private property. Some probably think they are doing what they were hired to do and doing a good job.

---

[88] As three examples each representing different victims. 1.) Collins-Maury vs. MEM 2, LLC. 2.) Interference with emails coming from the District Court to my hacked email account. 3.) Use of the Core Logic Equator computer-platform tied to Keller Williams for purposes of exchanging information, keeping everyone on the same page as theft perfecting tasks were accomplished or awaited completion at critical junctures.

[89] Per Facebook: https://www.facebook.com/joan.z.topp; up to 6/26/2019. *"Closer at Realty Title – Memphis. Paralegal Real Estate Closings at Parrish, Shaw & Brandon. Former Loan Assistant at Commercial Bank and Trust."*

[90] Warranty Deed No.: 06004794 Reads: This instrument was claimed to have been prepared by The Hewgley Law Firm, 6305 Humphreys Blvd, Suite 108, Memphis, TN 38120. Some instruments are created out of whole cloth to mean that nothing that is stated within is actually true.

Faxon Gillis, as the contractor, was not in the business of handing out empty lots, worth in excess of thirty-five thousand dollars to random people who show up and ask for them. So, what exactly is the point of this nonbinding Warranty Deed? How was it used as a fraud device?

The Warranty Deed tells any prospective lender that Mr. Andrews is the outright owner of the lot upon which the home, 35 Lewis Fairway Circle was to be built. He did not sign the Warranty Deed. A fundamental best practices requirement of any lender would be to: • *Ensure all parties sign the sales contract.* • *Ensure borrower signature on contract matches the loan application* *<u>and other file documents.</u>* • *Ensure earnest money deposits on contract match HUD-1.* The crony corrupt protectionist syndicate delivered that no lender greasing the chain of theft delved into the title history to uncover the fact that unsigned endorsements as legal contracts existed. James Andrews is not a party to how document fraud was used to obtain a mortgage. It is a federal crime to make any false statement in a loan application. This is a blatant example of "Asset Rental" that no lender should have missed. Asset Rental is a term coined by federal investigators.

ASSET RENTAL

Asset Rental is the rental of bank deposits or other assets, which are temporarily placed in the borrower's account, in order for a borrower to qualify for a loan. Asset Rental is a tool that can be used to commit mortgage fraud. ... Deposit rental is a means to inflate an individual's assets.

In a later search I found that 35 Lewis Fairway Circle was at one time claimed to be owned collectively by Charles L. Kelley, Lennie Faye Kelley, and Jeffrey L. Kelley. This suggests that 35 Lewis Fairway Circle was at one time parked in one of the Kelley family trust vehicles. Today, as a rental, it is being managed by Sherry Boyd. The chain of theft, where it originates, suggests coordination with the builder, Faxon Gillis.

At the cost of $44,950 the Andrews were charged twice for the same lot. Once in the original Countywide Deed of Trust (not found). Second in the phantom loan, debt, and lien. The fictitious lien will hibernate in the wings until that opportune time that it is needed. Usually it will surface only after the homeowners are gone from the theft asset. That said, in other examples, this practice was used by unscrupulous debt collectors to harass elderly victims into abandoning their homes.

This ploy places the REO Fraudsters in the first lien position. As we shall see, affirmed by a corrupt Fayette County judge, providing overkill that the message is not lost, "in the first **priority** lien position."

If there has been a back-door Ponzi scheme going on, selling the phony Deeds of Trust as a security worth investing in the Judge's order precludes any chance to file a separate claim. One must ask how often the theft asset is sold? Defrauded investors on the more local level would fit into this category; convinced that they have lost their investment. Sometimes their entire retirement savings as featured in an American Greed episode. Some will figure out how they were played, but shame and threat of even more losses keep them quiet.

Separating the house from the land was a common title theft practice. This served to fabricate a phantom debt leading to a fictious lien over the property. As we shall see, rubber stamped by a Fayette County judge.

FICTIOUS LOAN

A fictitious loan is the fabrication of loan documents or use of a real person's information to apply for a loan which the applicant typically has no intention of paying. A fictitious loan can be perpetrated by an insider of the financial institution or by external parties such as (REO Private Investor Groups), **loan originators, real estate agents, title companies, and/or appraisers.**

EQUITY SKIMMING

Equity Skimming is the use of a fraudulent appraisal that over-values a property, creating phantom equity, which is skimmed out through various fraud schemes. When a home is undervalued equity is skimmed via home improvement loans with loan funds not used for the stated purpose.

The interim period between initial acquisition of an interest in the mortgage and the final charade of Foreclosure and Illegal Seizure is highly lucrative for the REO Fraudsters. At least for a while they can pay dividends to investors in stolen property titles and additionally use house payments restyled as assignment of rents to pay off bank loans. These con-artists were not only looking for people like me who put down a substantial down payment; meaning that there was real, and not manufactured equity. The fraud scheme could be fitted to almost anyone. All that was needed was a warm body capable of signing the required documents. Or regarding the Andrews, Warranty Deed not sign them at all.

I have not been able to investigate how many other homes, as new construction in the Fair Oaks or neighboring areas had the lot severed from the mortgage as a conduit to theft of private property. Common sense would tell us that those trained to recognize these kinds of thefts should marshal whatever is needed for a deep dive into these practices.

This Warranty Deed reads that this parcel of land conveyed to Mr. Andrews was part of a larger tract of land that was sold to Faxon Gillis in a prior transaction of September 2005, for $778,500. This was merely the cost of the land. It does not reflect the cost of developing that land readying the various lots for the upcoming construction. Construction loans are usually short-term loans. Builders are pressured to build, produce, and sell quickly. This leaves contractors vulnerable to forming partnerships with white-collar criminals. It seems that other undeveloped lots were presold to the REO scam artists, but not disclosed to the homeowners. This gave the REO Fraudsters access to corrupt the chain of property title before the home was even built. This enmeshment between other builders and the REO Fraudsters surfaced in my research.

In theory James Andrews had a right to sell this land and pocket the cash. He did not try to sell it because he did not know that he owned it. The language in the Warranty Deed states that the contractor-grantor (Faxon Gillis) has the legal right to sell/gift this empty lot to Mr. Andrews upon which the house will be built. The passage reads that Faxon Gillis is: *"lawfully seized and possessed of said land,"* and thus, *"have a good right to convey it"* to Mr. Andrews. In the Andrews case the owner of the phantom debt as a duplicate sale of the lot, remained in the shadows.

Typical of all such contracts Faxon Gillis affirms that if challenged they will defend their right to sell, in this case to gift the lot to Mr. Andrews. To say that Faxon Gillis, as the contractor and rightful seller *(if they are in fact the seller or the only seller)* will undertake the cost of defending the Property title. The question is this. How long had the lot been sitting in one of the Kelley Family Trust vehicles? Just waiting for a prospective buyer to show up at the model house-sales office and be lured into purchasing a home that from the very start was a theft asset.

What we know for sure is that this lot was slid into the Andrews asset column of the loan application to be used as an asset-rental to commit bank fraud. It was later used to create a phantom debt upon which the Jones, Kelley, Boyd secret Note-Holders were able to assert a beneficial interest in the hijacked mortgage.

The language misleads to infer that there was a meeting. That Mr. Andrews handed over his ten dollars and signed the Warranty Deed at the same time that the signing officer from Faxon Gillis, *Michael E. Hewgley, Assistant Vice President for Faxon Gillis* as an authorized signing officer also signed it. The Warranty Deed is claimed to be prepared by: The Hewgley Law Firm.

Is this an endorsement created out of whole-cloth? It seems that there is another Michael Hewgley, also in Memphis, who goes by various other alias.' At this point in the book, I do not want to pick up the phone and call some of these people named. I'm merely reporting that they are named. This is because I've been personally threatened. I have outstanding complaints with the sixth circuit. Though the, RICO Criminal Enterprise may believe the catch and kill scenario has already been delivered by a corrupt clerk's office at the sixth circuit I do not want to put myself back in the cross-hairs of people I consider dangerous. I still have an outstanding void judgement at the sixth circuit. My appeal questions have never been addressed.

Like me, upon moving into the home the Andrews were immediately assigned a spy. Someone that would befriend Diane. A person who would monitor how well the ongoing shield of deception was holding up as secret back door transactions took place and equity was skimmed from the theft-asset; 35 Lewis Fairway Circle.

Deed of Trust Instrument No.: 06004795
Signed: May 10, 2006. Filed May 30, 2006. Filed on the same day that the unsigned Warranty Deed, used to establish the lot as an Asset Rental was filed.

This is not the first Deed of Trust. This is merely the first Deed of Trust filed in the Fayette County Register of Deeds Office in the name of James and Diane Andrews. It reads Diane and not Leslie. The James Andrews signature signing for himself and as legal proxy for his wife, under a Power of Attorney, is forged. Wherever the name "Diane" appears in these legal filings this is an example of Identity Theft.

The lender is claimed to be Southstar Funding. The amount of the loan: $179,800. This is the cost of the build absent the cost of the lot. The MERS MIN Number tells us that Bank of America is the Servicer of this loan. No where do we read that this loan started out as a Countrywide Home Loan. That Deed of Trust is buried or was never filed. According to the MERS site 35 Lewis Fairway Circle is now a, rental owned by a corporation. The REO Groups eventually transform into property managers reaping residuals from ongoing sources.

It may be that Southstar Funding is the servicer of the loan. They are not the Note Owner. It may be that Select Portfolio Servicing, Inc appearing later in the sequence of document fraud is the servicer accepting and processing house payments. It may be that GMAC is the servicer. The point is that nothing proposed is clear or straightforward. Everything stated is designed to confuse and conceal.

What homeowners believe are house payments going to pay down a valid mortgage are labeled "assignment of rents." This money will flow through the third-party mortgage servicer company hired by the REO Private Investors. The fraud narrative and dual claims of ownership become so imbedded in the system that even when homeowners do speak out, they are not heard. The avalanche of document fraud has done its work. The default will be laid at the doorstep of the Andrews while the REO Investors walk away with no charges filed against them for committing multiple felonies, mail and wire fraud, money laundering and bank fraud just for starters.

The MERS MIN Number appearing in some filings and not others inform us that at least at the beginning, before the REO Fraudsters acquired control of the mortgage, Bank of America was the actual servicer of this loan. After the mortgage is assumed premised on the fraud narrative, Bank of New York Mellon as the Trustee for the investors in the CWALT pool of securitized loans will be paid off at the agreed upon loss. From start to finish the secret REO Note Holder will continue to hide their identity behind that of Bank of New York Mellon, MERS, or some other entity. They will do so up to the charade of foreclosure and illegal seizure.

The best description of what and how the MERS MIN Number functions comes from: *McDonnell Property Analytics; City of Seattle Review of Mortgage Documents; Appendix "I" Definition of terms.*

MIN Number: The Mortgage Identification Number (MIN) is an 18-digit number that uniquely identifies a mortgage loan registered on the MERS® System. A MIN is permanently assigned to a mortgage at registration and cannot be duplicated or reused.

To process information on the MERS® System, you must enter a MIN. The 18-digit mortgage identification number ("MIN") required for each loan registered on the MERS® System must be placed in a visible location on the cover page (or first page if there is no cover page) of each of the following documents:

(a) Mortgage or deed of trust,
(b) Any other Security Instrument,
(c) Assignment of the Security Instrument to or from MERS,
(d) Lien release or reconveyance and
(e) Any other instrument recorded in the public land records in which MERS has a legal interest.

The 18-digit MIN Number shows up on the next Deed of Trust and on the Assignment of the Deed of Trust functioning as the identity theft Breeder Document.

The MERS layer is recent, has never been needed, and is needed now only to deprive the homeowner of a full and transparent history of their property title. After you locate the MIN Number log into the MERS Servicer ID site. Type in the eighteen-digit number. This will tell you what bank/lender originated the mortgage; whether that mortgage is active or inactive.

If the mortgage reads "inactive" but all communication still comes on the letterhead of your original lender something is seriously wrong. Your mortgage has very likely been off-loaded to criminals. When bringing up the MERS MIN Number associated with the Andrews address the MERS site does not tell us the date that the Countrywide/ Bank of America Mortgage was declared "inactive." This is intentional concealment. This is a key date that no homeowner can have because many of these mortgages are off-loaded to criminal partners while homeowners are still in their homes totally disenfranchised by the chokehold over disclosure. Intentionally precluded from fighting back as the Property Flip sequence gets underway.

Having this date is important. It tells the homeowner when a new Note-Holder took control, having the power to drive the mortgage into default. When the planned harassment begins and answers are sought the truth is concealed by the layers of deception infecting the official record that has gone before. When homeowners speak in lay terms they are dismissed and not thought credible. Signed and notarized paper cannot be wrong, right? Banks are always right, right?

When I typed in the MIN Number noted on what is wrongly postured as the first Andrews Deed of Trust, I found that MERS limited my search. According to MERS there have been so many loans secured by the Andrews property address that the history could not appear. This would be at least more than the incomplete six that appeared under my property address: 65 Pinehurst Drive. Just one secret flip of the property title, illegally laundering the chain of title, is one too many. The MERS search engine is created to frustrate any investigation with an incomplete digital footprint. Right away we know that MERS assisted in theft of 35 Lewis Fairway Circle. It is well past time that we dispense with the political script that sends a constraining message to federal law enforcement that certain entities and people are above the law and call them what they are. Willing and willful co-conspirators wrecking, havoc and heartache into the lives of hardworking Americans.

"There is no question in my mind that the officers of these banks and loan processing servicers made a conscious decision to commit fraud and participate in a scheme to deprive the public from knowing the true holder of their mortgage while at the same time avoiding paying billions of dollars in recording fees." John O'Brien.

So as to confuse the Andrew's further MERS is identified as the beneficiary. According to the McDonnell glossary of terms: "**Beneficiary" means the holder of the instrument or document evidencing the obligations secured by the deed of trust, <u>excluding persons holding the same as security for a different obligation.</u>**

The perpetrators of these thefts are shielded by those that create these endorsements. The term "foreclosure mill" has been coined to describe those law firms that churn out and, or, file a steady stream of document fraud for their clients. In some instances, not just for a fee, but for a piece of the action.

We read that this filing was prepared by: Katina Hoffman, 400 Northridge Road, Suite 1000, Atlanta, Georgia 30350. Who is Katina Hoffman? A random individual name substitutes for the company name. What appears fundamentally misleads depriving the homeowner of needed information. For this reason alone, the Fayette County Register of Deeds Office should have returned this filing to the law office that prepared it for clarification. Or to, Southstar Funding, LLC. Or to, Bank of America. Or to whoever it was that mailed it, wired it, or even walked it up the street or around the corner, into the county office controlled by criminal interests.

Mr. Andrews is identified as the borrower. *"Together with all riders to this document?"* Note use of the word "document" and not Deed of Trust. The "riders" most certainly refer to the fictious loan and lien just waiting in the wings to fulfill the purpose for which it was created. As we shall see the foreclosure mill attorneys did a lot of back stepping to cut any other potential lien holders out of any debt recovery outlay of funds.

Other creditors may have included local investors buying into a pyramid scheme. Having no idea that they were buying into a Deeds of Trust/Assignments of Rents Ponzi scam. These local investors are different from those who invest through the Wall Street securities industry. How many times will the SEC allow the same theft asset to feed an investment scheme founded on theft and fraud, oversold multiple times and therefore destined to fail?

There is no complete record of notarized paper. Broken chain of title with secret sales, transfers, and assigns of authority amongst conspirators are withheld from filing. What is selectively filed in the public record tells the public only what the REO fraudsters need told so as to nefariously conceal theft. In the Andrews example they did not do such a great job.

What made this couple attractive targets? They had the bad luck to choose *Lot 29, revised final plat, Phase 11, Fair Oaks Planned Development, i.e., 35 Lewis Fairway Circle,* owned by Jeffrey Kelley and his cohort. They were moving from another state. Diane was not present. Power of Attorney granted to the busy husband, starting a new job meant one set of eyes on the ball and not two. At this early juncture there was nothing to alert James and Diane Andrews that they had been targeted by ruthless, predatory criminals. Like most Americans the Andrews were unlikely to verify if the original Deed of Trust was actually filed. They would be unlikely to compare the written content of what they signed at closing with what was filed. They would therefore not stumble upon the Warranty Deed never signed that allowed the Jones, Kelley, Boyd lot to be used as an Asset Rental. Committing bank fraud in their names.

This Deed of Trust was recorded simultaneously with the fraudulent and prior, one-party unsigned Warranty Deed. It was filed on 5/30/2006 with the next falsely labeled Deed of Trust.

The Power of Attorney executed by Diane Andrews had a life of no more than thirty days. Thus, the first three filings had to appear to be signed and notarized within that thirty-day window. They were claimed to be signed, notarized, and filed on the same day. As another red flag that could have been picked up by an empowered Registry of Deeds Office what is proposed in these first three filings, as all taking place on the same day, is physically and administratively impossible.

Repeated misuse of the wrong name, replacing *Leslie, with Diane* worked perfectly well until some party upline decided that the chain of document fraud did not pass the straight face test; leaving the Criminal Enterprise operations too exposed. This person required a reformed Power of Attorney in the wrong name; rubber stamped by a court. As we shall see this had the effect of creating extra work for the Foreclosure Mill Attorneys which has left them exposed.

The original power of attorney was signed and notarized in the state where the Andrews family were moving from. That notary, a former Bank of America employee, told me that she lost that particular notary book. I did not believe her, but because I was told to back off, I did.

A forged Power of Attorney in the wrong name, *Diane*, affirming all the document fraud that had gone before was needed. James and Diane Andrews had no opportunity to be heard in any venue where they could be informed, heard, and where justice could be served. No due process equals no record.

Deed of Trust Instrument No.: 06004796
Signed: May 10, 2006. Filed May 30, 2006.
The same dates as the prior two Instruments;
an impossibility.

This is the third Instrument on file. It is labeled a Deed of Trust. This is not a Deed of Trust. Altering dates while applying deceptive labels is common to these schemes. The REO Fraudsters propose that this loan application and approval for this loan all came on the same day bypassing even the pretense of verifying the content of the loan application. This phony Deed takes back the lot that had been gifted to James Andrews and used as an Asset Rental. For a price. The price becomes the fictitious debt.

It would be rare indeed that an insurance company would agree to insure, a residential mortgage that was not collateralized by both the land and the build. Future redemption rights stemming from the fictitious lien, proposed by this take back of the lot, cannot survive until James Andrews is postured as giving back the lot. This instrument is not signed by any signing officer for Southstar Funding, LLC or for MERS. It is a made-up filing. The James Andrews signature is forged. His wife's name appears wrongly as Diane. Each time the fraudsters use the name Diane and not Leslie they dig the hole a little deeper. Like the Warranty Deed it bears no power to enforce because one party has not signed it and the other party signatures are forged.

The Notary stamp reads: William N. Griffin. The notary claim reads: *On this 10th day of May, 2006, before me the undersigned notary public in the aforesaid state and county, personally appeared James E. Andrews, Jr. To me known to be the person who executed the foregoing instrument on behalf of Diane Andrews and acknowledged that he executed the same as the free act and deed of, said Diane Andrews.*

These first three instruments paint a picture that on the same day, at different locations, James Andrews signed four sets of documents. The buried Countrywide Loan documents and the three proposed by these first three filings that serve to bury and smother the Countrywide Deed of Trust. That it exists at all is only suggested by the MERS Min Number. We are to believe that he appeared before three different notaries on May 10, 2006, including the unsigned and thus, void Warranty Deed witnessed and notarized by the loan closer: Joan Zinser Topp.

Even more bizarre we are to believe that James forgot how his wife's name habitually appeared in official documents; including their marriage license. Forgot how it appeared in the one and only true Power of Attorney. That the original Power of Attorney was not present upon signing which of itself would render the Instrument null and void. That suffering a lapse in mental clarity he signed the wrong name. That the local REO Fraudsters, having only heard Diane spoken in the neighborhood, forged the James Andrews signature and also forged James signing for his wife as "Diane."

The two labeled Deeds of Trust claim to take authority from the unsigned and thus, void, Warranty Deed. *The instrument constituting the source of the Borrower's interest in the foregoing described property was a Warranty Deed recorded SIMULTANEOUSLY HEREWITH in the Register's Office of Fayette County, Tennessee.* The Instrument Number: 06004794 is inserted by hand. This may have been inserted by a Fayette County Employee. This so-called Deed of Trust is yet another void endorsement, **not only because it takes authority from the prior unsigned, Warranty Deed but because the so-called lender, Southstar Funding as a named party to this transaction never signed it.**

This instrument pretends to be a kind of second mortgage. The fraudster use, of the labels like, "Mortgage" and "Deed of Trust," is intentional. It paints the take-back of the "Asset Rental" under a title that disguises the theft intentions of the REO Secret Note Holders.

For tax purposes the property was appraised at $211,100. Fayette County estimated the cost of the undeveloped lot, preconstruction, at: $37,000. The $44,950 amount is the second, duplicate charge for the same lot. To accomplish this set-up the lot had to be gifted and then immediately retrieved. This created the secret and fictitious loan, debt, and lien that will contrive to put the REO Fraudsters in the first lien position post foreclosure charade. Putting them ahead of any other locally defrauded investor having invested in Deeds of Trust under a kind of Ponzi scheme. Contributing to the indebtedness of this property, making default inevitable other loans are out there, concealed in the ether-world of the MERS E-Registry System.

The amount claimed to be borrowed is: $44,950. Payments will be made on this loan, "*with interest thereon providing for monthly installments of principal and interest with the balance of the indebtedness, if not sooner paid, due and payable on June 01, 2036.*"

Another sum under a different loan is referenced: ***Rehabilitation Loan Amount.*** Like me, I think Diane would have noticed if contractors showed up to make unneeded repairs on her home. We are to believe that the combined indebtedness of house and the lot is $224,750, despite the fact that other loans exist using 35 Lewis Fairway Circle as collateral including this mystery **Rehabilitation Loan Amount.** What was that sum? Seen as a, pattern in my home and the Turner property as well as others it was likely 100k flowing into the coffers of the Jones, Kelley, Boyd Perpetrator Nexus; some of it paying off satellite partners or at least for a time, any local investor-dupes feeding local leads into the system.

This Deed of Trust as well as the prior Deed of Trust do not reference or attach as an exhibit the Original Power of Attorney in the name of Leslie. Both are improper executions of what claims to be a Deed of Trust. They are evidence of identity theft and document fraud.

MERS claimed there were so many transactions tied to 35 Lewis Fairway Circle that when I tried to print the list it could not be printed. This is MERS limiting access to the digital footprint. Upon viewing the **"MERS Mortgage Industry's Utility"** list any homeowner would recognize transactions they had no part in. Any federal investigator would recognize the Property Flip – Equity Skimming – Title Theft sequence crying out for prosecutions.

What the Andrews imagine are house payments are actually assignment of rents. There are two stories. First that the homeowners are home buyers under a valid Deed of Trust. Secondly that they are renters with the REO dual claim of ownership smothering the first Deed of Trust indicated by the MERS MIN Number, under an avalanche of document fraud. Thus, assignment of rents used to guarantee illegally acquired loans equates to money laundering. Skimming equity restyled as rent-payments. The feds are very late to this party.

Any person who purchased a home in the Fair Oaks planned development. Or there about. Having experienced what seems to mirror part or all of the harassment associated with this same chain of theft. You may want to go back, only to discover that your former home is now a rental and, or, whether it was transferred to FREO TN, LLC; shell company for Pretium Partners, LLC. Or a company like it. *(Different named shell companies operating in different states.)* Launch your own independent investigation. It is very likely that you still own your home.

Assignment of the Deed of Trust Instrument No.: 11003920
THE BREEDER DOCUMENT
Signed July 20, 2011; Filed July 26, 2011;
Batch No.: 53310

This Assignment conveys the Andrews Deed of Trust from one party to another party. In the context of a Property Flip – Equity Skimming Scheme this transfer of authority is followed by a replacement of the original Trustee with the "Substitute Trustee" willing to circumvent the law so as to conduct the pretense of a valid Trustee Sale of the property to the general public.

Unlike any others, this "Assignment" of the Andrews, "Deed of Trust," to another entity, by law, is required to be filed and must appear in the public land records. You may or may not get a letter telling you that it has been filed.

What makes this a fraud device? Control of the mortgage had previously been off-loaded to the REO Private Investors before this Assignment is ever filed. Thus, regarding my home, Vernon "Wayne" Boyd and Sherry Boyd with all confidence could claim in a document in my possession that they owned my home for the prior three years before the charade of eviction ever took place. Homeowners must never learn who owns their Mortgage, what entity controls any default outcome, and with whom they are communicating with at any given time.

By the time this Breeder Document is filed the REO Fraudsters are already the secret, never disclosed, Note-Owner/Note-Holder calling the shots, having already hired the foreclosure mill attorneys.

This is the fourth transaction filed with the Fayette County Registry of Deeds Office. It was signed by MERS acting as nominee (proxy) for the secret REO Private Investor Note-Holders on 7/20/2011. For obvious reasons, at no time are the actual Note-Owners named. The fix is in. As the Breeder Document this instrument was dumped into the land fill of the Fayette County Registry of Deeds Office on 7/26/2011 purporting several lies. It is executed by the robosigner duo of Dominique Johnson and Deborah Beard. They did not actually sign this Assignment, but they did blindly sign many others making the signatures and notary seals easily accessible to the foreclosure mill attorneys.

ROBOSIGNERS

"We have defined the term "robosigning" as the practice of an employee or agent of the servicer signing documents automatically without a due diligence review or verification of the facts." United States Department of Housing and Urban Development (HUD).

Marie McDonnell wrote: ... it has been standard industry practice for mortgage servicers filing foreclosure actions to submit false affidavits, fraudulently backdated documents and other fraudulent documents in court for, at least the past fifteen years. ... In addition to false affidavits, mortgage servicers have also fabricated mortgage assignments and other documents on behalf of entities that no longer even exist.[91]

The signature of Deborah Beard and her notary seal has been "*electronically or photostatically copied*" and affixed to the Andrews Assignment of Deed of Trust, aka, the Breeder Document. The signature of Dominique Johnson is also a forgery. One of my pattern example groupings include Assignments of the Deeds of Trust, including my home, the Andrews home, and the Turner home (as well as others) all bearing the same photostatically inserted, and thus, forged signatures and notary seals. Below is the Marie McDonnell definition.[92]

BREEDER DOCUMENT, a.k.a., ASSIGNMENT OF DEED OF TRUST

"...in identity theft cases the birth certificate is often referred to as the breeder document because once fabricated, an imposter can use it to acquire a driver's license, Social Security Number, bank account, passport, etc. and obtain

---

[91] From: City of Seattle Review of Mortgage Documents © 2015 McDonnell Analytics, Inc., Appendix "1" Definition of Terms. Marie McDonnell is an acknowledged expert in the field of Mortgage Fraud; property theft enabled by our nation's largest banks.

[92] Marie McDonnell is a forensic property document examiner. McDonnell Property Analytics provides title and securitization reports and services to attorneys, consumers, registries of deeds, and government agencies. She is the leading authority in her field and has conducted numerous audits and served as an expert witness in mortgage fraud cases. https://www.mcdonnellanalytics.com

rights and privileges of citizenship to which he/she is not legally entitled. Translating this concept over to the realm of foreclosure fraud the most common breeder document is the fraudulent assignment of mortgage which purports to grant a title interest in the underlying real property to the fraudster, and serves as the basis for obtaining other documents necessary to extinguish the property owner's rights and transfer full legal and equitable title as well as possession to the fraudsters." From: City of Seattle Review of Mortgage Documents © 2015 McDonnell Analytics, Inc., Appendix "1" Definition of Terms.

Unlike Fayette County, TN rather than bury proof of widespread systemic fraud, John O'Brien and Marie McDonnell suggested that a grand jury be convened to look at proof that *"forged documents are intentionally and knowingly being used by banks and their lawyers to illegally remove Americans from their homes;"* Delaney Rohan[93]

From Affidavit of Marie McDonnell: ***The result of my investigation revealed widespread, systemic, methodical patterns of practice whereby the public land recording system has been used by the nation's largest banks to transfer title to real property that the banks do not own. This is especially true where a foreclosure is involved. ...This charade is being carried out by filing of a defective, often fraudulent conveying document, such as an assignment of mortgage, which becomes the "breeder document" that***

[93] Massachusetts Official Declares Registry a Crime Scene, written by, Rory Delaney Rohan. https://udolegal.com/udolegal-news/featured-articles/massachusetts-official-declares-registry-a-crime-scene.html O'Brien wants a Grand Jury to subpoena "both the past and present" CEO's of the Mortgage Electronic Recording Systems, Inc. (MERS), Bank of America, JP Morgan Chase, Citibank, Wells Fargo, Countrywide, Washington Mutual, and others." And... "There is no question in my mind that the **officers of these banks and loan processing servicers made a conscious decision to commit fraud and participate in a scheme to deprive the public from knowing the true holder of their mortgage** while at the same time **avoiding paying billions of dollars** in recording fees, O'Brien said. **"It is my opinion that they acted as a criminal enterprise."** That was 2012. How many decades will go by with these crimes enabled by corruption before American homeowners are protected from wholesale theft of their property? Unraveling this putrid ball of crime, putting criminals in jail must start somewhere.

enables the alleged assignee to obtain all other documents necessary to extinguish the property owner's rights and transfer full legal and equitable title as well as possession to the fraudster.

Aside from the fact that the notary and signing officer signatures are forged this Assignment of the Deed of Trust is also a void document, having no power to enforce, because it takes its authority from prior invalid, forged, one-party, unsigned Instruments. Business as usual at the Fayette County Register of Deeds Office.

Judge Martha Brasfield stepped up to the plate. She failed to notice the first unsigned Warranty Deed implying that she may not have required any proof but merely rubber stamped what the foreclosure mill attorneys needed. As we look at what happens next, we must consider the actions of this judge. It is hard to believe that Judge Martha Brasfield was ignorant of how the Breeder Document, functions in the common title theft scheme of operations?

We read: *"Recording requested by Bank of America."* Here is a red flag that should have led to a demand for the first Countrywide Deed of Trust which would have brought down this house of cards. As the quintessential source document, the Countrywide Deed of Trust starts the sequence of endorsements, signed and notarized paper. The claims and requests of the foreclosure mill attorneys had no legal standing without a full title history. Failure to verify the chain of property title represents a fraud upon the court; rubber stamped by this judge.

We read: *When recorded mail to Core Logic.* As the foreclosure charade juncture approaches there was likely a Core Logic Equator work order tied to the Keller Williams computer system, divvying up assignments, keeping all the fraudsters on the same page. This of course is wire fraud, a RICO Predicate Act.

As it turned out a confluence of scripted harassment induced the Andrews to move from their home before the brutal eviction that I experienced became necessary. Like me Diane Andrews had no idea that from the first day she moved into her new home she had been assigned a neighborhood spy. Reports went upline (up the street) to the Jones, Kelley, Boyd Perpetrator Nexus – REO Investors. The Andrews emotional state; what level of vulnerability were all reported. The stuff of betrayal.

Notice of Lis Pendens; Instrument No.: 12000429 In the Chancery Court of Fayette County Tennessee in the 25th Judicial District; Civil Action File No.: 15763 November 14, 2011

This is the fifth instrument filed with the Fayette County Registry of Deeds. It is only necessary because it was decided that the repeated use of the wrong name and the existence of the original Power of Attorney, which I do not believe was ever lost, left the theft scheme too exposed. The REO Holdings case let us know that the alteration of names, impeding any investigation, is a common feature in the tool box of these fraudsters. But it was not going to hold up in the theft of 35 Lewis Fairway Circle without a challenge.

What is Lis Pendens? I had no idea. It was often the case that I had to look something up. According to trusty Wikipedia: *In United States law Lis Pendens is a written notice that a lawsuit has been filed concerning real estate, involving either the title to the property or a claimed ownership interest in it. The notice is usually filed in the county land records.*

It is also described over the internet as: *a pre foreclosure formal notice filed by the lender against a homeowner with three months of unpaid mortgage. During the pre-foreclosure process the homeowner may try to refinance his mortgage or sell the property in order to fix his credit situation.*

Given a system that disenfranchises homeowners from all disclosures the Andrews could not have gotten the Jeffrey Kelley gangsters off their backs. They lacked the name of the Note-Holder. They had no idea with whom they were actually communicating with at any given time. Thus, they would never live at 35 Lewis Fairway Circle free from harassment. Amoral unfiltered capitalism had allowed criminal banks to commodify home mortgages. What did we think was going to happen? What is at stake today are property rights in America.

We read that the plaintiff bringing this Lis Pendens action is: *The Bank of New York Mellon, FKA, The Bank of New York Mellon, as Trustee for the Certificate Holders of CWALT, Inc., Alternate Loan Trust; Mortgage Pass Through Certificate, Series 2006-OC6.* Once again, the REO Fraudsters hide their identity behind that of Bank of New York Mellon. Bank of New York Mellon was the trustee for all the securitized loans acquired by Bank of America in the Countrywide bankruptcy. "CWALT" refers to Countrywide Alternate Loan Trust.

The Countrywide Deed of Trust is so troublesome to the success and concealment of the fraud scheme that it cannot surface. Informed by the existence of the MERS MIN Number, did Judge Martha Brasfield ask to see it? Theft of the Andrews property is obvious in the trail of document fraud never examined by this judge. If the fictitious lien will function as intended the Andrews Countrywide Deed of Trust, cannot be where anyone will find and read it. In the same vein if allowed Due Process the Andrews and any attorney would have realized it was missing. They had to be silenced. None of these crimes could take place as they do without Fayette County cooperation in shielding a billion-dollar theft industry operating nationwide.[94] Other counties across this country are holding the line; Fayette County crony corruptionism is not alone as facilitators of Title Theft.

A default judgment was achieved by the foreclosure mill attorneys because this judge allowed herself to be used, without examining the basis of any of the Note Holder claims; right to foreclose. Upon belief she knew exactly what was required of her.

A reformed copy of the original Power of Attorney needed to be produced without ever disclosing to James and Diane Andrews that it was needed. The signature of Diane Andrews would need to be lifted from another source and affixed to the "reformed" Power of Attorney. This charade must propose to Judge Martha Brasfield that Diane Andrews was informed and that she consented to the fraud perfecting use of her name, in multiple examples of identity theft, that was in every respect a departure from how she normally signed official documents.

Chancery Court must rubber stamp and declare valid the "reformed" Power of Attorney-fraud device enforceable, having the

[94] It was Judge Vescovo's hypersensitive out of context defense of the Fayette County Registrar of Deeds Office that caught my attention and caused me to go back and take a hard, more in-depth look at certain filings. I had only submitted one of the three pattern example groupings as an exhibit. I had cited errors specific to those filings pertaining to theft of my home without yet recognizing the full import of document fraud systemically corrupting the Fayette County land records. I had not named the Fayette County Registry of Deeds Office in the Civil RICO Case filed on 4/20/2016. I did however reserve the right to add defendants. When I tried to add JP Morgan Chase Bank the district court refused those exhibits. Under the weight of trailing corruption, the fix was in, following me to the Sixth Circuit Court of Appeals. No one wanted to rule on the truth, everyone was already groomed and committed to ignore.

same authority as that of the original when it was signed five years before on May 9, 2006.

We know how important the lost Power of Attorney was because the content of the Lis Pendens suit tells us. The lawyers for the REO Secret Note-Holders ask for permission of the court that the upcoming "reformation" of the original: ***"be declared valid, enforceable, and in first priority lien position."***

Informing the systemic culture of corruption Judge Martha Brasfield helps out. Keep in mind that as I repeatedly charged that the fraudsters had presented me with a forged Fayette County Judges Order of Eviction no one cared. This very serious crime was never investigated. Following pattern Judge Martha Brasfield will rubber stamp the request that anyone with half a brain would have recognized, at the very least, as an end run around the Due Process rights of the Andrews.

It might have been the securities broker that tossed this ball back to the local group of REO criminals. The person signing for the law firm, Rubin Lublin, PLLC and, or, any signing officer signing for a bank or mortgage company must show proof that they have actual authority to act in that capacity. The purpose of a designated signing officer meets the requirement that everyone is physically present when papers are signed and notarized.

Because this is such a big piece in creating phony documents the identity of signing officers must always be questioned. Who are they? Who do they work for? Is this a forged signature lifted from another filing and affixed to this one? Or... does this person even exist, is this an entirely made up identity? It isn't your job to prove all this beyond a reasonable doubt. It is the job of the foreclosing party to prove they have the legal right to foreclosure. Look for document fraud. Present it, but raise these questions in any court action you file.

At this crucial juncture, where illegal seizure of 35 Lewis Fairway Circle hung in the balance the REO Fraudsters are faced with a quandary. The entire house of cards could collapse at this tricky juncture if a default judgement that rubber-stamps the theft goals of the Criminal Enterprise is not achieved. No judge should ever make a decision premised on an incomplete record of filings. They should know enough that they can recognize when they are being conned. I would like to have been present as the REO Fraudsters worked out how to handle the need for a "reformed" Power of Attorney in the name of

Diane. Who would they propose lost the original? Because they are named as a co-defendant with the Andrew's we should believe that GMAC lost the Power of Attorney. GMAC came late to the game.

Letting the Andrews co-defendant immediately off the hook we read: ***GMAC is named in this complaint solely because it is the current servicer for the Deed of Trust from Mr. Andrews to Mortgage Electronic Registration System, Inc. as nominee for Southstar Funding, LLC dated May 10, 2006 and recorded May 30, 2006.*** Gobbledygook that regurgitates the fraud narrative.

Nowhere in the above statement do we read the actual, locally situated, REO Fraudster Note Holder identity. The judge does not require it, nor does she care to verify that GMAC was ever the actual servicer of the loan. These and other important questions were among those that GMAC should have been required to show up and answer. This cannot happen. A fraud partner would be under oath, required to lie and perjure themselves. At all times a minimal public records footprint is required. Solution: do an end run around the Fayette County justice system.

The fraudsters need the first Deed of Trust filed with the Registry of Deeds Office (Instrument No.: 06004795) taking its authority from the prior unsigned Warranty Deed (Instrument No.: 06004794) to be declared *"properly executed on behalf of Diane Andrews."* Sworn to uphold the laws of Tennessee and the integrity of the bench the judge is helping to perpetrate a fraud upon the court. Logical questions and multiple red flags flew by any filter she was equipped by education and experience to question and then, as a standard of care and duty, to act on.

Obstruction of the Constitutional Right to be heard in a court of law and the role of the robo-judge.

Conflict of interest-enmeshment amongst key players, with multiple roles played by the same people is standard operating procedure designed to reduce the risk of exposure. We see this played out by the law firm of Rubin Lublin TN, PLLC in filing this Lis Pendens suit and then emerging as the Resubstituted Trustee; flipping the property back to the secret REO Fraudster Note-Holders that hired them. This is arm in arm criminal collusion. These foreclosure mill lawyers will walk forward the charade of issuing a summons, notice to appear. Survival of theft at this tricky juncture require that the Andrews absolutely NEVER do, under any circumstances, show up to upset this applecart; speaking truth to the huge imbalance of power.

Because the foreclosure mill attorneys have to obstruct the right of the Andrews to be heard they are at first cast by the foreclosure mill attorneys in an uncooperative adversarial role to explain why they do not appear in this action. They are then cast as cooperative. This to justify the travesty of the default judgment signed off on by the Fayette County robo-judge.

The actions of Judge Martha Brasfield are in direct contradiction to those standards applied by Judge Arthur M. Schack in JP Morgan Chase Bank v. Butler (Chapter Twenty). Judge Schack actually looked at whether JP Morgan Chase Bank had standing. He declared Chase an improper plaintiff declaring: *Chase, the improper plaintiff, engaging in bad faith is "a waste of judicial resources."* Judge Martha Brasfield did not vet the legal standing of the smartly dressed, still not disbarred, foreclosure mill attorneys standing before the bench. Whose actions perfected theft of 35 Lewis Fairway Circle and I believe many other homes, on behalf of a RICO Criminal Enterprise.

Page-2 of what is filed as Instrument No.: 12000429 tells us what kind of trouble the Jones, Kelley, Boyd Perpetrator Nexus is in, in not being able to produce on demand a court sanctioned "reformed" copy of the Power of Attorney in the wrong name. As an established pattern of practice, the REO secret Note Holders, yet again, hide their identity behind that of Bank of New York Mellon.[95] And by extension behind that of the defrauded investors in the CWALT securitized trusts.

They request of Fayette County Chancery Court the following:

(a) *That the court issue an order allowing a copy of the Power of Attorney to be recorded in lieu of the original;*

[95] There needs to be a class action law suit filed against Bank of New York Mellon for allowing repeated use of their name to cover for that of the secret Note-Holders. The same principal holds true for MERS. Both entities are fully aware that they have no legal standing during the period that their names are used to conceal the identity theft needed to launder the chains of title. The REO fraudsters continued to hide behind the moniker of Bank of New York Mellon even after they and Bank of America had paid off the investors in the CWALT Trusts the year before. Look at pattern examples seen in this same timing; leading to illegal seizure of private property in violation of the Fourth Amendment to the United States Constitution.

(b) *That the court declare the First Deed of Trust record as Instrument No. 06004795, Fayette County, Tennessee records was property executed on behalf of Diane Andrews.*
(c) *That the First Deed of Trust recorded as Instrument No. 06004795, Fayette County, Tennessee records be declared valid, enforceable, and in first priority lien position against the Property; and*
(d) *That the Court award such other and further relief as may be just and proper.*

As we already know Instrument Number 06004795 is not the first Deed of Trust. The foreclosure mill attorneys are perpetrating a fiction upon the court. A painted pig is still a pig. *"Relief as may be just and proper"* is an outrage in that theft is so enabled by Fayette County corruption that the fraudster claims are just accepted at face value. If proper relief were going to be possible 35 Lewis Fairway Circle would be restored to the rightful owners, James and Diane Andrews.

The foreclosure mill attorneys could not call upon the Andrews to remedy this problem. Even if the judge was committed to rubber stamp theft, if allowed due process as was their right, I believe Diane would have noticed that the Warranty Deed was unsigned and a fraud on several points. That signatures appearing as "Diane Andrews" were forgeries. Any one of these lies might have led to recognition that certain notary stamps and signatures were lifted from other unrelated filings. A cooperating Fayette County judge, perhaps more interested in getting reelected than protecting the integrity of the court, delivered the needed outcome.

One must ask, how was the Diane Andrews signature acquired? I have an image in my mind of her assigned spy walking a card across the street. Building community, the Fair Oaks neighborhood was socially minded. The annual Christmas party took place at the golf club house. I taught a non-denominational Bible Study in the neighborhood only because a request went out from the social club. Get-well cards and birthday cards made the rounds. I believe that the Diane Andrews signature came from one of those sources. It was dutifully supplied by that person assigned to keep tabs on how well the behind the scenes multiple flips of the property title, the fraud narrative comprising the wall of deception were holding up. Were Diane and James Andrews worried? Did they suspect anything? Would anything come out of the wood-work to interfere with the theft-step-process? All this needed to be monitored.

The need to monitor targets of this scheme was real. I threw a wrench in the chain of theft when I put my home on the market, when I applied for HAMP, when I began communicating with the IRS and finally as a last-ditch effort to save the equity in my home, when I planned to file Chapter 13. All this was duly reported by Ann Jones to her criminal cohort. An IRS problem in the form of a lien threatened to derail theft of the Candace Turner home; our next example; Chapter Twenty-Seven.

Whether an IRS lien, a lost power of attorney, a last Will and Testament, any attempt to sell or move the theft-asset out from under the REO secret Note-Owners/Note-Holders control was met with extreme hostility and immediate action that included breaking even more laws. Whatever it was that threatened the theft-goals, it was business as usual to aggressively neutralize those threats.

Informing modus operandi two people I care about very much were approached by Sherry Boyd attempting to gain access to their personal lives under the pretense of building a relationship. When I was alone and dealing with Brett's relapse into addiction, they were more than kind to me. When one of them became ill, rebuffed on previous occasions, Sherry approached this woman asking if she had "the Holy Ghost." When Ann invited me to her church, she wanted me to invite this other couple. In her low-key way she kept after me about this until I finally did, the three of us accompanying Ann to her church for what she described as a special service. Upon reflection this was at the direction of Sherry Boyd looking for a hook, an access point, by which she could gather the information needed to steal the nicest home in the neighborhood. Her name appeared in the directory of several churches. One can only be offended when the pretense of faith is used to disguise predatory, greed obsessed motives. Career con-artists have this modus operandi well perfected.

After the Boyd's moved into my home as squatters they began to harass a neighbor who had just lost her husband after a long battle with cancer. I was told that they went so far as to park a van with a sign on the side proclaiming the United States Immigration Service. The neighbor, who spent some of her youth in another country was so unnerved that she went looking for her naturalization papers; proof that she was an American citizen. I had to wonder how often vulnerable immigrants functioned as straw buyers and, or, were targeted. Death of a spouse was a common feature in the pattern example groupings. The scripted harassment as a fraud tool grew so great that this friend and former neighbor kept her shades drawn and though she loved gardening stopped going outside for fear of being accosted over some minor, blown out of proportion dispute.

The Lis Pendens Civil Action was filed with intent to perpetrate a fraud. Not, withstanding another robo-judge this is a fraud upon the court. It is a fraud upon Diane and James Andrews. The bold and blatant nature of the Andrews fraud fits past and future patterns of practice and reflects how these dangerous perpetrators operate. When I sought help from those in authority I was cast in the role of troublemaker; the one doing the harassment. This deflection conceals who the real criminals are while ensuring that complaints are dismissed and not heard.

Permission for reformation of the lost power of attorney was filed by: Peter L. Lublin, Brian Linkowsky, J. Kelsey Grodzicki and Natalie Brown "Attorney's for Plaintiff Bank of New York Mellon" on **November 14, 2011.** Four (Rubin Lublin, PLLC) attorneys when all that was needed was one name. Look for overkill in these documents sending a subtle intimidating message to those victims inclined to challenge the fraud in what is proposed in these instruments. When did a law degree become a license to rob, steal, and thieve?

Lis Pendens suits are meant to serve notice to those named that a pending action will follow. At this juncture the Andrews still held a protected interest in 35 Lewis Fairway Circle because the charade of foreclosure as one of the last fraud perfecting theft-steps had not yet taken place. It cannot take place until the forged power of attorney covers for use of the wrong name.

Timing is everything. This filing reads: *Respectfully submitted **this 14th day of November 2011**.* It is stamped and signed by the "Clerk & Master," Vip D. Lewis, two days later on ***November 16, 2011.*** His signature is duly notarized. It was held back from filing with the Fayette County Register of Deeds Office until ***January 23, 2012.*** The ten-week delay before it was filed in the public land records as Instrument No.: 12000429 is no accident. Not until the Andrews have moved from 35 Lewis Fairway Circle. Not until they no longer live within easy driving distance of the Fayette County Register of Deeds

Office. Not, until they no longer live where the Sheriff's Officer serving the summons might actually find them... only then can it be filed.

The fraud scheme depends on the "mark" not thinking to periodically verify what is filed at the Registry of Deeds Office. The 70 **(seventy-day)** delay puts a choke-hold over the flow of information. At every juncture where any public records footprint could unravel the putrid ball of big-picture-deception, exposing a Criminal Enterprise, victims must never be heard in any venue that produces a record. These dangerous characters threaten and resist all legal challenges with the ferocity of an invading army. They have the cooperation of lawyers willing to catch and kill these cases; impeding access to due process.

Crony corruptionism is grafted into West Tennessee as firmly as the out of control kudzu smothering the vibrancy of what is living and beautiful. Next time you park your car facing the charming Somerville court square. Sit for a spell at the cute little gazebo and breath in the scent of summer flowers. I believe you may also pick up the scent of nothing being what it seems. It takes a lot of people not doing their jobs, subjugating morality both personal and professional, willing to put their critical thinking skills on hold, forgetting that there is a higher authority, for this level of white-collar theft and assault to function as it does.

DETOUR / Summons "Civil Paper" Notice to Appear

Now we break away from the sequence of filings to consider how Diane and her husband were claimed to have been served notice of this law suit. When in fact, by intentional design they were never served, "Civil Paper" by the Fayette County Sheriff's Office. This would be the same Sheriff's Office that violated my civil rights by refusing to take a police report.

The Summons reads: *You are summoned to defend a Civil Action Filed against you in Chancery Court, Fayette County, Tennessee. Your defense must be made within thirty (30) days from the date this summons is served upon you. You must file your defense with the Clerk of Court and send a copy to the Plaintiff's attorney at the address listed below. If you fail to defend this action by above date, judgment by default can be rendered against you for the relief sought in this complaint.*

This is exactly the needed outcome. Everyone knows that the Andrews no longer live at the theft-asset address of 35 Lewis Fairway

Circle. Jeffrey Kelley lives at 85 Lewis Fairway Circle. It appears that they owned seven lots on the same street including 35 Lewis Fairway Circle which explains how the lot was severed from the mortgage and then folded back into a phantom mortgage. Max Jones lives in the same very small neighborhood. The person I believe was the Andrews designated spy, though the house faces a different street, can stand at the end of the driveway and watch for the mail delivery. The Kelley's are tied to the former Sheriff. If Jeffrey Kelley wanted the Summons delivery sabotaged this was easily accomplished. Not least of all by a short walk down the street to retrieve anything left at the doorstep or in the mail box. The Sheriff's Office claimed that Diane and her husband were each separately served by Officer Kenneth Hunt, a physical impossibility.

At the bottom of the page we read that: *James Andrews was served on 1/22/2012 by K. Hunt (2418).* Mr. Andrews signature does not appear.

Under Serving Data section we read: *Paper Status: SERVED.* We read; *Who Served: Diane Andrews.* No signature appears.

The Lis Pendens action which generated the Notice to Appear Summons was delivered to Chancery Court on 11/14/2011. Unlike immediate notice of service to GMAC two months went by before there was any attempt to serve the same Summons to the Andrews. This coincides with the 70-day delay before the Lis Pendens suit was filed with the Fayette County Register of Deeds Office... after it is confirmed that the Andrews have moved.

Though the outcome is described as Diane having been served. And at the bottom of the Fayette County Sheriff's Civil Paper form: *James Andrews was served on 01/22/2012 by K. Hunt (2418)* no signatures appear.

Sheriff's Officer Kenneth Hunt having already falsely claimed to have served Mr. Andrews then submitted the Summons back to the Chancery Court. Doing so on January 10, 2012, twelve days before he claims to have successfully served it. *I hereby return this summons as follows: (name of Party Served). Date of Return: 1/22/2012.*

Officer Hunt then affixed his signature in the designated box. Unlike the GMAC acknowledgment of receipt of summons, the Andrews designated space is blank. Though there was no proof of service this was good enough for the Fayette County Judge, Martha Brasfield who allowed what is essentially a blank form to be submitted as an exhibit by the foreclosure mill attorneys.

Fayette County government is so corrupt that I have to say the following. If anything, that I have referenced by instrument number or otherwise is not found or appears to state something different ask me for my copies placed off site in a secure location. Is Fayette County corrupt beyond repair? I was not joking when I said that crime scene tape should be placed around the Fayette County Register of Deeds Office with a grand jury impaneled. It is up to the good people of Fayette County to restore honor, trust, and morality.

Consent Order and Final Judgment as to James E. Andrews and Diane Andrews. "Filed and Entered" by, Chancery Court April 12, 2012. Fayette County Register of Deeds Instrument No.: 12002794; filed on June 11, 2012.

In this filing we read again that Bank of New York Mellon is the: *current holder of the Deed of Trust... recorded May 30, 2006, at Instrument No.: 06004795, Fayette County, Tennessee records. ...and securing the real property located at 35 Lewis Fairway Circle, Oakland, Fayette County, Tennessee.* NOTHING – no part of – this statement is true. Start out believing nothing that you read. The Note Holder is the Jones, Kelley, Boyd Perpetrator Nexus. The Investors in the securitized trust have already been paid off at the agreed upon loss (securities fraud).

The entire sequence of filings is premised on the illegally contrived debt of the lot incurred by a fictious loan. This phony debt has been labeled as a Deed of Trust so as to bury the Countrywide Deed of Trust; concealing identity theft. Along with everything else this robo-judge lets slide, she quashes the first Deed of Trust as a legal contract between the Andrews and their lenders allowing it to be replaced by a fraud. Why? She cannot be this stupid. Has she, or anyone in her family, personally benefited from theft of private property in West Tennessee? The REO Fraudster, holders of this fictitious debt are again, hiding their identity behind that of Bank of New York Mellon.

We read in this Consent Order: *Whereas, upon information and belief, the original Power of Attorney was lost prior to recording.* It was not lost. It just needed to be buried since it exposed repeated use of the forged wrong name.

Further Reading: *Whereas, on July 20, 2011, the First Deed of Trust was assigned from Southstar Funding to Bank of New York*

Mellon ***via that certain assignment recorded July 26, 2011 as the Instrument No. 11003920****, Fayette County, Tennessee records (hereafter the "Assignment;" and...*

Go back and read the section of this chapter that addresses **Instrument No. 11003920, Assignment of Deed of Trust**, and how as the Breeder Document the forged "Assignment" functions to grant those who do not actually own the property pretended authority to re-title the Property in their names. Allowing the Trustee Sale and pretense of Foreclosure as the well-worn theft-step-process to go off without a hitch.

Among the many lies we then read: **Whereas, the Bank of New York Mellon, Mr. Andrews, and Mrs. Andrews have consented and agreed that the real estate records of Fayette County, Tennessee should be reformed by recording a Power of Attorney in lieu of the Original; and...** So ordered, entered and filed, *April 12, 2012*. If truth were a standard upheld by this court the Bank of New York Mellon name would be stricken and the names of the actual REO Private Investor Group should appear.

Perfection of this theft is then signed off on by Judge Martha Brasfield who, ignoring multiple red flags agrees that the phony Deed of Trust can quash the first Deed of Trust. Existing to replace, taking authority from the unsigned Warranty Deed and the forged identity theft Breeder Document; "Assignment of the Deed of Trust." We read that this fraud device should be declared "**to be properly executed on behalf of Diane Andrewes;"** Diane as the identity theft moniker. Judge Brasfield functions as expected.

On the following page (Instrument No.: 12002794) states that on February 4, 2012 Diane Andrews consented to the Reformation of the lost Power of Attorney that will now be used to back step the theft-step-process assigning an authority that did not then, up to today, or ever exist. We read page-278; **CONSENTED TO:** Signed: **Diane Andrews.**

We are invited to believe that Diane traveled on February 4, 2012 so she could appear before a Tennessee Notary: Cynthia L. Hubbard. Abandoning a history of signing her birth name she cooperated with the theft-agenda by signing "Diane." We are to believe that the Notary verified her identity. It appears that the notary signature was lifted from another filing and affixed to this one. The year of the notaries signature is altered to read: 2012. The "2" is superimposed by hand over what appears to have previously read as "1." To falsely read; **Witness my hand, at office, this 4th day of February 2012.**

Exhibit A attached to this filing, is a copy of the forged Power of Attorney. The notary signature was lifted from the Original Power of Attorney that was in fact, never actually lost.

We then read that copies of this order, rubber stamped by the Fayette County Judge, were mailed to James and Diane Andrews at 35 Lewis Fairway Circle. At this point they no longer lived at this address. But Jeffrey Kelley and his wife Carrie live a short distance away on the same street at 85 Lewis Fairway Circle. Just as I believe Ann Jones took papers off my desk and out of my mail box the Kelley's were positioned to do the same. Diane and James Andrews were obstructed from and denied Due Process. They were denied knowledge of the conveyance of their property accomplished via a fraud upon the court.

Obtaining an assignment through fraudulent means invalidates the assignment. Fraud destroys the validity of everything into which it enters. It vitiates the most solemn contracts, documents, and even judgments. Walker v. Rich, 70 Cal. App. 139 (Cal.App.1926).

Was the Andrews property ever a HUD owned property? The Fayette County Registrar of Deeds Office had no Instrument on file letting me know that my home was at one time owned by: **"Secretary of HUD"** and registered over: **"The HUD Information Systems, Shepherd Mall Office Complex, 2401 NW 23red Street, Oklahoma City, Oklahoma."** With the fraud riddled HUD-1 declaring, "HUD is the Seller."

The HUD fraud is the start of the Property Flip – Equity Skimming theft-step-process for some, but not all of the examples I looked at. The HUD acquisition is important and crucial information for any victim to have. No filing at the Registry of Deeds Office of these HUD transactions renders every homeowner profiled and targeted for these theft schemes a sitting duck. HUD should be required to file legal instruments whenever homes are assigned to their authority however temporary. This should be done directly by HUD and not left to criminals and foreclosure mill attorneys to selectively withhold. Because HUD gets away with this and other failures of oversight, fraud is rampant. HUD can only restore integrity by returning these homes to their rightful owners. I'd like my home back.

I submitted multiple FOIA requests.[96] I isolated six properties to highlight as examples that replicated the same chain of theft that I experienced; fraud upon and use of HUD programs to commit in part, bank fraud. These six homes were the subject of some of my HUD FOIA Requests.[97] Even on appeal the HUD resistance, up to this writing, continues. Though on appeal I was told some information would be forthcoming that directive has been utterly and completely ignored. This is control of federal programs by powerful financial industry players concealing the national footprint of the Bank Theft Delivery System.

HUD has no interest in making public how they have facilitated white-collar theft of private property via misuse of federal programs meant to benefit the poor. Homeless veterans would be grateful for the chance to buy or rent homes going into HUD-Vash programs, stabilizing at risk families across this country. Not growing the personal wealth of the borderless financial industry criminals.

Default Judgment and Final Order as To GMAC Mortgage, LLC Instrument No. 120002793; filed May 11, 2012

This is the sixth filing. The entire exercise of naming GMAC as a co-defendant with James and Diane Andrews is a complete farce. GMAC

[96] Fayette County Register of Deeds Office; Filing BATCH NUMBER: 53310.

[97] I narrowed repeated FOIA requests to six properties, including my own. There were many commonalities including the forged Assignment of Deeds of Trust prepared by the same law firm to function as the Breeder Document; all dumped into the land fill of the Fayette County Register of Deeds office on the same day. I already knew they were subjected to a Property Flip – Equity Skimming Scheme. But I wanted to know, and had a, right to know, if like my home, the other five homes were pooled into HUD programs and repurchased out of those programs by the same REO secret note-holders. These select properties from the larger "batch" all needing investigation were: 1.) Adams-1400 Jones Chapel Drive, Moscow, TN; Straw Buyer: Mark A. White. **2.) Andrews-35 Lewis Fairway Circle, Oakland, TN; Straw Buyer: Laura Wolf. 3.) Clair and Stancil-65 Pinehurst Drive, Oakland, TN; Straw Buyers: Vernon "Wayne" Boyd and Sherry White Boyd.** 4.) Joyner-395 Oakland Hills Drive, Oakland, TN; Straw Buyers: Jerry Lee Lewis and Beverly Parkinson. 5.) Barnicle-70 Garden View Drive, Oakland, TN; Straw Buyer: Chernica J. Turner. **6.) Turner-40 Valley Oaks Cove, Oakland, TN; Straw Buyers: Darnell L. Bradley aka Brad Monroe Darnell.**

was served notice through its registered agent. There was no threat of exposure in serving them. Unlike the Andrews who might actually show up if they'd actually received notice, the REO Fraudsters knew that GMAC would not bother to hire an attorney so as to have a presence in any courtroom. They knew better than to testify under oath. Judge Martha Brasfield did not see their absence as a red flag. For failure to appear a default judgement was entered against GMAC as well as against the Andrews. GMAC could care less.

Now that Fayette County Chancery Court has allowed the reformation of the Power of Attorney in a wrong name per forged signatures and notary stamps, having conspired with the local bad actors to obstruct the Andrews Constitutional Right and access to Due Process, the phony foreclosure charade can get underway.

Next steps require that a Substitute Trustee must be appointed to replace the first Trustee. A Trustee who, in conducting the Trustee Sale of the property will ensure it is never offered for sale on a level playing field to any member of the buying public as the law requires. It will end up back where it started. Fed through The Bank Theft Delivery System to the Wall Street securities market.

Appointment of Substitute Trustee
Instrument No.: 13005287; signed June 3, 2013.
Filed 80-days later on August 22, 2013.

What went on during that eighty-day hiatus? The mountain of document fraud in the wrong name can appear as valid. The lawyers for the REO fraudster clients can pick up the phone and tell whoever it was that worried about identity fraud as a fly in the ointment that the robo-judge had issued the phony consent order; green lighting the reformed Power of Attorney in the forged, wrong name. Everyone is off the hook if a federal prosecutor, a remote possibility in the minds of these career criminals, will come knocking.

The Jones, Kelley, Boyd Perpetrator Nexus are not too worried. They've been getting away with these crimes for at least, two decades.

Trustee means the person designated as the Trustee in the Deed of Trust. Our fraud scheme requires removing the original Trustee and replacing that Trustee with a Substitute Trustee willing to break the law. This eighth filing tells us that the Substitute Trustee is Rubin Lublin, PLLC. This is the same law firm that told the Fayette County Chancery

Court that the reformation of the Power of Attorney was consented to by, Diane Andrews when it was not.

The term "Foreclosure Mill" means law firms that have a history of breaking the law. As the Substitute Trustee it will now be the job of Rubin Lublin, PLLC to conduct the bogus and illegal Trustee Sale. This is set up for the physical seizure of 35 Lewis Fairway Circle that has been a theft-asset almost from the beginning.

A Trustee has authority to act based on the information provided to them by the mortgage company. In this case provided by the REO Criminal Enterprise. In theory based on those instruments validly executed and filed in the public domain. Yet again... Without ever actually naming them, the REO Fraudsters are described as, "Holder." To mean Holder of the Deed of Trust acquired by fraud, premised on the forged Breeder Document, taking authority from the fraud device of the unsigned Warranty Deed.

This "Holder" is not Bank of America, not GMAC, not Bank of New York Mellon. Some of the people as "Holder" lived down the street from the Andrews. The holder is not Southstar Funding and it is most certainly not Select Portfolio Servicing, Inc. The various illegal flips of the Property title are suggested by these connections. When reading filings and claims over the Andrews property the names of these companies appear only to deceive, out of context to the roles they actually played or, despite what is claimed, never did play.

Rubin Lublin, TN PLLC has already been acting in a criminal capacity under color of law. All the paperwork filed by them, even to an untrained eye, is a fraud tool. The lawyers showing up have not been disbarred. They are nicely dressed, bearing all the accruements,' of elitist authority. Exposure of the lies appearing in the avalanche of document fraud cannot be allowed to bring down this house of cards.

The Substitute Trustee Deed, again conceals the REO Fraudster identity. The Jones, Kelley, Boyd Perpetrator Nexus are referred to as: "Holder." ***Now therefore, Holder, pursuant to and in compliance with the Deed of Trust, does hereby name and appoint Rubin Lublin TN, PLLC as substitute trustee under the Deed of Trust, and declares that they shall have the same powers and authority as the Trustee (as such term is defined in the Deed of Trust).***

Select Portfolio Servicing, Inc., is the signing officer. This filing reads that they are: *The attorney-in-fact for The Bank of New York*

Mellon FKA The Bank of New York Mellon, as Trustee for the Certificate Holders of CWALT, Inc. At this juncture appointing Rubin Lublin, TN PLLC as the Substitute Trustee. Again, we see that the REO Note-Owners/Note-Holders are hiding their identity behind that of Bank of New York Mellon. Everything claimed is false.

So, who is Select Portfolio Servicing, Inc.? In November 2003 Fairbanks Capital Holding Corp were sued by the U.S. Department of Housing and Urban Development (HUD) and separately by the Federal Trade Commission.[98] They agreed to pay $40 million dollars in settlement fees to the homeowners who had been overcharged. The suit addressed those mortgages driven into default by illegal practices that included tax sales and claims of forced placed insurance.

Sound familiar? At the same time the federal prosecutors for HUD[99] allowed these white-collar criminals to skate on admitting wrong doing.[100] Thus, they lived on to act as, in this capacity, the third-party mortgage servicing entity that in the context of fraud stands as a barrier and layer between the homeowner and the secret REO Private Investor Note-Holder. After the law suit Fairbanks Capital Corp as a criminal enterprise merely changed their name (common practice) to that of Select Portfolio Servicing; this name is thus, affixed to the Appointment of the Andrews, Substitute Trustee, filing.

For those very serious criminal charges brought against them by the Federal Government no person went to jail. Thus, Select Portfolio Servicing, Inc. lived on to appear as the "attorney-in-fact" appointing the foreclosure mill attorneys, Rubin Lublin TN, PLLC, as the Substitute Trustee. That is, if anything about this instrument is factual and true.

---

[98] United States v. Fairbanks Capital Corp. alleged misconduct that "resulted in substantial overpayment of fees and charges in connection with their mortgage loans, and has exacerbated delinquencies and caused unnecessary or illegal foreclosures." Class Action Rebates Web Site.

[99] Department of Housing and Urban Development (HUD) Program Compliance Division. Programs utilized by REO Private Investors. The role of the third-party mortgage servicing companies plays, a crucial role in the thefts described in this book.

[100] In the United States District Court for the District of Massachusetts. The United States of America, Plaintiff vs. Fairbanks Capital Corp., a Utah corporation, Fairbanks Capital Holding Corp., a Delaware corporation, and Thomas D. Basmajian, Defendants. Findings: page-2, paragraph-4: *"Defendant has not admitted any of the allegations of wrongdoing set forth in the Complaint, and entry of this Order is not an admission of any such allegations of wrongdoing or violation of law. Nevertheless, Defendant stipulates and agrees to entry of this Order in order to settle and resolve disputes."*

It appears that the Notary seal and signature as well as the signing officer has been lifted from another document and applied to this instrument by the foreclosure mill attorneys.

Today Select Portfolio Servings, Inc. are owned by a foreign holding company. Theft of private property in the United States so lucrative that foreign criminals have flooded this breach allowed by law makers who should be protecting the public welfare.

There is a common sense fairness principal that most of us learned on the playground as children. A principal that under law has made the chop-shop sale of auto parts taken from stolen cars, gold melted down from stolen jewelry, the resale of stolen guns and electronics via the conduit of a pawn shop a crime punishable under law; sending people to jail. To say that no one can give (sell) what he does not own. And that no one receiving or buying stolen goods can claim rightful ownership over that property.

Nemo Dat Quod Non Habet. The NEMO DAT RULE reads: **"no one gives what he does not have. States that the purchase of a possession from someone who had no ownership to it also denies the purchaser any ownership title in that property.** (Black's Law dictionary.) **"The baseline principal of our system of property regarding transfers of ownership is nemo dat quod non habet – "no one can give what he does not have."** City of Seattle Review of Mortgage Documents, Definition of Terms, McDonnell Analytics, Inc.

The Andrews still own 35 Lewis Fairway Circle. No future sale of, or purchase of, this property is valid. I still own 65 Pinehurst Drive. Candace Turner may or may not be the rightful owner of 40 Valley Oaks Cove. The jury is out as to whether her ex-husband was a straw buyer who behind the scenes made sure she could never keep the property granted to her in her divorce settlement by yet another robo-judge.

Substitute Trustee's Deed; Instrument No.: 14001319
Signed March 5, 2014; Filed March 12, 2014

A new Deed of Trust has to be produced. This Deed of Trust evidences the illegal seizure of private property in violation of the Fourth

Amended to the United States Constitution. This Deed of Trust will stand until yet another appears to replace it in the name of Straw Buyers.

The REO secret Note-Owners waited nine months before they pretend to auction off 35 Lewis Fairway Circle so that they could turn around and repurchase (flip) the same home back to themselves. The straw buyer waiting in the wings moved into this property on March 26,2014 if not before.

This document was prepared by the foreclosure mill attorney's, Substitute Trustee, Rubin Lublin TN, PLLC. It is signed by them at a location in Norcross, GA; the same location as the Notary, Marshall Clarke. To state that Victor Kang, the signing officer was physically present in Georgia having proved his identity *"to be a Member of Rubin Lublin TN, PLLC."*

The foreclosure sale of 35 Lewis Fairway Circle, was claimed to have taken place 389 miles away on the same day, on the court house steps in Somerville, TN. Checking on another foreclosure sale I found that chairs were set up in the lobby of the Court House, but no bidder appeared. There is in fact no auctioneer, no Trustee presiding. There is no lawful foreclosure since these homes are off-loaded to the REO Fraudsters by the Banks, long before the charade of Foreclosure, followed by the illegal seizure becomes necessary. Every act is a mock exercise in deception.

The foreclosure mill attorneys hired by the secret Note Holders, Rubin Lublin TN, PLLC, claims to have opened the *"the floor for competitive bids."* This evokes a word picture of buyers gathered at the court house steps check book at the ready. In fact, nothing could be further from the truth. Letting an average citizen buy these properties in any genuine arms-length transaction, absent all conflict of interest totally negates the fraud-goals of where these homes are destined to end up. Morphed into a rental, pooled into a Wall Street security, bought and sold by the criminal banks to their investor depositors.

Regarding the theft examples described in this book Bank of New York Mellon is not the lender. They are not the Note-Holder. They are not the Note-Owner. They no longer have any beneficial interest in the mortgage because at some point. Establishing the needed degrees of separation. Bank of New York Mellon as Trustee over the CWALT Trusts have already been paid off at the agreed upon loss. This is securities fraud. In my case they were paid off in 2011 before start of the

HAMP Fraud Scheme. Like the name of MERS, their name is merely used as proxy to conceal the Jones, Kelley, Boyd Perpetrator Nexus. Or whatever Private Investor Group you identify as having assumed your mortgage. Driving that mortgage into default via use of the Bank Theft Delivery System.

I have an image in my mind of James Andrews signing what he believed were genuine closing documents for himself and his wife under the original Power of Attorney. Happy and excited he perhaps phoned Diane to share the moment she could not be present for. It is a milestone in life when homes are purchased. But before he was even out of the parking lot the groundwork of the fictitious loan and lien were in place as the excuse for Bank of America as the servicer, to grant the REO Fraudsters a beneficial interest in the mortgage.

We read: *Whereas demand was made for payment of the Note secured by the Deed of Trust, referenced above.* There is no valid note. The note is the fictious loan.

The Fayette County Judge allowed the identity theft; rubber stamping the fraudster request that the REO criminals be put in the first lien position under the Lis Pendens action, Civil Action No.: 15763; **and in the first priority lien position against the Property.** The first lien position is not the mortgage. It is the lien, stemming from the fictious loan, over the lot, gifted, promptly retrieved; used as an asset rental.

The REO Fraudsters request of the corrupt judge, as documented in the Lis Pendens Action, Instrument No.: 12000429: **That the First Deed of Trust recorded as Instrument No. 06004795, Fayette County, Tennessee records** (which is not the First Deed of Trust) **be declared valid, enforceable.** But, as you already know, it is not valid nor enforceable since the authority is taken from the unsigned Warranty Deed.

We know what Note (so called Deed of Trust) this foreclosure is premised upon because page-2 (two) of this filing (lacking actual page numbers) tells us. The Rubin Lublin, PLLC foreclosure mill, trusting that corruption is so accepted that no party will actually go back and read the void Warranty Deed and least of all Judge Martha Brasfield. Notice that the Warranty Deed, simplistically and incorrectly is labeled "DEED" to assign invalid authority over a fraud device. **Being the same property conveyed to James E. Andrews, herein by Deed**

of record in Instrument Number 06004794, in the Register's Office for Fayette County, Tennessee.

Instrument Number: 06004794 is the Warranty Deed that gifted the lot owned by the Jones, Kelley, Boyd Perpetrator Nexus to James Andrews for ten dollars. James Andrews did not sign the Warranty Deed. Every document filed after, including this one is null and void.

This filing appears just as a valid Trustee Deed should appear. Anyone can download these forms and load them onto their computers for repeated use. Everything claimed in this filing is a lie. There is no valid foreclosure. One cannot take possession of what one never owned. **"The baseline principal of our system of property regarding transfers of ownership is nemo dat quod non habet – "no one can give what he does not have."** City of Seattle Review of Mortgage Documents, Definition of Terms, McDonnell Analytics, Inc.

Whereas, by that certain Deed of Trust dated May 10, 2006 and recorded May 30, 2006, at Instrument Number 06004795, Register's Office for Fayette County, Tennessee (the "Deed of Trust"), Diane Andrews and James Andrews ("Borrower,") ... This is another fraud perfecting statement. This statement, which when taken at face value simply because it reads as one would expect, buries recognition of the Countrywide Deed of Trust and replaces it with a fraud device. We expect more from courts and judges. They are in place because, "We The People," believe they will stand in the gap against tyranny. When they fail us, they fail all of their peers as well.

Within this filing is a veiled threat. We read the intimidating language meant to deter any victim from fighting back. To say that Bank of New York Mellon as proxy for a Criminal Group of REO Fraudsters is: ***...free from any equity of redemption, statutory right of redemption, spouse's elective share...*** To say that the law does not matter.

The illegal seizure of 35 Lewis Fairway Circle could not survive even a limited challenge. It was illegal on every claim. Therefore, the Andrews Due Process rights had to be obstructed. Another deterring statement seeks to let the Fayette County Registrar of Deeds Office off the hook to say that the Andrews have no right to bring suit against, or right to challenge, ***...the accuracy of the Index Book of said Register's Office.***

If this were true Leader, Bulso, & Nolan, PLC would not have filed and won their case against REO Holdings, LLC. Hagans Berman Sobol Shapiro, LLP would not have won a victory at the Tenth Circuit Court of Appeals ruling that Bank of America could be declared a, RICO Criminal Enterprise. Evil people intend for these messages to forestall any victim from fighting back, to say that victims are out-gunned before they even speak up. Justice has to be worth fighting for.

After the phony pretense of foreclosure, this is when Straw Buyers are needed. It is at this juncture that straw buyers temporarily live in these homes still owned by the REO Private Investor Groups. The REO Investors, by law, are to sell these homes on the open market. The rigged system, in part enabled by HUD, has meant that average citizens are cut out as back door deals, illegal appraisals, and price fixing rule the day. The relationship between the REO secret Note-Holders and the straw buyers are conspiratorial and illegal.

STRAW BUYERS, circumvent legal restrictions while enabling fraud. For our purposes these are people that apply for bank loans in order to buy a home as proxy for the REO Criminal Investment Group. Doing so they conceal the real Note-Owner Identity. They conceal conflicts of interest, arm in arm transactions, price fixing, and fictitious appraisals that either over-value or in the majority of my examples coming out of Fayette County, initially under-value the theft-asset. This allows for the lucrative home improvement loan with loan funds not used for the stated purpose. The Straw Buyer(s) appears to be just an average purchaser with no prior financial interest in the stolen property.

Some straw buyers are bribed. I found one identity that appeared to be prison at the time he was purported to be buying a home. At a specific juncture my home, the Andrews property and the Turner property were occupied by straw buyers tied to the Jones, Kelley, Boyd and Keller Williams-Chamberwood group of bad actors.

The Andrews sequence of filings, inform us that theft of 35 Lewis Fairway Circle was planned even before a warm body showed up to select this particular lot.

Different mistakes were made in our next example. The push back to cover them up was just as aggressive and equally reckless. When roadblocks surface the fraudsters do not have the option to walk away. A property theft not carried out to completion draws too much attention. The primary fear is always federal investigators and prosecutors.

The lawyers that filed the case against REO Holdings, Eugene N. Bulso, Jr. and Paul J. Krog warned that these crimes are taking place all across the State of Tennessee. Bulso and Krog filed their case in 2015. I've been fighting my battle for recognition of these crimes up to today. The Examples that I write of and researched took place between 2009 up to 2019. The sixth circuit refusal to hear my last motion for a void judgment and the unaddressed complaints I filed with the sixth circuit are gasping for breath on the vine of inaction. As I edit this it has been over sixteen months that I filed complaints with the Circuit Executive at the Sixth Circuit. It seems that the MERS strategy to *resist, limit, and delay,* are common fraud tools that should have no presence in any American court. The sixth circuit is even above any requirement that they address issues of administrative corruption. Who will hold them accountable? United States Judicial Oversight Committee: www.judiciary.senate.gov It cannot be that corruption and infiltration of our federal court system is the new normal.

CHAPTER TWENTY-SEVEN

"Investment finance math is sales math. It doesn't matter that you don't need it or that everybody interprets it in their own way. You're using it to impress clients. ... The financial industry uses mathematics in a manner that would be mortifying to any other field of science. Academic literature and industry research are rife with pseudo-mathematical nonsense. You don't have to look far to see where the motivation lies: Many of the authors are either employed by or retained by richly paid investment management and consulting firms. ..." From: The Wall Street Math Hustle: How the financial industry's embrace of bad math is BS by, Richard Wiggins and Michael Edesess

40 VALLEY OAKS COVE
The Asher and Turner Property

Fayette County Instrument No.: 12000565; 40 Valley Oaks Cove, Oakland, TN. Letter from the REO Fraudsters to IRS Agent: Ellen Dolby; Notice of Federal Tax Lien/Consent to Sell.[101] *"...against certain parties thought to be the owners of the property."*

In keeping with how these Property Flip – Equity Skimming Schemes operate the actual Private Investor Note Holders are not named. Here they hide behind the phrase: *"certain parties thought to be the owners of the property."*

The foreclosure mill attorneys know who hired them. It is their job to conceal their client's identity in every endorsement and document that they file.

Is Ellen Dolby a real IRS Agent? I don't know. I wrote to her and never heard back. The purpose of dropping this letter into the Fayette County land records was to establish the notion that the IRS issues are handled. This lets the bank (Bank of Fayette County) off the hook for their part in laundering money. To later explain why they failed to file a Suspicious Activity Report (SAR). The bank, perfecting one of several illegal flips of the property title, will make money as they launder

[101] Internal Revenue Service (TN); C/O Ellen Dolby, 801 Broadway, MDP53, Nashville, TN 37203-3804. From: Rubin, Lublin, Suarez, Serrano, LLC.

income via assignment of rents and other business thrown their way by the REO Criminal bad actors. We'll get to that a little further along.

Informed by the signed and notarized paper dumped into the landfill of the Fayette County Register of Deeds Office we have a picture of how this property was stolen. We see how the larger community of REO fraudsters network and cover for each other, with complete confidence that they will always escape consequences. Every document filed exists to tell a story that deflects from the truth.

In the history of this property there was a Countrywide Loan and Deed of Trust. Because the REO Fraudsters assumed that mortgage from Bank of America this is the quintessential source document. It cannot be named without linking to the original homeowner identity; not Candace Turner. For this reason, two phony source Documents are created. They replace and quash from recognition that original Deed of Trust. Fraud in what postures as the source document(s) invalidate everything that comes after. Until proven otherwise regard everything filed after your Deed of Trust as a potential red flag. *A red flag is an indicator that calls for further scrutiny. One red flag by itself may not be significant; however, multiple red flags may indicate an operating environment that is conducive to fraud.*

The Pooling and Servicing Agreement

40 Valley Oaks Cove, like almost every mortgage in America is securitized and pooled under the terms of a Pooling and Servicing Agreement. There is a beginning and an end-date that properties can be entered into a Pooling and Servicing Agreement forming the Mortgage Backed Security. The SEC makes it impossible for homeowners to track who exactly owns an interest in their mortgage and therefore has a motive to corrupt the property title while leaching equity via a theft scheme. The protectionist syndicate that has built up around the borderless financial services industry means that the SEC cannot reliably say what outside investors own any single piece of any American mortgage.

The terms of the Pooling and Servicing Agreements define the responsibility and rights between the Servicer, the Trustee, and over the pool of mortgage loans controlled by the financial industry. Rights of the homeowner are entirely disregarded. Any pool of loans, combining the value of these properties, represent millions of dollars. Unbridled capitalism view, every mortgage as a product. Mortgages traded like poker chips many times over far exceeds in importance and authority that contract between the homeowner and the original lender that is the Deed of Trust. As we saw in the Andrews example the original Deed of Trust is an impediment; treated as an inconvenience that needs to be undermined, buried, and corrupted before American homes can be fed through the Bank Theft Delivery System described in this book.

"The important thing about the Pooling and Servicing Agreement is you will find in virtually every case that all the parties who are involved violate nearly every provision of their own Pooling and Servicing Agreement."[102]

Homeowners do not know that they can opt out of allowing the corrupt financial industry to securitize their mortgage. As the consumer you can decide that you wish one lender to hold your mortgage until it is paid off or you decide to sell your home. You can have input into how any contract Promissory Note and Deed of Trust reads. At the very least get confirmation in writing that there will be no secret flip, transfer, sale, or assign of temporary authority putting your property title at risk of theft that is not also copied to you. Not additionally disclosed by filing at the Registry of Deeds Office. In fact, no lender can agree to these stipulations. If securitization is not stopped on the front end, the day you sign your, closing documents the runaway fate of any single mortgage is no longer under the control of that lender.

If once approved for a loan and then abruptly you are offered less favorable terms because you make this choice. If suddenly you are turned down altogether you can sue the bank for discrimination and violation of your civil rights in that you do not choose to risk being defrauded by a predatory system that views the home buying middle classes as a lost gazelle on the African savannah. "**We the people**" can and must take back our power.

When overwhelmed and beleaguered homeowners try to understand how they lost their home they are often directed to the securitization process and the pooling and servicing agreements to prove fraud. Courts recognize that the FDIC and the SEC are not enforcing the terms of the Pooling and Servicing Agreements. A lot of union and pension funds are invested in this industry largely controlled

[102] http://4closurefraud.org/2013/05/08/wells-fargo-bank-n-a-v-erobobo-non-compliance-with-pooling-and-servicing-agreement-psa-voids-assignment-of-mortgage/

via the mafia-like chokehold of criminals. If the FDIC and the SEC won't prosecute a message is sent to the lower courts. Destabilizing and keeping a free-thinking American populace so preoccupied with economic survival that they are less likely to impact reform, less likely to vote, more likely to accept the censorship of media is part of the globalist agenda to control every aspect of American life.

Plaintiffs and their attorneys should by all means look at and use whatever comes out of an examination of the Pooling and Servicing agreements. However, do not put all the eggs into this single basket. Victims of these fraud schemes and their attorneys should concentrate on the massive amount of Document Fraud dumped into the public record. They should get everything filed with the MERS E-Registry System that is selectively withheld from victims of these fraud schemes. This would include the third-party servicer and bank vendor records. Banks are required to perform an on-site review of the servicer loan documents, all servicing records, before they approve loans that launder the chains of title. They are not being held accountable. This is not an accident. This is part of a larger conspiracy with obvious racketeering implications.

The facts you accumulate are the unfiltered road map. The lie fed to HUD that I had abandoned my home. The Andrews fictitious loan and lien. The, Linda Howard accumulation of bogus fees and then refusal to accept her house payments. The, fraud narrative, whatever it is establishes the premise for the engineered default. Whatever that slander is, it has to be repeated both in declarative statements and in the spirit of what follows within the company of trailing documents. Fraud in the endorsements, filing instruments, tells you that everything after is null and void. You still own your home.

The foreclosure mill attorneys are the same as seen in the Andrews theft. Here the name reads the longer version of: Rubin, Lublin, Suarez, Serrano TN, LLC. To avoid confusion, hereafter I refer to them as Rubin-Lublin. Read MERS and think Fraud. Read Rubin-Lublin connected to any mortgage and think up to no, good until proven otherwise.

The series of documents filed in the Turner example tell us that although Candace Turner believed she had acquired a home under the terms of her divorce settlement, 40 Valley Oaks Cove was already, an REO Owned Property. Whatever Deed of Trust was referenced in her divorce case, she did not end up with a house. She was merely granted the lot upon which the house was already sitting. This is the same hook seen in theft of 35 Lewis Fairway Circle. What was different is what prompted the extra fraud perfecting filings and how some of them appear; dumped indiscriminately into the Fayette County Registry of Deeds Office. So as to meet head on the push back. This time from the Internal Revenue Service (IRS.) As always, the veneer of legitimacy was robotically provided by giving these thinly veiled fraud perfecting filings and endorsements a Fayette County Registry of Deeds Instrument Number. Fayette County helped perpetrate a fraud, not only upon Candace Turner, but upon a federal agency.

In the Turner example the Asher Countrywide Deed of Trust covering both the lot and the house as a traditional mortgage must not surface. This is because its existence contradicts the fraud narrative trailing forth in what is filed, that all Candace Turner gets in her divorce settlement is an empty lot. To wrongly communicate that the house has not yet been built.

Attorneys and the judge signed off on the divorce scam. I've wondered if Candace was prevailed upon to share an attorney with her ex-husband. If she had her own attorney, he/she was either inept or prevailed upon to assist these fraudsters. The secret REO Note Holders used Candace Turner and the circumstances of her divorce to extend that period that house payments could be skimmed from the theft-asset of 40 Valley Oaks Cove. Candace thought she was in good shape; she did not owe more on her home than it was worth. Nothing she believed was true, actually was true.

The REO Fraudsters used the Fayette County Register of Deeds Office and the court system to perfect their crimes with, as it turns out the reasonable expectation that they were shielded by the toxic and systemic culture of corruption they had helped to create. The primary difference between Candace Turner and the Keller Williams Straw Buyers who are today still squatting at 65 Pinehurst Drive and whose influence to control and conceal these crimes extended all the way up to the Sixth Circuit Court of Appeals, is that Candace Turner did not know she was a straw buyer. She thought she was a homeowner.

The problem is that Steven Turner could not give what he did not own. The court judgment that rubber stamped this scheme were bound by the same rule. **"The baseline principal of our system of property regarding transfers of ownership is nemo dat quod non habet – "no one can give what he does not have."**

McDonnell Analytics, Inc. There is no statute of limitations on a void judgment.

Aside from the loss of any settlement value her character was besmirched. As the designated scapegoat a default judgement is filed in the Fayette County Register of Deeds Office; Instrument No.: 17003854. The Internal Revenue Service came calling with misplaced blame assigned to Candace by slick Criminal Enterprise attorneys. Another cooperating Fayette County Judge was yet again, willing to accept everything proposed by the smartly dressed attorneys standing before the bench.

We start with the Turner PROPERTY RECORD CARD

According to the Property Record Card the home was appraised at: $191,500. The first transaction listed within the Fayette County Property Record Card deflects from and by design, conceals the actual first transaction. Candace Turner is shown as the single mortgage holder with that transaction taking place on 6/25/2010. Helping out Fayette County does not list Steven Turner. Early in the planning Candace is to be the designated scapegoat. As we shall see this was a theme.

Only four transactions are shown on this Property Record Card. There is no disclosure as to the limited nature, why a limited list, or where to find a more complete list. The REO Fraudsters, influence how this information presents and Fayette County cooperates. The point is that the entire set-up is not citizen use friendly. Nor is it reliable. The protocols, if in fact any exist, are too easily adapted to conceal fraud.

This list conceals the Asher Countrywide Deed of Trust, as the quintessential source document from which the Turner claims flow. The Asher Deed of Trust is buried. The *Note Section* on the Property Record Card is left bank. In some examples it is not blank. The property is claimed to be abandoned or vacant. A statement that if read by a homeowner like me, still living in my home when this claim was made, would have equipped me to defend my property title. Regarding 70 Garden View Drive, straw buyer, Chernica J. **Turner,** we read: "House Vacant 10/3/2014."

Does Fayette county provide instructions regarding use of this comment box on the Property Record Card? Is there accountability for the inconsistent application in how it is used or not used? Another example is 1400 Jones Chapel Road; Moscow, TN. This house is claimed to have been vacant: reading *HSE Vacant*. Upon belief that this was a home assumed upon illness and death of one Margaret Dorse. Were there any rightful heirs that should have inherited this home? I don't know. The appraised value of this home is: $316,900. As a red flag the original Deed of Trust does not appear. Three Warranty Deeds and one (Substitute) Trustee Deed takes up the four slots allowed serving to bury the original Deed of Trust.

Thus, when one goes back to try and determine who is the straw buyer(s) and who is the homeowner first targeted nothing is clear. I believe this was the case with 40 Valley Oaks Cove. A goal of the theft-step-process is to smother that first targeted and relevant Deed of Trust from recognition, i.e., the quintessential source document. It cannot be a coincidence that Fayette County repeatedly falls short.

I spoke on three occasions with Candace Turner. She believed that 40 Valley Oaks Cove came to her from her husband, Steven Turner in their divorce settlement. When I explained how the Property Flip – Equity Skimming Scheme operated it was she that jumped ahead to ask: "Where did the house payments go?" Smart question.

The Turner divorce agreement represents another fraud upon the Fayette County Court. A judge was required to sign off on what was presented; granting that divorce. Lawyers inducing judges to sign off on theft under color of law is a serious crime not to mention a disbarable offense.

According to the Property Record Card the house was built in 1999. Although a Quit Claim Deed implies something different this home was already built when Steven and Candace Turner purchased it via a Warranty Deed from Chad Asher and Kimberly Green Asher on 4/26/2006. A so called "second mortgage" functioning as a, fictitious loan, over the phony sale of a lot, puts the Original Deed of Trust in jeopardy. In today's unprecedented culture of corruption, until proven otherwise, Warranty Deeds and Quit Claim Deeds should be regarded as a red flag. How they are used in the fraud context was addressed in a previous chapter, but merits repeating.

Quit Claim and Warranty Deeds may be used by someone who is transferring the Property title, but is not the owner or the owners' representative. The purpose of such a transaction is to sell the property outright or to refinance the debt in a

cash-out transaction to collect loan proceeds. A fake Power of Attorney may be used as authorizing the deed transfer.[103]

The Asher name does not appear in the Property Record Card. This was a home destined to go into default. Upon belief that Candace Turner was innocent of how she was used as Steven Turner's wife to perfect this theft, burying the Asher Deed of Trust under the Turner claims. The Instruments filed in the Fayette County Register of Deeds Office support only that Candace was the rightful owner of the lot. Not the house built on that lot. A proposal so ludicrous that it does not pass the laugh test. And yet, no Fayette County employee looked twice at what was proposed. And if any did, they were not empowered to question the intent of this filing and return it for clarification. While the tax office is diagonally across the way a copy of the Turner divorce agreement was a short walk upstairs. But no Fayette County employee in the Registrar's office is empowered to look for fraud, let alone report it. It is the height of irresponsibility that in an electronic age with massive opportunity for corrupt practices to take root the public welfare falls by the wayside while white collar criminals, some appearing the most respectable, wreak havoc into a community.

Perhaps Candace would have wanted to work with the IRS to save her home. She was not afforded any opportunity to do so. Per modus operandi she was always in the dark as to whom she was communicating with at any given time. She could not have accurately described her position to the IRS. However, it is absolutely true that Candace, like me and others, posed a very real threat. The IRS needed to be neutralized before anyone thought to interview or communicate with her directly. Candace might have decided to phone IRS Agent, Ellen Dolby, who may or may not be a real person. But in any case, getting someone on the phone; starting any kind of back and forth dialogue was unacceptable to the REO Fraudster, secret Note Owner clients of the Foreclosure Mill Attorneys with oh so much to hide. Therefore, the REO Fraudsters, via the foreclosure mill attorneys, stepped in to handle the IRS.

---

[103] The Detection and Deterrence of Mortgage Fraud Against Financial Institutions: A White Paper. FFIEC Fraud Investigations Symposium; page 36. https://www.ffiec.gov/exam/Mtg_Fraud_wp_Feb2010.pdf

Who is the rightful owner of 40 Valley Oaks Cove?

As I write about this property the question will always be, who is the rightful owner. Is it Chad Asher and his wife Kimberly Green Asher? Did this start out as a builder buy out scheme that positioned this property to be repeatedly flipped?

I raise this question because, informing pattern, the Chad Asher name is tied to that of Steven Turner in yet another suspect property. This is 650 Canadaville Loop; Eads, Tennessee. Grantor/Debtor Asher, Chad. Chad Asher then conveyed the property by Warranty Deed to Candace Turner, Instrument No.: 06003768. There was then a Deed of Trust Instrument No.: 07007187; Borrower: Steven Turner, Jr. and Candace Turner.

As I write this 650 Canadaville Loop, Eads, TN 38028 is currently for sale. Any new owner should not accept any superficial claim that there is a clean chain of title by which they can assert ownership. They should acquire the full MERS record. If going ahead with this purchase it would be wise to file Quiet Title. In fact, the Fayette County title history of many homes, including many in the Fair Oaks neighborhood, have been so corrupted that almost anyone should do the same.

Quiet Title: Any purchaser of a property wants a guarantee at purchase that they have a clear property title that will not later be challenged by any liens, levies, or any secret dual claims of ownership. They want to know that their Deed of Trust is a true and valid contract. That house payments will never appear as assignment of rents with money laundered by secret private investor claims of ownership. At purchase this guarantee should appear in writing by your lender and by the seller's agent. A notice can appear in newspapers and also filed at the Registry of Deeds Office. Any incomplete and corrupt property title would require a law suit and judgment leading to a Quiet Title notice. Quiet Title in today's corrupt culture has to mean something far more comprehensive than it previously has.

Some of the homes I looked at were conveyed directly from the builder to straw buyers connected to the REO Fraudsters. We are then led to question how the Chad Asher name was used in both 40 Valley Oaks Cove and 650 Canadaville Loop.

As a pattern of practice, the stolen property titles flip these homes to the limits of the equity skimming potential. We are now going to look at the sequence of public filings that flushed what I am calling the Candace Turner property, 40 Valley Oaks Cove, through The Bank Theft Delivery System.

Warranty Deed; Instrument No.: 06003768
Signed March 17, 2006; Filed April 26, 2006

Neither this Warranty Deed nor the fake Power of Attorney that follows can stand up under scrutiny. Fayette County lets the REO Fraudsters get away with broken chain of title as a ploy to deflect any investigator from easily bringing up a complete history tied to 40 Valley Oaks Cove.

This Warranty Deed reads that the Asher's also received 40 Valley Oaks Cove per a transfer by Warranty Deed. ***Being the same property conveyed to the party of the first part by Warranty Deed of record at Plat Book 6, Page 179, in particular description of said property.***

This Warranty Deed reads that it is prepared by attorney, Brian K. Smith. Once assigned an Instrument Number it is to be returned to Jeffrey McEvoy. Attorney McEvoy is the owner of Home Surety Title and Escrow, LLC. Reducing risk, in the same way, Mark Miesse is tied to his own title company. Remember the McEvoy name. The property owner is named in bold print as Candace Turner. The name of her husband, Steven W. Turner appears to have been added as an afterthought. His name does not appear in bold text. This is deliberate. By design Candace is the designated scapegoat. Further along Candace will be offered up to the IRS as the primary bad actor.

Contempt for Candace likely existed even before the marriage went south. Her value to the Criminal Enterprise is that she can be used to assign misplaced blame, pushing her name forward, while keeping the Stephen Turner name in a minority position. The same pattern of contempt is revealed in how Max Jones and the Criminal Enterprise used Ann. Perhaps also in how Denise Martin is being used.

We read that the value of the property transferred by Warranty Deed on March 17, 2006 to the Turner's, for $10.00, *whichever is greater is $189,500.*

This is another one-party transaction. For a legitimate conveyance of real property there must be an agreement attested to by all parties signing their names. This one-party Warranty Deed is not signed by Candace or Steven Turner. The Asher's have signed. The Turners do not indicate by signature that they receive the property. This is a red flag missed by every lender. It is yet another fraud device having no power to enforce. The fraudsters need not worry. Fayette County has already proven that they will file almost anything.

This Warranty Deed will replace the actual first Deed of Trust. It will masquerade as the source document from which trailing documents, perfecting the chain of theft, claim authority that does not exist. This might as well be reading that Donald Duck conveys the property at the cost of $10.00 to former deceased President Harry Truman... who because he is in the grave failed to sign it. Antiquated laws compounded by a culture of corruption have hamstrung reporting.

Deed of Trust; Instrument No.: 06003769
Signed March 17, 2006; Filed April 26, 2006

The Lender is America's Wholesale Lender. According to various court rulings America Wholesale Lender (AWL) is a fictious entity that has no standing to foreclose. The loan amount is: $151,600. This may be the amount that Candace thought was outstanding on the original Countrywide/Bank of America Loan. Candace made house payments that never went to pay down a valid mortgage. This phony Deed of Trust is claimed to be prepared by Meghan P. Shanley; an employee at AWL. Once filed with Fayette County and assigned an instrument number it is to be returned to Countrywide Home Loans, Inc. It is also to be returned to Home Surety Title and Escrow; Jeffrey McEvoy. Though she did not know it Candace was now the illegal owner of the lot absent the build, a ridiculous proposition.

At this point Arnold W. Weiss is named as the Trustee. He is actually the Substitute Trustee. As we shall see under the travesty of the fake Power of Attorney, Rubin-Lublin is the resubstituted, third Trustee. A third Trustee distances the conflict of interest actions of the former and should always be regarded as a red flag. Appointments and assignment of multiple trustees and repeated use of the same connected professionals unlikely to break ranks, informs that secret flips of the property title have gone before; not found in the public filings where any harassed and beleaguered or merely interested homeowner might find them.

Arnold Wiess was the eviction specialist named in the Core Logic Equator work order bringing to completion the illegal seizure of my home; 65 Pinehurst Drive. His name appears in other pattern examples. As the Substitute Trustee he will oversee the illegal seizure of 40 Valley Oaks Cove under the buried Asher Deed of Trust. Arnold Wiess does not seem to mind that his professional credentials are used to perfect theft of private property. He is an active part of the Jones, Kelley, Boyd – Keller Williams (MEM 2, LLC) – ERA Chamberwood Realty – Perpetrator Nexus.

A worthwhile question is whether 40 Valley Oaks Cove may have already been transferred to Pretium Partners, LLC, a.k.a., FREO Tennessee (shell company) by Warranty Deed or Quit Claim Deed? If true, courts have ruled that a REMIC Trust does not have standing to foreclosure. This timing can be significant to any defense.

Though the heading reads that once filed this Instrument should be returned to Countrywide Home Loans, Inc., it is stamped in bold that it should be returned to Home Surety Title and Escrow tied to Jeffrey F. McEvoy. When reading something like this, ask the Registrar of Deeds Office if a copy was returned to both. Ask to see the outgoing mail or communication records pertaining to your property address. Walk out the door with copies adding to your exhibit file. You are entitled to full disclosure. The common excuse I heard was that to share information with me, would be a violation of the privacy of those persons named in the public record. This is hogwash. No state or federal agency should be protecting what skims the surface of recognition as a fully functioning RICO Criminal Enterprise operating within a national footprint.

McEvoy, has prepared and filed the two key instruments needed to bury the Asher Countrywide Deed of Trust. These two falsely postured source documents are fraud devices. They include the Asher Warranty Deed which the Turner's did not sign; Instrument No.: 060037**68**. And the Deed of Trust Instrument No.: 060037**69** America's Wholesale Lender as an illegally postured mortgage company; reading that it should be returned to McEvoy's title company. He has also prepared the next Deed of Trust which names Arnold Weiss as the Trustee (actually the Substitute Trustee) Instrument No.: 060037**70**. All three are filed on the same day noted by the sequential instrument numbers; last two digits 68, 69, 70. This is a red flag. Banks that help to launder any chain of title are required to see this as a red flag. Ask yourself if what is claimed to be accomplished by what is signed, notarized, and filed all on the same day could have reasonably been accomplished within that time span. In this case within eight hours.

There is also the unearthed forged Power of Attorney (Power of Attorney No.: 11004022) not filed under the Turner name, but significantly claimed to be witnessed by Kaitlyn F. McEvoy and used as phony authority for appointing foreclosure mill attorney's Rubin-Lublin as the third "Resubstituted Trustee."

I write about this Power of Attorney in detail further along. It is referenced but, by intent, it cannot be filed in the Turner sequence of filings because it is so very obviously a repeatedly repurposed fraud device. It cannot stand up under scrutiny. It has been used as phony authority to foreclose on thousands of other Tennessee properties. Brought forward as an exhibit by any homeowner defending their property rights pre or post foreclosure, any judge upon seeing it, unless they are lazy, corrupt and paid for, would throw it out.

This America's Wholesale Lender (AWL) loan compounded to the Countrywide loan means that the total indebtedness brought about by the equity skimming practices far exceeds the value of the property.

"Equity Skimming is a type of real estate fraud scheme that became popular in the early 2000s following the mortgage crisis. It basically involves a person or (REO private investor) **investor gaining title to another person's home, then refinancing the home and taking out all the equity in the property." "... also, equity skimming cases are sometimes intertwined with other types of scams, such as home improvement scams, second mortgage loan fraud,** reverse mortgage scams **and other issues." (from: Legal Match Law Library)**[104]

Deed of Trust; Instrument No.: 06003770
Signed March 17, 2006; Filed April 26, 2006

This is not a second mortgage. This is not a valid Deed of Trust. ***Arnold M. Weiss, Attorney*** is claimed to be the ***(herein Trustee) and the Beneficiary***. The unsigned Asher one-party Warranty Deed filed by McEvoy establishes the pretense of authority upon which this

[104] www.legalmatch.com/law-library/article/what-is-equity-skimming.html

phony Deed of Trust stands. This loan, $37,900, is collateralized by the lot severed from the home already built. This is the same lot already secured by another loan and in any case no bank that is not helping to launder income for criminals would grant a loan secured by the lot when a home has already been built on that same lot. Such a scenario would be set up for multiple conflicting claims that would put at risk both loans. Somewhere in this mix, there is a corrupt title insurance company.

This begs the question, did the Jones, Kelley, Boyd Perpetrator Nexus purchase these lots pre-build from the contractor or from the original owner of these tracts of land as part of the set up? I think they did. Did the REO Fraudsters present the lender with a purchase agreement to imply that the Turner home had not yet been built? I believe this has been common practice in the Fair Oaks neighborhood and elsewhere.

What seems clear is that the REO Fraudsters anticipated that an upcoming divorce would take place. They did not want Candace Turner walking off with any theft asset they had plans for. Candace had worked with her husband and father-in-law. They had to be seen to give her something. A disgruntled spouse knowing too much would always be a threat. The same issues would have presented when Michael Harlow died and his widow, who likely knew far more than Candace Turner, needed to be managed, somehow neutralized, or brought into the fold (if she was not already there.) This harks back also to Ann's preoccupation with Max giving her a house in her name alone untainted by the pool of REO owned homes repeatedly flipped.

There was no clean chain of title. The entire house of cards could collapse if at any time in the future Candace decided to sell 40 Valley Oaks Cove. Just as I had to be aggressively obstructed from selling my own home the REO secret Note Holders skimming equity had to proactively defend against any possibility that Candace would try to do the same. This Deed of Trust, singularly covering the cost of the lot ($37,900) is a phantom debt. It is used as set up to claim a beneficial interest over the fictitious outstanding mortgage. This leads to the foreclosure charade and illegal seizure as set up for the next flipping sequence.

Candace then needed to be ejected from 40 Valley Oaks Cove, leaving a minimal public records footprint guaranteed by the corrupt Fayette County machine. But first there were house payments to skim which I imagine appeased the bitterness of Steven Turner and his cohort... the Jones, Kelley, Boyd Perpetrator Nexus, this time more directly involving Loretta Martin and therefore ERA Chamberwood Realty Group.

We see that the cooperating Title Company inserts an escrow/closing number and loan/document ID number where the MERS MIN Number should appear. No one will make payments on a loan they do not know they are liable for. Thus, at least for a time the REO Fraudsters use house payments morphed into assignment of rents to pay these loans. The Ponzi scheme aspect of these crimes will survive as long as complicit banks accept the inevitable losses, knowing they will make money on the backend laundering income.

Three Fair Oaks neighborhood properties fitting the same chain of theft is evidenced by, Warranty Deed in Lieu of Foreclosure; Instrument No.: 10007010. The secretly owned REO properties featured in this transaction are: **235 Pinehurst Drive, 250 Lewis Fairway Circle, 560 Fair Oaks Drive all fed to the Property Flip – Equity Skimming step theft process.** All three properties were pooled into the rental market. Someone needs to do a deep dive into these homes.

The REO Private Investor Group I looked at have evolved over time to be more and more sophisticated and yet due to their success they are also prone to be sloppy. In Steven Turner they settled on an interim straw buyer already in trouble with the IRS. Steven Turner worked for Wells Fargo Bank and is tied to the Mike Carey; Generation CRM[105] group; a breakaway group stemming off from the David Osborn, Keller Williams, MEM 2, LLC – Jones, Kelley, Boyd Perpetrator Nexus, but making use of all those networked bad actors who have traded their professional credentials to, for a price, perfect these thefts.

---

[105] CRM Central Properties, Southern Serenity Homes; Mark Miesse / SunTrust Bank / CRM Capital Corp; brokerage firm. Warranty Deed in Lieu of Foreclosure Instrument No.: 10007010, 12/15/2010 from builder Faxon Gillis to CRM Central Properties, LLC. Giving the REO Fraudsters means to fabricate the fictious lien and the fictious debt. Three REO Owned properties feature in this transaction including 235 Pinehurst Drive, 250 Lewis Fairway Circle, 560 Fair Oaks Drive all fed to the Property Flip – Equity Skimming theft-step process. Preparation of this instrument tied to the former law practice of Judge Oscar Carr. Also, Special Warranty Deed No. 11006142; 11/28/2011 Grantor CRM Central Properties flipping the property to straw buyers. Scrivener's Error: No. 11006384 – Shelby County to Fayette County.

Candace Turner told me that she suspected that her father-in-law was behind the loss of her home. Steven Turner, Sr. and Jr. appear to have meshed identities. I'm not writing more about this because I cannot distinguish between the two. I am not, after all, the white-collar crime unit of the FBI. If, in fact, such a department is viable at the FBI Memphis Field office. Have they been told to stand down? Just as I gave up trying to gain the help of HUD, at some point I had to give up on them. Under Civil RICO you are armed to act as a citizen prosecutor. More Americans encountering corruption in multiple areas should look at Civil RICO and especially when law enforcement arms of government refuses to even hear us out.

I've always believed that appraiser Larry Lane Billings is an alias for Jeffrey L Kelley. I'd like to be proved right or wrong in this. This seems a possible explanation for why the State of Tennessee was induced to manipulate the outcome that I was prevented from attending that meeting where we would have come face to face. If that had happened I would have recognized Larry Lane Billings, a.k.a., Jeffrey L. Kelley as the person I met in the Jones home. I cannot say to what degree the Asher name or other names showing up in my pattern examples function as an alias. There is much I wish I had answers for.

Quit Claim Deed; Instrument No.: 10004680
Signed: June 25, 2010; Filed August 31, 2010

Two urgent issues as flies in the ointment needed to be handled. First the Turner divorce. Second the pending Turner IRS Lien that may have listed this property amid the asset list. Bringing dangerous, unwanted scrutiny, not to Stephen Turner alone, but to the actual group of secret Note-Holders/Note-Owners flipping and skimming equity from this property.

Once the phony Deed of Trust establishing the phantom debt has gone unchallenged Steven Turner can grant Candace the lot separated from the build. This is accomplished per this Quit Claim Deed. It has no power to enforce. It is a fraud device. In theory Candace could have put up a little shed in the corner of that lot and rightfully lived there until someone objected. On paper she was a squatter living within the walls of a home she did not actually own. The incongruity of this arrangement flew by the Fayette County Registrar of Deeds.

Steven W. Turner claims to grant Candace Turner ***...the following described lot or parcel of land.*** Conveyed by Warranty Deed to Steven Turner and Candace four years before on 3/17/2006 and which instrument they failed to sign; ***(lot 5, section A, Oakland Woods Subdivision, as shown on plat of record at Plat Book 6, Page 179); Instrument No.: 06003768.***

To now, at the divorce juncture, wrongly communicate to any cursory reader of these filings that the house has not yet been built. We know from the Property Record Card that the house was built in 1999. This Quit Claim Deed is signed by Steven W. Turner. We then read what likely comes from an entirely different document; not filed. Steven Turner signed this filing on June 25, 2010. Sixty-eight days later, on August 31, 2010 an Affiant whose signature is unreadable and whose name does not appear neatly printed below the signature affirms the following: ***I, or we, hereby swear or affirm to the best of the affiant's knowledge, information and belief, the actual consideration for this transfer is $-0, pursuant to parties Final Decree of Divorce, Docket Number: 15337 entered with the Fayette County Chancery Court Clerk.***

Minor, Johnston, Douglas, PC prepared this Quit Claim Deed. They likely walked it across the street for filing with the Fayette County Registrar of Deeds Office.

No disclaimer can fully absolve attorneys that have assisted the commission of a crime. Lawyers are not to cross certain lines. So that we do not miss the disclaimer that functions to absolve Tom Minor of blame, we read in capital letters and bold print: **THIS INSTRUMENT BEING PREPARED WITHOUT THE BENEFIT OF A TITLE OPINION.** Why the hell not? Read, overkill like this and understand that these lawyers know, they would have to be brain dead, not to know that they are perfecting a con-artist hoax for their clients. A real and true vetting of this property title would reveal the Property Theft – Equity Skimming theft step process that as the ongoing pattern of title theft must go unrecognized. The Mark K. Waterbury notary signature appears to be electronically or photostatically copied.

The purpose of this Quit Claim Deed which grants nothing, worth nothing to Candace Turner sets her up to be the required scapegoat for what follows. Once the divorce is handled and Candace is happily unpacking. Paying what she imagines are house payments under false pretenses, siphoned off as assignment of rents, the looming issue of an IRS audit representing the more significant threat, has to be stopped in its tracks. Fayette County will accept county taxes no questions asked. A walk across the hallway would have told them that she was the victim of a scam.

House payments will be fed as income through BAC Home Loans as the Bank of America Third Party Mortgage Servicer Company to the REO secret Note Holders. They will not go to pay down a mortgage that in fact does not exist. This Quit Claim Deed is not worth the paper it is printed on, but it does serve to build the fraud narrative. Upon a cursory examination people believe what they read. Big mistake!

We read: ***...and mail Deed to: Ms. Candace Turner, 40 Valley Oaks Cove, Oakland, TN 38060.*** There is no Deed of Trust that is remotely enforceable. What Deed of Trust is referenced by this statement? This statement appears for the sole purpose of misleading any that read it. The explanation later sold to the Internal Revenue Service (IRS) is that this is still the original Asher, Countrywide/Bank of America Deed of Trust. The REO Fraudsters do not even try to sell the IRS on the fallacy that the loan from America's Wholesale Lender (AWL) is the valid Deed of Trust. When communicating with the IRS lies are kept to a minimum. There must be a more delicate, sophisticated conflating of the truth.

Assignment of the Deed of Trust, a.k.a., The Breeder Document[106] Instrument No.: 11003924 Signed July 20, 2011; Filed July 26, 2011; Batch No.: 53310

Everything I have already stated about the Andrews, Assignment of the Deed of Trust functioning as the Breeder Document, applies here.

The REO Fraudsters are now ready to move forward with the pretense of a Foreclosure under a Deed of Trust that does not exist. They have conned Candace out of at least two years of house payments laundered as Assignment of Rents. If the IRS had not come knocking

[106] Read the definition of the Breeder Document and how it functions in the previous chapter.

this interim period may have been extended. With the IRS reviewing the Turner asset list the property needed to be devalued and flipped. Candace was evicted from a home she never actually owned.

According to Marie McDonnell, ***"...the most common breeder document is the fraudulent assignment of mortgage which purports to grant a title interest in the underlying real property to the fraudster, and serves as the basis for obtaining other documents necessary to extinguish the property owner's rights and transfer full legal and equitable title as well as possession to the fraudsters."***

The MERS MIN Number tells us that Bank of America is the servicer of what began as a Countrywide Deed of Trust. We read that America's Wholesale Lender (AWL) is the original lender. As we have already established this is a lie. The Original Borrower is named as Candace B. Turner. This too is a lie. Steven W. Turner's name is omitted though he is the co-borrower named in the phony Deed of Trust, Instrument No.: 06003770. Steven Turner is shielded from recognition of the part he played in perpetrating a fraud upon the IRS, the court, and upon his ex-wife.

This Assignment of the Deed of Trust was dumped into the landfill of the Fayette County Register of Deeds Office as a batch of other Assignments all essentially appearing the same. Like the other Assignments the signature of Deborah Beard and her notary seal has been "*electronically or photostatically copied*" and affixed to the Candace Turner Assignment of Deed of Trust, a.k.a., the Breeder Document. The signature of Dominique Johnson is also a forgery. ... ***"forged documents are intentionally and knowingly being used by banks*** (and REO secret Note Holders) ***and their lawyers to illegally remove Americans from their homes."*** Marie McDonnell

Aside from the fact that the notary and signing officer signatures are forged this is also a void document because it takes its authority from the two documents that are falsely claimed to be the source documents. Which according to the fraudsters provide ongoing authority for all future filings. Smothered from recognition is the Asher Countrywide Deed of Trust that may or may not link to what I suspect may have started out as a builder buy out scheme. Proxy, substitute, phony and forged source documents appear in all these theft examples.

Fraud Device – Power of Attorney; Instrument No.: 11004022 Signed on June 16, 2011; Filed on August 1, 2011; Batch No.: 53388 Signed and notarized at both earlier and subsequent dates, at numerous other locations, even different states.

This Power of Attorney proposes that it is an assignment of authority from The Bank of New York Mellon to any party that wants to foreclose on a home, including those homes whose mortgages have been assumed (taken over) by REO Private Investors.

The set-up is such that this repeatedly repurposed Power of Attorney can be used as a fill in the blanks' kind of fraud tool, in theory forever. At least until it is challenged and thrown out of any courtroom where it makes an appearance.

Foreclosure Mill Attorneys, Rubin-Lublin have filed it with Fayette County as a "Batch;" **Batch No.: 53388.** This tells us that multiple copies of this fraud tool were filed on August 1, 2011. Each one is separately linked to illegal foreclosure actions as set up for the physical seizures of multiple Fayette County homes under color of law and by authority that does not in fact exist.

The Note Holder is not Bank of New York Mellon as claimed. The Note Holder are the REO Fraudsters. If you are a Fayette County victim of this scam look to see if this "batch" links to your property address. Is this fraud device referenced in any endorsement filed under your name or property address? To thus, claim illegal authority to perpetrate a phony foreclosure action followed by illegal seizure of your home. Or to appoint the foreclosure mill attorneys, in this case Rubin-Lublin, as a Trustee. Upon belief that this same repurposed fraud tool has been used to steal thousands of Tennessee homes in multiple Tennessee counties. Not all uncovered by my very limited investigation.

This Power of Attorney was not signed by Bank of New York Mellon on June 16, 2011. A former copy appears to have been signed by them on January 29, 2009. The State of New York Notary Stamp on the Fulton County, Georgia copy and every other copy stemming forward is so faint and partially obscured that it is unreadable. This is a forged notary stamp lifted from another document, interfered with, and affixed to this 2009 Power of Attorney.[107]

So, what is the point? Why take, this risk? No one is paying attention. Laws are not enforced. Fayette County is so far removed from protecting the public welfare from title theft that as a ludicrous example, not far removed from what actually takes place, they would likely file a birth certificate for a farmer's cow labeled a, Quit Claim Deed. They should account for every example where this fraud device corrupts their record keeping. Every homeowner that lost property tied to its appearance should be alerted as should the states attorney general office. The likelihood of Fayette County doing so without fundamental reform rooting out corruption is remote.

Without this fraud tool in place Rubin-Lublin cannot appoint themselves the Resubstituted Trustee, replacing Arnold Wiess who in fact was the second Trustee. Without this pretense of authority, the REO criminal enterprise cannot complete what they were hired to do. That is... to unlawfully foreclose and orchestrate under the fraud device of this, forged Power of Attorney filed as a, *batch*, meaning that it was used to perfect theft of other Fayette County homes tied to the same Foreclosure Mill Attorneys, hired by the same REO secret note holder, white collar criminals.

Like me, Candace Turner needed to be bullied and induced to leave her home so as to achieve a, minimal public records footprint. Meaning no opportunity to recognize and challenge the chain of document fraud.

Because this Power of Attorney cannot stand up under scrutiny Fayette County helps out. They fail to file it with the Candace Turner series of filings linked to 40 Valley Oaks Cove. That list which passes for a complete list of linked filings and endorsements was printed by me on 8/14/2017. What appears is a list of no more than five instruments. I write this because, when this book comes out someone with illegal access to do so, may decide to clean up and back step some of the more overt theft assisting maneuvers.

So as to conceal theft, Fayette County also fails to include on

[107] Norman Yu, Notary Public, State of New York, Qualified in Queens County; LIC# 01YU6183731; Expires 3-24-2012. "Diane Pickett, known to be as a Vice President, and Mauro Palladino, known to me (to) be a Managing Director of the Bank of New York Mellon..."

this print out Warranty Deed No.: 06003768. This is the transfer of 40 Valley Oaks Cove from Chad Asher and Kimberly Green Asher to Candace and Seven Turner. The fraudsters cannot risk having the Asher name appearing on this digital list. Fayette County helps out yet again when they fail to connect back to the original Asher Deed of Trust as the quintessential source document.

It is hoped that this incomplete digital list of filings, upon bringing it up on the computer screen, will be all that anyone will ever look at, scanning the list to say, "all appears in order." Just as the Property Record Card serves as the first fire wall, this list, how it reads and what is omitted, what is wrongly labeled so as to mislead any citizen investigator functions as the second fire wall.

Thus, we see that the America Wholesale Lender Deed of Trust, Instrument No.: 06003770, is mislabeled. It is called a Countrywide Home Loan to infer that this is the Asher Countrywide Deed of Trust. This implies crony corrupt intent stemming from Fayette County employees. This ploy anticipates and helps to satisfy any question about the MERS MIN Number linking to Countrywide and Bank of New York Mellon appearing on the identity theft Breeder Document; the Assignment of the Deed of Trust. Someone would look at the five instruments, never read the Asher name and be wrongly led down the garden path to imagine that the Countrywide source document was filed when upon investigation of what is filed, it would be found to be missing.

Controlled by crony corruptionism, Fayette County is taking a page out of the MERS play book. They are presenting a broken chain of title which deflects investigation. This Power of Attorney has had a life in New York, Florida, Arizona, Tennessee, and Texas. The McEvoy Warranty Deed, the forged assignment and this Power of Attorney perfected theft of this home. Secret sales, assignments and transfers of authority are buried in the MERS System, to, thus guarantee no possibility that Candace Turner, can uncover the truth. Finding that house payments were stolen and despite how her divorce settlement may have read, she was never the actual mortgagee.

We read the usual hogwash. The REO Fraudster identity hides behind that of Bank of New York Mellon. Authority is granted from Bank of New York Mellon to, among others, the REO Fraudsters without actually naming them. This is where, any judge, upon being presented with this crowded, messy, obviously forged Power of Attorney should ask for a complete chain of title. In a sane world it should never have been assigned a Fayette County Instrument Number.

This Power of Attorney is a fill in the blanks back door pass. It functions vaguely and ***"necessary to effect...; (ii) disposition of an REO Property."*** It grants illegal authority for what has already taken place; any REO Fraudster to assume (take over) any mortgage prior to the forced default and illegal seizure. No current, real time disclosure to homeowners. There is no caveat that reads that homeowners have been, or will be at any time notified. Nor that the REO Fraudster-Note Holder is accountable to any lawful process. In Orwellian double-speak this fraud device reads that what is illegal under both state and federal law is, in the altered world of white-collar title theft legal.

Other assignments of authority have been filed over the MERS system and withheld form the public record. This includes appointment of the third-party mortgage servicer companies. These Mortgage Servicer Companies can process house payments laundered into the coffers of the secret REO Note-Holders. Lots of opportunity to skim equity when by design homeowners are left entirely in the dark.

By the time this fraud device moves on from New York, through Georgia to be used in other Tennessee counties stealing other homes out from under valid homeowners the first page is so crowded with phony affirmations of authority that Fayette County had to place their stamp to sit alone on a second page. This fraud device, making an appearance in Fayette County, is linked back to McEvoy. A name that I asked you to remember.

The Jones, Kelley, Boyd Perpetrator Nexus operating with impunity and within the protectionist syndicate of West Tennessee, and their conspirators (other REO Groups) went fishing for a usable fraud device. They stumbled upon this one. The same practices are well established, described by the lawyers that filed suit against REO Holdings, LLC. **Family Trust Services, LLC v. REO Holdings, LLC (Case no.: 15-780 IV).**

The Georgia copy is signed by Howard Harlow and, or, the signature may be Howard Harlan. Below the signature we read that it is not valid unless signed in red ink. Is it signed in red ink? Did any judge ask for the original to verify this stipulation? It is my belief that as a very low standard, all they cared about, was that it was claimed by the suits standing before the bench that it existed. Any Judge that would actually take this fraud device in hand and look at it would have thrown it out... unless of course they are party to the crony corrupt protectionist syndicate helping to feed homes acquired by theft to the securities market.

The Cathelene Robinson (Georgia) Registrar affirmation-stamp, affirming that this is a complete and accurate copy of the original that was filed with her office and signed by Howard Harlow does not appear on the original Fulton County copy. It only appears on that copy used in various Tennessee Counties. This raises the issue of another alias worth investigating. Michael Herbert Harlow, a.k.a., Howard Harlow/Harlan?

By the time this fraud device gets to Fayette County we read that it has been filed in at least three other Tennessee Counties. It has been used to perfect theft of, lacking a forensic review of Tennessee Registry of Deeds Offices by an unbiased expert of the caliber of Marie McDonnell, only God knows, how many other homes.

There is no start date. There is no end date. Thus, it can be repurposed, adapted and forged to any theft perfecting circumstance, in theory, for years to come. Unless a smart judge would take it in hand, be justifiably outraged. Call it an unenforceable, forged, theft tool and throw it out. Unless Tennessee counties search and purge this Power of Attorney from their records; notifying homeowners that they and their homes were targeted for title theft. Restoration of integrity has to start somewhere.

The crowded first-page Power of Attorney reveals that it has been filed in three Tennessee countries, one Georgia County, and at least one New York County. Did this Power of Attorney have a life before Queens County, New York?

Like Fulton County, Georgia, Montgomery County, Tennessee helped out the Criminal Enterprise by also stamping and signing that this was a ***"true and exact copy of a Power of Attorney that appears in my office."*** This tries, but fails in every respect to substitute for a valid notary signature and seal. Its purpose is to deceive unwitting homeowners. Connie W. Bell, Montgomery County Registrar's stamp is in effect affirming the use of a fraud tool. One that has likely brought heartache to some that elected her.

It is no accident that Fayette County did not file this fraud device with the Candace Turner filings. The registrar at the time, and I understand back in control, was Edward Pattat. It may be that a few Tennessee Registry of Deeds Offices will need to be sued before laws change. Too often financial consequences must weigh in before integrity makes an appearance.

On the face of what presents in this Power of Attorney, as a fully functioning theft tool, we read the following. It was filed:

1. Montgomery County 6/16/2011, county seat Clarksville.[108] We don't know when it was notarized. All the notary seals are unreadable. Multiple illegal seizures <u>and counting, up to today</u> have taken place using this fraud tool.
2. Grundy County 7/13/2011, county seat Altamont.[109] Multiple illegal seizures <u>and counting up to today</u> have taken place in Grundy County using this fraud tool.
3. And Fayette County 8/01/2011, county seat Somerville. The Fayette County receipt is stamped alone at page-2 there being no room to place it anywhere else on this messy and crowded first page, which of itself is a red flag. Multiple illegal seizures <u>and counting up today</u> have taken place using this fraud tool.
4. With no detail disclosed it was also filed in Queens County, New York. Any Instrument Number, book and page number, has been scrubbed. We saw in the REO Holdings case that many documents were created out of whole cloth.
5. Additionally, this Power of Attorney, was filed in Fulton County, Georgia, county seat Atlanta, Cathelene Robinson, Clerk of Court.[110]

This Power of Attorney, given traction as a fraud device by the Fayette County Instrument Number, claims to grant ***"unto said attorneys-in-fact and agents, and each of them, the full power and authority to do and perform..."*** whatever is necessary to effect in our theft examples ***"the disposition of an REO Property."*** The attorney-in-fact is not named. Again... this is a fill in the blanks, kind of deal; a retooled, fabricated, forged Power of Attorney fitting any "attorney in fact," who happens to have larceny in their hearts.

---

[108] Registrar Connie W. Bell; Montgomery County, TN, claimed to be filed: Volume 1385; pages 104-104. Filed June 16, 2011.

[109] Registrar Gayle VanHooser; Grundy County, TN, claimed to be filed as Instrument No.: 75175; Record Book 1032; page 640-640. Filed: 7/13/2011.

[110] Referenced as appearing in Deed Book 47712; page 6. Filed by Cathelene Robinson, Clerk of Superior Court 2009; 0056192.

The Fulton County, Georgia filings reveal a hauntingly familiar pattern. Multiple lots owned by an REO agent. A lien over a lot severed from the original mortgage. Assignment of Leases and Rents painting the original homeowner under a secretly assumed mortgage as a renter and not a homeowner. The Breeder Document reads: *Transfer and Assignment of the Deed to Secure the Debt*. The debt being a fictious loan secured by the lot; charging twice for the same lot. A homeowner that is claimed to have, "Waived Borrowers Rights." His/her signature does not appear on the lender's affidavit nor on the closing attorney's affidavit. The broker is tied to that person that used the lot to establish a fictitious lien.

There are three notary stamps crowding this one-page Power of Attorney.

- None of them are legible.
- Someone has taken a black pen and moving parallel to the length of the page made two of these notary stamps and signatures deliberately illegible.
- No county caring about the integrity and reliability of the title recordation process should have filed what is so obviously a forged, unenforceable fraud device.

Fayette County allowed the repeated use of this fraud device. The sole purpose of which is to deceive homeowners, concealing the pre-assumption of mortgages, title theft, and the interim Property Flip – Equity Skimming Schemes.

On the top left corner of the page we read that the Power of Attorney was filed by Countrywide Home Loans, a.k.a., BAC Home Loans. Countrywide and BAC Home Loans is a third-party mortgage servicer company. The Federal Trade Commission sued Countrywide Home Loans and BAC Home Loans in 2012.

Diane Pickett is the signing officer, calling herself a vice-president with Bank of New York Mellon. Once again Bank of New York Mellon lends their identity so that the REO Fraudsters can conceal their identity behind the intimidating moniker of a powerful bank. It is all about intimidating victims, deterring any overwhelmed homeowner as they navigate and seek to understand a field they have not been trained to deal with.

- The Diane Pickett signature is witnessed by Kaitlyn F. McEvoy. It was Memphis attorney Jeffrey F. McEvoy that prepared the substitute proxy source documents.

- Because there is no end date, as a fraud tool this Power of Attorney is perfectly suited to repeated use reading: ***disposition of an REO Property***.
- Giving the Criminal Enterprise blanket authority, ***ability to assume a mortgage,*** i.e., any mortgage. Leading to illegal seizure in violation of the Fourth Amendment to the United States Constitution.
- Every filing conceals when the mortgage was first off-loaded to criminals, forward dating a chain of events. No real time disclosure, current to the title theft and flipping sequence, ever disclosed to homeowners.

Very significant to this fraud scheme we then read that the secret REO Note Holders who are never actually named have the power to appoint *"substitution and re-substitution of a trustee,"* inclined to break the law. It gets too hot, too risky for a single trustee to exercise control over the entire sequence of title flips.

The continually repurposed Power of Attorney then covers use of the lot severed from the build which has established the fictious lien. The fictious lien waits in the wings for the opportune time; when it is known homeowners are obstructed from access to Due Process. The salient passage reads: ***Releasing the lien over any mortgage in connection to the transactions contemplated in those certain pooling and servicing agreements by CHL Servicing, CHL, and CWABS, Inc.***

The usage of the word "contemplated" in the prior passage is highly offensive. In this context to say that it is permissible under the Pooling and Servicing Agreements; (CWABS, Inc.) To say that whatever adaptation of the fraud scheme "contemplated" and put in action the Title Theft schemes (transactions) continues on; ostensibly and in theory forever. Taking place under color of law and in the petri dish of no fraud detection practices putting the fundamental rights of American homeowners below that of criminals.

As we shall see 40 Valley Oaks Cove, controlled by the same REO Investor Group will flow through Chad and Kimberly Asher, Steven and Candace Turner, Candace Turner per her divorce settlement, and then Darnell and Diane Bradley, and then to one Kevin Powers. Each person can be tied by relationship to the racketeering criminal enterprise. If Keven Powers or anyone else was told that they were "renting to own" they should look twice at that con artist sales pitch. Upon belief none are actual owners under a valid Deed of Trust. With or without their consent all are renters and, or, straw buyers.

11-03166

Nm:H-8-8-400(1401777), Rq:432.10

RECORD AND RETURN
COUNTRYWIDE HOME LOANS
2505 W. CHANDLER BLVD
CH-DLR-D30
CHANDLER, AZ 85224

Old Republic Title
Suite 450
1100 Lakewood Parkway
Alpharetta, GA 30005

FILE FIRST

Deed Book 47712 Pg 6
Filed and Recorded Mar-16-2009 12:28pm
2009-0056192
Cathelene Robinson
Clerk of Superior Court
Fulton County, Georgia

POWER OF ATTORNEY

The undersigned, as Trustee under the *Pooling and Servicing Agreements (as defined below)*, hereby constitutes and appoints Countrywide Home Loans Servicing LP and its authorized officers (collectively, "CHL Servicing") and each of them, its true and lawful attorneys-in-fact and agents, with full powers of substitution and resubstitution, for and in its name, place and stead, in any and all capacities, for the limited purpose of executing and recording any and all documents necessary to effect (i) a foreclosure of a Mortgage Loan, (ii) the disposition of an REO Property, (iii) an assumption agreement or modification agreement or supplement to the Mortgage Note, Mortgage, or deed of trust, and (iv) a reconveyance, deed of reconveyance or release or satisfaction of mortgage or such instrument releasing the lien of a Mortgage in connection with the transactions contemplated in those certain Pooling and Servicing Agreements (the "Pooling and Servicing Agreement") by and among the undersigned, CHL Servicing, CHL, and CWABS, Inc. The undersigned also grants unto said attorneys-in-fact and agents, and each of them, the full power and authority to do and perform each and every act and thing requisite and necessary to be done in and about the premises, as fully to all intents and purposes as might or could be done in person to effect items (i), (ii) and (iii) above, hereby ratifying and confirming all that said attorneys-in-fact and agents or any of them, or their substitutes, may lawfully do or cause to be done by virtue hereof. Any capitalized term not otherwise defined herein shall have the meaning assigned to such term in the Pooling and Servicing Agreements.

THE BANK OF NEW YORK MELLON, as Trustee

Witness: ______________ Kaitlyn F. McEvoy

By: ______________ Diane Pickett, Vice President

Witness: ______________ Steven Chrysanthis

By: ______________ Mauro Palladino, Managing Director

STATE OF: New York
COUNTY OF: Queens

On the 29th day of January, 2009, before me, Norman Yu, a Notary Public in and for said, personally appeared Diane Pickett, known to me to be as a Vice President, and Mauro Palladino, known to me be a Managing Director of the Bank of New York Mellon, a New York banking corporation that executed the within instrument, and also known to me to be the persons who executed said instrument on behalf of said New York banking corporation and acknowledged to me that such New York banking corporation executed the within instrument.

IN WITNESS THEREOF, I have hereunto set my hand and affixed by official seal the day and year in this certificate first above written.

______________ Notary Public

Norman Yu
NOTARY PUBLIC
STATE OF NEW YORK
Qualified in Queens County
1YU6110183731
Comm. Exp. 2012

NOTARY PUBLIC

Connie W. Bell, Register
Montgomery County Tennessee
Rec #: 133230
Instrument #: 591089
Rec'd: 10.00
State: 0.00
Clerk: 0.00
Other: 2.00
Total: 12.00
Recorded 5/23/2011 at 11:29 AM
in Volume 1385
Pgs 104-104

I hereby certify the within and foregoing to be a true, correct and complete copy of the original that appears in Deed BK 47712 PG 6 in this office this 17th day of May 2011
Cathelene Robinson Clerk of Superior Court, Fulton County, GA
By ______________ Deputy Clerk
not valid unless signed in red ink

I, Connie W. Bell, Montgomery County Register do hereby certify that this is a true and exact copy of a Power of Atty, as appears of record in my office in OR Book 1385 Page 104

Witness my hand and seal of office this 10th day of June, 2011

CONNIE W. BELL, Register
______________, Deputy

Gayle VanHooser, Register
Grundy County Tennessee
Rec #: 69784
Rec'd: 10.00
State: 0.00
Clerk: 0.00
EDP: 2.00
Total: 12.00
Instrument #: 75175
Recorded 7/13/2011 at 3:41 PM
in Record Book 1032 Pgs 640-640

Volume 1385 Page 104

Instrument Number 11004022

STATE OF: New York
COUNTY OF: Queens

On the 29th day of January, 2009, before me, Norman Yu, a Notary Public in and for said, personally appeared Diane Pickett, known to me to be as a Vice President, and Mauro Palladino, known to me be a Managing Director of the Bank of New York Mellon, a New York banking corporation that executed the within instrument, and also known to me to be the persons who executed said instrument on behalf of said New York banking corporation and acknowledged to me that such New York banking corporation executed the within instrument.

IN WITNESS THEREOF, I have hereunto set my hand and affixed by official seal the day and year in this certificate first above written.

Notary Public
Norman Yu
NOTARY PUBLIC
STATE OF NEW YORK
Qualified in Queens County
LIC. 01YU6183731
COMM. EXP. 3-24-2012

Connie W. Bell, Register
Montgomery County Tennessee
Rec #: 233220
Instrument #: 891099
Rec'd: 10.00
State: 0.00
Clerk: 0.00
Other: 2.00
Total: 12.00
Recorded 8/23/2011 at 11:29 AM
in Volume 1385
Pgs 104-104

I hereby certify the within and foregoing to be a true, correct and complete copy of the original that appears in Deed BK 47772 PG 6 in this office this 17th day of May 2011
Cathelene Robinson Clerk of Superior Court, Fulton County, GA
By ____________ Deputy Clerk
not valid unless signed in red ink

I, Connie W. Bell, Montgomery County Register do hereby certify that this is a true and exact copy of a Power of Atty, as appears of record in my office in OR Book 1385 Page 104

Witness my hand and seal of office this 16th day of June, 2011
CONNIE W. BELL, Register
____________, Deputy

Gayle VanHooser, Register
Grundy County Tennessee
Rec #: 69784
Instrument #: 75175
Rec'd: 10.00
State: 0.00
Clerk: 0.00
EDP: 2.00
Total: 12.00
Recorded 7/13/2011 at 3:41 PM
in Record Book 1032 Pgs 640-640

Volume 1385 Page 104
Instrument Number 11004022

Appointment of Substitute Trustee; Instrument No.: 11006304 Signed on November 30, 2011; Filed on December 6, 2011

This endorsement replaces Arnold Wiess with the foreclosure mill attorney's Rubin Lublin, Suarez, Serrano LLC (Rubin-Lublin) as the "Substitute Trustee." The heading of this filing serves to deliberately mislead. As a red flag, multiple trustees suggesting a, property flip scheme, they are actually the, *"re-substituted trustee."* At minimum they are the third trustee. Authority is claimed to stem from the Power of Attorney filed into the Fayette County Registry of Deeds Office as a batch; each singularly greasing theft of other Fayette County homes.

Does the Rubin-Lublin name appear as orchestrating the Trustee Sale of your home? If so investigate. Is any attorney you hired networked to protect the operations of the lucrative Criminal Enterprise described in this book?

Just as any appraiser is part of the Criminal Enterprise network, so too are the Trustees. We saw previously that a Trustee in another title theft scheme was an employee of the Title Insurance Company. The need is to replace the first Trustee with a cooperating fraud partner.

Substitute Trustee Deed; Instrument No. 12000565 Signed on January 18, 2012; Filed on January 27, 2012 Claimed to have been sold at Auction on January 3, 2012

All the salient details regarding the role of the Substitute Trustee described in theft of the Andrews property apply here. The form itself looks as it should. Only because any citizen investigator would actually read what is filed, vet for fraud, explore the title history, establish the *Enterprise Plus Relationship* connections, would they realize that this too is a fraud device used to grease the ongoing Property Flip – Equity Skimming – Title Theft of American homes, many of them fed to the Bank Theft Delivery System.

There is no valid foreclosure sale. In violation of the law there is no offering to the public on a level playing field. No auction on the court house steps. This is an arm in arm, illegal, conflict of interest flip of the property back to the REO Fraudster, Note-Holder, cohort of bad actors. No random bidder would be allowed to buy this home.

With Candace Turner, as the designated scapegoat and mark, ejected from 40 Valley Oaks Cove, The Substitute Trustee's Deed, paves the way for straw buyers, waiting in the wings, to move into these premises.

Defrauding the Internal Revenue Service (IRS)

The illegal seizure of the 40 Valley Oaks Cove could not take place until the issue of an IRS Lien was addressed. In part it is addressed in the public filings at the Fayette County Registrar of Deeds Office. The local bank helping to launder income for the REO Criminal Enterprise operations can point to what has been addressed in the public record to say that they vetted for fraud when in fact they did not.

Fake tax returns are a frequent piece that perfect interim home improvement loans, and other transactions that skim equity. In other instances, amendments to tax returns may be made to further the scheme. Crony corrupt enablement and a decades long history of getting away with these crimes tell these REO Fraudsters that no verifications will occur. Whatever it was that triggered an IRS investigation of Stephen Turner that attention was likely not coming from any Suspicious Activity Report (SAR) complying with the terms of the Bank Secrecy Act filed by any bank.

Conning the IRS is a kind of minefield. At this point the Fraudsters must reference the first Asher Countrywide/Bank of America Deed of Trust. It is the quintessential source document though it is not identified as such in the Candace Turner filings. The fraudsters do not even try to sell the IRS on Americas' Wholesale Lender as the bank that held the original Deed of Trust or for that matter any Deed of Trust. The broken chain of title is not explained because it cannot be without revealing that 40 Valley Oaks Cove is an REO owned theft-asset and any money owed is not due from Steven Turner alone, but from the Criminal Enterprise group of thieves and con-artists having swallowed up many other properties.

If the IRS had dug a little deeper, they would have realized that:

- the Note Holder/Note Owner calling in this lien represented by the lot is not Bank of New York Mellon.
- They would have realized there was a phantom loan and a fictitious lien.
- They would have seen what they are extensively trained to recognize and report. Patterns of practice operating as a Property Flip – Equity Skimming – Title Theft Scheme whose bones are disguised by year-end tax filings.

- They might have gone back and looked at the year-end expenses and write offs of the Jones, Kelley, Boyd Perpetrator Nexus and their cohort of conspirators.
- They would have found home improvement loans with funds not utilized for the stated purpose.
- House payments laundered as Assignment of Rents.
- Skimming equity via bank loans collateralized by homes that these groups do not actually own.
- Leading to the mountain of document fraud.
- Leading to the needed referrals for prosecution.
- Leading to return of stolen property to their rightful owners; an outcome that has yet to happen.

The highest and best bid was claimed to be $148,500. **Borrowers source of title is that certain Quit Claim Deed dated 6/25/2010 from Steven W. Turner and Candace Turner of record on 8/31/2010 in Instrument # 10004680...** This is: The said lot or parcel of land by no means worth $148,500. The fraudsters are counting on the fact that the IRS will not look at what is proposed in the public filings to say that the IRS problems are handled. The actual source of title represented by both the land and the house is concealed. The IRS must be conned not to recognize what is going on here.

Authority to foreclose is also premised on: **...and that Warranty Deed from Chad Asher and Kimberly Green Asher to Candace Turner and Steven W. Turner of record on 4/26/2006 in Instrument # 06003768.** This is the unsigned Warranty Deed that begins the process of burying the Countrywide loan picked up by Bank of America; buried under the avalanche of document fraud.

Rubin-Lublin play their part. They premise their authority to foreclose on the fraud device that presents as the fake Power of Attorney. We read that this so called "sale" is subject to eight caveats. The IRS do not go so far that they delve into the title theft history of this property. They know who owes the money. They just don't know that Stephen Turner, Jr. was in effect a straw buyer in the same camp as Vernon "Wayne" Boyd and Sherry Boyd.

Number seven addresses the IRS claim. A conflict of interest appraisal that undervalues the property by 40K invites the IRS to look elsewhere for money owed. We read that there is a federal tax lien. That the IRS has a right of redemption ***pursuant to 26 U.S.C. § 7425(d).*** We read that they have ***been, notified of the foreclosure sale***

pursuant to 26 U.S.C. § 7425(c); and any other matters that an accurate survey of the Property might disclose.

"Accurate" the key word. The Criminal Enterprise cannot survive the IRS looking beyond the surface of what is proposed as lies. To find that almost nothing dumped into the land fill of the Fayette County Registry of Deeds Office is, indeed, accurate. Entrenched power constricts justice. It plunders and breeds contempt for the rights of ordinary people.

As with my home ERA Chamberwood Realty Group; Hattie Brawley and Loretta Martin played a role. The sale is claimed to have taken place at auction on 1/3/2012. Two weeks later there is the pretense of a sale on 1/18/2012. Quick turnover of property to straw buyers, never offered to the public on a level playing field, is another red flag. Once they get Candace Turner out they will move Diane Bradley and though it appears he never lived in Fayette County, her husband Bradley Darrnell, a.k.a., Darnell Bradley from (on paper) another stolen property location into the 40 Valley Oaks Cove theft-asset address.[111]

This Instrument was signed and notarized by the Rubin Lublin Suarez Serrano TN, LLC, (Rubin-Lublin) agent, Lisa Caplan, in Norcross, Georgia. The notary name is Najur Bowser also in Georgia. His last name on the Notary Seal is partially obscured by lines bleeding over from the outside circle. The Affiant's signature, that person approving the sale amount, is unreadable though it is likely Lisa Caplan.

---

[111] Someone should look at: 120 Janis Marie Road, Oakland, TN 38060. Straw buyer, Diane Cameron Darnell, is postured as a relative of deceased couple Calvin and Elizabeth Wilbanks moving from this address into 40 Valley Oaks Cove. Styled as having purchased the Turner home at auction. If she is in fact, an actual relative I could not find it. Calvin died on: 4/25/2010. Even before that date, "send tax bill to: "Loretta Martin (CHWO)." Same chain of theft beginning with an absent and elderly Calvin Wilbanks targeted as too sick to fight back. A decoy realtor is used to establish a degree of separation from Loretta Martin, a.k.a., Loretta Chambers (possibly Lynn Martin) and ERA Chamberwood Realty Group as the secret and actual Note Holders. Each MLS represents a flip of the property title. Who were the rightful heirs of Calvin and Elizabeth Wilbanks? How did the Calvin Wilbanks, Last Will and Testament, actually read? Was the law firm that probated it tied to the property thefts taking place in Fayette County? I saw other examples where I felt rightful heirs were defrauded, victims profiled as unlikely to dispute what was proposed with those homes fed to some version of the same title theft sequence of events. Via the Wilbanks-theft, we see the same straw buyers willing to be used at different locations. There were many properties that for one reason or another did not fit my research criteria. I had to maximize limited time and resources. 120 Janis Marie Road and the elderly couple that lived there has continued to occupy my thoughts. It is directly linked to 40 Valley Oaks Cove and together paint a more complete picture of how the money laundering portions of this fraud scheme operate.

Rubin Lublin Suarez Serrano, LLC (Rubin-Lublin) Exhibit A Re: Notice of Federal Tax Lien/Consent to Sell /File No.: 11-06679 Correspondence Dated: November 9, 2011 Instrument No.: 12000565 / Filed on January 27, 2012

A lot of money is owed the IRS. The IRS need to be conned into looking elsewhere for the collection of monies owed the United States coffers. My IRS problem would have eventually been handled. Though small and insignificant it was aggressively handled by Max Jones who, through his wife, intruded into my life in order to gain control over any outcome. They needed the IRS to go away and go away fast. The real threat is not the money that may or may not be owed. The threat is to the national footprint of the billion-dollar Criminal Enterprise operations skimming along the surface of exposure.

The REO Private Investor Groups operating in West Tennessee cannot have any federal agency delving into the tangled web of how equity is being illegally skimmed from homes that conspirators do not own. They cannot begin to recognize how that very specific chain of operation set in play by our nation's largest banks is founded on a mountain of document fraud, all neatly signed and notarized and dumped into Registry of Deeds Offices across this country.

I've watched the Frontline documentary called: *"Abacus Small Enough to Jail,"* more than once. It highlights the unequal application of justice and chain of corruption which I am currently experiencing extending to the Sixth Circuit Court of Appeals. A public relations scapegoat was needed to appease the growing unrest centered on public awareness of how our nations, largest Banks and the Wall Street financial industry led our country to the brink of financial collapse. Now just three decades forward a repeat performance is looming centered on manipulation of the mortgage and housing markets. In the Obama era culture of "banks too big to fail" a Chinese-American family whose small successful bank serving the immigrant community of New York was singled out, indicted for mortgage fraud, while the biggest banks on Wall Street who created this crisis avoided charges all together.

The degree to which American citizens are considered stupid, easily manipulated and appeased never ceases to amaze me. Abacus was selected to take the hit because it was thought they could not absorb the huge expense associated with any defense. It was believed that they could be bullied into the position of scapegoat, accepting extortionist settlement terms that would destroy their reputation. I believe that the financially stable Abacus customers were jealously coveted. It was hoped that Abacus Bank depositors would be forced to do business with New York branches of other banks. I can almost imagine the board meeting where it was decided the public relations disaster could be appeased by dropping their name to federal prosecutors willing to be used in this way.

Abacus as the designated scapegoat did not work out as planned. Jurors proved once again that Americans are not as stupid as the elite, power entrenched globalist bureaucrats, needing a one world banking system believe we are. The Sung family bravely took on Goliath and won. The Sung family felt that a duty was owed to the community they served. The documentary is compelling and worth watching. The following quote comes from Director-Producer, Steven James.[112]

"You know, a lot of people look back on 2008 with some bewilderment and even anger, like 'Why didn't those banks get prosecuted?' FRONTLINE has done its share of great reporting on that whole crisis. But I think it helps to see the other side of it, where this one, small bank was singled out. And I think that story has relevance today, given that no justice was ever brought as it related to the bigger banks. The other thing is that a lot of economists remain concerned that what caused the collapse in the first place hasn't been solved. Not only were the big banks not prosecuted coming out of that crisis, they were not regulated in a way to ensure that we're not going to have more of these problems."

So how much money does the IRS claim is owed by Steven W. Turner, Jr. Per these limited filings, at minimum, at this point in time,

[112] Inside the Making of Abacus with Steven James. Interview by, Patrice Taddonio: Assistant Director of Audience Development. Frontline / September 12, 2017 http://www.pbs.org/wgbh/frontline/article/inside-the-making-of-abacus-with-director-steve-james/

March 15, 2011, it is: $478,000.[113] 40 Valley Oaks Cove is assessed for tax purposes at: $191,500. It was sold at auction back to the REO Fraudsters at what is claimed to be the last and best bid: *$148,500.* The IRS are in the first lien position. It must appear that there is no money to be got out of this theft-asset. The lot-scam as a fictitious lien and secret behind the scenes debt cannot surface. Nor can it be known that this was price fixing. A home never offered to the buying public on a level playing field. The fraudsters cannot allow the IRS to oversee the sale of any one of these homes. Thus, in all cases I looked at where it appeared the IRS were being manipulated or offered an excuse to look elsewhere, they are aggressively dealt with.

It cannot be that we defend or ignore a dual system of justice because it has not yet impacted us personally. It isn't just me. It is the countless others who cannot write a book like this, imperfect as it may be, and are never heard from again.

The Harvey Weinstein strong arm tactics that controlled media reporting. The powerful elitist machine that protected him for decades is described in Ronan Farrow's book, Catch and Kill. Speaking to these levels of corruption seeping into other areas Ronan Farrow wrote: ***"But mostly messages came from stranger after stranger, saying they, too, had stories... All whispered of abuses of power and of the systems – in government, media, law – deployed to cover them up."*** *Catch and Kill; page 287.*

The Jeffrey Epstein escape from prosecution in Florida denying his victims a voice after they had worked with law enforcement and put their safety on the line is described in the book, Filthy Rich by, James Patterson. Because of this dual system of justice, the impact of crony-corruptionism, normalized in America, Epstein went on to abuse even more victims.

---

[113] Fayette County Instrument No.: 12000565. Featured as an Exhibit, one page from Fayette County Instrument No.: 09000144 "Notice of Federal Tax Lien," encumbering the sale of 40 Valley Oaks Cove. Also featured as an Exhibit "Notice of Federal Tax Lien;" one-page Instrument No.: 11001553. Person noted as responsible: Steven W. Turner, Jr. Do these two pages filed as Exhibits reflect all that was owed ($478,000)? I don't know. Selected filings tell us only what the REO Criminal Enterprise must file so as to superficially make it appear that the newly appointed Substitute Trustee, Rubin-Lublin, are complying with the law.

The stranglehold over justice and truth began in Fayette County, Tennessee and followed me all the way up to the second highest court in the land. The power of the financial industry to override the citizen access to justice made certain that a treasury investigation was shut down. That HUD failed to comply with all but one of my FOIA Requests. That a corrupt magistrate judge could get away with slandering the content of my Civil RICO complaint, rubber stamped by her superior, Judge Lipman. The same thread of corruption traveled forward in the form of administrative corruption at the sixth circuit who are above addressing their own mistakes.

The IRS Lien does not name Candace Turner. As the designated scapegoat her name is introduced by Rubin-Lublin reading: ***Name per Client: Candace B. Turner and Steven W. Turner.*** I could not help but notice that the foreclosure mill attorneys routinely place Candace's name first, sometimes even in bold print over that of her ex-husband. They repeatedly place the Steven Turner name in a minority position as if to say that they have access to privileged information that paints Candace as the primary bad actor. It is clear who the Rubin-Lublin client is that needs protection. Steven Turner possibly one in the same as Chad Asher.

The REO Fraudsters acknowledge to the IRS what they fail to state – cannot state – in the Turner sequence of public filings. They acknowledge the existence of the Countrywide/Bank of America Loan which they assumed for purposes of driving the property into default. They acknowledge the actual role played by BAC Home Loan Servicing, LP. They then shift gears and lie to the IRS so as to impede them from unearthing the real property title theft history of 40 Valley Oaks Cove. They state: ***The recording information for the Security Deed and subsequent assignments, as well as the terms of the sale and additional information, can be found in this notice.*** This is a crock of... lies.

They then acknowledge the clouded chain of title to say there are other liens and claims over this property. This may be a reference to those that have invested in these Deeds of Trust, oversold locally by the REO Investment Group to friends, relatives, and those drawn into the chain of theft? Operating as a kind of first tier Ponzi scheme.

The REO Fraudsters propose that they have already done the property title search to say that the IRS should not bother. Big Mistake!!!

They write: ***The title search of the Fayette County records indicates that federal tax lien(s) has/have been found***

against certain parties thought to be the owners of the subject property.

Who are the other, "certain parties?" The problem is acknowledged without naming individual REO Private Investors. The, other "certain parties" include the RICO Criminal Enterprise cohort of bad actors. Rubin-Lublin is proposing to the IRS that Steven Turner, though he appears as the owner, of 40 Valley Oaks Cove, he is not the sole owner. They cannot lie to the IRS as boldly as they do to Fayette County citizens and Judges in the fraud perfecting series of endorsements that they file.

If the REO Fraudsters will continue to skim equity from this home it needs to be held onto. The property title history cannot be unearthed. The names of ***certain other parties thought to be owners of the subject property*** must not surface. No hint of the existence of the Family Trust vehicles holding these titles as income is laundered, as money is disbursed in the form of dividends can be hinted at or disclosed. The IRS unearthing the truth could lead to an alert going out to the SEC and Treasury. And if any reporting did take place would the protectionist syndicate that has built up around these crimes be ignored by the State of Tennessee and the FBI white collar fraud unit at the Memphis field office?

Through the foreclosure mill attorney's, Rubin-Lublin, the IRS Fraudsters then tell the IRS that they are wasting their time. ***The unpaid principal balance is approximately $156,795,75. Interest through the sale date is approximately $500.00. Costs associated with the sale should be approximately $590 and the attorney fees will range from $500.00 to the maximum allowable by Tennessee Law.***

As already stated, the real threat is not this IRS Lien. It is that a smart IRS Investigator might be led to examine the title history of this home. Following that string back and then forward they would be led to identify a group of victims. They would recognize that the Private Investor Group, operating as a criminal enterprise, collectively have committed tax fraud. They could build a Criminal RICO Case.[114] This would lead to what must be avoided at all cost. Any examination of the REO Private Investor Group(s) year-end filings linking to the big picture seated in The Bank Theft Delivery System operations.

If we don't act to reverse the mafia-like reach of these crimes

---

[114] Only the Federal Government can bring a Criminal RICO Case.

the same criminals that created the former mortgage crisis will be responsible for creating the next, even bigger financial crisis. "**Not only were the big banks not prosecuted coming out of that crisis, they were not regulated in a way to ensure that we're not going to have more of these problems.**" Director-Producer Steven James echoes the same sentiment as that of many others.

Flip to the Straw Buyers

After the phony foreclosure straw buyers Bradley Darnell and Diane Darnell acquire the property by Special Warranty Deed No.: 12003929. The value of the Property is claimed to be $94,000. Undervalued this is set up for the next home improvement loan with funds not used for the stated purpose.

The source of the title is claimed to be: Instrument No.: 12000565 (not the unsigned Turner Warranty Deed.)

The secret REO Note Owners then take out two loans against the value of the property. They do so in two separate amounts of: $80,775.64 and $19,224.36 which together total: $100,000. As a red flag even amounts are to be questioned and reviewed in context to the Title History. Bank of Fayette County helps to bury this particular "red flag;" the standard equity skimming amount of $100k seen in many other properties. Including 65 Pinehurst Drive per the JP Morgan Chase Bank Loan to Keller Williams straw buyers Vernon "Wayne" Boyd, and Sherry Boyd.

- Assignment of Leases and Rents. Instrument No.: 14002462
- Assignment of Leases and Rents. Instrument No.: 14004889

The Bank of Fayette County is laundering money derived from illegal sources. Preferred Auto Insurance Company, Inc. is owned and operated by Jeffrey L. Kelley, Charles L. Kelley, and Lennie Faye (Boyd) Kelley amongst others. It will be remembered that Max Jones is listed as serving on the Audit Committee.[115] If one had to account for a lot

[115] State of Tennessee Department of Commerce and Insurance *"As of December 31, 2012"* report on examination of Preferred Auto Insurance Company page-5. Audit Committee: Jeffrey L. Kelley, Clinton B. Haley, Max L. Jones. I found this department very difficult to work with. For one thing they refused to send me a copy of the last report as well as requests for other information. They treated me in a defensive, manner even telling me that I had no right to be asking questions or seeking information. I complained to Lamar Alexander. I cannot be the only Tennessee citizen treated in this manner. It is not the job of state agencies to protect the ongoing operations of white-collar criminals.

of cash derived from illegal sources an insurance company, which is required to keep large cash reserves on hand in order to maintain a high rating by insurance regulators and analysts would fill the bill.

The report on Preferred Auto (December 2012) reads: ***The company executed a Custodial Agreement***[116] ***with the Bank of Fayette County effective December 19, 2013. The agreement supersedes the custodial Agreement effective May 1, 2013. The agreement was again revised and signed by the Bank of Fayette County on January 30, 2014. The Company and The Bank of Fayette County executed a new Custodial Agreement on January 30, 2014, to comply with all provisions required Tenn. Comp. R & Reg. 0780-1-46-02.***

As already stated, smaller banks are less likely to come under scrutiny by regulators. Compliance requires the bank to know their customer. Are they clean? Are they dirty? Even the suspicion of criminal activity requires any bank to report improper or questionable activity. What is the compliance history of Bank of Fayette County? Upon belief that a smart federal investigator could look at loans made to the REO Private Investor Group(s) and track those loans to the chain of document fraud by which thefts of these homes are perfected. Cooperative lenders willing to forego fraud detection practices are needed. Filling out the required paperwork for the benefit of deceiving regulators is not the same as complying with the law. Bank of Fayette County is not alone. Risk has to be disbursed. If the superficial façade of bank records were examined by smart Treasury Agents the cesspool of corruption would be uncovered.

I've selected just a few properties from my pattern example groupings to highlight. I must stop somewhere. My ongoing prayer is that federal agency(s) will prosecute these crimes. Tennessee will not protect its own citizens. My hope is that this will change. That Tennessee and other states will place white collar theft of private property high on their agenda. States must clean up the cesspool of corruption operating and stemming out from these theft schemes. Tennessee must adopt a

---

[116] These agreements direct payments to the individual company or group. Upon belief that this is just another avenue by which illegally gotten gains can be disbursed to the REO Criminal Enterprise Group of bad actors. Upon belief that Bank of Fayette County is helping to launder income held by the bank.

culture of transparency. They must change how they process, link, and investigate consumer complaints.

Just for starters I'd like my home back. I'd like to see many other homes returned to their rightful owners. I'd like to see JP Morgan Chase Bank prosecuted for handing over 100k of my equity to the Jones, Kelley, Boyd Perpetrator Nexus; no questions asked. Other banks who assisted the Property Flip chain of theft need to be held accountable. With the long game of how and why The Bank Theft Delivery System operates recognized and prosecuted.

I'd like a lawyer to look into that Avernatti-brand of a bogus settlement made in my name that enriched criminal attorneys; letting the racketeering Criminal Enterprise (shadow clients) off the hook. How much money did they get?

I want to know why the sixth circuit is sitting on my complaints failing to investigate the very serious issues I raised. Why have they failed to rule on my outstanding motion for a void judgement? The reason is that they cannot do so without acknowledging administrative corruption and a biased dual system of protocols unevenly applied.

Though HUD promised to comply with part of a FOIA request I want to know why and how they have not done so? Why are they allowed to continue stonewalling so as to protect REO white collar-criminals they have enabled to steal many other homes feeding product to a billion-dollar theft industry.

I'd like the Tennessee Bar Association to stop sitting on the fence.

There have been interludes when I know that I have been surveilled. Times when I was certain that my phone was hacked or while living in Fayette County that my car was being followed. Letting me see this was a form of intimidation. People on the same calls have noticed the same odd noises and an echo that when remarked upon will suddenly switch off. It is hard to describe how this primitive instinct kicks in and we know that we are being surveilled; not safe in our own communities or homes.

I want criminal banks regulated and prosecuted; sending more of the kingpins to jail. I want the SEC to do their job backing these stolen properties out of the securities they have been pooled into, returning them to victims.

Most of all I want this book to assist the reader to recognize if and when they are targeted by these schemes, fully armed to face the enemy and keep what is rightfully theirs.

I hope this book raises questions about what is wrong with American jurisprudence today? Summed up in the following quote which of itself negates the right of ordinary citizens to be heard in a court of law, under an equal standard of care. And which in the absence of that care makes a mockery of those rights conferred under the United States Constitution to every American. I've held onto this fantasy that someone who loves the Bill of Rights, will help me. ***"The Summary may be... the only part of the brief some judges will ever read, whether because they find the case simple enough to decide without further study or because they are too over-loaded with work, or simply unwilling to work very hard."*** **Robert L. Stern**

THE END

Made in United States
North Haven, CT
07 November 2026

21928351R00240